MW00562112

THE DARKEST PLACES

THE DARKEST PLACES

UNSOLVED MYSTERIES, TRUE CRIMES, AND HARROWING DISASTERS IN THE WILD

THE EDITORS OF *OUTSIDE* MAGAZINE

GUILFORD,
CONNECTICUT

FALCON®

An imprint of The Rowman & Littlefield Publishing Group, Inc.
4501 Forbes Blvd., Ste. 200
Lanham, MD 20706
www.rowman.com
Falcon and FalconGuides are registered trademarks and Make Adventure Your Story
is a trademark of The Rowman & Littlefield Publishing Group, Inc.

Distributed by NATIONAL BOOK NETWORK

British Library Cataloguing-in-Publication Information available
Library of Congress Cataloging-in-Publication Data available

ISBN 978-1-4930-3988-3 (hardcover)
ISBN 978-1-4930-3989-0 (e-book)

∞™ The paper used in this publication meets the minimum requirements
of American National Standard for Information Sciences—Permanence
of Paper for Printed Library Materials, ANSI/NISO Z39.48-1992.

Printed in the United States of America

CONTENTS

WILD CRIMES

INTRODUCTION

CHRIS KEYES

When you're dealing with a tale of intrigue and suspicion in which nothing wants to be what it seems, the best place to start is at the beginning, before everything about the Mystery of the Feet got complicated.

So begins Christopher Solomon's "Foot. Loose.," a true-crime masterpiece and one of the strangest tales we've ever published in *Outside*. In 2010, the magazine's longtime contributing editor proposed investigating a frightening case that was unfolding a few hours north of his home in Seattle. Seven detached human feet had washed ashore over the span of fifteen months in the coastal waters surrounding Vancouver, British Columbia. Authorities had no idea whether these macabre discoveries were evidence of an active serial killer or just a strange coincidence. We were just as baffled—though we were clear about one thing. Missing feet? Seven of them? We needed to assign this immediately.

Solomon's eventual story, which begins on page 164, is a wild ride. It's also a prime example of the kind of can't-look-away events and peculiar crimes *Outside* has spent forty-one years chronicling. Decisions on whom or what to cover in our magazine are generally informed by our original mission statement: to inspire active participation in the world outside. So I'll acknowledge up front that this sunny, positive outlook appears to be in direct conflict with an anthology comprised of grisly crimes, horrifying mysteries, and terrifying, unexplained phenomena. On the surface, at least, the only thing the subjects of these stories—murder, violence, disappearances, and general mayhem—should inspire is an extreme compulsion to stay inside. Go deeper, however, and you'll discover that these pieces reveal hidden truths about the natural world and ponder the yin-and-yang realities of exploration in the wild. We champion the idea that time spent in nature is one of the most effective antidotes for the stress and anxiety that afflict our plugged-in, tech-inundated era. But we also recognize that terrible things sometimes happen in the same places that promise refuge, and to ignore that fact—to not examine it closely or wrestle with its implications—is to ignore the essence of nature itself. Besides, who doesn't love a scary story told around the campfire?

We're not cable news, however. We don't aim to exploit the tragic suffering of others for entertainment value and increased circulation. To that end, there are some basic themes and ingredients we look for before we tell a writer to spend months following leads into creepy and dangerous territory. Scrutinize the stories we've selected here, a representative sample of some of the scariest pieces we've ever published, and common traits emerge that point to why we took the time to tell them. Take, for example, "Foot. Loose.," which is cataloged under the heading of Strange Phenomena—stories that gamely attempt to explain the unexplainable. When we gave Solomon the green light, we knew it was unlikely that he'd solve the mystery. Didn't matter. It was the setting, the noir backdrop of the Pacific Northwest, that gave the story such obvious potential. "It's very possible that a macabre killer isn't on the loose, of course," Solomon wrote in his original pitch. "But the certainty of a killer is beside the point, really. This is a mood piece—a heavily reported mood piece—about a region, its dark history, and its unique relationship with death." To which we replied: Go for it.

Similarly, in 2010, when Tim Zimmermann set out to report on the death of a SeaWorld trainer during a performance with a captive orca, the goal wasn't to simply recount the horrific event itself. The grim details could already be found in a pile of national news stories covering the tragedy. Instead, Zimmermann wanted to explore a larger question: Could an orca commit premeditated murder? The question is too preposterous to really answer, but we knew that grappling with it would lead Zimmermann to pull on some fascinating threads, including a sober examination of the questionable ethics involved with training and breeding wild sea creatures in captivity. His eventual story, "The Killer in the Pool," was one of the most widely read pieces in *Outside*'s history. It also led to the acclaimed documentary *Blackfish*, and important changes in the way SeaWorld and other marine parks treat their animals.

Sometimes stories that fall into the Strange Phenomena category offer no mystery at all, but an overlooked angle or surprising wrinkle serves as the narrative engine. In 2011, Dean King pitched us on the tale of an eight-year-old boy named Robert Wood Jr., who went missing in a forest in northern Virginia. By the time King sent his proposal, Wood had already been found, and it was a different element in the story that made it worthy of pursuing: Wood was autistic. Unlike the vast majority of people who get lost, the boy was likely trying to *evade* being found, because of a hardwired fear of contact with strangers. As King explained, that meant the frantic search-and-rescue teams charged with finding Wood had to scrap their standard playbook and completely rethink their approach. Their tactics make "Catch Me If You Can" a fascinating look into the science of search operations and human behavior.

The common threads you'll find linking the stories in the book's Wild Crimes section are quite different. These pieces all involve some combination of heinous acts and dastardly behavior, ingredients that have been driving narratives for eons. But it's the writers' efforts to figure out what makes the perpetrators tick—what separates these criminal masterminds from any of us—that often elevates them beyond mere disaster porn.

In 2007, that kind of quest landed writer McKenzie Funk in prison. Well, as a visitor. For months, Funk corresponded by phone and through letters with convicted ecoterrorist Chelsea Gerlach, a former member of the Earth Liberation Front who participated in the group's 1998 arson at Vail Resort in Colorado. Few *Outside* readers would ever condone her actions. The fires not only caused $12 million in damage, but they could have killed Vail employees. Still, many of our readers are environmentalists, and Funk was curious to understand how a young woman interested in protecting wild places became radicalized to the point that she was willing to put lives at risk to achieve her goals. What does that evolution look like? "Firestarter" succeeds in answering that question, in large part because Funk chose to tell it in Gerlach's own words.

You'll find a similar approach in the story "Hornswoggled" (page 365), by Paul Kvinta. For several years we looked for a compelling way to tell a story about big-game poaching in Africa—emphasis on *compelling*. Magazines and newspapers, after all, were already stuffed with dry reports citing the grim statistics of charismatic megafauna getting slaughtered at the hands of greedy poaching syndicates. But Kvinta found a way to take us inside one of those syndicates by earning the trust of a repentant bit player willing to share his story. South African Johnny Oliver had witnessed—and frequently played a part in—the extensive crimes of an international wildlife trafficking kingpin. His detailed and extensive recollections reveal an impossibly complex scheme involving illegal hunts, gambling, imported prostitutes, and the slaughter of dozens of rhinos. I'm confident you'll never read a more compelling story about poaching.

On rare occasions, we've even been able to get a glimpse inside a criminal's head while he's still on the lam. That was the case for Brendan Borrell when he went in search of Jeff Caldwell, a prolific con artist. Caldwell had spent years roaming the American West, building relationships with women—often bonding over a mutual love of the outdoors—and then delivering a well-rehearsed sob story to scam them out of cash or other belongings. One of Caldwell's recent victims gave Borrell his cell-phone number, and after weeks of unanswered texts, Caldwell suddenly replied. He not only agreed to talk; he was also introspective about his actions. "There has got to be a reason why I'm here," he tells Borrell at a time when he was still running from the law. "There's got to be. It can't be to keep scamming people." After he was finally caught, Caldwell called Borrell from jail, and perhaps not surprisingly tried to con the writer out of money, too. Suddenly Borrell had an intimate understanding of how other victims fell for Caldwell's scams. "I knew he was starting to see me as another mark," Borrell writes, "but I still felt guilty about saying no. I saw how easy it was to be charmed by him. . . . I wanted to believe that he was ready to turn his life around."

Borrell's experience points to a critical ingredient you'll find in many of the stories filed under Mysteries, the last section of the book: a personal connection. Consider "In a House by the River," in which Megan Michelson researches the murder of her stepfather at a kayaking lodge in a remote pocket of Northern California. Only fourteen at the time of the tragedy, Michelson was kept in the dark about many of the details. Her mother was understandably trying to protect her young daughter. But once Michelson became an adult, her desire to make sense of the murder was no longer possible to suppress. Her story is a devastating reflection on how tragedy can alter one's life and a commendable illustration of bravery in reporting. Toward the end of her investigation, Michelson shows up unannounced at the killer's work site for an interview. "Hi, I'm Megan," she rehearses to herself in the car. "You killed my stepfather. Got a minute to chat?"

Writer Earl Swift was also haunted by a decades-old murder. In 1990, he was on the Appalachian Trail when two fellow hikers were killed by a drifter outside a well-known shelter. Swift knew the victims; he'd run into them on the trail. He'd also spent time at the shelter just a few nights before the tragedy. His story, "Up on Cove Mountain," bolstered by Swift's own vivid memories, reveals how one crime could affect a season's worth of hikers for decades. On similar quests to confront painful memories, Caroline Alexander revisits a shooting that took place at the beloved Tennessee camp where she spent several summers as a child ("A Shot in the Night"), and David Vann returns to a notorious and lawless stretch of Mexican coastline he'd once sailed to investigate the final days of an Irish sailor whose beaten and bruised body was found floating in the same waters ("Last Voyage of the *Cúlin*").

Sometimes a personal connection is simply a result of close proximity or individual obsession. In 2007, novelist Tony D'Souza had just arrived in San Juan del Sur, Nicaragua, to pursue his passion for surfing and fishing when a fellow American expat was arrested for murdering his local girlfriend. Fascinated by the case, D'Souza threw himself into covering it, befriending the suspect and sitting through the trial in which he was eventually convicted. "The Boomtown, the Gringo, the Girl, and Her Murder" is a harrowing look at how one expat's dream became a nightmare. You'll find other writers getting caught up in events throughout the Mysteries section, whether it's Mark Sundeen becoming obsessed with the disappearance of a marine in the wilderness near his Montana home ("Why Noah Went to the Woods") or Brandon Sneed heading to North Carolina, where a feud between violent poachers and an elderly woman who lived with bears turned a small town upside down ("What Killed the Bear Lady?").

Of course, beyond all of these common themes, what really ties this collection together are the unique voices you'll encounter along the way. I am grateful to writers like Solomon and Kvinta and Sundeen and Alexander—not only for bringing us their original ideas to begin with, but for delivering on that promise of these stories time and again. Once you've finished reading the harrowing tales they've produced, I'm certain you'll be grateful, too. And, sure, a little terrified, as well.

MYSTERIES

LONG GONE

BRYAN DI SALVATORE AND DEIRDRE MCNAMER

~~~~~~

When a promising young runner went missing in Wyoming's Wind River Range in 1997, everything changed for the community of athletes she left behind. Authorities immediately suspected the boyfriend—but had they overlooked a serial killer prowling this rugged stretch of the American West?

~~~~~~

Gatorade was on sale at Safeway for 89 cents a 32-ounce bottle, and Mr. D's, just along Main, had knocked down country-style ribs to $1.39 a pound. The school district and the Gannett Grill needed cooks. It was Thursday, July 24, 1997, in Lander, Wyoming, and the twice-weekly *State Journal* had thunked onto porches the afternoon before. Its lead story: Police chief Dick Currah was pressing the city council to crack down on street parties. Jesse Emerson of the Spirit Freedom Ministries would speak that evening about family alcoholism and drugs. Here was a one-bedroom apartment for rent: $350 plus utilities. No pets. Someone in northern California wanted a nanny. By midafternoon, thermometers would crawl toward 90. It would be lip-cracking dry, under a ferociously blue sky. Clouds big as counties would bunch up to the northeast, where the Owl Creek Mountains meet the Bighorns, and just west, in the Wind River Range, Lander's backyard. They might shape themselves into massive anvils and shoot lightning down to the high plains. Or they might just light up gold as the sun fell away and be gone by morning.

To all appearances, it was going to be a spectacularly ordinary high-summer day.

What happened instead was something strange and nightmarish, the kind of nightmare that begins with innocuous moments that become harrowing only in hindsight. A casual good-bye kiss. Three quick glances at a wristwatch. A cheery wave.

It would be the day that a Lander resident named Amy Wroe Bechtel—twenty-four years old, 5-foot-6 and 110 pounds, Olympic marathon hopeful, amateur photographer, friend, employee, daughter, sister, wife—fell off the face of the earth.

~~~~~~

At the northwestern edge of Lander, past the Toyota dealership, on a rise above the tidy town, ten identical frame houses face the Wind River Range. Small and scraped-looking—former company houses from some gone-bust outfit in Rock Springs—they line one side of a street called Lucky Lane. The residents, many of them, are young, ardent, competitive rock climbers. An intense little bohemia of mountain-town athletes.

Todd Skinner, their de facto captain, lives in number 10 with his wife, Amy Whisler, also a climber. Skinner, thirty-nine, has led four of the most notable first free ascents of recent years: Half Dome's northwest face, the Salathé Wall of El Capitan, Proboscis in the Yukon, and the Nameless Tower in Pakistan's Karakoram Range. Mike Lilygren, who accompanied Skinner on that 1995 Pakistan climb, lived last summer in number 7. (He recently moved in with his girlfriend down in town.) Skinner's sister Holly lives in number 8. And until July 24, Amy Wroe Bechtel lived with her husband, Steve, one of Skinner's Half Dome and Nameless Tower partners, in number 9.

When they woke on that morning, Steve and Amy faced a busy schedule. They had the day off from Wild Iris Mountain Sports, the local outdoor equipment store where both had part-time jobs. Steve's plan was to drive with his yellow Lab, Jonz, to Dubois, 75 miles north, meet his friend Sam Lightner, and scout some possible new climbing routes at Cartridge Creek. Amy drove her white Toyota Tercel station wagon to the Wind River Fitness Center, another of her part-time employers, and taught an hour-and-a-half kids' class in weight training. She was upbeat, says owner Dudley Irvine, though "a little high-strung because she had a lot to do."

Indeed. Three days earlier, Amy and Steve had closed on a new house a mile toward the center of town from Lucky Lane, and she was busy organizing a 10K hill climb, scheduled for September 7. The runners would puff up a series of switchbacks not far out of town and then jump into Frye Lake and finish up with a picnic.

Her to-do list was long: run & lift, recycling, call phone co., electric, gas, insurance, get photo mounted or matted, flyers for race, get more boxes, mow lawn, call Ed, close road?, have Karn do drawing.

We know this: Amy taught the fitness class and picked up the center's recycling. She contacted the phone and electric companies. She stopped in at the Camera Connection on Main and asked owner John Strom about several photographs she planned to submit in a competition.

She was eleven days short of her twenty-fifth birthday, thirteen months into her marriage—a radiant young athlete, small, lithe, determined, thoughtful, even-tempered, trusting. That's the capsule description, and it varies not a whit, whether the describer is an acquaintance, like Strom, or a family member, or a close friend.

Strom, reserved and bespectacled, remembers that Amy was in running togs: yellow shirt, black shorts, running shoes. That she seemed cheerful and busy. That he sent her to the framing shop upstairs to see about matting. That it was midafternoon.

She talked with Greg Wagner at Gallery 331 about her photos. He says that in the course of twenty minutes or so, she looked at her watch two or three times. She left the store. Call it 2:30 p.m.

At this point, while quotidian life went one direction in Lander—while the shopper at Safeway reached for discount Gatorade and the fisherman eyed the gathering clouds and the golfer double-bogied the difficult fourth hole at the local municipal and Jesse Emerson rehearsed that evening's presentation—life for Amy went another.

At this point, everything about Amy Wroe Bechtel—her movements, her well-being, her very existence—becomes subject to speculation.

Lander is one of those pleasant, historically undistinguished Western towns that borrows most of its reputation from what it is near, and what it is not. It is 7,500 souls living a mile above sea level. Butch Cassidy was once arrested here. Its most famous resident was an old buckaroo, Stub Farlow, whose image atop a sunfishing bronc adorns Wyoming's license plates.

What it is near is the spectacular eastern front of the Wind River Range—fierce, sharp peaks that give onto gentler ones that give, in turn, onto the oceanic high plains. It is terrain of such starkly heroic proportions that it can make other American vistas—the silo-anchored fields of the Midwest, the nubby Appalachians, even the punched-up Pacific Coast Ranges—seem like the Land of Toys.

And what is Lander not? It's not rich-thick Jackson, 160 road-miles northwest—though like many small Western towns with a view, it fears it may become that. Landerites cast wary glances at Jackson's log palaces, its sleek fleets of celebrities and wannabes and wealthy kids who fall from the sky in Western costumes and $300 haircuts for some quality mountain time.

But truth be told, that's a transmutation Lander won't have to worry about anytime soon. It has no downhill ski area and no prospect of one. Its snowfall, relative to much of the mountainous West, is sporadic and undependable, and its periodic winds are the kind of hellers that make it sad to go outside. ("Due to high winds please return carts to corral in parking lot," pleads a sign outside the Safeway.) Fishing is fine, but hardly world-class. Hunting is seasonal. Snowmobilers have been part of things for a long time, and the hipness quotient, measured in the New West by the ratio of cappuccino to Folgers, is negligible. The modest Magpie is still the only sit-down coffeehouse in town.

What else is Lander not, besides Jackson? It is not the gritty, extractive, assault-and-battery West of, say, Rock Springs. Or the university-town West that is Laramie. Or the strafed and struggling Indian West of the Wind River Reservation, just north of town.

Lander was the original home of *High Country News*, the feisty biweekly environmental newspaper (it moved to Colorado in the early eighties). In 1965, the National Outdoor Leadership School, which trains about 2,800 students each year in outdoor skills, was established in Lander. A few years before that, prosperity had descended on Lander in the form of a US Steel iron-ore mine. In 1985, increasing foreign imports and other economic woes, so said US Steel, prompted the company to pull out, putting 550 people out of work. The streets were suddenly dense with For Sale signs.

Lander, however, took stock. Regrouped. Hired some crackerjack community resource personnel, and realized that its big selling points were its size, its civility, and its proximity to forest, wilderness, and mountains. NOLS stayed and prospered. The town promoted itself as a friend of small business. It aggressively advertised for "vigorous retirees." It expanded the golf course. It upgraded and modernized its sewer and water systems and remodeled Main Street with tasteful streetlamps, flower boxes, and litter baskets.

In the early nineties, the rock climbers began to arrive, drawn by some of the most accessible and difficult walls in America—notably the 2-mile-wide dolomite, sandstone, and granite cliffs of Sinks Canyon, 9 miles from town, and a higher area known as Wild Iris, with its two hundred bleach-white climbing routes (featuring difficulty ratings from 5.9 to 5.14), 26 miles from town.

Business is good now, based mostly on recreation and light industry; growth is steady and calm. Lander keeps its boots shined and its troubles to itself.

The town's resident climbers—perhaps two-thirds of them male, most of them from west of the Mississippi—are a furiously healthy, adrenalized, unironic group. They describe themselves as factionless middle-roaders of the sport—not the somber Brahmins, forever talking about how it used to be done, and not the young punks who scramble up the rock walls, headphones blasting, knocking a cliff all to hell in search of a few kicks.

The Lucky Lane bunch appears to waste little time on bad habits or generalized angst. Any outright oddnesses or furies seem to get channeled into climbing, and what's left over is small-town camaraderie (potlucks, fireworks on the Fourth), lots of rock-talk, and the edgeless high jinks of a platoon in the movies, of the spirited kids on the team bus. They tend to keep their doors unlocked and share equipment, climbing plans, social lives, workplaces. Skinner and Whisler are part owners of Wild Iris, the outdoor-gear store where Amy and Steve Bechtel and Mike Lilygren were on the payroll, and they own the house that Steve and Amy were renting. (Steve also works as a sales rep for DMM, a climbing hardware company, and for Stone Monkey action wear.)

At times, the in-without-knocking, postcollegiate communalism wore against Amy's need for privacy and order, according to Jo Anne Wroe, her mother. Amy wanted a home of her own and couldn't wait to move into the crisp ranch-style house they had just bought—an in-town place with flowers, a lawn, space for a darkroom. In fact, Amy's original plan for July 24 was to drive three hours north to her parents' home in Powell, Wyoming, to pick up furniture that her father, Duane, had been refinishing for the young couple.

Jo Anne remembers that Amy called the night before and said, "Would you feel really bad if I didn't come tomorrow? I've got about a million things to do, and it's my only day off." Jo Anne, her voice taut, adds, "Later I thought, Why didn't we just make her come that day? Those 'almost' moments. They're the things you think about."

Steve Bechtel says he returned from his rendezvous with Sam Lightner about 4:30 that afternoon to find the house empty. He and Amy were not in the habit of leaving notes about their whereabouts, and anyway, Steve had returned earlier than he'd planned. No reason for alarm. After a bit, he spoke with Todd Skinner and Amy Whisler next door, but they hadn't seen Amy since midday. He turned down an invitation to go for pizza with some of the Lucky Lane bunch, and waited. Had she gone climbing? No, her gear was still in the house. Had she gone to take some photographs? No, her camera was in the house. Her jeans and T-shirt were on the bedroom floor, and her running shoes were gone.

At about 10:00 p.m., he called her parents to see if perhaps Amy had driven there on the spur of the moment. When they asked him if anything was wrong, Steve, who later said that he was starting to worry at this point, replied with a casual white lie: "No."

Skinner and Whisler had gone to the 8:45 p.m. showing of *Con Air*, and they arrived home around 11:00 to find that Amy still wasn't back. By this time, Steve had called the Fremont County sheriff's office, which sent two deputies to the house, alerted the night shift, and began to organize a search-and-rescue team to head out at daybreak. Skinner and Whisler, meanwhile, went to look for Amy's car. They drove downtown, turned right at the Safeway, and followed what's known locally as the Loop Road, a 30-mile affair through the Shoshone National Forest.

At about one in the morning, Whisler used her cell phone to call Steve: They had found Amy's white Toyota Tercel station wagon at a place called Burnt Gulch, up in the mountains about forty-five minutes from town. The car was unlocked. The keys were under Amy's to-do list on the passenger seat, next to her $120 sunglasses. Her wallet was not in the car. Nothing—except Amy's absence and the wallet's absence (she never carried it running)—seemed awry. It was as if she had simply parked the car and stepped away for a breath of night air.

Steve and his friend Kirk Billings grabbed lanterns, a sleeping bag, and matches and drove to Burnt Gulch. The little group arrowed flashlights past tree trunks, into blurry undergrowth. They called and called Amy's name, were answered with wind through the trees. They summoned more searchers.

Long before dawn and the arrival of the official search party, a dozen friends were looking for Amy-with-a-sprained-ankle, Amy-with-a-broken-leg, or Amy-attacked-by-a-bear. No attempt was made to preserve the integrity of what would later be presumed to be a crime scene. This was merely a lost runner. "I expected her to come stumbling out of the woods," said Billings. In retrospect, that assumption would seem disastrously naive.

Certain couples can look to outsiders like some platonic combination of health, beauty, and uncomplication. There is Amy in their wedding photo, smiling serenely, almost remotely—as if she's listening to a happy story she's heard before. Her pale blonde hair is a shiny cap, her skin golden, her carriage slim and erect, her dress a simple, sleeveless column of white.

And there is Steve, strong-jawed and smoothly handsome in a tuxedo. And shorts. And Tevas. He's the cutup, the counterpoint.

Steve and Amy met at the University of Wyoming in Laramie in December 1991, took exercise physiology classes together in the spring, and were dating by the fall of 1992.

Amy is the youngest of four closely spaced siblings, allies and friends during their growing-up years. Their father, Duane Wroe, sixty-six, is a retired city administrator—intelligent, gaunt, testy, chain-smoking, a former big-time drinker (he gave it up twenty years ago). The family moved to Jackson in 1973, not long after Amy was born, and Duane was city manager there, and later, in Douglas and Powell. These days he keeps his hand in politics—he's been spearheading an initiative that would codify ethics requirements for Wyoming officeholders—and he tinkers with furniture and works on his and Jo Anne's modest house.

Jo Anne Wroe, twelve years younger than her husband, quiet-voiced, is a dark-haired version of her three towheaded daughters. She can seem tentative, forthcoming, and insightful, almost in the same breath. She worked as a teacher of handicapped preschoolers for many years and now substitutes in the Powell school system.

A large photograph of Amy in kindergarten, part of the hallway display that Jo Anne calls her "rogues' gallery," shows a canny, appraising child of five, looking out from under a shock of white-blonde hair. Even then, her parents say, she was thoughtful, orderly, highly focused—the kind of kid who sets goals and when she does, says Duane, "you better get flat out of her way."

Amy got the running bug in sixth grade. She wasn't, by all accounts, very good, but she kept at it through high school in Douglas and at the University of Wyoming. By her junior and senior years in college, Amy started winning everything in sight. She was captain of the UW cross-country and track teams, got named to the Western Athletic Conference's all-star team, and still holds the UW record in the 3,000 meters: 9:48.9. After college, she continued to compete in both regional and national competitions. In 1996, she ran the Boston Marathon in 3:08:33. Though Amy finished 41 minutes behind winner Uta Pippig, and though her time was 33 minutes behind the 1996 American Olympic marathon qualifying time, Steve Bechtel would matter-of-factly tell anyone who asked that his wife was hoping to qualify for the 2000 Olympics. He and her friends pointed to her heart, her drive. What, in the face of willpower like Amy's, is 33 minutes?

Steve, twenty-seven, grew up in Casper, the son of Thomas Bechtel, an architect, and Linda Bechtel, who is the director of a school for developmentally disabled children. Steve has a younger brother, Jeff, and an older sister, Leslie.

In his teens, Steve turned his back on team sports and skiing and pointed himself at rock-climbing, the sport that has obsessed him since. And, like Amy, he progressed through sheer doggedness.

"Steve doesn't have the natural build of a climber," says Mike Lilygren, who was his college roommate. "You want to be lean, skinny, wiry, small, compact, like me. Steve is big, barrel-chested, and he's got those big legs to haul around."

Steve is talkative, quick, and, according to his friends, engagingly zany. He knows by heart the lyrics to the complete works of They Might Be Giants. He programmed his computer so that when it came on, it screamed out one of Holly Hunter's lines from *Raising Arizona*: "Where's Junior?" By Lucky Lane standards, these are examples of full-frontal madcappery.

When it comes to his sport, however, Steve is known for a singularity of purpose unusually intense even for a big-wall climber. When Skinner began assembling a five-member team for the celebrated 1995 scaling of the Southeast Face of Pakistan's Nameless Tower—a 3,000-foot granite spear, also called Trango Tower—he picked Steve for his bulldog tenacity, his "mono-focus," his ability to Be Positive.

"An expedition team is an organic unit," Skinner says. "I guess I'm the mind; Lilygren, the good spirits, the sense of humor. Steve is the heart." Skinner speaks emphatically and with much eye contact. He is often out of town, giving motivational speeches to various organizations, corporate and noncorporate.

Steve was dropped from the expedition at base camp because of a severe sinus infection and eye hemorrhages. It was a bitter disappointment. The rest of the team spent two months on the Tower, waiting out storms in hanging tents or on narrow ledges, before completing an ascent in which they relied on no climbing aids—only their hands, their feet, and safety ropes.

If there is a moral to their adventures—and you hear it from the Lucky Lane climbers again and again—it is that tenacity buys victory, that you can hang for a long damn time 4 miles above sea level and still make the top, that hopelessness, failure of will, can be lethal.

Positive mental attitude. Focus. Your mind on the task, on the problem and nothing else. Quitting is not an option. Those were the mantras at Lucky Lane, even during the best of times. When Amy disappeared, climbing a cliff became finding a person.

"Amy is the summit," said Skinner, the motivational speaker, during the early days of the search. "We're trying to get to that point."

~~~~~~

Getting lost or injured near Lander is like having your house catch fire next to the fire station. Scores of rescuers, fit and mountain-wise, live within a rifle shot of city hall. Amy's disappearance prompted an all-out response from the county's search-and-rescue volunteers, many of whom are NOLS staff and students; from Lander's extended climbing community; and from Amy and Steve's family members and a number of their college friends. By the weekend, the company of searchers grew to nearly two hundred.

"We know what we're doing," says Dave King, the Fremont County sheriff's deputy who became the case's lead investigator. "We have fifty activations a year. We have specialists in steep-angle searches, swiftwater searches, cave rescues. We have trackers, air spotters, and what are called cadaver dogs, which supposedly can catch scents even underwater. We can bring people out via Life Flight or horseback or on a stretcher. Me? I round up the volunteers. I provide the authority, and I take the blame for bad decisions, but I'm not the expert. I feel foolish sometimes— directing traffic that includes people who have written books about mountain search-and-rescue."

King is forty-one years old, squarely and solidly built, with a spiky haircut that looks like something his thirteen-year-old daughter urged on him in the interest of with-it-ness. He's Lander-born and -bred, with such an engaging lack of bluster or antagonism that it's easy to overlook the fact that he keeps his cards very close to the vest. He summarizes, he confirms, he returns calls, he expresses his frustration at being literally clueless.

Investigators had discovered, on the bottom of the to-do list found in Amy's car, a milepost description of landmarks that she apparently jotted down, while referring to her odometer, along the first section of the proposed 10K race route—one more indication that Amy herself drove the Toyota up into the mountains before she disappeared. Therefore the search centered on the upper sections of the Loop Road, which begins as a paved highway flanked by ranchettes on the immediate outskirts of Lander. It parallels the Popo Agie River through Sinks Canyon State Park, where visitors can watch the river vanish into a mountain cave and then walk a quarter-mile to watch it emerge at a quiet pond called the Rise of the Sinks. Water should make this underground trip in a few minutes; instead it takes two hours. More water emerges than has disappeared. Go figure.

Beyond Sinks Canyon, the pavement turns to gravel and switchbacks, rising 1,500 feet in 6 miles to Frye Lake—the hill climb Amy was scoping out for her 10K.

Still heading up through the Shoshone National Forest, the road passes campgrounds, firewood-gathering areas, Louis Lake, snowmobile and hiking trailheads. It crests above 9,000 feet and then descends to connect with Wyoming 28 near the skeletal mining hamlets of Atlantic City and South Pass City.

The Loop Road is essentially a horseshoe tipped on its ends. A vehicle has one way in, one way out. During the day, traffic is sporadic but not infrequent. At night, the Loop feels very empty, very close to the stars, suspended in a soft rush of tree-top wind. About halfway along the road, in the westward shadow of Indian Ridge, the loop passes through a fire-thinned forest of lodgepole pines. A rutted side road used by firewood cutters heads off into the trees toward Freak Mountain. This is Burnt Gulch, the place where Skinner and Whisler found Amy's Tercel.

In the days that followed, searchers painstakingly staked out and scoured roughly 20 square miles around Amy's car. They almost literally combed the 5-square-mile area closest to the Toyota. They walked, four abreast, the length of the Loop. It was both a "wallet toss" search—covering the distance that someone could discard a wallet—and a "critical separation" search, in which volunteers, depending on the terrain, maintain only enough distance between themselves so as not to miss anything: The "critical separation" might be ten yards on a sandy plain, ten inches in a rain forest.

Horses joined the hunt, and then the cadaver dogs and the National Guard. ATVs scampered over the land. A search plane buzzed overhead. Helicopters, including one equipped with infrared sensors, thwacked over the mountains for hours, days. Radios crackled. Passing motorists were stopped and questioned. It went on from dawn to dusk for more than a week.

She should have been found.

If she had been attacked by a mountain lion or a bear, searchers should have found disheveled underbrush, scraps of clothing, blood, remains. If she had become injured or lost, the searchers—who went everywhere she could have managed to take herself—should have come upon her, and come upon her fast. It was a Rolls-Royce of an operation—nothing haphazard or skimpy about it—and it yielded not a flicker of Amy Wroe Bechtel.

The first day, the second day, the fifth day. Searchers returned to camp exhausted, pained, and baffled. There was not, according to King, a snip of cloth, a drop of blood, a single verifiable track, a sign of a scuffle—anything to indicate unambiguously that Amy was physically present, alive or dead, on the mountain. There were only a car, some keys, sunglasses, and a to-do list, with four of its thirteen items checked off.

Landerites like to say that they live in a town that's free from big-city crime—the kind of random or serial mayhem that seems most possible when everyone's a stranger. But that's not strictly accurate. Beneath Lander's just-folks exterior is a town that, like most others, has not been able to fence itself off from trouble. A terrifying series of break-ins and rapes that began in the fall of 1993 prompted women's self-defense classes. In 1995, a self-described "hobo" was committed to the state hospital after being convicted of four of the attacks.

In February 1994, a local teenager was shot five times in the head and torso in the Sinks Canyon parking lot by a drug dealer who thought the victim was a police informer. The editorial headline: "Have Big-City Problems Invaded Our Secure Little Mountain Town?"

There have been unsolved murders. A woman and two children disappeared in 1980, and her blood-spattered car was found 30 miles outside of town; the bodies were never found. There was a brawl after the Lander–Riverton football game a few years ago. Shots were fired. Authorities confiscated bats, metal pipes, and a nine-millimeter pistol.

Still, Lander retains a sense of itself as a friendly, essentially innocent sort of place. Its motto could be "Bad things happen, but they are not who we are." And always, the piney mountains just outside town have seemed some kind of antidote to human poisons and sorrows. That's where you could go to relax, to breathe in deep, to listen to your best self.

So, five days after Amy disappeared, when the search turned into a full-blown criminal investigation—when twenty-five FBI agents arrived from Denver and Virginia and from elsewhere in Wyoming, set up shop in the sheriff's office, and began to question anybody who knew anything about the young woman who seemed to have evaporated from their midst—Landerites reacted with fresh shock, followed by the scramble to impose some kind of logic on an inexplicable event. Very quickly, everyone seemed to have an opinion: the skinny, insistent drunk at the Gannett Grill who said the husband did it; the hacker on the twelfth hole who was sure that someone with the wiles of a Ted Bundy had taken her away; the customer at a restaurant who said Amy was at the bottom of a nearby lake with a chain around her neck; the store owner who wondered if "maybe she just ran away." There was the half-remembered story of another young, athletic, blonde woman named Ann Marie Potton, who vanished without a clue in British Columbia three years earlier after setting out for a hike on Whistler Mountain, and vague recollections of the "mountain men" who abducted a young blonde athlete named Kari Swenson while she was jogging on a Montana mountain road in 1984. (In a curious coincidence, it turned out that one of Swenson's cousins is married to the owner of the Wind River Fitness Center, where Amy worked.)

Hikers and runners in the Lander area and beyond, especially women, began to look over their shoulders, to run in pairs or with dogs or with pepper spray.

And then the yellow ribbons appeared. Yellow ribbons on parking meters, on telephone poles, on trees, on tee-marker signs at the golf course: Come home, Amy. We're here. Come back, and the mountains will be safe again.

There are no yellow ribbons anywhere on the Wind River Reservation, which begins a few miles north of Lander. It is as if the Shoshone/Northern Arapahoe reservation occupies another country and another time, and the drama of Amy Bechtel plays faintly, far, far away.

Captain Larry Makeshine, at tribal police headquarters in Fort Washakie, heard about Amy's disappearance soon after it happened, but Fremont County authorities never contacted his office directly. Makeshine also heard that the FBI had sent in twenty-five agents, and he was mystified.

"I'm not questioning it," he said, several weeks after the FBI had come and gone, "but if I'm going to be quoted, I'd say I've never seen it done that way before."

Makeshine, a wry and circumspect man in his forties, said two agents from the FBI office in Riverton conducted interviews after several mysterious deaths on the reservation during the past year, including the hit-and-run homicide of Daniel Oldman Jr., the teenage son of another tribal policeman. But Makeshine said that he doesn't know the status of those investigations, because "they didn't keep us posted."

Not far out of Fort Washakie, there is a little cemetery on a hillside where the Shoshone say Sacagawea, the heroic guide and interpreter for the Lewis and Clark Expedition, is buried. A number of historians say otherwise—that the evidence points to an early death at Fort Manuel, far to the east in the Dakota Territory—but the Shoshone story is that she wandered for years after the expedition and came home finally to her people, who had long given her up for dead. They called her *Wadzi-wipe*: Lost Woman.

A month has gone by. Thousands of man-hours have been expended on generating publicity and following up on the hundreds of tips that have come in. By now, Steve and his friends have learned to discriminate between the promising and the ludicrous.

Two or three dozen psychics have offered their services. Some want money up front. Some just offer their insights. Some of the insights are theoretically helpful. "Let's say someone says, 'Check out a yellow mobile home off the highway ten miles from Lander,'" Steve says. "We can do that. If someone says, 'I see a white pickup in Utah,' well, tell me another."

Jim and Wendy Gibson, owners of Lander's Pronghorn Lodge, have told investigators they passed a slender blonde woman wearing dark shorts running in the same direction they were traveling on the Loop Road—away from town—late on the afternoon of July 24. They had taken some visiting relatives, Nebraska flatlanders, up to the mountain for some predinner sightseeing.

"That's unusual," Wendy recalls saying as they drove by. "Someone running, way up here."

The runner was swift, swifter than any town jogger clomping the pounds away. Jim made a little joke: "She looks like she's running away from something."

On the way back to town, at Burnt Gulch, Wendy noticed a "dirty white vehicle" but had no reason to connect it with the young runner they'd seen earlier. Wendy remembers seeing "something red" in the car, something that reminded her of camping. A little farther toward town, they noticed a gray truck with half a load of logs and a man standing nearby, shirtless, holding a plastic container.

There was a report of gunfire on the night of July 24 at Louis Lake, 8 miles from Burnt Gulch, and a voice yelling, "Come on, you sissy, do it, do it!"

A kid found a bottle in the river near Main Street in Lander. Inside the bottle was a note: "Help. I'm being held captive in Sinks Canyon. Amy." The handwriting, predictably, was not Amy's.

Wavery memories, contradictory as dreams. Dots to be connected. Frail clues. Cruel hoaxes. Shadows demanding to be tackled, to be pinned in place.

It is the end of August, then early September. Search headquarters has moved from the mountains and into town, and the taciturn, professionally noncommittal FBI agents, after an investigative blitz that lasted a week and a half, have returned to Denver and Cheyenne and Quantico.

A room in the sheriff's office has become the new command post. The walls are thick with time lines and topographic maps. In one corner sit three computers; in another, a small table with a pair of size-eight Adidas Trail Response running shoes and a mannequin torso wearing a yellow Stone Monkey T-shirt and black running shorts.

The concrete world of a physical search—gullies, cliffs, thick copses—has given way to the more abstract realm of an investigation: theories, networks, possible sightings, criminal profiles.

The vast majority of violent crimes against women are committed by a friend, an acquaintance, or a relative of the victim. The authorities quickly became interested in Steve and in a small number of men who had exhibited particular interest in Amy or her running career, but no one has emerged as anything approaching a clear suspect. Sam Lightner, the climber whom Steve drove to Dubois to meet on July 24, corroborated Steve's account of his whereabouts that day; still, no third party as yet has provided firm independent corroboration of the two climbers' account.

Meanwhile, Steve Bechtel and Amy's friends and relatives are doing what they compel themselves to do, acting as they have trained themselves to act.

They have converted Todd Skinner's garage on Lucky Lane into a search headquarters. The place is hot, cluttered, airless. Two women, including Steve's sister Leslie, stuff envelopes with canary-yellow flyers—a photo of Amy, her vital statistics, the date and place of her presumed abduction, a phone number to call, a heading: HAVE YOU SEEN AMY? $10,000 REWARD.

The group has mailed out or directed "satellite" volunteers to mail out more than 80,000 flyers. Addresses are gleaned from e-mail chain letters and Internet phone directories: bars, pawn shops, convenience stores, truck stops, motels, bus lines, Adopt-a-Highway sponsors, film processors. There is an Amy website; more than two hundred other websites have links to it, and there is a goal of one thousand links. The search is out of the woods, onto the computer screen.

Aphorisms are handwritten on the garage walls: "Miracles come after a lot of hard work." "You wouldn't want to quit and then find out later you only had inches to go . . ." Kipling's "If" is taped to a cupboard door.

A separate room at the back of the garage is the Lucky Lane climbing gym. One wall tips forward in a dizzying replica of an overhang. Mattresses cover the floor. On a side wall, scores of routes are listed by category: Easy, Tricky, Hard, Desperate, Savage, Hoss. Scattered randomly are yet more aphorisms: "Die Young! Die Strong!" "Life is Pain / I want to be insane." "No prisoners / No Mercy!" "You must Get Weak to get strong!"

In Steve and Amy's house, across the street, taped to the group's central computer, is another: "You've got a date with the ultimate burn."

There are few mysteries more potent than that of someone who vanishes without a clue, who seems to inhabit an ordinary day and then does not, who becomes the presumed victim of a crime only because the other alternatives seem less likely.

A missing person is not fully alive or fully dead. She does not age. She exists in a shadowland that we, the waiting, invest with both our fantasies and our nightmares. What if she simply slipped out of her life and started another from scratch? It's a theme that runs deep in America—the idea of leaving behind the complications and sorrows of one's day-by-day existence to make a fresh start as someone new, to lose one's past.

The FBI's National Crime Information Center listed approximately 35,000 adults missing at the end of 1997. But if history is any guide, the majority will return on their own or will otherwise be accounted for. Only 2 or 3 percent of the missing will turn into outright, long-term mysteries involving assumptions of foul play.

No one who has known Amy Bechtel seems to believe that she would simply cut all the traces and disappear, that she could impose that kind of open-ended pain on those she left behind. And so the imagination moves into a more dire realm, but one in which it is still possible to invest the missing person with the qualities of one's own, most survivable self. Maybe she is a prisoner, waiting for her chance. Or she is wandering in an amnesiac state but will someday recall her name and her history and reclaim them in triumph after a strange, long time in which she was lost to her searchers and to herself.

Beyond that, there is murder. That is the first terror-dream when a person is missing, and it is linked to a second: that of dying in such a way that one is never conclusively missed, never completely mourned.

~~~~~~

Steve Bechtel enters the garage from across the street. He is wearing a T-shirt, shorts, sandals. In the weeks since Amy disappeared, his perennial tan has faded, though his face remains preternaturally smooth and unlined. His demeanor has taken on the alert exhaustion of an air traffic controller. With reporters, his manner is energetically neutral, like a young surgeon describing a harrowing operative procedure. A fancy new anesthetic gets the same buoyant description as the details of sawing through a limb. His cheerful tone of voice, his amiability, remains constant, whether he's talking about the details of rock-climbing or the possibility that his wife has been raped and murdered.

"He's hurting," says his friend Marit Fischer, in Denver. "But he will never show them he is."

"Them" could be the reporters, or the volunteers in the garage. Or they could be those who are angry and confused by Steve's refusal to take a lie-detector test.

Early on, the authorities—the FBI, chief investigator Dave King, sheriff Larry Matthews—and many townspeople, and even Amy's parents, took the position that if Steve was innocent, he had nothing to lose by sitting for a lie-detector test. Steve, most of his intimates, and his lawyer—Kent Spence, stepbrother of one of Steve's climbing acquaintances and son of that Spence, Gerry—felt quite differently. They said that Steve had already submitted to four formal interviews with the investigators, and they pointed to study after study about the unreliability of polygraph tests.

Further, Steve and Spence accused the cops of picking at straws in the wind, of relying on "profiles" of perpetrators, of wasting their energy badgering and frightening Steve when they could be tracking down potentially fruitful leads and suspects.

"The FBI in their usual sensitive manner attacked Steve Bechtel when they became frustrated with their failure to come up with any clues," Spence said shortly after taking on Steve as a client. "They pointed their cannons at him and accused him of being involved, when they had no evidence whatsoever."

Steve speaks of an FBI agent who he says told him, point-blank, just two weeks or so after the search for Amy began, "We have evidence you killed Amy." Steve uses the words "preposterous" and "unbelievable" to describe the situation. What he seems to be saying is that he has been put in a predicament in which he has to bear not only the loss of his wife, but also the open-ended suspicion that he was her killer.

"This sounds strange, but we hope that she's been abducted," he says. "With that option, there are unlimited scenarios. One is that she was grabbed, raped, and killed . . ." He clears his throat. "We think that is unlikely. We think she's still alive, being kept alive, and has left the area. Maybe she has amnesia. That she is being kept by someone infatuated, obsessed with her. That is why we're making this a nationwide search.

"She's a very trusting person. She thinks that people are generally good. I think her thinking will change, has changed."

Nine miles from town, in the Sinks Canyon State Park Interpretive Center, among other exhibits, is a mounted photograph of a rock climber. The photo, shot by Amy Wroe Bechtel, placed third in the action category in a local contest. The climber, leaning against air, seems to be hanging onto the mountain by his very fingernails.

~~~~~~

Two months after she disappeared, the Amy Bechtel Hill Climb took place. One hundred and forty-six runners stretched and shivered and high-stepped in a parking lot not far from Sinks Canyon State Park. Soon they would head off, climbing past killing switchbacks, toward Frye Lake, 10 kilometers distant.

You know the drill: large dogs barking, tights, running shorts, sweatpants, ski caps, singlets, gloves, Marmot, Columbia, Patagonia, The North Face, prerace babble.

There was Steve, greeting friends, being hugged. There were Jeff, Steve's brother, and Jo Anne and Duane Wroe, and Todd Skinner. There were Tom and Linda, Steve's parents, and Casey and Jenny, Amy's sisters.

Steve, in shorts, bareheaded, raised his hands and quieted the crowd. "Amy has wanted to do this race for a couple of years," he said. "She was always told the only people who would show would be eight of her former track teammates."

Laughter. Cheers.

"We're in this together. We know Amy's alive."

Cheers. Yes.

"Okay . . ." His voice quavered. He paused. When he spoke again, it had returned to full strength.

"One last thing: Please wait for me after you get to the finish line." Laughter.

Ray Candelaria, Lander Valley High School cross-country coach, said, "Runners, on your marks," and pointed his starter's gun to the sky.

~~~~~~

We are not an especially admirable species. We are suspicious, violent, maladroit. We leave unholy messes wherever we go, despite our best intentions.

By the start of the hill climb, everyone was tired. They had been a long time on the mountain. Things had gone wrong. The original 800-number on the missing posters—all 120,000 of them—turned out to be invalid when dialed from out of state. Todd Skinner and Steve blamed the cops. The cops expressed surprise at this, claiming that Steve and Todd had told them the mistake wouldn't really matter, since a correct local number was also printed on the poster.

While the climbing community in Lander remained solidly loyal to Steve, things had unraveled badly among the family. Tempers had shortened. Alliances had frayed. A few weeks before the race, Amy's parents and siblings met with the FBI and the Fremont County sheriff's office and poured out their anxiety. Why were they so focused on Steve? Where was the investigation leading?

The authorities produced Steve's journals, or portions of them, selectively highlighted (or not—it depends on who's telling the story). As volatile and intriguing as the journals may be, they have not been made public, and the import of their contents varies wildly with the account of each possibly unreliable witness. Nels Wroe, Amy's brother, and his wife, Teresa, who is the director of a center for domestic-abuse victims, were shocked at what they felt were indications of violent tendencies in the writing, of obsessive thinking on Steve's part. Soon after, Nels restated—for a reporter from the *Casper Star-Tribune*, and on a Wyoming public radio news program—his fervent wish that Steve would take a polygraph test. Duane Wroe agreed. Jo Anne said little. Amy's sisters, on the other hand, remained publicly loyal to Steve.

"It's not within me to be angry at someone for having feelings or thoughts and for dealing with them by placing them on a piece of paper," Casey Wroe-Lee told the *Star-Tribune*.

Nels said that Steve denied the journals' currency, that Steve said they were written in high school. Steve denied Nels's version of his denial, and stated that while the entries do run up to a week or so before the disappearance, some of the disturbing entries were only gonzo song lyrics, written in high school.

Nels pointed out, as an example of Steve's obsessive jealousy, that Steve had refused to accompany Amy to Nels and Teresa's wedding because of the likely presence of a possible former boyfriend of Amy's.

Nels and Teresa didn't attend the hill climb. They said they didn't want to cause a stir, to have the families' choppy sorrows upstage an event that should focus exclusively on Amy.

So, as the runners headed toward Frye Lake, what had been envisioned as a day of sad but positive solidarity, of communal bolstering, had become—certainly for the families of Amy and Steve—grim, stiff, heavy, angry. The grand blue Wyoming skies had curdled.

～～

Winter would arrive.

Steve would start working again at Wild Iris, and he would begin fixing up the house he and Amy have yet to occupy together. He described himself, wearily, as "functioning, able to work and continue living." When asked about his anger at the cops, at Nels, he said, "I don't really have the energy to get pissed off at anyone these days."

The mouth of the Sinks was searched by divers. Old mine shafts in Atlantic City, Wyoming, were explored.

At a University of Wyoming football game, the scoreboard lit up with Amy's photo, the familiar phone number, the request for any information.

Todd Skinner and Amy Whisler headed south to their winter climbing headquarters in Texas. Skinner went on to Mali to climb Fatima, a 2,000-foot quartzite tower.

In mid-November, Skinner was asked about "Amy as the summit," about never giving up. He replied that in the absence of new clues, the primary task had become supporting Steve. "We never really started climbing anyway," he added. "We were stuck at the base of the mountain, walking in place."

Steve and Nels met at a race for Amy held in Laramie. They spoke briefly, cautiously, civilly.

Dean Chingman, a young Indian from Ethete, on the Wind River Reservation, went missing in early November. The search-and-rescue effort included search dogs and one airplane. Two FBI agents were assigned to the Chingman case.

Everyone waited for news from NASA on whether photographs that might have been taken by Russia's Mir space station on the day of Amy's disappearance would reveal new clues. Eventually word came that no such photos existed.

In mid-October, the FBI and the local investigators, having dropped their demand that Steve Bechtel submit to a polygraph test, asked him to come in for another general interview, but on the advice of Kent Spence, his attorney, he declined. "They're just trying to poke and poke, and hope that they get something," Spence said recently. "They've made it look like Steve has something to hide."

The Bechtel case was on the docket of a grand jury, convened in Casper in late November. Grand jury proceedings are unnervingly secret affairs. None of the officials involved would comment on the deliberations, though one of the subpoenaed witnesses said that the jury was mostly interested in a former acquaintance of Amy's whom authorities have been unable to locate.

The reward for information leading to the recovery of Amy Wroe Bechtel now stands at $100,000.

~~~~~~

All of these strands, these smears, shadows, whispers, shards—they have come to naught.

Early storms arrived, left. Deer hunters—objects of an intensive, dedicated, but fruitless flurry of Have You Seen Amy? publicity—came and went.

The Loop Road became impassable and was closed.

Winter lasts a long time in Lander. Forget the brochures, forget Jackson Hole. It is a punishing time. It is not the winter of whooping skiers and snowboarders, of fresh flocks of pink-cheeked tourists. It is unfathomably cold. It is knife-blade winds. It is the season of iron silence. Time to take shelter. To regroup. To gain faith—faith that the snow, the cold, will vanish. It has to.

It is also the season of memory's distortion. The golds of autumn become more golden; the greens of summer, greener; the warm, clear days, warmer, clearer.

But not this year; not in Lander. A woman is still lost. Friends and loved ones still grieve, wonder, rage: Where is Amy? And so her life, and the lives of those who care most about her, are suspended. In place of logic, movement, and resolution, there is stasis: a young face on a poster, a dusty Toyota station wagon, blinking cursors.

These won't do—not at all. They don't recall Amy, and they don't convey the knee-buckling anguish of this bottomless mystery. To glimpse even a measure of these things, you could return, perhaps, to a moment in September, nearly three hours after the first runner in the Amy Bechtel Hill Climb crossed the finish line at Frye Lake. The last four walkers are approaching the line as one, holding hands: Amy's mother, Jo Anne; Amy's sister, Casey; Casey's young daughter, Jillian; and Jillian's friend, Hanna.

Jo Anne Wroe's face is pulled long. She is limping. Strands of her rich black hair stick wet to her face. She looks bewildered, beyond exhaustion, like death itself.

THE BOOMTOWN, THE GRINGO, THE GIRL, AND HER MURDER

TONY D'SOUZA

~~~~~~

In 2007, a local beauty turned up dead in Nicaragua's San Juan del Sur and the dream of paradise became a nightmare for one expat American surfer. He got thirty years and, predictably, a media melee ensued. Our man was on the scene from day one. This is the story you haven't heard.

~~~~~~

San Juan del Sur, Nicaragua, is a fishing-and-tourist town of colorfully painted wooden homes laid out on lazy Pacific-coast streets where bicycles outnumber vehicles, where kids set up goal markers out of rocks for afternoon games of *fútbol*, where locals pass the evenings exchanging gossip on their stoops or attending mass. Always now, too, half-clad gringa girls stroll past in flip-flops on their way to Marie's Bar, where the party on the weekends spills out the door, or Big Wave Dave's, where expats line the counters trading notes on the day's sailfish catch, on the going price for laborers, on the quality of the local beauties, of which there are many.

Los Años Ochentas, as the Sandinista–contra war of the 1980s is carefully referred to here, is long over, though the memories of it remain. The men go out in their narrow pangas for tuna, for roosterfish, for bonito, for whatever they can pull in on their hand-lines. The women hang up their laundry to sun-dry.

I'd come, like others before me, looking to pitch a hammock on a stretch of untrammeled beach. Hearing reports of Nicaragua's beauty and safety from a fellow former Peace Corps volunteer, I'd left Florida in my Ford Ranger in early October with a couple of fishing poles, driven slowly through Mexico, Guatemala, El Salvador, and Honduras, and arrived in San Juan del Sur on a dusty Sunday afternoon six weeks, five border crossings, and 4,000 miles later. I'd been disappointed before by tales of paradise that turn out to be tourist traps, but my first view of the bay, hemmed in by two sets of cliffs like the Pillars of Hercules, left me diving into the surf as the sun set, wearing a smile as warm as the water around me. By noon the next day, I had a little house with a view of the Pacific for $250 a month.

San Juan is small. Officially, twenty thousand people live here; according to the local barber, Roberto López Mora, it's really just a few extended families—Lópezes, Chamorros, Calderons, Sanchezes, Danglas—tracing their roots to the time "before records." It doesn't take more than a day to start recognizing faces: the oldest beer-bellied expat with his young Nica girlfriend, the Rastafarian trinket hustler who promises he can get you "any-ting, any-ting." But also, the carpenter who makes furniture across from the park and the expat and his local wife taking their tawny-haired kid down to the beach for a swim.

Nine days after I arrived, on Tuesday, November 21, I walked down the hill into town in the evening to buy a few cans of beer. In the street outside the Miscellania Calderon, where I'd buy all of my sundries over the next three months, a huge crowd had assembled, everyone hushed and looking at something I couldn't see. Gatherings like this are ubiquitous in Central America; I passed it off as a religious event, a Purisima procession of a statue of the Virgin. Then I saw the cops. They came in and out of the doorway of the Sol Fashion boutique in their neat blue uniforms, taking notes.

In the coming days, the shocking details of what was alleged to have happened were splashed in tawdry headlines in *El Nuevo Diario*, the left-leaning national paper. Doris Ivania Alvarado Jiménez, twenty-five, a pretty, popular San Juan native, was reported to have been raped, sodomized, and strangled with a ferocity that spoke of specific hatred. It was an audacious crime. Last seen alive in front of her shop at 11:30 that morning, Jiménez was found shortly after 2:00 p.m. when the building's watchman, noticing that the boutique was closed, let himself in with a key. What he found inside has threatened to boil resentments between locals and expats into open hostility: the woman's body, hog-tied with bedsheets, asphyxiated with wadded-up paper and rags.

The first newspaper reports pointed to a robbery gone wrong, that Jiménez had happened upon—and recognized the criminals—that they'd killed her because of it. That premise quickly fell apart as the police issued warrants for four men.

Two of them, local surfers who ran in the same posse, were picked up soon after the murder: Julio Martín Chamorro López, thirty, better known as Rosita, was nabbed after a policeman remembered seeing him wandering near Sol Fashion shirtless, bearing what appeared to be fresh scratches and "acting nervous." Nelson Antonio López Dangla, twenty-four, who goes by the nickname Krusty, was arrested shortly after Chamorro. The third man, twenty-year-old Armando Llanes, had been casually dating Jiménez, her friends said. A student at Ave Maria College of the Americas, near Managua, whose family has ties to both Nicaragua and South Florida, Llanes was never taken into custody. He was dropped from suspicion when he produced a statement from his university registrar accounting for his whereabouts during some of the time of the murder.

But what made this case so dramatic was the fourth suspect: Jiménez's ex-boyfriend, a twenty-eight-year-old expat from Nashville, Tennessee, named Eric Stanley Volz. Bilingual, with a degree in Latin American studies from the University of California at San Diego, Eric had moved to San Juan del Sur in 2005 and become a Nicaraguan resident. Until his bio was removed from the Century 21 website several weeks after the murder, he was listed as associate manager of the company's San Juan office, and had also made a name for himself publishing a glossy new bilingual lifestyle magazine called *EP* (short for *El Puente*, or "The Bridge"). Eric and Doris had dated for a little over a year, but by the summer of 2006 they'd split: He moved to Managua to devote himself to *EP*, while she remained in San Juan to run her business. After her death, Volz canceled a Thanksgiving business trip back to the States to attend her funeral. Police arrested him shortly after the ceremony.

Local opinion convicted Eric Volz immediately. YOUNG BUSINESSWOMAN VICTIM OF JEALOUS GRINGO, blazed the *Diario*. US EMBASSY ADVISES ACCUSED GRINGO TO KEEP QUIET. As reported in the paper, and as I later read in court documents, what Rosita Chamorro told police in an unsigned statement—one that he and his lawyer would later insist to me had been coerced through torture—was that Volz, apparently jealous of Jiménez's new relationship with Llanes, had offered Chamorro $5,000 to go with him around noon to Sol Fashion, where the American attacked Jiménez, then raped, sodomized, and killed her. Krusty Dangla, who would become the prosecution's main witness, said Volz came out of the shop at one p.m. and paid him 50 cordobas (about $2.75) to put two garbage bags full of what felt like clothes in a white car.

Volz's family quickly disseminated detailed accounts of his alibi—that at least ten witnesses placed him two hours away in Managua the whole time—on a website for supporters called FriendsofEricVolz.com. But the people of San Juan had made up their minds: At Big Wave Dave's, the long-haired beauties tending bar began casually rebuffing expat advances with the simple and musical refrain *Gringos son asesinos*. Gringos are murderers.

~~~~~~

Things have been changing quickly in San Juan over the past five years. Sixty major housing developments are either under construction or soon to break ground, from the Costa Rican border, a half-hour south of town, up to and well beyond the fabulous Popoyo reef break, an hour north. More than $400 million in foreign investment has poured in. Land that was next to worthless as recently as 2002 is now flipped with ease; one-third-acre ocean-view lots go for hundreds of thousands. The franchises have followed: The first Subway opened three weeks after I arrived.

An estimated seventy-eight million Americans will retire in the next twenty years, some of them dreaming of deals down south. On the higher end, this could mean a $500,000, 2,500-square-foot house in a gated community overlooking one of these stunning beaches, with its own restaurants, swimming pools, shops, clubhouses, DirecTV, wireless Internet, and full security. The expats need not speak Spanish or even notice much that they are in Nicaragua. All the while, the real estate ads promise, their investments will increase at rates that would make the stock market look silly.

A quick scan of back issues of *Between the Waves*, a local quarterly English-language magazine geared toward tourists, reveals three things nearly all of these ads tout: investment potential, concern for the environment, and sex. *Between the Waves* covers feature lovely, light-skinned young Nicaraguan women emerging like Venus from the Pacific foam, some of the shots proving so popular they've been reprinted as local RE/MAX ads: a tall girl stepping from the sea in a bikini and hoop earrings, smiling at someone off camera, no one else on the beach. Other developers take the green approach. One outfit, Nica Dev, promises that they "develop with a conscience," advertising green communities built around ecological reserves, and Century 21's ads exhort readers to "preserve the beaches."

It's not hard to see why there's an air of expat guilt about what's going on here. In December, I drove out to one of the bigger new projects, Cantamar at Playa Yankee. While many developments can't be seen from the gatehouses where guards stop prying visitors, this one is too big to hide. Carved into the forested hills overlooking an untouched beach are clear-cut terrace after clear-cut terrace, heavy machines at work, the ground rumbling beneath their weight. When Cantamar is eventually finished, it will be a sprawling community of luxury homes, but when I went back in March, it still looked like what it was: deforested land.

Nicaragua is a World Bank– and International Monetary Fund–designated "heavily indebted poor country," with little legal ability to control its economic future: Everything is for sale. And once Nicaraguans decide to cash in and sell their houses or farms, they have to look far inland for anything affordable. Many who sold four and five years ago realized less than 5 percent of what the same properties sell for now. A prominent development appraised by the owner at $26 million was built on land bought for $80,000, according to a son of the family who sold it.

Some of these sales are contested. "The foreigners come here knowing the titles are in disarray," one San Juan man told me late one night at L'Mche's Bar, where the local restaurant and hotel staff unwind after work. He was home for the holidays from the job he held, legally, in Texas. "They have the money to win any lawsuit. We can't afford to fight them in court. And do you know how we are treated when we go to the United States? We can't even jaywalk without being harassed by the police."

This huge and growing disparity in wealth has begun to reveal itself in ugly ways. Though Eduardo Holmann, San Juan's Sandinista-party mayor, dismissed a *Diario* report that local fishermen have been shot at when they drop anchor in bays fronting private developments, he admitted that new laws have to be written to protect beach-access rights, which some foreigners have been trying to deny. Petty theft is a persistent annoyance. Crack is a growing problem. One Wednesday night late in January, a block from Big Wave Dave's, a celebrated local hustler and avowed user stabbed a prominent expat twice in the stomach with a pair of barber's scissors, the culmination of a long-running feud. The expat recovered after surgery; the hustler was arrested and released, and a few weeks later he left town.

Meanwhile, the boom continues, despite foreign anxiety surrounding the November 2006 reelection of former Sandinista president Daniel Ortega. Ortega, after all, led the nationalization of private property following the 1979 revolution, which overthrew US-backed dictator Anastasio Somoza. The Ortega of today is not the Ortega of the past; he has been actively reassuring investors that the favorable business climate here will not change. Still, few deny it comes with a price. "You've seen these developments," said Mayor Holmann. "Where is that sanitation going to drain? We are trying to support all of this with the same infrastructure that we had thirty years ago. If we don't get help from the national government, we are going to have critical situations with drainage and electricity."

The mayor is not anti-development. "If the foreign investors behave with social responsibility," he said, "community relations will turn out okay." But, he cautioned, "what we don't want to see is a San Juan del Sur of America."

Into the fray of this fevered market came Eric Volz. Speculation had become so rampant by 2004 that Internet investors who'd previously never left the States were visiting regularly on real estate tours, getting the hard sell while enjoying the delights of the bay, the 70-cent beers, the heady idea of financial windfall, the sight of all the pretty girls. Everywhere, the air was full of the sounds of construction, the money crashing in like the big breakers rolling onto shore. It says a lot about San Juan's unregulated, unlicensed real estate market that it could not only make room for the youthful and inexperienced Volz, but also allow him to thrive. By all accounts, he had a knack for closing the deal; he was gathering capital, more than $100,000 of which he'd use to fund *EP*.

According to friends, Volz is a diversely talented individualist, a traveler and outdoor enthusiast. When he was ten, his family moved from Sacramento to Nashville, where his divorced parents both still live. Volz's father, Jan, is a country-music-tour organizer and founding member of an alternative Christian band called the 77's; his mother, Maggie Anthony, is an interior decorator. He has a younger sister, plus a stepsister from his mother's second marriage. His mother's side of the family is of Mexican descent, and it's from them that Volz became "receptively bilingual," as he put it when I spoke to him in March. "I understood what they said, but I only produced English."

Volz took up climbing at a local gym when he was eleven, as a way to deal with his parents' divorce. "It really began to mean something about freedom, learning my limits, learning to trust myself," he told me. After high school, he moved to Meyers, California, near South Lake Tahoe. He worked in carpentry, took classes at Lake Tahoe Community College, DJ'd at a local bar, and built a reputation as an exceptional free climber.

While many of his Tahoe friends remained in the mountains, Volz chose a different path, ultimately pursuing Latin American studies at UCSD. "I reached a point where I was ready to be a little more responsible socially," he says. "I realized that hanging out in the mountains and staying in shape was great, but I wasn't really doing much."

Volz's climbing friends would be among the first to come to his defense after his arrest. "He had a view you don't see as much in mountain towns," Chris McNamara, a Tahoe climber who made bouldering films with Volz, wrote me in an e-mail. "He was concerned with global issues and was looking for the opportunity to address them. He thought Nicaragua was the place to do this. And that's the incredibly tragic irony of this case. Eric was working to get beyond those divisive cultural and political relations. Everything that he now seems to be in the middle of."

In 2004, Volz joined his father for a ten-day trip to Iraq, photographing country singer Chely Wright's tour as she entertained the troops. He met Iraqis, interviewed soldiers, and flew in Black Hawks. He soon finished his degree. In early

2005, having visited San Juan off and on for six years, he decided to move to Nicaragua. In the waterfront Rocamar Restaurant, where he often ate, Doris Jiménez was a waitress. Volz's résumé was already filled with travels; she was a local girl of very modest upbringing. "Her dream, from when she was fifteen years old," says her aunt María Elena Alvarado, "was to have a shop." Jiménez studied business administration at the UPOLI University in nearby Rivas, taking computer and English classes. While Volz, as one friend puts it, "had the world by a string," Jiménez, according to everyone, was the prettiest girl in town.

Just one year later, Jiménez would be running Sol Fashion, while Volz focused on the launch of *EP*. The magazine, as he wrote in his first publisher's letter, would be devoted to everything from "the explosion of surf culture" to local anxiety over the "oncoming waves of foreigners, construction, and the almighty dollar." Professional, bilingual, and printed on expensive paper, the premiere edition appeared in July 2006, boasting a 20,000-copy run, a viable presence in five countries, and a look to rival *Vogue*. That first issue includes a nine-page "fashion documentary" called "Maria's Journey," following Nicaraguan model Maria Mercedes in various states of dress and undress in Victoria's Secret, Prada, and Benetton—beginning as she wakes with a yawn and a long tumble of black hair in what is clearly a campesino shack and ending with her posed outside a modern office building, a powerful CEO. "Where you come from," the text reads, "does not determine where you can go." Doris Jiménez appears on page 59, standing in the countryside in a traditional skirt, the wind in her hair. The words beside her read, "We are rising in the ranks of power, breaking new ground.—Women of Central America."

Before *EP*'s glossy incarnation, Volz had produced two issues of a community newsletter called *El Puente*, in March and October 2005, with Jon Thompson, an Atlanta native who began going back and forth to San Juan in 1999. Earnest and crew-cut, with fluent Nicaraguan-accented Spanish, Thompson, thirty-two, now directs the upscale Pelican Eyes resort's A. Jean Brugger Foundation, which provides educational opportunities to students. The original *El Puente* was Thompson's idea, his ticket to moving here full-time. "Let's say I come to San Juan and I don't know there's an eco-stove project going on," he said in December. "That's what *El Puente* was going to be for—to connect resources and interest with local leadership and sustainable projects."

Thompson and Volz met here in 2001, when they were both still visitors. "He told me about his films, that he'd been a DJ," Thompson said of his onetime friend. "I told Eric, 'I'll hire you to come down, take pictures.'" Their close partnership lasted well into 2005. "Then Eric wanted to grow," said Thompson, who clearly regrets the loss of his project. "San Juan wasn't big enough for him. His Century 21 money poured in, and eventually it grew beyond a local newsletter and became the international *EP* magazine."

When they first started *El Puente* and money was tight, Volz shared a house with Thompson and his local girlfriend, Arelis Castro López, now his wife. Volz and Jiménez began dating; Jiménez moved in, too. The arrangement lasted several months, and both Thompson and his wife say they didn't see anything that would make them think Volz is a murderer. Thompson knew Jiménez three years longer than he knew Volz; he says what everyone says—that she was nice.

Though sentiment in San Juan is unanimously positive concerning Doris Jiménez, opinion about Volz is mixed. People close to her family invariably say that his foreign ways led her into behaviors considered shameful here. Her mother, Mercedes Alvarado—who sold her San Juan home in 2006 and moved inland to Rivas with Doris's two younger sisters—says she took exception to what she describes as Volz's lack of communication with the family, to her daughter's willingness to leap out of bed "when he would call in the middle of the night." Jiménez's grandmother Jacinta Lanzas told the *Diario*, "With these people you have to be very careful, because you don't know anything about them, nothing of their past, and in this case I always sensed something bad. I never felt good about this guy." Volz, for his part, says Jiménez was never close to her mother.

Volz's business associates insist he is "a great guy," that he couldn't possibly have done this. A few other expats, people who had unsuccessful real estate dealings with him at Century 21, readily vilify him in open anger. Many others simply say that he seemed aloof. "A lot of the expats in San Juan," Volz explained, "quite frankly, I don't connect with them. So I could see how they could see me being an arrogant person. I wasn't your normal expat. I worked pretty much all the time."

Volz and Jiménez's split, both he and Thompson insisted, was amicable. "I had a lot of love for her," said Volz, who says that he ended things around June 2006. "It wasn't like I moved to San Juan del Sur and was just, Oh my God, a Latina—sexy. I knew I wasn't going to be in Nicaragua forever, and I was always very up front and honest with Doris about that."

"Doris was Miss San Juan a couple years ago," Thompson said. "Eric wasn't even her first American boyfriend. Eric is innocent. The town didn't know him; that's why they were so quick to condemn him.

"Have you heard the expression '*Pueblo pequeño, infierno grande*'?" he asked. "'Little town, big hell.' There is a lot of jealousy here. Who knows what's really going on?"

Two days before Volz's December 7 arraignment in Rivas, a car with loudspeakers circled through San Juan exhorting people to "bring justice to the gringo!" A huge crowd jeered as he was escorted into the courthouse; during the hearing, a woman outside could be heard shouting, "Come out, gringo, we are going to murder you!" Expecting the worst, Volz and the US Embassy regional security officer, Michael Poehlitz, exchanged clothes while Volz's father, Jan, who'd flown in from the States, looked on.

As Volz left the arraignment, the mob saw through the ruse and rushed him. "A couple punches flew out of the side," Volz told me. "I don't know if I dodged them or if they just missed me. I felt a rock fly by my head." He ducked into a nearby gymnasium and hid in an office. With the mob surrounding the building, Poehlitz ran in behind him, making calls on his cell while Volz frantically stripped off one of the handcuffs and kicked through a wall into a room where they would be more secure. An hour later, police retrieved them.

"It was utter chaos," Jan Volz told me this spring. "Eric had said to me, 'Dad, do not come over here; there are guys with clubs.' I was not going to leave my son. They were taunting and jeering." As Jan left with two legal advisers, he recalled, "people were pounding on our car, hitting it with clubs. I'm convinced that if they had caught any one of us, they would have killed us."

Under Nicaraguan law, the defense may choose between a trial by judge or jury. With sentiment tilted so heavily against Volz, and because a jury trial rules out the possibility of appeal, the defense opted for a judge; the trial was set for January 26. Meanwhile, Volz was held in various jails and penitentiaries. According to his parents, he wasn't fed for a five-day stretch; he spent a week in a medical ward; he was repeatedly threatened. Then, at a special hearing on January 16, the pretrial judge, Rivas district judge Dr. Edward Peter Palma Mora, ordered Volz released to house arrest. If he'd had all the facts at the arraignment, Palma stated, he would have thrown the case out due to lack of evidence. As it was, the trial was postponed until February 14, with a designated trial judge, Dr. Ivette Toruño Blanco, officiating. Until then, Volz would remain at a friend's house in an undisclosed location.

Middle-class by US standards, Volz's parents say that they've spent their life savings defending their son. In January, friends brought a host of Nashville musicians together for a benefit concert. Dane Anthony, Volz's stepfather, has left his eighteen-year career at Nashville's Belmont University, where he was an associate dean of students, to focus full-time on the case. Volz's team would eventually include Jacqueline Becerra, a lawyer with the multinational firm Greenberg Traurig and president-elect of the Federal Bar Association's South Florida chapter;

Simon Strong, of Holder International, a company specializing in risk management; Melissa Campbell, a music-industry publicist and family friend; private security from multinational Corporate Security Consultants (CSC); and Ramón Rojas, a prominent Nicaraguan lawyer who successfully defended Daniel Ortega in a civil case in 2001.

From the first days, the family seemed out of their element. Early comments they made about the legal system were used by the Nicaraguan media to ill effect, and local coverage was so one-sided—with the people of San Juan relying on the *Diario* and an incensed Mercedes Alvarado for most of their information—that Volz's parents would finally pay to run his side of the story as an ad.

Sometime in the second half of December, Volz's defense team called a meeting at the Crowne Plaza Hotel in Managua to give San Juan mayor Holmann Volz's account of his whereabouts on the day of the murder, hoping he could intervene with local reporters. What quickly transpired, however, was anything but positive. Holmann expanded the invitation to include Krusty Dangla's lawyer, Cesar Baltodano, and commissioner Yamil Gutiérrez, of the Rivas police. Agreeing to try to arrange a tête-à-tête between Jiménez's mother and Volz's defense lawyers, Baltodano invited Mercedes Alvarado to lunch at the Gran Diamante restaurant, near Rivas on Lake Nicaragua. According to Alvarado and her lawyer, Erick Cabezas, who was also present, Baltodano told the woman, "Your daughter is dead. She's not coming back. How much could she have earned in her life? Fifty dollars a day? Over forty years?"

Cabezas alleges that Baltodano told Alvarado that if she would make a public written statement attesting to Volz's innocence, a cash settlement of $1,000,000 would be placed in her bank account, to which Cabezas, as her lawyer, would be entitled to 20 percent. While Baltodano denies offering a settlement, he admits the subject came up. "You know," he told me, "this sort of thing exists everywhere in the world. I said to her that her daughter would never live again; maybe we could do something." Volz's family, his defense team, and Holmann all emphatically deny having suggested a settlement.

Nevertheless, Alvarado went to the press. "I don't need a million dollars," she would cry in every subsequent radio and print interview. "I need my daughter!" Local sentiment turned darker. "He's rich! His powerful family is trying to buy him out!" became a local mantra.

The Volz family seemed totally confused. "I'm a guy who makes a salary," Jan Volz said. "I'm broke now. Doris's life was worth a lot more than a million dollars. I'm deeply sorry that she's gone. I want justice, too. If Eric was guilty, I'd tell him, 'You'll pay in here because you made a choice.' Had I a million dollars, I wouldn't have given it to her. Eric is innocent—I'm not trying to buy his innocence."

Meanwhile, they kept up their vigil. "Today is day 23 for Eric in jail," his mother, Maggie Anthony, wrote from Nicaragua on the website on December 16. "That is the way I start each day. I've been waking up at 5:00 each morning wondering how many days has it been, and if Eric is sleeping. I then quietly go downstairs to check my e-mail for any news from our attorneys or a message from someone who is sending us love or support."

Volz was able to contribute one posting himself, on January 4. "I still don't know exactly why I'm being forced to walk this path," he wrote. "Some have mentioned 'karma'—I say bullshit. This is me being formed through a heavy spiritual and physical journey. The ultimate purpose is not yet clear, but in the meantime I have become a lightning rod for politics, compassion, prayer, and love. A campaign and a movement have emerged."

~~~~~~

Surfing is a good way to escape the complexities of the world, especially on the empty waves of Nicaragua. When a swell rolls in, there are double overheads, left breaks, right breaks, beach breaks, reef breaks. The water is warm and clean, the sand soft. Looking south, you can see the dense mountains of Costa Rica; just off-shore, islands rise out of the ocean like the buttes of Monument Valley. Fish leap from the water in schools. Humpback whales breach in the distance.

Playa Madera, 4 miles north of town, is where they all surfed—Volz, Chamorro, Dangla. During the rainy season, the road is an axle-bending, suspension-wrecking gash through the rain forest, but, to be fair, once the rains stop and the government grader comes through, you can get into third gear. Here and there are the signs of development—tarmac-long clear-cuts and completed gated communities—along with modest truck-shed *fincas* with chickens and pigs in the yard, the municipal dump crowded with turkey vultures, and long swaths of forest resplendent with parakeets, butterflies, and monkeys.

My truck made me lots of "friends" in Central America, and among my more-regular passengers out to Playa Madera were Roque and Rex Calderon, the half-dozen members of their entourage, and everyone's surfboard. Roque, twenty-one, and Rex, fourteen, are two of Nicaragua's best surfers—Roque led the national squad to second place at the Central American Championships in Costa Rica last July—so that at any given time, I'd be driving the majority of the Nicaraguan national surf team to the beach. Day after day in the months leading up to Volz's trial, the Calderons, their friend Juan, and I waxed our boards and paddled out to the 4-footers. Duck-diving back out through the set, I'd get to watch Roque's surgical dissection of the whole line, Rex's skateboard aerials.

One Saturday night in early December, Roque and I had a drink on the rooftop of the La Dolce Vita Hotel, getting started on what usually wound up at four in the morning in the low-key and hidden L'Mche's Bar. Roque has begun to appear in the surf magazines; his mentor, American board shaper Tom Eberly, believes in him so much that he quietly paid for Roque's initial English lessons, getting him ready to succeed on a larger stage. As we looked down at San Juan's central intersection, where European and American girls in sarongs passed in pairs and threes under the yellow streetlight, Roque told me, "Thanks to surfing, lots of people here are making a living: hotels, restaurants, the beach taxis, the surf boats. It's expat surfers who are building many of the developments here. Twenty percent of tourism in San Juan depends on surfing." For himself, he'd like to open a surf shop.

About the murder? "Rosita is my cousin. I used to see Eric surfing."

In other words, Roque didn't want to talk about it. Nobody does: Fear of blood feuds looms large in San Juan, and Chamorro's and Dangla's extended families are enmeshed in everything. One shopkeeper took me into a back room so she could cry and tell me how awful she feels for Volz; she wouldn't let me use her name. "[My store] is a public place," she said. "I'm afraid."

"The people in town—they're angry," another echoed. "Eric didn't do it. I am afraid of people here. Of vendetta."

Meanwhile, the sidewalk in front of the Arena Caliente hostel and board shop is busy night after night with the local surfers and the twentysomething backpacker girls who hook up with them.

"'Do you think he really loves me?'" mimicked American ESL teacher Mara Jacobsohn, rolling her eyes at the foreign girls the surfer guys go through like soap. Jacobsohn has taught hundreds in the town; she lived with a local family so long that they still get approval over whom she dates. While Nicaraguan attitudes don't seem to condemn casual encounters between local men and female tourists, the reverse situation, she noted, isn't viewed in the same light. When it came to this case, she said, "It's been very important that it must be someone not from here. What's most important about Eric is that he lacked a community; it seemed to me like he was one of those people here to make money. At the same time, I don't think he did it. Even with Doris, although pleasant and nice, she was rewritten. She was beatified. It's disgusting to see Krusty as a witness. A parasite on the whole community."

A few men in the surfer crowd, I noticed, had turned to hustling, befriending tourists and intimidating them into paying for the night's drinks or staging phony drug deals in which the tourists got burned. One expat woman, who would not allow her name to be published, told me that she once pursued a restraining order against Chamorro after a violent encounter; when I asked him about it, he said that she'd hit him first. Chamorro's lawyer, Geovanny Ruiz Mena, denies any history of violence on his client's part, aside from a bar altercation four years ago.

Down on the street when Roque and I left the Dolce Vita, four young men in blue shirts, all bouncers from the Otangani disco, at the edge of town, were passing out photocopies of Jiménez's picture. "We are friends of her family," they explained. "We want these tourists to know that this happened." One shouldered past the others and said in a low voice, "When Eric is convicted and sent to the real prison, he will be killed there for sure." He drew his finger slowly across his throat. "But I hope they rape him first."

In early February, after repeatedly and persistently being turned away, I was finally given access to the Doris Jiménez murder-case file in the Rivas courthouse, by Judge Toruño herself. For forty minutes, she allowed me to sift through the nearly four hundred pages of documents while two of her staff looked on. I have to admit that all the rumors, coupled with the *Diario* articles, the number of people who said they didn't know or like Volz, and the certainty of Jiménez's family and friends, had led me to have little doubt of his guilt. But when the clerk called time, I closed the file sure that, whoever he was or wasn't, Eric Volz was innocent.

In the file were the original charges against Volz and Armando Llanes for the rape and sodomy of Jiménez, as well as murder charges against Volz, Llanes, Chamorro, and Dangla. These were amended on December 6, and what was read at the December 7 arraignment was that Eric Stanley Volz and Julio Martín "Rosita" Chamorro López were accused of killing Doris Jiménez. Charges against Armando Llanes and Nelson Antonio "Krusty" López Dangla had been dropped. Dangla was now the prosecution's principal witness.

As I'd already read in the papers, Dangla's police statement alleged that at ten a.m. on the day of the murder, he was standing outside the Costa Azul hotel when Volz stopped in a low, white car with another man in the passenger seat and told him to come to Sol Fashion at one p.m., where Volz allegedly came out of the shop, handed him two black garbage bags full of what felt like clothes, and told him to put them in the car. Dangla said Volz gave him 50 cordobas and sped off in the direction of Managua.

The police statement attributed to Chamorro was also in the file. Volz, it alleged, had offered Chamorro $5,000 to go to Sol Fashion, where the American hit and kicked his ex-girlfriend, then raped, sodomized, and killed her. It wouldn't be until after the trial that Chamorro's lawyer told me the statement had been coerced.

Then there were the crime-scene photos: Jiménez's body, bound at the ankles and wrists; her mouth, forced open so wide from being stuffed that it seemed frozen in a perpetual scream. A first forensic exam by the "supplemental" examiner in Rivas, Dr. Isolde Vanesa Arcia Jiménez, described vaginal and anal scratches. A second examination, by Dr. Óscar Bravo Flores, the official forensic examiner, found none. Toxicology put Jiménez's blood alcohol content at 0.3, a bizarrely high level. In the photos, her belt is unbuckled and the first two buttons of her fly are undone, revealing the waistband of her underwear. The official police report states that the perpetrators undressed her to rape and sodomize her, then put her clothes back on because of a "sentimental" attachment, and finally hog-tied her the way she was found. Volz's blood type was entered as O, then as A, which is what he is. (Jiménez was also A, while Rosita Chamorro is O.) The Nicaraguan criminal-justice system does not yet test for DNA, and I found no fingerprint evidence against any of the defendants.

In official physical exams recorded in the files, the police say that both Chamorro and Dangla bore "fingernail" scratches on their arms. According to these files, Krusty Dangla was scratched on seven different parts of his body, including the head of his penis. Volz, the reports noted, had a number of thin, straight lines, one more defined than the others, on the unbroken skin of his right shoulder.

And then I read the evidence regarding Volz's alibi: cell-phone records, a time-stamped instant-messaging log, page after page of statements by the ten people—most of whom I would later interview myself—supporting Volz's account. Shortly after 9:00 a.m., Volz maintained, he walked into the *EP* offices from his living quarters—the building also served as his home—and was seen by the security guard, the housekeeper, and various *EP* staff. From 10:30 to 11:00, model Maria Mercedes and a friend said they met with him. At noon, Ricardo Castillo, a Nicaraguan journalist who has contributed to the BBC and other news outlets, arrived; he and Volz then initiated a teleconference to Virginia with consultant Nick Purdy, a cofounding publisher of the music magazine *Paste*. As the conference progressed, Purdy and Volz exchanged instant messages on their impressions of Castillo, a potential contributor to *EP*. The call lasted nearly an hour. Following it, at roughly 1:15 p.m., Volz, Castillo, and Adam Paredes, *EP*'s art director, sat down to a lunch of curried fish served by the housekeeper, Martha Carolina Aguirre Corea. Castillo left at 2:00. At roughly 2:45, Volz received a call informing him of Jiménez's death; more calls would quickly come in confirming it. Meanwhile, a local hairstylist, Rossy Elena Estrada López, had arrived to cut Volz's and another employee's hair; she found him talking on a cell phone, she said, "afflicted and crying." According to these witnesses, Volz left the office at roughly 4:30.

Volz's cell-phone records precisely match his account of what happened next: that he left Managua and drove to San Juan. At 4:38 p.m. the first call outside Managua appears on the log, the following eleven calls tracing the trajectory of someone driving quickly, arriving in the San Juan cellular area at 6:34. (I've since done this drive twice in the same amount of time. It requires driving fast but not inordinately so.)

Only one document cast suspicion on his alibi: a rental agreement from Hertz. Volz had called Hertz to rent a car to go to San Juan. (His, he said, was unreliable.) The agreement was printed at 3:11 p.m. at the Hertz office. But when the vehicle was delivered, *EP* assistant Leidy de los Santos, not Volz, signed the agreement. She went inside and returned with a credit-card slip bearing what appeared to be his signature, but the delivery driver never saw Volz himself.

The case for Volz's innocence seemed obvious, irrefutable. The day before the trial, the Volz family asked visitors to their website to pray for the "safety of all involved in and surrounding the trial: Eric, witnesses, press, attorneys, bystanders, security, police; [the] health of one of Eric's key defense team, who is sick with the flu; [the] judge; Doris's mother & family; that the trial is swift and that Eric will be free on Friday!"

~~~~~~

At the Rivas exit on the morning of February 14, police searched my truck for weapons. In town, a two-block circumference around the courthouse was sealed off. I was patted again for weapons, given my press pass, and allowed to walk into the deserted heart of the downtown commercial district. Most of the businesses would keep their steel doors shut for the next three days.

The courtroom was small, frigid with air-conditioning. The cramped gallery was separated from the prosecution and defense tables by a narrow wooden rail. Black-armored special-operations police blocked the door, while six armed national police were stationed at different points in the room. When Lésber Quintero, the *Diario* reporter, arrived, I sidled over to him and asked, "Lésber, why do you always use the word *gringo* instead of *norteamericano* or *estadounidense*?" Quintero blushed as everyone around us laughed. But he quickly found his footing. "*Gringo, chele, norteamericano*—for us Nicaraguans, it's all the same thing."

Soon enough, Volz and Chamorro arrived, and the cameras began flashing. Volz's lawyer, Ramón Rojas, would always be the best-dressed man in the room, save the three US Embassy observers taking notes in the gallery corner. Volz wore a jean jacket, the outlines of a bulletproof vest visible underneath. Chamorro wore his bulletproof vest over a long-sleeved black shirt.

The proceedings opened with efforts by the prosecution, led by Isolda Ibarra Arguello, to establish the time of the crime. A university student who lived next door to Sol Fashion testified that he'd heard someone knocking on Jiménez's door at around 11:45 a.m., and two loud sounds like something heavy hitting the floor at around 1:00 p.m. Another neighbor said that Chamorro had been hanging around Jiménez recently and that something had happened between them. Five days before the murder, he told the court, he'd overheard an angry Chamorro say, "I don't give a damn about this Doris; she's a gringo chaser. She and her beauty can stay that way." Jiménez's mother and close friends testified that Volz was motivated by his jealousy, which increased, they claimed, when Jiménez told him about Armando Llanes. Mercedes Alvarado waved around a receipt from the Gran Diamante, crying out, "I don't need a million dollars. I need my daughter."

Other witnesses were brought forth to call Volz's alibi into question, including the Hertz delivery driver, Victor Morales, who testified that one of Volz's friends had asked him to say that he saw Volz at the *EP* office that day when he didn't, at which point the prosecution spoke at length about why Leidy de los Santos would have signed Volz's rental agreement. Chamorro was never called; the statement he would later recant did not factor into the trial in any significant way. Therefore, the only witness tying Volz to the crime scene was Krusty Dangla. In testimony that made everyone in the courtroom laugh—even the judge—the excitable and often confused Dangla again and again couldn't follow simple directions to hold the microphone up to his mouth. The one coherent thing he managed to do was point his finger at Volz and say, "He gave me 50 cordobas."

"I may be an alcoholic," Dangla stood up at one point and said to Rojas, "but I'm not a liar!"

After declining to cross-examine nearly everyone but Dangla, to the groans of the US Embassy observers, Rojas questioned the forensic witnesses. They explained that the misrecording of Volz's blood type was a typo, and acknowledged that fluid from Jiménez's vagina and anus revealed no presence of semen. We also learned that, between the two forensic examinations, Jiménez's body had been partially embalmed, at her mother's request.

Court adjourned at one p.m. Alvarado, dressed in black, rushed outside to lead a mob of a hundred San Juan residents, calling the police "whores of the gringo" for keeping them back. Volz left the court as he arrived, protected by a Nicaraguan detail of Corporate Security Consultants bodyguards, including a Caucasian man carrying an AR-15 machine gun. The *Diario* would quickly run article after article asking why foreigners were carrying military arms in Nicaragua. That was the last time CSC guards appeared at the trial, though the damage had been done.

Back in San Juan, I found Dangla where I knew he would be: hanging with his friends outside his house. He was jubilant, laughing. On the stand, he had adamantly said that he did not know Jiménez at all beyond seeing her now and again. Now, back in town, with his role in the trial over for him, he said something different. "Yeah, I knew her—at the beach, when I'd pass her shop. I'd see her every day." Asked how he felt, Dangla said, "Very good. I didn't do anything. I have my version. [Eric] has his version. You'll have to talk to my lawyer."

The next day, February 15, Rojas presented the defense. Consensus among the embassy staff and the other two foreign reporters present was that the prosecution's case was too weak to have been brought in the first place. But the judge had tossed out all but three of Volz's witnesses as redundant, allowing him only Nick Purdy, the consultant; Ricardo Castillo, the journalist; and Rossy Estrada, the hairstylist. Purdy went first, testifying through a court translator that he'd been in phone and instant-message conversations with Volz throughout the time of the murder, which Castillo confirmed, testifying that he was actually in the *EP* office with Volz. A frightened Estrada testified that she cut Volz's hair. In the cross-examination, the prosecution hammered away at the point that both Castillo and Purdy had incentive to see Volz free, as they had business dealings with him.

Then Volz took the stand. He was calm and looked directly at the judge. He discussed his relationship with Jiménez in fluent Spanish. He talked about the competitiveness of the real estate market. When he described the $3 million an average San Juan real estate office made in annual sales, a ripple went through the gallery and a woman gasped, "In dollars?" Volz looked at the judge and said he was innocent. When Rojas asked him why Dangla was lying, he said he didn't know.

Then Rojas asked how he had gotten the marks on his shoulder. Again looking directly at the judge, Volz gave an answer that was wholly in keeping with the telenovela elements of the case: "I got it carrying Doris's casket at the funeral."

In the total fifteen hours of the trial, less than forty minutes would be spent on Chamorro. He wasn't called to the stand in his own defense or Volz's prosecution; when his lawyer demanded that his client be called by his legal name, not Rosita, the judge shook her head and smiled, "But that is how we Nicaraguans refer to each other." Chamorro kept a blank face as he watched his only witness, a bleached-blond surfer named Yamil "Coky" Brook Gonzales, testify that he and his Canadian girlfriend had eaten with Chamorro in the market from 9:00 a.m. to around 11:45 the day of the murder. During recesses, he would come to the rail and exchange hugs with his mother and aunt, who always brought a sweater for him, which he didn't wear. He didn't like his picture being taken, and menaced the photographers the first day. But by the second day, he seemed resigned to it.

Volz spent time during court breaks calmly talking to his lawyers; after the first day, he wore a heavy coat against the cold. No members of his family ever appeared in the courtroom; after what had happened at the arraignment, Maggie Anthony told me in Managua in March, they were afraid. Indeed, a terrified Nick Purdy looked at the door after being dismissed from his testimony and said, "I ain't going out on the street."

In closing statements, the prosecutors summarized their case. Nelson "Krusty" Dangla had seen Volz at the scene of the crime. The Hertz delivery driver's testimony and the rental agreement signed by Leidy de los Santos had called Volz's alibi into question. Blood-typing had found both A and O on the sheets used to hog-tie Jiménez; Jiménez and Volz were type A, Chamorro type O. The first forensic examiner found evidence of rape and sodomy. Cell-phone records could not prove Volz was the one using the phone, the prosecution claimed, nor could instant messages. And then there were Volz's injuries. "How can one be scratched by a coffin while wearing a shirt?" the prosecutor asked. The judge looked at the picture of Volz's shoulder, case photo number 21, for a long time.

Rojas presented an impassioned closing statement. Point by point, he went through the prosecution's evidence, highlighting the changes in the original charges, the scratches on Dangla, the conflicting findings about sodomy and rape, the shoddy police-lab work, which included Volz's incorrect blood typing as well as the failure to collect testable material from under Jiménez's fingernails, though her fingers showed signs of defensive injuries. He talked about the credibility of Purdy and Castillo, about the phone records. His voice rose to a crescendo as he slammed the national police laboratory. About the marks on Volz's shoulder, he said, "Of course that could happen—he has white skin." (Later, Mercedes Alvarado would play me a DVD of the funeral. The video shows the sharp edge of Jiménez's coffin resting on Volz's shoulder.)

Just as Rojas was about to finish, there was a sudden commotion, and the special-operations officers barricaded the door with their bodies. A court clerk shouted, "There is shooting outside!"

"Nobody leaves the room," the judge said, and everyone flipped open their cell phones. Jiménez's mother held out hers for us all to hear the shouts of the mob confronting the riot police, which sounded as chaotic as it should. It was amid this tension that the case concluded. Volz's final statement was "Nicaragua has a lot of heart. I believe in her justice." Chamorro said, "God knows I was not there." The judge told the court she'd have a verdict in two hours.

It was hot outside; the street was a shoulder-to-shoulder line of riot police in armor, helmets, and shields. Halfway up the block was another line of blue-uniformed national police, and facing them was an angry crowd of hundreds. I had only two real questions left: Would the judge find a way to convict Chamorro even though she would have to let Volz go? And how violent would the mob get?

Security for the 4:00 p.m. verdict was tighter than it had ever been. A wooden fence had been placed in the hall upstairs, and the riot police made us wait behind it until the accused had taken their seats. The folding chairs in the gallery had been removed so that now the space seemed like a pen. The judge did not come in until 4:15. Then she sat and began to speak.

What I can say is this: The reading of the verdict was long and theatrical. Judge Toruño went through the charges against the two men in a loud and emphatic way, rolling her r's just a touch longer than necessary, letting the names of the accused settle around us in their length. The cameras rolled; it would certainly play out well on local television, which it soon did. The judge threw out Purdy's testimony, because he was in Virginia during the phone call. She threw out the cell-phone records because she said they didn't prove Volz's physical location. She said Ricardo Castillo wasn't credible; she said Dangla was. She admitted that the police lab had done a terrible job and chastised them for it. And then she said two things to Volz. "You were in Managua at 5:00 p.m. and arrived in San Juan at 6:30. You want me to believe that you can move around very fast." And as far as the scratches on his shoulder were concerned, she said, "You can't get scratches from a coffin." Volz hung his head. Chamorro was stoic.

Judge Toruño pronounced both defendants guilty. The prosecutor asked for the maximum penalty for both men, thirty years. Alvarado burst into tears and said, "Thank God! Thank God! This is what a mother wanted—not a million dollars, but justice," as the cameras flashed and rolled. I passed Chamorro's mother in the hall as I left. "It's better this way," she whispered. "It's better that it's both of them."

Outside on the street, the mob was jubilant. Jiménez's uncle pointed his finger at the sky and said, "This is justice for our small town, for Nicaragua, and for all of Central America!" As Volz and Chamorro were hustled into waiting police trucks, the crowd hung off the walls of the surrounding buildings, whistling and shouting that one word: "Justice!"

~~~~~~

Early on the morning of Tuesday, March 27, I sat in a rental car in the parking lot of the Modelo National Penitentiary, just outside the town of Tipitapa, thirty minutes east of Managua. A half-dozen dusty boys, their hands and faces pressed to the windows, waited for me to get out so they could "guard" my car for a tip. This was my fourth attempt to get into the prison in two weeks; what was different about today was that I finally had a letter from Judge Toruño, extending me access to visit Volz, for which I'd had to lobby all the way to the office of a Supreme Court magistrate. Meanwhile, the first international TV crews, from *Dateline* and the *Today* show, had arrived in Nicaragua. Outside the warden's office, seven or eight of them were already waiting their turn to see Volz.

I'd been thinking a lot about Doris Jiménez—about what dark thing descended on her that November day. On March 16, her family commemorated her birthday at the San Juan cemetery. A mariachi band played a haunting traditional song, "Very Pretty Doris," as her relatives tearfully decorated her grave with plastic flowers and ribbons. While I still disagreed with Alvarado that Volz had killed her daughter, I understood her sorrow, her furious desire to see someone pay for this crime.

Entering the Modelo grounds, I saw industrial penitentiary buildings in need of paint. Barbed-wire-crowned walls surrounded the facility, punctuated here and there with towers manned by armed guards. A line of older women were waiting to enter the grounds, carrying plastic shopping bags of toilet paper, rice, and beans. From somewhere, I could hear the echo of men singing.

I was led into a spartan office; Volz was waiting at the desk. He wore a blue Hurley baseball cap and a black T-shirt with the letters EP embossed in green; he'd placed a small voice recorder on the desktop. We shook hands and sat in folding chairs; a guard observed us from a chair in the corner. Volz was calm and collected. He began our interview with this statement: "I've been misquoted a lot; that's why I'm recording. . . . I have an army of attorneys that are willing to step up in any way that I ask. So it's not a threat, but I just want that to be understood."

Over the next two hours, Volz and I talked about the case, about his relationship with Jiménez, about his hopes for the appeals process and his future. (Ramón Rojas filed Volz's appeal shortly after the verdict; by press time, in mid-April, the Rivas court had sent the paperwork up to the appellate court in Granada, where three judges were expected to rule on the case by the end of the month. If Volz's conviction was upheld, the final decision will be decided by the Nicaraguan Supreme Court.) "The best-case scenario for Nicaragua right now is to undo the injustice, release me, absolve me, continue the investigation, and find the real killers," Volz said. "And ultimately, I should be compensated. I've lost a lot. I've worked for two years, really hard, and as soon as I get released, I've got to leave the country."

When the verdict was read, he recalls, "Oh, man, it was a horrible feeling. It's just a dark, dark place that I've gone to on several different occasions. You just have to . . . you close your eyes, just have faith, and you pray." He has a cellmate. Like all of Modelo's two thousand prisoners, they are locked in their cells from four p.m. to four a.m. The rest of the time, the penitentiary keeps a guard near him; he worries about his safety. While still in police custody, he told me, he'd been tortured, but he refused to elaborate. The federal pen was better; still, he said that he had told his mother, "If I die in here and they say it's suicide, don't believe it."

Volz rejected the San Juan rumor that if he wasn't the actual killer, then he must have contracted Jiménez's murder. "It's a town that is hurt," he explained. "Collectively they want to fill their heart with somebody who's the culprit. I didn't pay to have Doris killed; I had nothing to do with her death. I'm one of the people that has been most hurt by it."

The experience had, obviously, changed him. "I'm stripped down," he said. "Day-to-day life in prison is just that: day to day. There's days that I feel confident, I feel good, I get exercise, I get to go out in the yard. And there's days that I don't feel good. . . . Even the strongest person—eventually it gets to you." He relies, he said, on the letters he receives from friends and strangers alike. "People tell me they're in the grocery store looking at which kind of juice to buy and they think about me," he said. "They all of a sudden feel very appreciative for what they have. . . . Those are the kind of things that really make me feel this is not all for nothing. Yeah, Eric Volz is a man in prison, but Doris is the one who lost her life. It's been really hard for me that she's been lost in this tailspin of cultural and political—this divide."

Finally, the guard told us to wrap it up—a film crew was waiting outside. "I'm a warrior," Volz told me. "It's prison, man. Survival of the fittest."

There was one last person I wanted to see: Rosita Chamorro. He was being held in the Granada penitentiary, a facility off the highway that houses eight hundred prisoners on small grounds. Once the guards approved my papers, I walked past long cement buildings, the barred windows revealing prisoners in hammocks, clothes and towels hanging everywhere. At the far end of the yard, I suddenly realized that I was surrounded by inmates, no guards in sight. I entered a narrow corridor, passing the prison chapel, where fifty men prayed, and came out into an area busy with prisoners. A uniformed guard, the only one there, pointed me down a flight of stairs and into a long, dark room, where I could make out the tall and imposing figure of Chamorro.

Alone in the room, we sat together on a bench. Chamorro seemed much affected by prison life, often to the point of tears. "It's hard to be in here," he told me. "I have a lot of enemies. . . . They steal my money, my food. Right now I have nothing. . . . Thirty years, they say to me: thirty years, thirty years, thirty years."

Indeed, prisoners looking down through the barred door at the top of the stairs whistled at us; one of them barked. Chamorro is being held in an overcrowded dormitory cell; the fifty-three men of his wing, he said, share two toilets. Again with great emotion Chamorro told me, "I don't know who killed [Doris], but I know that it wasn't me. I can never go back to my town. Little town, big hell. . . . It's like San Juan doesn't exist for me anymore."

As his lawyer had told me, Chamorro recanted the statement that Volz had offered him $5,000 to go to Sol Fashion. "I was tortured by the police," he said. "They hit me and hit me." Does he think Volz is guilty? "I can't say," he replied. "I can't decide justice for another person." What about his friend Krusty Dangla? "A friend?" Chamorro laughed. "An enemy. We were arrested together, he went free. He's laughing out there. He had scratches. Why didn't they put him in jail?" When I asked if he had any message for Dangla, Chamorro nodded slowly. "Walk carefully," he said. "One day I'll leave here. . . . Watch yourself."

When the guards called time, Chamorro and I exchanged a hug. He asked me to say hello to his family, and if I could give him a little money to buy a soft drink, he'd like that. His voice broke again as he told me, "Don't ever in your life let this happen to you."

As I left, I thought back to Modelo and the last moments I spent with Volz. Our time was drawing to a close, and I would soon walk out into the bright day, while Volz would not.

"Do you think this could happen to anyone?" I asked him.

He nodded. "Yeah. Oh yeah. And it has."

LAST VOYAGE OF THE *CÚLIN*

DAVID VANN

~~~~~~

John Long was living the greatest adventure of his life, sailing home from San Fran-cisco to his native Ireland in 2007. But when his beaten and bruised body was found floating off the lawless, empty coast of Chiapas, it was a scene our writer, an expe-rienced sailor, knew all too well.

~~~~~~

According to villagers, John Long's boat sailed itself all night before crashing onto the beach, a ghost ship with all its lights on. They were afraid to approach because of the giant waves rolling in off the Pacific, but in the morning, when the tide went out, they found gold rings and bracelets in the sand and American dollars every-where, the beach littered with riches. They said they found keys made of pure gold—ancient sailors' keys for opening chests.

Everyone gathered, until eventually there were nearly one hundred people standing on the beach, worried that a family might still be trapped inside the hull. Perhaps it was not a ghost ship at all, but a ship of death.

Local fishermen said they found the body near the mouth of the Río Cahoacán— a white corpse as large as two men, with no clothes and a light beard, mouth open as if it might speak. Villagers went to find the judge, because he was the only one with a phone, and he called officials from larger towns to come take the body away. This village was only a few *palapas* made of sticks and bamboo, with palm-frond roofs.

It was like a story from Gabriel García Márquez: the carnivalesque scene on the beach. The sea that brings gifts of the First World, conquistadors, and death. This body floating naked and larger than life—John Long, literally a big man, now become legend. But this tale is real. It happened in February in the village of La Cigüeña, on the west coast of Chiapas, 7 miles from Mexico's border with Guatemala. Long, a seventy-eight-year-old Irishman who'd spent his adult life in California, had dreamed of this voyage for sixteen years. He'd left San Francisco three months earlier on his 48-foot ketch, *Cúlin*, heading south to the Panama Canal and then home to his native Ireland.

Long's EPIRB, or emergency position indicating radio beacon, went off at 12:49 a.m. on February 2. And contrary to all the colorful stories from the villagers, with their invention of gold and claims of finding the body, the Mexican navy actually discovered Long's corpse around 11:00 a.m. the next morning, floating 2 miles offshore near the town of Puerto Madero, 7 miles north of La Cigüeña. His body was naked and bruised, with cerebral hemorrhaging, broken ribs, and a broken neck.

Long's story was disappearing even as it was happening, and soon legend would be all that was left. I know this because his story is a version of what could have been my own. Ten years ago, I ran into trouble in these same waters.

My sailboat was a 48-foot ketch, just like Long's, and in the late fall of 1997 I hired another captain to deliver it from San Francisco to Panama while I finished a semester of teaching at Stanford. My plan was to pick up the boat in Panama and continue to the British Virgin Islands, where I would run winter charters. This boat, *Grendel*, was my business and my home.

But the captain I'd hired, an accomplished sailor in her thirties, took on some bad diesel in Acapulco, diesel with water in it, and limped into the town of Puerto Madero on a bit of wind. For some reason, she waited a week before calling me. Then the cook took off on another boat for *la pura vida* in Costa Rica, and took my $2,000 in emergency cash with him.

None of this made any sense, of course, and it was the beginning of the most outrageous four months of my life. I arrived in Puerto Madero figuring I'd be on my way in about a week. But soon enough, I was the center of attention in the town's backwater shrimp port, a tiny village of its own, without a name. I'd fallen down the rabbit hole, into a place where, everywhere I turned, I heard newer and less believable stories, and they were all about me.

My sailboat was large and broken, tied to the one crumbled chunk of concrete on the shoreline, visited by rats, snakes, begging children, prostitutes, the police, the navy, drunken fishermen, and the crooked port captain's men. At first I tried to have the engine fixed, but a mechanic with a disco shirt, gold chains, and a group of thugs at his shop held the high-pressure injection pump for ransom, demanding $900 instead of $100 for the repair. So I tried a new tack, spending $3,500 to buy a used engine and have it trucked down from California. This engine was stolen before it ever arrived, only to reappear mysteriously months later, a 500-pound hunk of metal dumped on the beach in the middle of the night.

The outboard engine for my dinghy was also stolen, a theft I came to believe was arranged by my one friend in port, a young Guatemalan named Santiago who was also my interpreter. When I alerted the port captain, a formal and evasive man in his sixties, he told me I could report my stolen engine officially, or unofficially. *Officially* meant he'd have six agencies come strip-search me. *Unofficially* meant he'd do nothing, even though I could tell him who'd stolen the engine and where it was being kept.

As a week turned into a month, I started paying protection money to Gordo, a Buddha-like crime boss, but even then I was threatened by his own toughs, who beat a prostitute nearly to death right in front of me. I was harassed constantly by a Nicaraguan guy who had an imagined rivalry with me over a waitress at the port's only restaurant, a misunderstanding based on one nervous smile. Almost every day at dawn, a Mexican navy captain came aboard to search my boat and give me advice on how to do my hair, which was already so short it was almost military. One morning, his men bound my hands and beat me as he looked for drugs.

Ultimately I spent four months in Puerto Madero, out of options and out of money. I was referred to locally as "the ATM machine," bleeding cash, on the edge of ruin. Even when I'd take a taxi from Tapachula, the larger city 15 miles inland, the drivers knew who I was and every detail of my story. They knew the mechanic and his men. They knew what I paid Gordo. They knew who had my outboard. They knew I had tried to escape once, putt-putting away at 1 knot on a broken diesel engine belching black grime into the water, and that pirates in pangas had rammed my boat and threatened to board it for drugs. They knew I had sailed straight to sea that night like a coward with my lights off, then limped back into port to go through it all again.

In other words, I became familiar with Puerto Madero. By the time I finally left, I was enraged and terrified. Ten years later, when I heard about Long, I knew I had to go back, as much to resolve my own story as to find answers to his.

~~~~~~

John Long was three months into the biggest adventure of his life. He'd loved boats and the sea since his childhood, on the coast of Ireland, and now he was on his way home, planning to finish his voyage at the oldest sailing club in the world, the Royal Cork Yacht Club, in Crosshaven, a few miles upriver from his native Myrtleville. "If you sail into Crosshaven, you'll die a happy man for having made it," his brother, Michael, told him when he left San Francisco. "And if you die along the way, you'll die a happy man for having tried."

Long and his wife, Julia, had come to America in 1965 on their honeymoon. They didn't intend to stay, but Long saw that he could make good money as a carpenter, so they decided to stick around long enough to earn the cash to buy a Volkswagen van back in Ireland.

The momentum of a life is something few of us can control, however. The Longs ended up raising their three sons—Aaron, Philip, and Jason—in California, and John never missed a single day of work. His was a good life, a rich life, but in his retirement, the dream of this yacht, *Cúlin*, and the dream of this voyage took over.

"It became an obsession, almost an obligation," says his youngest son, Jason, a thirty-five-year-old English professor in Merced, California. In 1992, Long bought a bare hull made of Cor-Ten steel and used his skills as a master carpenter to finish out the interior in teak and other hardwoods.

He and Julia were separating, though the family would still spend holidays together, and *Cúlin* was a labor of love after all those years of steaming and bending, carving and fitting.

Then there were his half-dozen attempts to make the voyage. Long was delayed over the years by family events, such as the birth of a granddaughter, but also by having to turn back many times. Though he'd served in the merchant marine as a young man, sailing around the world delivering bananas and coffee, he didn't know navigation or his boat's equipment very well. On his first attempt, he sailed north instead of south after he left San Francisco Bay. The next trip was the same; he ended up near Tomales Bay, more than 40 miles up the coast. The next time Long tried, he found himself out in the Farallon Islands, almost due west.

Each time, he'd say he was done. "I'm sick, I'm tired, my hand is hurt," he said after the Farallones. "I'm done with this. This is it."

Then, the next day, there would be another voice mail, saying he knew now what had gone wrong and how to fix it. "I think I can do this."

When Long left on his final voyage, on October 14, 2007, there was no party. No one saw him off. Sailors at the dock had ridiculed him for years, and his family had lost faith. For the early attempts, they gave going-away parties. After a while, though, they stopped believing he would ever really go more than a few miles outside the Golden Gate. Jason hoped he might just sell the *Cúlin* and get a condo and season tickets to the Oakland A's. "We felt okay," he told me, "because we thought he would never go."

But this voyage had become, to some extent, a grudge match against the naysayers. This time, Long had taken classes. He knew navigation and his equipment, and he surprised everyone by making it down to Santa Barbara to visit his oldest son, Aaron, a business student. He was on his way. He was anxious to continue on, sailing for Mazatlán within a week.

"I've got my sea legs back," he said. "I'm feeling good. I'm going."

I never thought I'd set foot in Puerto Madero again, and arriving back in town is disorienting. The small port area, where I was stranded, has been renamed Puerto Chiapas, and the government has put in a cruise-ship dock, which Holland America is using for its Panama Canal trips. On the surface, Puerto Chiapas is an innocent place of coffee and fruit and friendly people, with a tremendous fake pyramidal marketplace and a pool. But the pangas are still here, and the fishermen, and I suspect things haven't changed all that much.

I've got a letter from Jason Long giving me full authority to try to salvage or sell the *Cúlin*. Armed with this, I take a taxi to the harbor, to the small port captain's compound, and go inside. The old port captain has passed away, the secretary tells me. The new one, Captain Andres Ordaz, a good-looking man in his forties, is a bit slicker but seemingly up to the same games. He claims Long was sailing north from Central America, had never been in Mexico (he says he confirmed this with officials in Manzanillo and Mazatlán), and was cooking some fish on deck when he tripped overboard. He even claims that parts of the dinner were found.

I have only a few facts, provided by the Longs before I left: a photo of the *Cúlin* taken a few days after it hit the beach, showing all three sails up; the US Coast Guard's report of when and where the EPIRB went off; directions to the spot where the *Cúlin* is beached; and a summary of the autopsy report provided to the Longs by the US consulate in Mexico City.

Trying to match these facts with the port captain's account creates a fairly preposterous scene: It's one a.m. and Long is on deck, with his three sails up. The jib is back-winded, though, held out on the wrong side, which stops the boat dead in its tracks, like a giant air brake. Yet somehow the *Cúlin* has been able to defy the laws of physics, sailing hundreds or even thousands of miles north from Panama or Costa Rica or wherever Long teleported to after he left California. To celebrate this miracle, he is fixing a lovely fish dinner in the middle of the night, naked, but suddenly trips overboard, managing to hit his head so hard that his brain hemorrhages. Midair, the abrasions on his left cheek, described in the autopsy, have time to quickly scab. He breaks his neck and ribs and instantly stops breathing, so that when he hits the water none of it gets into his lungs.

I'm guessing the port captain's fable is a fair preview of what I'll find as I try to follow the local investigation, if there is one. So I decide to go directly to the boat.

The last few miles to La Cigüeña are down a narrow dirt road through low plantain trees, unspoiled and remote but also a little spooky, given what happened to Long. The village is beautiful, though, when it appears, a collection of bamboo-and-wood huts stretched along the slow Río Cahoacán. No garish paint, no abundance of concrete. The few attempts at that were wiped out in 2005 by Hurricane Stan. There are goats and pigs and dogs in the road, and when I get out of the car, everyone stares. The first man to offer help is a drunken fisherman in a yellow shirt. His name is Israel, his eyes are marbled, and he's full of claims. He'll take me to the boat.

"*Hay un problema?*" he keeps asking. Do we have a problem? And then he answers himself in English, "No problem, my friend."

We walk through the village to where the river turns north and divides the jungle from a long beach and the sea. Israel's two sons have a small wooden canoe they've built by hand. It's narrow and tippy, with yellowish bilge water and a blue crab huddled inside the bow. I board and squat low. The Cahoacán is known for its crocodiles, but one of the boys walks beside the boat in waist-deep water, pulling the bow.

It's late afternoon, the air warm and humid but not hot, not stifling. There's a light breeze coming from the ocean, and a few fishermen throw hand-nets into the water. Small, thin fish skip across the surface to escape us. There are trees overhanging to our right, driftwood like sculpture on the beach to our left. It's lovely here, like parts of Puerto Madero ten years ago, and it doesn't feel dangerous at all. We land on the beach side and walk 100 yards across sand to the Pacific, where slow rollers are coming in.

After a few minutes, I see the *Cúlin* ahead. The boat is only a hull, more than half buried, lying on its side. A group of men are standing on her cabin, bent over, perhaps removing something. They're several hundred yards away, and they remind me where I am, what this place is capable of. As we come closer, they see us and immediately leave, walking away fast. I can't tell whether they're carrying things or not.

Up close, the boat is heartbreaking. Waves washing over it, everything stripped and carted away. I had wanted to help Long's family salvage something, but there's nothing left.

From Acapulco south to the Guatemala border lie hundreds of miles of yellow-sand beaches, from the surf towns of Puerto Escondido and Puerto Ángel to the undeveloped coast of Chiapas, where you might see a few palm-frond-roofed palapas and then another 100 miles of nothing. Conventional sailing wisdom advises keeping close to land here as you pass through the enormous Gulf of Tehuantepec: They say the "Tehuantepeckers"—60-knot winds that scream across the narrow, flat spit of land separating the Gulf of Mexico from the Pacific—can blow you 300 miles to sea. This is myth, in my experience, but the sailing world is full of myths, and this one puts every yacht in close to shore, where it becomes a target for pirates.

The pirates of southern Mexico don't quite merit the name. Those off the coast of Somalia have .50 caliber machine guns and rocket-propelled grenades. They operate out of a country that hasn't had a stable government in more than a decade, so they are in fact much like the seventeenth- and eighteenth-century pirates of the Caribbean, powerful enough to capture entire ports and operate out of them untouched. The pirates of most of the world, though, and certainly the Central American coast, would never think of themselves as pirates per se; they are merely opportunists, poor fishermen and petty thieves. A passing yacht can be worth a hundred times what a Mexican fisherman will make in his lifetime; when I was here ten years ago, the average wage was $25 a month.

Add in the fact that this coast sits right on an active smuggling route. Acapulco lies between the Colombian port of Buenaventura and California, and with crackdowns in the Caribbean, smugglers have moved out into the Pacific, its vastness hiding merchant ships towing submarines full of cocaine, cigarette boats running fast and invisible to radar in the dark, semisubmersibles riding low, only their periscopes sticking up. In October 2007, Mexican law enforcement seized 23.6 metric tons of cocaine from a ship docked in Manzanillo, a record seizure on land or at sea.

It was just outside Manzanillo that Long had his first brush with pirates. He'd made it all the way down the 1,100-mile coast of Baja California and stopped for a few repairs in Mazatlán. But just north of Manzanillo, at sea, at night, his electrical system died. His alternator was out. He also had a recurring mechanical problem: The prop shaft would slip back and jam against the rudder and make him go in circles.

Long set off his EPIRB, which alerts rescue agencies by satellite. This is a serious piece of equipment, an international cry for help that should not be set off unless the boat is sinking or there's some other life-threatening emergency. Problems with an electrical system don't usually qualify. But Jason says his father was worried that without power, he wouldn't have lights or radar and was in danger of collision.

The Mexican coast guard came out immediately. They'd been watching Long, because sitting there in one place with his lights off, he looked as if he were on a drug rendezvous. The officers boarded with machine guns and made him leave his boat. Then they sped away, leaving the *Cúlin* drifting, and stopped and waited. Pirates were tracking the boat, apparently. "It was kind of left as bait for a while," Aaron says. The coast guard watched on radar, but the pirates had radar too, and they could see the coast guard waiting, so they turned back. The officials returned Long to his boat and gave him a free tow into Manzanillo, and there he began an ordeal of repairs and scams and paperwork that lasted more than a month.

When Long finally left Manzanillo, in January, he planned to sail straight to Panama. He continued to have mechanical and electrical problems, though, so Aaron thinks he may have been looking for a port to pull into for repairs. He was hugging the shore, sailing no more than a few miles out, avoiding the Tehuante-peckers. This put him right in the drug route, not only for big loads to Acapulco, but also for local traffic making quick trips over the Guatemala border. He presented an opportunity to everyone.

The ironic thing is that Long had built the *Cúlin* specifically to withstand pirate attacks. He'd placed his helm inside and could lock himself behind a massive slid-ing steel door and windows of thick bulletproof glass. All his lines to control the sails ran inside as well. I've never seen or heard of another sailboat quite like this. Most sailors just hope they won't run into pirates, but Long was prepared.

~~~~~~

The truth may be elusive in other places, but here in Puerto Madero and La Cigüeña, I believe it never actually exists. Even as events occur, they immediately become something else. An outsider can never know anything for certain, and this is partly because we are mythological creatures, born of conquistadors and sitting on our mountain of gold in El Norte. We aren't believable ourselves, even our existence, so we're told stories, and every story is about one thing: money. It made perfect sense for everyone to try to take my boat. And it makes perfect sense now that Long's story should be buried.

I have to admit, I still feel a bit of the old fear as I walk through the *palapas* along Puerto Madero's waterfront to the fishing area, where the pangas line the beach. I never saw any fish brought into port ten years ago, but this time I actually see a few, and the man cleaning them suddenly calls my name and smiles. It's my old friend Santiago.

It's difficult to know the nature of this place. I like Santiago, and he still feels like a friend. He has the nicest house in town now, cement and tile, painted a light blue. He tells me what happened to all the people I knew from before. Gordo was killed a year after I left, he says, picking up drugs over the Guatemala border. At least four others were killed, too. Santiago shows me who he says the drug runners are now, a row of identical pangas with new 115-horse outboards. He says they run small loads along the coast, usually to Acapulco, but sometimes all the way up to California.

Listening to Santiago very nearly got me killed ten years ago. I tried to recover my stolen outboard engine from his friend's house at night and found a Glock in my face, cocked. It was right here along the slough where these pangas are kept. But I decide to trust him now, because I have few other options.

Santiago says yes, he will go to La Cigüeña and ask around. I pay him generously for this, in advance, which is a mistake. The next day he tells me he's found someone there who will tell him the truth and even cross into Guatemala to find out what he can, since the pirates, Santiago says matter-of-factly, are Guatemalan. This extra day means more money, of course, and I feel all the old scams revving up. But Santiago does go to La Cigüeña the next day, and then, the day after that, I go with him.

It turns out his contact is Israel, the fisherman who originally took me to Long's boat. He isn't drunk this time, but his version of things keeps shifting. First he says he saw Long's boat at 4:00 a.m., sailing with the lights on, and that it crashed ashore around 5:00 a.m. The waves were huge, the winds high, and he had to wait several hours for the tide to go out before he could try heroically to get to the boat to rescue whoever might be trapped. Then, a few minutes later, his story is that the boat hit the beach at about 8:30 a.m., and the waves weren't very high at all. There was money on the beach, or no money, or just two dollar bills and a ten. He didn't take anything, of course. The guys who did this are from Guatemala, and then they're not. Drug traffic here is constant, he says, or maybe there's no drug traffic at all. The pangas only go out with gas to refuel larger drug boats.

Talking with Israel is like talking with the new port captain in Puerto Madero. But I'm hoping I'll learn more from the Mexican navy. They recovered the body, and they had divers in the *Culin* for an hour, looking for other victims. They must know something.

The navy base is in Puerto Chiapas, opposite the new cruise-ship port. They take my passport and misunderstand that I'm part of Long's family. Nobody can read my official letter, as it's in English, but the existence of a signed document in multiple copies means everything here. Half a dozen guards melt away.

I wait in an air-conditioned lobby, and Lieutenant Jorge Castillo Hurtado finally comes out. I ask where the body was found, and he refers me to the police. I ask what might have happened, and he refers me to the police. I ask about the EPIRB, but he says the navy has no information about an EPIRB.

Hurtado is a tall man, in a beautiful white uniform. He remains consummately polite, even when I push with questions. The funny thing is that I like him. The whole show works. And as he walks me out to the taxi, he actually opens up a bit. Their force is too small, he says. They're not a big base, like Manzanillo, and they're overwhelmed, unable to deal with all of the local drug trafficking. Sure enough, several months later, the Mexican newspaper *El Universal* will report that the coast of Chiapas has become so dangerous the navy has "initiated a land, sea, and air operative," mobilizing helicopters, airplanes, and blockade ships in search of boats running drugs up from Central America.

My own experience with pirates on this coast came a week or two after I'd arrived, when I left Puerto Madero in desperation on my broken engine. I knew it was stupid, but my friend Julie had come down as crew, and she'd be leaving if I didn't try. We made it 50 miles, going slowly along a beautiful and abandoned coastline, before we saw two pangas coming at us from the Puerto Madero direction.

"Great," I said. "Visitors."

Julie looked nervous. "I'm going below," she said. "If anyone asks, I'm not here."

"Ha," I said. "Can you look around in the cabinets above the chart table and find the two flare pistols, please?"

"Are you kidding?"

"No, I'm not kidding. Please get them quickly. And cartridges."

The pangas came right for us. Julie found the flare guns just in time to slide them to me and disappear again below. I put the pistols on deck, loaded, down low where the guys in the pangas wouldn't see them.

They came up fast, one on each side, 75-horse outboards roaring. They crossed behind my stern, circled back, and throttled down to my speed, which was no speed at all.

"*Coca*," one of the men shouted, pushing a finger into a nostril, tilting his head back. He had no fish on board, no fishing gear. Just gasoline and *cervezas*. The man was drunk and possibly on drugs, weaving a bit as he stood braced against the throttle arm of the outboard.

On my other side, the driver of the second panga was making the same gesture, poking his finger into his nose.

"*No tengo*," I said. "*Lo siento*." I was trying to sound polite. I glanced down the companionway at Julie, who had one hand to her mouth and was hiding behind the stairs. She looked terrified. I felt the enormity of how stupid I'd been. I know it sounds crazy, but despite my experiences in Puerto Madero, I hadn't even thought about piracy.

"*Cerveza,*" the man on the starboard side said. He made a gesture of drinking. He was wearing a bandanna, his face beat up. I knew without a doubt that if he climbed onto my deck, I was going to shoot him.

I wanted to just toss him a beer, but I didn't have any beer, or cocaine. "*No tengo,*" I said. I tried to gaze ahead, hoping they'd leave us alone.

The guy on my right zoomed off a few hundred feet and circled around to come up fast behind me. He rammed into the stern, which luckily was rounded, so that his bow glanced off. The other driver saw this and circled around to do the same thing. Like sharks bumping.

"Get on the VHF," I told Julie. "Try calling the coast guard."

Julie opened the cabinets and grabbed the mic. She held it up and started gesturing wildly. She had no idea how to use a VHF radio.

The guy on my port side came up close. "*Coca!*" he yelled. I put my hand on the pistol on that side. He was climbing partway out of his boat to hook an arm on my rail.

I heard the other man behind me, so I turned around to look, and then I realized my back was to the first man, and they were going to get me.

But they didn't take the opportunity. In a high falsetto, pretending to be a woman, the leader sang out to me, "*En la noche.* I come back for you. *Con armas,*" which meant with guns. Then as quickly as they had arrived, they were gone, and Julie and I motored straight out to sea, sails down and lights off, and hid all night.

~~~~~~

The police in Puerto Madero keep Long's case in a homicide folder, on a messy front desk littered with other homicide folders. Public-ministry lawyer Teofilo Esteban Perez Sala takes me over, then hands me the police report. I'm so shocked, I can't speak. I finally manage a "*Gracias.*"

Perez says Long's injuries were so extreme that his entire skull was basically "pushed over" to the side. I ask whether I can photocopy the file, and to my amazement he says yes. It turns out there's absolutely nothing useful except the full autopsy—but I'm in the right place, finally.

The only problem is that there was never an investigation. We should know, for instance, whether there were any traces of blood on the boat. The injuries happened somewhere, and there must have been evidence before looters literally sawed it off the boat and carted it away. But even Perez, with his homicide folder, caves in to the official line and says he thinks it was an accidental death.

When I leave Puerto Madero after a week, I have little more than the facts I arrived with. But here's what I believe happened to John Long. He was sailing sometime before midnight, only a few miles from shore. Despite what his son Aaron says, I don't think he was planning to go into Puerto Madero for repairs. If that had been his plan, he would have been wearing clothing, and he would have furled his sails.

But Long was flying full sail, including main, mizzen, and his largest jib, in light air and small waves, making probably 4 or 5 knots. It was hot, so he may have been naked as he rested or tried to sleep below, and he had his pilothouse door all the way open for breeze.

Close to Puerto Madero, he heard a panga roaring up, heard its outboard over the sound of water against the hull. And he most likely had already experienced this a dozen times, day and night, pangas coming up asking him for things all along the coast. So he turned on his deck lights and climbed out his side door to tell them to scram. The pirates could have come aboard quickly, easy to do from the bow of a panga.

According to Jason Long, his father was no longer very physically able; even climbing bleachers at ball games had become difficult. And his guns, which were illegal in Mexico, were too far away, stored not in the pilothouse but in the lower section of the boat.

Long was hit hard on the left side of his head by a blunt object, perhaps a club used for killing fish. He had cerebral hemorrhaging, a broken neck, broken ribs, a bloody nose, and large bruises on his right thigh and stomach, one of them a foot and a half long. His skin wasn't cut, however, so it's possible he was stripped before being thrown overboard.

I think it's fair to say there's no chance that Long's was an accidental death. The boom swinging over on an accidental jibe could fracture a skull and break a neck, but all of Long's controls were below: During a tack or jibe, he would have been in his pilothouse. He also couldn't have fallen from a mast, because he had no mast steps. He couldn't have been deploying his dinghy, because all of his sails were up. It's hard to imagine he simply fell, because he moved slowly and his injuries were so extreme.

The *Cúlin*'s EPIRB went off briefly at 12:49 a.m., and again, at 12:59 a.m., then went silent. Its position was where the boat lies now, on the beach. But the navy recovered Long's body 2 miles out to sea. I think it's most likely that looters set off the EPIRB while fiddling with the buttons.

Long's body would have drifted at about half a knot per hour south, so my guess is that he was killed around ten p.m., within a few miles of Puerto Madero. After an hour or so, his boat must have turned toward land. Even if the malfunctioning autopilot had been turned on, the boat could have slipped off course, toward the beach. At that point, the *Cúlin* became a true ghost ship, sailing itself into La Cigüeña, its captain lost at sea.

~~~~~~

At the end of my own saga, after finally installing that replacement engine and escaping north to Ixtapa, I had to change the propeller on my boat. I was in the water with mask and snorkel and wrench, the underside of the hull a hairy, green, shadowy thing in water that was murkier than I had expected.

I adjusted my mask and was about to dive down to try to loosen the old propeller when I happened to glance across the surface of the water behind the boat. I don't know why I took that glance, but I saw the bumpy end of a snout cruising toward me, just barely breaking the surface, creating only the smallest wake, and behind it, two prehistoric eyes. It was a crocodile, a big one, nearly invisible, coming after me.

I somehow managed to leap vertically onto the dock. That's the way it seemed, anyway. One moment I had been in the water, about to die, and the next moment, I was safe. There was no transition that made any sense. The crocodile was in very close, only a few feet away, much larger and heavier than I would have dreamed, and then it was gone.

IN A HOUSE BY THE RIVER

MEGAN MICHELSON

More than twenty years ago, the man who helped raise writer Megan Michelson was shot to death at a remote kayaking lodge in Northern California—a nightmare episode that her mother had refused to discuss until the author decided to investigate the story for herself. Knowing that the killer is still free and living in the area, Michelson embarked on a painful search for answers about what really happened, and why.

"This is Kayaker Nine," I announced. Jerry was teaching me trucker slang, and Mom laughed. "We're heading downstream on the South Fork at mile 11. Over and out."

"You've got a future in radio, kid," Jerry told me, cracking sunflower seeds in his teeth. He cranked up Tom Petty's "Learning to Fly" on a mix tape my mom had made, and we sang along. Jerry was tall and strong, wearing sunglasses attached to a cord around his neck. Mom's dark, wavy hair hung to her chin, and her legs were lean from cycling.

Somewhere up the road was our cabin on California's Salmon River, one of the very few undammed rivers in the state, and a spot so remote—deep in the 1.7-million-acre Klamath National Forest—that electricity still doesn't reach it. The closest town, Forks of Salmon, consists of a post office, a tiny elementary school, a herd of wild ponies, and an oak-shaded picnic table that serves as the local pub. Fewer than one hundred people lived out there then, and fewer now: gold miners, pot growers, Native Americans, hippies who come to stay at the nearby Black Bear Commune, and, thanks to the world-class whitewater, a handful of kayakers.

A couple of miles downstream from Forks, Jerry turned left at the wooden sign marking the entrance to Otter Bar Lodge, the whitewater kayak school where he had met my mom. The lodge shared a road with our cabin—a small, wood-framed loft with a gas stove and no walls, perched on a cliff overlooking a quiet bend in the Salmon.

That year, I took a boogie board down a mellow stretch of river, roasted marshmallows, and swam in the ponds while Mom and Jerry kayaked. It was one of the last times that things were really good.

On our first night at the cabin, Jerry and I carved our names into the picnic table out front. Jerry used his middle name, Raymond, which was also his trailer-park alter ego. When he and Mom—married for two years at that point—went on vacation, they used to make home videos pretending to be Marge and Raymond, a redneck couple out for a good time. Our Christmas card that year featured the whole family, including my fifteen-year-old brother, Miles, and thirteen-year-old sister, Erin, dressed in rags in front of a dilapidated shed. It read, "Merry Christmas. How was your year?"

It was all an act, of course, but the kind that softens the truth by exaggerating it. You see, Jerry had a violent side that came out when he drank. One minute he'd be playing fetch with our dog, the next he was shattering plates. I only remember snippets of the fights—of him smashing a dresser and hitting Mom in the face with a full Diet Coke can, blackening her eye. Once he got so mad at Miles that my brother ran out of the house and then moved back to Dad's place a few weeks later.

Jerry had been drinking on February 18, 1995, the night he died just a few hundred feet from our cabin. He was alone there that weekend; my mom and I were skiing in Tahoe. I was thirteen, old enough to feel the calamity of his death, but too young for anyone to entrust me with the details. At the time, Mom told me Jerry had gotten into a fight and that his body had been found in the doorway of the Otter Bar owners' private residence. The few times I asked for specifics, Mom's response was short: "You don't want to know."

But I'm twenty-eight now, and I do want to know. Jerry was flawed, but he wasn't a monster. He raised me from age four to thirteen, and even though his death gave my family a twisted kind of peace, I still loved him. I want to know what happened to him and, more important, why. Over the years, I've looked up the stories from the *Siskiyou Daily News*. The first articles ran the day after the incident:

> *Jerrold Raymond Davidson, 40, was shot after an argument over a trespassing incident. John Douglas Greiner, 35, was arrested after he called 911 and reported*

that he had shot Davidson. Greiner reportedly was care-taking [the] property at Otter Bar Lodge. The victim owned the property next door and reportedly spent weekends there.

Another headline appeared thirty-eight days later, when Greiner, who goes by J. D., was released from jail: MURDER CHARGES DISMISSED AGAINST SALMON RIVER MAN.

Last summer, when I went to Mom for answers again, she agreed to talk. We decided there was only one place to do it.

It's a sticky afternoon in June when we arrive at Otter Bar, two kayaks stacked on the roof of my Subaru. Peter Sturges, the lodge's owner, is pedaling his mountain bike up the driveway when we pull in. He doesn't recognize me at first, but he sees my mom in the passenger seat and swings off the saddle.

"That's Megan, all grown up," she says.

"Of course," says Peter. "Welcome. The river is running great right now."

In her prime, Mom paddled Class V. She's sixty now, graying and showing the sun and wear in her hands, but still shockingly fit.

The last time I was here was five years ago, but Otter Bar has a timeless gloss to it: a white clapboard lodge surrounded by green lawns, with two small ponds where instructors teach kayak roll sessions. It's edged by giant firs and a river that still supports healthy salmon runs. It's a wildly beautiful landscape darkened by the cloud of what happened to my family here.

That night Mom and I set out lawn chairs on the bluff overlooking the river and drink chardonnay from plastic wineglasses. We both know what we're here to discuss, but there are barriers that must be moved. She's survived the deaths of a child and a husband, as well as her younger brother to the first AIDS outbreak among San Francisco's gay community. I think we're both pondering the sanity of her unloading the weight onto me. Finally she sighs, gulps some wine, and begins to talk.

In 1980, my parents' third child, a girl named Macey, born two years before me, died of SIDS at three and a half months. I'd known this was an inflection point in their marriage. Afterward, Mom would go to the basement, where Macey's baby clothes were stashed, and sob. My dad, Steve Michelson, went back to work, perhaps too quickly, at the San Francisco video-production company he and Mom had started. It was a multimillion-dollar operation that produced national TV programs, commercials, and even segments for the Olympics. "That business was your dad's mistress," my mom says.

They tried to save their marriage. My own birth, in 1982, was one attempt to fill the void. They tried in other ways, too. In March 1984, after reading a story in this magazine about a new lodge called Otter Bar, Mom booked a week of kayak lessons for both of them. They returned the following two summers. On their third trip, in June 1986, my dad left Otter Bar early to finalize the sale of their company, and Jerry, a substitute instructor, arrived. He flirtatiously mistook Mom for a former Miss Florida, who was also a guest that week. Mom says there was something electric about their connection. This is the first time she's told me how it all happened.

Jerry was thirty-one then, and had a square jaw and an athletic build. "Can I share your pillow with you tonight?" he asked her. "I'm a married woman," she responded, but she still gave him her phone number when he asked for it over milkshakes the next day.

Jerry called Mom at home a few days later and invited her on an overnight trip down the Class III Chili Bar stretch of the South Fork of the American River. She asked a friend to take care of us. I was four, my sister was eight, and my brother was ten. "I just want to have some fun," she told her friend. She told Dad she was going kayaking but didn't mention Jerry.

They met by the river, ate pizza, and set up camp. "Are we going to have an affair?" he asked. "I certainly hope so," she replied. When she returned home at one a.m. the following night, Dad asked, "How was the boating?"

A few months later, after sixteen years of marriage, my parents got divorced. I barely remember it, but it was a big deal for my brother and sister. Mom moved us from the Bay Area to Nevada City, a sleepy Northern California town known for its proximity to gushing rivers. I spent occasional weekends and holidays with Dad and, oddly enough, he went on to date that former Miss Florida. But what I remember most about that time is Jerry. My earliest memories are of him teaching me to throw a softball and make grilled cheese sandwiches.

And I remember that he made Mom ridiculously happy. Her notes in the margins of an old, weathered copy of *A Guide to the Best Whitewater in the State of California*, which she gave me, read like diary entries: "January 9, 1987. Middle Fork of the Smith River. Evans's first adventure into winter boating. I like winter boating, kissing in the eddies and riding bikes for the shuttle. We're still smiling the same at each other. I love Jerry."

In 1988, Peter Sturges offered to sell 10 of his 40 acres to his best client—my mom—for $150,000. With some of the proceeds from the sale of the video company, she tells me, she bought the property that she and Jerry named Otter Bar. That she paid for the property always bugged Jerry. Mom had grown up in a world of boarding schools and trips to Aspen. Jerry came from a middle-class family and wanted to pull his weight. So Mom let him design the cabin—without exterior walls, like he wanted—and that seemed to placate him.

They got married in May 1989, and for their honeymoon they bused fourteen members of our family to Otter Bar for a week of rafting and kayak lessons. A home movie shows me, at age seven, sitting in a kayak in the pond. "Did you go boating today, Megan?" Jerry asks me. I had rafted that day, clinging to the boat with all my might, but I pretended that I had kayaked. "Yeah, I kayaked," I said. "How did you handle that big rapid? Straight down the middle?" Jerry joked. "Yeah, straight down the middle," I giggled.

Then things started to corrode. The fights usually happened late at night. Yelling and loud thuds from their bedroom, followed by unexplained bruises and broken furniture. My mom was mortified when my sister and I would see it. Sometimes she'd apologize to us the next morning.

During one particularly bad fight, Mom threw their wedding album into the fire. I couldn't stand the sound of their rage, so I walked into their bedroom in the middle of one ferocious war and asked Jerry if he wanted to play cards. That seemed to ground him, at least momentarily. Mom says I always had a calming effect on him.

By 1993 Jerry had undergone knee surgery and quit his job as a physician's assistant, and he was clearly depressed. He drank more, saw a therapist, and put on weight. One day, I wore my hair down with the top half pulled into a barrette. "I like your hair like that," Jerry told me. "I want you to wear it like that at my funeral."

In the fall of 1994, just a few months before his death, Mom finally told him to move out. He packed his things and got a job in Medford, Oregon. After he died, Jerry's sister found a journal in his apartment, which Mom copied and gave me earlier this summer when I told her I wanted to write about Jerry's death. One late entry read, "How long can I sit here and not blow my brains out? What's the reason for being here? Life goes on and I go down, down to the depths of such despair."

Fortunately for my family, the last time we saw Jerry he was the gentle, sweet man Mom had first met. Two days before he died, Jerry showed up unexpectedly in the middle of the night. He brought Mom two dozen roses for Valentine's Day and a note that ended, "Let us put all our troubles behind us. The new, improved Jerry wants peace, love, and kindness, especially with you." The next morning, he drove me to school and gave me a bigger-than-usual hug at the curb of my junior high.

The following week, I cried while putting my hair half up for his funeral.

The morning after our beach-chair chat, Mom and I are floating in a calm eddy near the shore. Just downstream, the Salmon drops into Indian Crossing, a rapid that requires a clutch move to avoid a nasty keeper hole. Keepers are made when the river dumps over a boulder and forms a chaotic vacuum at the bottom. Water—and, by extension, boats and people—that should be flowing downstream are instead sucked back upstream in an indefinite cycle. Not far below the rapid is the take-out at our porch.

"Go right down the middle," Mom says. "Just above the hole, brace hard with your right blade and cut left." Then she arcs into the current with me on her tail. We both run a clean line, maneuvering around the chaos.

After we peel off our wet gear, I walk over to Otter Bar and knock on Peter and Kristy Sturges's door, which is just next to the lodge where the guests stay. Originally from Rhode Island, Peter moved here in 1972 from Alaska, where he'd been working as a commercial fisherman. Kristy was a local schoolteacher. They got married and bought the property on the Salmon River in the early eighties. They raised their two children here, and their son, Rush, has gone on to become a well-known kayaker and action-sports filmmaker.

Peter, now sixty-one, invites me into their kitchen. For an awkward moment, I pause in the doorway, knowing that this is where Jerry took his last breath. In front of me, there's an old gas stove and a cluttered countertop. To my left, a staircase leads up to the home office where J. D. placed the 911 call that night. Kristy has found the typed 911 transcript in her filing cabinet and hands it to me. I take a seat on the couch and flip cautiously through the first couple of pages.

J. D.: I have a man in my house that will not leave.

DISPATCHER: Okay, he's trespassing?

J. D.: I've asked him to leave several times, and he thinks it's funny. He's laughing at me. I think he's maybe slightly intoxicated.

DISPATCHER: Okay, what is your name, sir?

J. D.: I'm J. D. Greiner. I'm staying at Otter Bar Lodge.

DISPATCHER: Okay, and who's the man?

J. D.: He's the next-door neighbor who has assaulted me before.

Peter is leaning over an armchair with the afternoon light filtering through the windows. I stop reading and ask him when things went bad with Jerry. He tells me that Jerry had worked at their doctor's office in Arcata and they all became friends.

J. D., who did odd jobs around Otter Bar, met Mom and Jerry in 1989, when they hired him to do some work around the property.

J. D. and Jerry became pals and occasionally boated together. The first time they quarreled was when they were building the septic system for the cabin. The engineers had screwed up the leach lines, and Jerry angrily blamed it on everyone else around him. J. D. had pulled Mom aside and asked, "Are you going to be okay driving home with him?" She said she'd be fine.

Before the house was built, there was another incident, Peter says. A few kayak instructors camped on our property, later telling Jerry that Peter had told them it was fine. (Peter had in fact instructed them otherwise.) "Jerry called me and he sounded uptight," recalls Peter. "Jerry said, 'I hear you've been renting out my place.' He sounded like a completely different person. That was the start of this whole thing. That's what set Jerry off. I had the feeling that I was going to be dealing with a nightmare for a while."

Jerry became increasingly upset over an access issue on the property. The 10 acres that Mom had bought included the shared driveway that accessed both properties. Peter had an easement, of course, but Jerry would often place large stones along the driveway, marking our property line.

Jerry got confrontational after that, and Peter claims he threatened to bomb the lodge and turn him in to the county for illegal construction projects. J. D. and Jerry were still friends, but that all changed one day a few months before Jerry's death, when he padlocked the gate at the top of the driveway. Lodge guests had no way of getting in.

J. D. often carried a gun, and that day he had a .357 caliber revolver on him. He fired a shot, either at the lock or at a squirrel, depending on whom you ask. "J. D. is a gun guy," Peter tells me. "Which isn't that rare up here." Jerry heard the shot and became irate, blasting J. D. for having a gun on his property. Then Jerry knocked him to the ground and kicked him.

After our talk, I leave Peter's house and sit outside on a rock wall to finish reading the 911 transcript alone. A few pages in, Jerry gets on the phone to talk to the dispatcher.

JERRY: This man drove across my property. He fired a weapon at me this past summer.

DISPATCHER: What do you want from J. D. today? I mean, why did you come over to his house and knock on the door?

JERRY: I did not come over to his house.

DISPATCHER: All right. Are you not—

JERRY: This is not his property. He's not on his own property.

DISPATCHER: Okay, Jerry, why don't you just hang up the phone and go home then.

JERRY: Well, I don't know, this is my property—I have as much right to be in this place. I mean he's stirred the pot; he's definitely stirred the pot.

I can't tell from the written transcript if Jerry is angry or drunk, and the audio file has long since been discarded. But Mom remembers listening to it after the incident. "Jerry sounded pretty calm to me," she says. "I didn't know how drunk he was until the autopsy came back." His blood alcohol level was .22 percent, nearly three times the legal driving limit.

Jerry gets off the phone, and the dispatcher talks to J. D. again.

DISPATCHER: We've got a unit en route.

J. D.: I'll just stay on my side of the room and he stays on his. Jerry, leave. Go away, Jerry.

DISPATCHER: Keep the situation under control.

J. D.: I'm trying.

DISPATCHER: Disconnect the phone and go outside until we can get a deputy there.

J. D.: Ow . . . ow . . . He just kicked me in the balls.

DISPATCHER: J. D., just leave the house. Hang up the phone and seek safety. Go upstairs and lock yourself in a room. Do that, okay?

J. D.: Leave, Jerry. Ooooooh. He's on one side of the door, I'm pushing against it [heavy breathing]. Come on, Jerry [heavy breathing].

Then the line goes dead. Nearly two minutes later, J. D. calls 911 again.

J. D.: Oh man. Send a coroner, please.

DISPATCHER: What happened?

J. D.: He was beating me back.

DISPATCHER: What do you mean, send a coroner? Mr. Greiner.

J. D.: I had to shoot him.

By the time I was fourteen and in eighth grade, it was just me and Mom in the big empty house in Nevada City. My brother and sister were both in college, so when

Mom went away on yet another of her weeklong kayak trips that spring, it was just me. One of my sister's friends was staying with me, but she used the grocery money to buy beer.

I never told my mom how much her absences upset me. I wrote diary entries about how I felt totally alone in the world, which is probably what every fourteen-year-old girl feels. But Jerry was dead, and my mom wasn't around to talk about it. I began shutting her out, giving her the silent treatment even when she was around.

Later that spring, Mom held her annual kayak party. The place was overrun with Toyota trucks, ratty tents, and dirty shirtless guys wearing Tevas. Everyone was drinking beer or some cocktail involving Red Bull. I invited some of my friends, and we wandered in awe as strangers smoked pot on my trampoline and skinny-dipped in the swimming pool. By the time I was seventeen, my mom's younger guests began hitting on me and my friends. After one of her epic parties, a drunk twentysomething stumbled into my room and asked for my friend Hilary, who was sleeping over. I kicked him out.

And it wasn't just the parties. Our house was continuously infested with free-loading boaters who smelled of mold, ate our leftovers, and brought me presents in an effort to seduce my single mother. I hated kayaking—hated how it had torn my family apart and turned my mom from a successful businesswoman into a hard-partying widow who occasionally hucked herself off waterfalls.

I became a case study for the effectiveness of reverse psychology in parenting: the more she rebelled, the straighter I became. She smoked weed several times a day; I refused to touch the stuff until my last year in college, when friends finally persuaded me to nibble a pot brownie. Most of all, I refused to let her teach me to kayak.

"After Jerry died," my mom says now, "the only way I could make it stop was to go kayaking. Because then I had to think about the river, and it took my mind off everything else."

While I was struggling with the loss of Jerry and Mom's frequent disappearances, she met Dieter King. I was seventeen. He was some kind of California whitewater pioneer. When he moved in, I packed up my things and lived in the apartment above the garage.

Mom was happier, but this all seemed too familiar. I still can't bear the sound of even mild argument. Raised voices cause flashbacks to the fights, the broken glass, the house-shaking tremor of Jerry's body moving toward hers. Dieter seemed like a gentle man—he is—but I didn't want to risk it. I stayed above the garage until the fall of 2000, when I left for Middlebury College, in Vermont. It was the farthest place I could find from California.

Eventually I did learn to kayak. At Middlebury, I hiked and skied—and met some of the school's young kayakers, who made the sport seem, well, fun. In 2004, after graduating and moving back to California, I mentioned that I might want to try kayaking. Mom did the only logical thing and signed me up for a class at Otter Bar.

~~~~~~

The night of the shooting, J. D. was arrested and charged with first-degree murder. Desperate for help, he called his fishing buddy, Eric Bergstrom, a local criminal defense attorney. Bergstrom's case was so weak—J. D. having confessed to shooting an unarmed acquaintance—that if Peter Sturges hadn't put up the cash to hire Michael Thamer, a respected private defense attorney who'd moved to the area from Orange County, J. D. would likely be serving a life sentence.

I meet Thamer at Nordheimer Campground, a couple of miles downstream from Otter Bar. He's wearing canvas pants and a Wilco T-shirt from a 2004 tour. He's fifty-four, a year younger than Jerry would have been. When he refers to Jerry as my father, I don't correct him.

"I never met your father," Thamer says, sitting at a picnic table. "When I met John Greiner for the first time, he was in custody. John is a quiet, reserved, different person. Anyone who wears a gun is a different kind of person. But when you're a couple hours away from 911 out here, people think they need to protect themselves."

Thamer tells me that, according to the police report, Jerry went to Nordheimer Campground hours before he was shot, and on his way home he drove his truck into a tree, where it was later found by a sheriff. Earlier that afternoon, Jerry had met up with his friend Bill Wing, an outfitter and early manufacturer of polyurethane rafts, who was leading a group of hemophiliacs down the river. "Jerry didn't seem drunk when I saw him," Wing says when I call a few weeks later. "Sure, he was going through some problems. He seemed stressed. But he was as friendly as ever."

Wing testified before the grand jury—one of the few who defended Jerry—and he still thinks there's something fishy about how the case played out. "The police didn't do a very good job investigating," he says. "To do what J. D. did was way over the top. Jerry was murdered. That's what I felt."

According to Thamer, that's what investigators originally believed, too. "The police came and in a matter of moments they decided what happened," says Thamer. "Was Jerry armed? No. Were there any visible wounds on Greiner? No. They see that Greiner shot someone between the eyes with a .357 and that the victim is unarmed. So they arrest Greiner for first-degree murder."

The case was the biggest thing to happen in Siskiyou County in ages. RARE SLAYING ROCKS ISOLATED RIVER TOWN, blared the *Sacramento Bee*. Some reports even likened the trial to the still-recent 1994 O. J. Simpson ordeal. "It totally shocked everybody," said Gladys Stanshaw, the local postmaster.

Two weeks after the shooting, the headlines got interesting again: NEW EVIDENCE FOUND IN SALMON RIVER CASE. I ask Thamer what it was. "This is indelicate," Thamer says. "Do you really want to hear this?" I nod. None of this has been easy to hear.

Thamer's investigator, Woody Schamel, found some cranial fluid and blood from Jerry's head above the door in the Sturgeses' kitchen, which placed Jerry inside the house. The original investigators had simply noted that his body was in the doorway. Schamel also found an indentation on the kitchen wall where the door had slammed the phone into the drywall—breaking the receiver and disconnecting the first 911 call—which showed that Jerry had forced his way in. Thamer tells me that, under California law, if someone who doesn't live in your house uses force to get in, it's legal to kill him if you fear for your own life. Lucky for J. D., Thamer proved that Jerry had crossed the magic line.

A handful of witnesses testified before the grand jury, including Peter, my mom, and Bill Wing. Mom says she was ready to defend Jerry on the witness stand, but then she learned how intoxicated he'd been when he died. In the hearing, Thamer asked her whether Jerry was suicidal and wanted this to happen. "I told them Jerry didn't do this on purpose," she says. "He wouldn't have done that. But in some ways, I think he did want to die."

Thamer presented the evidence they'd found at Peter's house, as well as a few other damning details: Jerry's police record contained incidents of threats and battery; he'd stopped taking his antidepressants; he'd driven his truck off the road that night; and of course, there was the 911 call. A day and a half later, and less than two months after the shooting, the grand jury decided that J. D. had acted in self-defense.

~~~~~~

It's my last day at the Salmon, and there's one person left on my list—the only man who knows what happened in those two minutes between 911 calls.

J. D. isn't in the phone book, he doesn't have an e-mail address, and Google shows no record of him. But Peter makes a few calls and sends me to T&T Construction, in the town of Orleans, about 20 miles downstream from Forks of Salmon. During the drive, I nervously rehearse what I'm going to say. "Hi, I'm Megan. You killed my stepfather. Got a minute to chat?" I consider turning back, but don't. When I ask for J. D., the man behind the counter points me toward the mill yard out back.

When I spot him, he's hunched over a saw, guiding planks of redwood across a whirring circular blade. He's five-nine, maybe 160 pounds, wearing Levi's, work boots, and a T-shirt. He has a full beard and long gray hair that sticks out the back of his baseball cap. He's fifty-one now, and the sun and labor have left their marks on him.

Once J. D. spots me, he shuts down the saw and walks over. It turns out Peter called to tell him I might show up.

"Hi. Sorry to interrupt. Are you J. D.?" I ask.

"It's been a long time since I've seen you," he says.

"I must have been too young," I say, embarrassed that I don't remember. "Do you have a minute?"

He nods, pauses, and offers: "I think the man your mom first met on the Salmon River is a different person than he was at the end."

"Are you willing to talk about it?"

He nods again and we sit on a sap-covered log. I don't know where to begin, so, thankfully, J. D. takes over. Once he starts talking, he doesn't stop for a long time. He's not the reclusive man people have made him out to be. He's talking about how he and Jerry were friends once, how they used to paddle together, but there's really only one story that I've been waiting more than fifteen years to hear.

"That night in February . . ."

"I was just sitting down to eat a bowl of ice cream and there was a thud at the door. And there's Jerry. He has this look on his face, like there's something up. I was talking to him in a normal voice, and he starts ranting and raving about me doing this and that. And I say, 'None of this is true. You've got to leave.' And he says he doesn't have to leave. So I walk upstairs and grab the cordless phone and punch 911. The look on his face when I called 911 was like 'You're calling the cops on me?' And then he says real quiet, 'You're dead.'"

J. D.'s recollection matches the transcript, but then he gets to the part where the phone gets crushed behind the kitchen door.

"Jerry kicks the door so it jams my hand back. I can hear the screen door breaking off the hinges. I'm like 'Jerry, come on. You already hit me, and now you're breaking Peter's door. This is enough.' He has this real demon-looking face. The phone is jammed between the door and the drywall. I back up into the kitchen, where I left my .357 on the countertop, in a holster. So I pick up the gun, flick it open with my thumb, and I take the speed loader—put it in, twist, lock, load. And I've got it down like this."

J. D. holds his thumb and forefinger like a gun near his waist. "And Jerry goes, 'Oh, you got your gun.' And I say, 'Yeah, and you just saw me load it. I'm through, Jerry; just leave.' And he looks at me right in the face and goes, 'I'm going to shove it up your ass.' And he starts stepping forward. So I let one go and caught him right up in the left part of the forehead. He did a 180, took a step, and sat down."

I'm feeling dizzy, and I can barely comprehend the fact that, for my benefit, J. D. is getting down on the ground to act out Jerry's 190-pound body falling—his left leg underneath him and his upper body collapsing forward. I feel a sense of curdling sadness settle over me. This is how Jerry left the world: not gracefully or heroically, but with a hollow-point smashing through his head. No fairy dust or white light. Just the cold tile of Peter's kitchen floor.

I hate J. D. for telling me this. I hate him for pulling the trigger instead of running away. I write the word *coward* in my notebook next to his name. I can't stand how small and worn-out he looks, the smell of sawdust and sweat coming off his skin. And I can feel a sudden urge to leave and speed down the twisting roads.

But I've seen for myself how a dozen or so beers could transform Jerry from a loving father to a screaming, baseball-bat-swinging maniac. Mom would have killed him herself if he'd ever touched us.

Once J. D. is done talking, I hammer out a choppy good-bye—"Thanks," I say, awkwardly and regrettably—and run for my car.

Mom and I don drytops, helmets, life jackets, and spray skirts at the put-in of a Class IV section called Butler, on the Salmon's main canyon. The granite walls sling upward on both sides of the river.

"I paddled this stretch the day I met Jerry," Mom tells me. "It's one of my favorites."

The canyon walls have been polished smooth over the centuries, and the river, now joined by two tributaries, flows heavier than it did upstream on the South Fork. I tell her that worrying about the rapids feels joyfully distracting. She says she understands, and I feel some of the old bitterness wash away. Coming out here, I'd kind of hoped to vindicate the man who raised me, but instead I feel a new sense of understanding for my mom, who did the best she could no matter how life and the people in it failed her.

Mom is happy now. She and Dieter have been together for more than ten years, and she owns a successful motel in Nevada City.

Later in the summer, a few weeks after our return from the Salmon, I will find a note I once wrote, crammed into a box at the top of a closet. It's dated February

20, 1995, two days after Jerry's death: "I pray each day that I will not forget the happy times. Jerry must stay in my mind always. I write this down privately in order to remember how I feel and how much I love him."

It's like a message my thirteen-year-old self wrote to my twenty-eight-year-old self. Don't forget—who you are now is partly who Jerry helped you become: writer, kayaker, cyclist, triathlete, telemark skier. When he wasn't destroying himself and the people he loved, Jerry was the ultimate adventure dad.

Back on the river, things flow as they should between mother and daughter. We're finally headed downstream again. Mom gives me tips on getting through each rapid—pointing out the nasty holes and the sketchy eddy lines. She is part guide, part mentor, part friend. At the take-out, we change and she offers me a beer from the cooler in the car.

The cabin has walls now. Soon after Jerry died, Mom decided to add them to block the wind and rain. On my last night there, she tells me how, when the walls were being built, she put a small box between the wood and the insulation near the front door. Inside, she placed a handful of Jerry's ashes, a photo of the two of them, and a note written on lined yellow paper. "I put the box there for the people who decide to update this house one hundred years from now," she says. "Then they'll know who built this house and everything that went along with it."

I ask my mom if I can see the box, somehow break into the wall and read the letter and see his ashes. "No," she says. "It's not really for you. It's for the next generation to discover."

WHY NOAH WENT
TO THE WOODS

MARK SUNDEEN

~~~~~~

He was a proud Marine who survived three brutal tours in Iraq and had plans to redeploy with the National Guard. But when thirty-year-old Noah Pippin left his parents' home in Michigan in the summer of 2010, announcing he was on his way back to California to report for duty, he vanished inside Montana's remote Bob Marshall Wilderness, leaving behind a trail of haunting secrets—and a mystery that may never be solved.

~~~~~~

Vern and Donelle Kersey aren't the type of parents satisfied with hauling their kids to a national park and pitching a tent beneath the floodlights of someone's motor home. Native Montanans both, when they go to the great outdoors, they get all the way there.

In the summer of 2010, when Vern's only week of vacation was pushed into September, the couple was not cowed by the threat of early snow. Along with their two youngest kids, sixteen-year-old Shelby and eleven-year-old Trevor, they set out to hike 30 miles to the Chinese Wall, one of the most magnificent and remote features in the country, a 1,000-foot-high, 26-mile-long spine splitting the Rockies of western Montana.

The Bob Marshall Wilderness Complex—known in these parts as the Bob—is 30 miles wide by 80 miles tall, accessible only by foot and horse (and, in dire circumstances, plane), population zero during winter, then inhabited July through

September by five fire lookouts perched like lightning rods on isolated vantage points. At night the lookouts find their only human conversation over the airwaves, their tiny voices crackling in static beneath black skies and swirls of clouds close enough to touch.

The Kerseys brought mummy bags, rain gear, and overnight packs, as well as a four-person tent, rain tarp, lightweight stove, and water filter. They weighed out nine days' worth of freeze-dried food. The Bob is one of the few places in the Lower 48 with a robust population of grizzly bears, so the Kerseys packed pepper spray and a 9mm handgun. With no cell coverage, a minor injury like a sprained ankle or hypothermia could be serious.

And that's why it was strange when, on the fifth evening, shortly after setting up camp and heading off to collect wood, Vern and Trevor came across a man who looked simply unprepared. He wore army fatigues with a nylon poncho over his backpack. He knelt on the trail, filling a plastic milk jug where water trickled through the rocks, pouring it straight into his mouth. The men exchanged hellos. Vern sensed that the stranger wanted to be left alone, so he kept moving, but just to be safe, as the man entered the Kerseys' camp, where Donelle and Shelby were firing up the stove, Vern lingered on the rocks and listened.

"How you doing?" Donelle sang out. She was vivacious and fit, with a hint of country in her throaty voice.

The man smiled and made a motion to the holster on his hip. "Just to let you know, ma'am, I'm packin'."

Big man! Donelle thought to herself. Her own 9mm lay on the log in plain view. But as she studied the man's face, he looked less dangerous than hungry, thin in the cheeks, maybe as young as her twenty-two-year-old son.

"How long you been on the trail?" she asked.

"Thirteen days."

"Wow!" she said. "Where did you start?"

He told her he'd walked from Hungry Horse, then spent three days at a lake. Hungry Horse was at least 100 miles away, a tiny town on the northern edge of the wilderness. She asked the man where he was headed.

"I'm just going to follow the Wall," he said.

Donelle felt her maternal instinct kick in. This is not right. "There's no trail along the Wall," she said, showing him on her map where the trail diverged. "And once you get a little down the trail, there's no camping or fires allowed for four miles."

The man just nodded.

"There's plenty of good places around here," she said, making a welcoming gesture.

"I'm going to keep going."

"But it's almost dark."

"I'll just curl up under a tree," he said with a smile.

"We're going to cook dinner," Donelle said. "We brought way more food than we can eat."

"I'm fine."

"We really don't want to carry it all out with us."

"No, thank you, ma'am," he said.

The man bade them good-bye, and mother and daughter watched him disappear down the trail.

"What if he's some kind of psycho who's going to come back and kill us?" said Shelby.

"Nah," said Donelle. "He just has some things on his mind he's trying to work out."

The next morning a storm blew in, icy rain that soon turned to snow. The Kerseys broke camp and trudged out, chilled to the bone even in their new jackets and fleece. Vern built a fire at lunch. The next day the storm was worse, and the waterlogged family still hadn't reached the trailhead. They spent the seventh night shivering in the tent. Donelle hoped the stranger in his cotton fatigues and surplus poncho had found a place to stay dry.

~~~~~~

On August 17, 2010, thirty-year-old veteran Noah Pippin arrived at his parents' home outside Traverse City, in northern Michigan, for a weeklong visit. Earlier that summer, after nearly three years as an officer with the Los Angeles police department, Noah had quit his job and told his parents, Michael and Rosalie, both sixty, that he planned to redeploy with the military. He said he was going to vacate his LA apartment, haul his possessions to Goodwill, and live out of his car at the National Guard Armory until he could transfer to a unit that was deploying to Afghanistan or Kosovo.

It was an abrupt decision, but not out of character. Noah was already a veteran of three fierce combat tours in Iraq as a marine, and had always seemed most at home among the strict regulations of military life. Many vets can't tolerate the tedium of a civilian existence, and servicemen routinely discard their possessions before tours, then buy new stuff when they return. Nor did it seem strange to Noah's parents that he planned to live out of his car. In 2007, after his honorable discharge, Noah had lived in his Buick sedan in a rest area on the freeway near Camp Pendleton, California, while he covered shifts at Lowe's and gathered letters of recommendation for jobs. No big deal. Rosalie and Mike were thrilled that they had convinced their eldest son to rent a truck and haul his belongings to their house near Lake Michigan. They were doubly thrilled when Noah arrived a day early. He and his dad and his brother Josiah, twenty-nine, unloaded the boxes into the basement. Then Noah announced that he would spend that night in a motel.

"It was just plain weird," said Rosalie, "the beginning of some weird things we did not understand." But like family often does, the Pippins found ways to explain their son's behavior. Noah Pippin had always lived by his own code—of duty, structure, and minimal possessions and attachments. He did not date and had never had a girlfriend, or, for that matter, a boyfriend. Noah's father likened the code to that of a samurai warrior. And so it was on this visit. Noah's plan had been to arrive on August 18, and he meant to stick to it.

Despite the curious beginning, it was a wonderful week. The family took their fishing boat and puttered around the lake. (The youngest of the three brothers, Caleb, twenty-seven, lives in Texas, and wasn't there.) Noah's weight had ballooned the previous year after a knee injury, and Rosalie was so pleased to see him back in good physical shape, smiling and basking in the northern summer sun. She forgave him for listening to his iPod instead of chatting. "Listen to this!" he said, placing the buds on his mother's ears. Wagner's *Ring* cycle, as usual.

Eight days after he arrived, Noah hoisted his backpack into a taxi. Mike and Rosalie had offered to drive him to the car-rental office, but he refused. The date was August 25, and he was due in San Diego for National Guard drill on September 10. He did not mention any plans for the drive home. His parents encouraged him to make a vacation of it. The cabdriver snapped a picture of the family, in which Noah looked intensely serene, his arms draped over the shoulders of his mother and brother. They hugged him good-bye and off he went. Minutes later Josiah found Noah's watch—an expensive Swiss Army model—and Rosalie called her son's cell. "Just give it to Josiah," he said.

For the next few weeks they heard nothing, but that wasn't unusual. On September 11, 2010—four days before the Kerseys encountered the stranger at the base of the Chinese Wall—the Pippins' phone rang. It was the sergeant from the California National Guard. Noah hadn't shown up for drill in San Diego. He was AWOL. Did they have any idea where he was?

The Pippins were alarmed. Given their son's strict adherence to his moral code, a scenario in which Noah had intentionally shirked his military duty was nearly inconceivable. After several calls to his phone went straight to voice mail, they began to investigate, discovering that they knew far less about their son than they had imagined.

From the car-rental agency, the Pippins learned that Noah had returned the vehicle just two days after his departure—not in San Diego, but at the airport in

Kalispell, Montana, more than 1,000 miles shy of his stated destination. Noah had never been to the state, or even mentioned it. His phone records showed that on August 30 he had called a pizza parlor near Kalispell. The final call, placed on August 31 at 10:45 a.m., was to a different area code and had lasted four minutes. Mike dialed the number and explained to the man who answered that he was looking for his missing son.

"Dad," said the other voice. "This is your son, Caleb."

Caleb's own phone bill confirmed that he had received the call—although his records indicated it had lasted only two minutes. Caleb had no recollection of it. He sometimes works nights and sleeps during the day, and he remembered a call from Noah that woke him up, but he couldn't be sure it was on the day in question.

That fall, Mike Pippin flew to Kalispell, met with Flathead County detective Pat Walsh, and posted homemade signs around town featuring a color photocopy of a family photo with the handwritten words MISSING VETERAN, and an arrow pointing to Noah. After the Kalispell news aired a story about the disappearance, a hunter named Bob Schall called in. He and his buddies had seen Pippin near the Chinese Wall on September 15 and offered him a cup of coffee, which he accepted, and a hot meal, which he declined. Pippin had walked into their camp late that afternoon, a few hours before he met the Kerseys. His bearing was military: "yes, sir" and "no, sir." The men talked firearms. When Pippin revealed that he was carrying only a .38, a tiny five-shot revolver with a 2-inch barrel, Bob Schall let out a hoot. "Well, son, if you come acrost a griz, you better save the last bullet for yourself!"

With Schall's help, Detective Walsh tracked down others who'd seen him. Earlier that same day, a backcountry ranger with the US Forest Service named Kraig Lange had been leading a string of horses up a set of switchbacks near the Wall, on a section of the Continental Divide Trail, which runs from Canada to Mexico, when he came across a man sleeping smack-dab in the rut of the trail. Lange asked him to move aside. "Yes, sir," said Pippin. "I'll take care of it right away, sir."

Surveying the small pack and spartan gear—Lange remembers Pippin wrapped in a poncho or bivy sack, perhaps without even a pad—the ranger asked if Pippin was a through-hiker. "What's that?" said Noah.

"It was pretty weird," said Lange, who has worked twenty-nine years in the Bob. "I've never seen anyone sleep in the trail." Still, Lange felt no reason to be concerned. "He seemed to be very fit," Lange said. "Not malnourished or at the end of his rope." After they passed, Lange and another ranger speculated that they'd just met some sort of "Special Forces kid."

The Pippins set up a Facebook page called Have You Seen Noah Pippin? A woman called from Missoula to report seeing a homeless man in fatigues who looked just like Noah. A Missoula cop questioned a look-alike on the sidewalk, but when the man stood up he was 6-foot-3—3 inches taller than Pippin. The case had gone cold.

The following summer, his photo appeared on the cover of the weekly newspaper in Missoula, where I live, 80 miles southwest of the Chinese Wall. The mystery was irresistible. I picked up the phone and called Mike Pippin.

~~~~~~

Back in Traverse City, the Pippins had spent the long winter looking for clues at home. Noah was a methodical man, and in the wastebasket of the guest bedroom his parents found evidence of his planning: an instruction manual for a GPS unit, a package for a waterproof carrying case for the device, a sales tag for a Gore-Tex rain jacket, and a plastic bag from a new pair of Magnum-brand "Professional Boots for Tactical Operations."

Mike and Rosalie sifted through Noah's boxes in their basement. They discovered pamphlets about Montana hiking trails that had been mailed to his home in Los Angeles. In his notebook, printed in neat block letters, they found this:

SOUTH FROM HUNGRY HORSE ALONG THE EASTERN EDGE OF THE FLATHEAD RESERVOIR TO THE SPOTTED BEAR RIVER. THEN EAST ON SPOTTED BEAR RIVER (TRAVELING ON ITS NORTHERN BANK) UNTIL BLUE LAKE(S) IS REACHED.

Here was the first confirmation that Noah had not just wandered into the woods but had plotted his hike for weeks, possibly months. On the next page he had written:

WATCH
BINOCS
X2 PONCHOS
GPS
COMPASS
X5 HONEY BOTTLES
WATER
BEEF JERKY
FLOTATION DEVICES

A serious wilderness expedition. But it raised questions. How long did Noah expect to survive the Bob Marshall in September on just jerky and honey? And what was he planning to do with flotation devices? Did he mean a personal flotation device—a life jacket? Why would he need more than one? More puzzling was his destination. Blue Lakes is a nondescript waypoint about 20 miles northwest of the Chinese Wall, and would not present itself to someone browsing a guidebook or Googling "hike Bob Marshall" or "isolated wilderness Montana." Probably the only way Noah could have learned of the existence of Blue Lakes was if somebody had told him about it. But who?

Other discoveries were just as ambiguous. Another to-do list, scrawled on scratch paper in the wastebasket, included "Return vehicle to Toyota Financial." But Noah had not returned the 2002 Corolla that he still owed a couple thousand dollars on—and which he planned to live in. Instead, he had left it in the lot of a Los Angeles shopping mall, where it was promptly impounded and auctioned. The list also included "Close e-mail account(s)." When he was in Iraq, Noah had regularly written his parents from his Yahoo account. If he had been planning to deploy again, why close it?

Months after the disappearance, the Pippins and Detective Walsh were asking the same two questions: Why had Noah walked into the Bob? And where was he now? The simplest explanation was that he had gone hiking, only to be overcome by the elements, a fall, a bear, freezing, or starving. But that didn't explain why he had concealed his plans from his family.

Suicide was a possibility—especially given Pippin's recent military service. While only 1 percent of Americans have served, recent studies have shown that vets account for 20 percent of the suicides in the United States. According to his parents, Noah had seemed preoccupied when they last saw him. He had canceled his accounts on Audible and iTunes and Steam (a video-game site) and given his mother his Kindle, with its eighty nonfiction books—ranging from de Tocqueville to Noam Chomsky, Naomi Klein to Nietzsche—saying, "I won't need this anymore." It had not struck Rosalie as strange; Noah often gave her his gadgets when he upgraded. But in retrospect his words were ominous. Still, his final known actions did not indicate suicide: Why would a man wanting to die buy all-new gear and plot a 100-mile hike?

Maybe, then, Noah was still alive. Perhaps he had faked a disappearance and was living a new life, on the streets or in a different country, or under a new identity, free of debt and military obligations or some other secret burden he could not share with his family. He was equipped to travel and had last been seen within walking distance of the Canadian border. The Pippins, like any family, clung to this hope, wondering if he had just decided to check out for a while and think things over. His brother Josiah imagined Noah alive and well, and told me, "It will be amusing to hear his reaction to all of this."

The Pippin home was once a cafe and boardinghouse for a railroad depot and village that were swept away by a tornado half a century ago. When I visited last October, a homemade sign on the lawn read EGGS $3 DOZ. With a hand-cranked coffee grinder and a woodstove, the house had that comforting smell of plank floors and the old-timey tick-tock and hourly yodels of a cuckoo clock. Even with the computers and fax machine, the Pippin home resembled the 1800s as much as the twenty-first century.

In 1988, after stints in Memphis and Berkeley, the Pippins moved to northern Michigan, where Mike landed a job as a pension adviser. They are devout Christians, and Rosalie said the move was partly a retreat from the chaotic and corrupt world around them. "We wanted more control over our children's exposure to people," she told me. "When you see bad influences, you think: Let's not take them into our home." Both Mike and Rosalie had grown up with the television always on. They wanted their boys to be outdoors, climbing trees. They required Noah and his brothers to clean the chicken pens and collect the eggs.

The Pippins created a sheltered haven. Noah was a hardworking kid who tromped miles through the forest to the golf course, where he was a groundskeeper. He never so much as sampled a joint. But for Noah, the pastoral idyll was mostly a proving ground for his real passion: the worlds he created in his imagination. With his brothers and friends, the woods became fantastic battlefields for ninjas, warriors, commandos, and space creatures. At night the boys played long games of cover and concealment, searching for one another with flashlights.

Soon enough, Noah discovered the dreaded television and video games. "I had everything at my place he wasn't allowed at his," remembers Patrick McDonnell, one of his closest childhood friends. "Cable TV, video games out the wazoo, freedom of expression, swear words. It was his escape into the world he'd often read about but wanted to experience. He'd spend all weekend at my house, glued to the television in my room, channel-surfing and soaking everything in like a sponge."

A big kid, Noah played on the high school football team, but by then he was mining the experience for irony. While he liked the discipline and physical training, what he seemed to relish most—to boast about—was the fact that, in his two years on the squad, the team didn't win a single game.

In 1998, Noah went off to Central Michigan University, a three-hour drive from Traverse City. He changed his major from journalism to philosophy. Noah had chosen to be baptized when he was eighteen, but now, citing Nietzsche and Richard Dawkins, he declared first that God did not exist, and then, putting a finer point on it, argued that because the existence of God could never be scientifically proven one way or the other, it wasn't worth debating. Unlike his Christian parents, who tried repeatedly to bring him back to God, Noah was a Man of Reason. After two years, he transferred to Michigan State University for prelaw, a move that his father now thinks was a mistake. "He just didn't fit in," said Mike Pippin. "Noah would like to go running—in a snowstorm—and then he'd come back to the dorms and everyone was sitting there smoking pot." Noah's grades declined, and in the summer of 2002 he left college without a degree.

Pippin was inducted into the Marine Corps on January 22, 2003, just as the nation was preparing for war in Iraq. He joined less for political or patriotic reasons than for the discipline, strength, and adventure it promised, and—above all—the honor. It was a word Noah used often, one he applied not just to his heroes from war memoirs and science fiction, but also to the authors—Plato, Darwin, Adam Smith—whose strict adherence to truth had altered the course of civilization.

"In a very Aristotelian sense, he tried to have a good habit," said fellow marine Aaron Nickols, who described Pippin as principled, deliberate, and intentional. Aristotle tells us that we are what we repeatedly do, and therefore excellence is not an act but a habit. "He never wavered from what he believed," said Nickols. "At all."

Noah shipped to Iraq in 2004. There, in the presence of his fellow marines, he seemed embarrassed by his doting parents, letting their care packages sit unopened while his comrades jealously imagined the home-baked brownies and local dried fruits inside. In his two tours in Fallujah and one in Ramadi, Noah saw some of the worst fighting of the war, but he didn't speak much about it to his parents. During the thirty-day leave between his first and second tours, he didn't even visit home, choosing to remain in the barracks, reading and gaming.

Although aloof, he could be tender with his mother, addressing her as Mutti and Madame Le Goose. From Fallujah he sent chatty e-mails about care packages ("I gobbled the cherries right up!"), about the family getting a new animal ("A FREAKING COW???!!! . . . LOL! Ohhhh man, I thought we had trouble with the chickens"), and about their mutual struggle to maintain their weight.

On September 29, 2006, during his final tour, Noah was almost killed. While he was manning the turret of a Humvee patrolling Fallujah, an SUV sped out of an alley. "Truck in convoy!" came the warning on the radio, but Noah and his team never even saw it. The SUV detonated, and the Humvee erupted in flame, lifted on two wheels, then somehow managed to land flat. The men were knocked unconscious but quickly came to and leaped from the burning wreckage. Noah was confined to the camp for medical observation but returned to work within twenty-four hours. "It was just a matter of time in my line of work," he wrote to his father. "I've made a full recovery except for my hearing, which is pretty much shot. . . . Please don't tell Mom, 'cause I know she'll just make trouble for me!"

Mom learned soon enough. "Noah, God saved your life in this last blast and those of your buddies," she wrote. "For the last 4 years, your dad and I have been asking Him to save your life until your surrender to him. Oh Noah, turn away from your life of self-will!"

But Noah did not surrender. His rejection of his parents' religion bordered on defiance. The dog tags he wore in combat were stamped just below his name and blood type with the word ATHEIST. During one visit home, he told his parents that he had employed the services of prostitutes. He also showed them photos of dozens of Iraqi corpses, the results of his efforts as a mortar man. One night his father told him how they had looked up at the moon above Michigan and realized that Noah had seen the same moon from Iraq, and they wondered what their son was thinking. "The only thing I thought about was that there are people out there who are trying to kill me," Noah laughed, dismissing the chance to confide any more.

"Ever since he was a teenager, he just never liked what we put out on the buffet," said Mike Pippin. "He did not accept our belief that Jesus is the Messiah. It just wasn't for him. I think it's obvious in retrospect that he is well suited to be a soldier or a policeman, and I wasn't that kind of person myself and I found it difficult to recognize."

When I visited the Pippins, fourteen months after their son's disappearance, they were beginning to accept the possibility that Noah was dead and were combing their memories of his last visit for clues about his emotional state and intentions. As a child he had been diagnosed with attention-deficit hyperactivity disorder and medicated with Ritalin, and during his visit it had seemed to Rosalie that his symptoms were returning. As he sat at the dining room table, Rosalie mentioned a new book about the condition, which she suffered from as well. The author proposed that people with attention deficits were gifted in ways not always appreciated by society.

"Being this way is not an advantage," he snapped at her. "I'm defective."

"He was just so hard on himself," said Rosalie. Three days before his departure, at a party at Good Harbor Beach, she tried to spring Noah from his shell by introducing him to a family friend—also a marine, also a vet. The men debated religion until Noah cut it short. Later he complained that discourse with the marine had been like wrestling a beanbag. Any time Noah won a decisive point, the man rehashed the same emotional appeal. He inserted his headphones, oriented his lawn chair toward the sunset, and returned to his hardcover, *A House Built on Sand: Exposing Postmodernist Myths about Science.*

Noah simply hadn't been himself that week. "Normally, he would have laid on the couch and I would have scratched his back and he'd tell me the things deep in his heart," said Rosalie. "But this time we just never got to it. He just didn't open up."

Phone and credit-card records subpoenaed by Detective Walsh reveal the activities of Noah Pippin's final week in civilization. After leaving his parents' house mid-morning on August 25, Pippin ate the next day at a diner in Moorhead, Minnesota, nearly 800 miles away. Late that night, he called a motel in Hungry Horse. The following day he dropped off the car at the Kalispell airport, another 1,000 miles to the west. A taxi shuttled him from the airport to Hungry Horse, a settlement of 934 souls on the Flathead River.

For Walsh, a Flathead native and a veteran detective whose father had once been county sheriff, the records presented as many questions as the clues at his parents' house did. Flanked by such jewels as Flathead Lake, Glacier National Park, and Whitefish resort, Hungry Horse is not a destination but a waypoint, offering little more than two gas stations, two diners, and two motels. Why, after such a deliberate drive west, did Pippin spend five days there?

He took meals at the Huckleberry Patch, a tourist magnet that hawks huckleberry jams, pies, syrup, soaps, lotions, and saltwater taffy. He bought groceries—not expedition provisions but casual fare: sandwiches, apples, roast chicken, a couple of cans of Coke Zero. By all accounts Pippin hardly ever drank, yet in three days he bought a bottle of red wine, a bottle of white, a corkscrew, two cans of hard lemonade, and a premixed screwdriver. He placed calls to three credit-card companies. Pippin purchased food in Hungry Horse each day between August 27 and 31, but he didn't check into the Mini Golden Inns until the 29th. Where had he spent the first two nights? Detective Walsh canvassed the other motels, with no luck.

On the morning of August 31, Pippin left without checking out, leaving behind three pairs of pants, a laptop case, a sheet of camouflage netting, and car chargers for his cell phone and laptop. His computer has not been found. From the menu at Elkhorn Grill, where the most expensive breakfast item is $9.95, he racked up a bill of $23. Was Noah with another person? Walsh couldn't find any waitresses who remembered him. At 10:45 a.m., Noah placed the lost call to his brother. And there the paper trail ends.

After that, if what he told the Kerseys is true, he walked 64 miles on a dirt road to the Spotted Bear trailhead, then another 30 miles to the Chinese Wall, where he was last seen fifteen days later.

Through the long winter and into the spring of 2011, as authorities waited for snowmelt to allow a search, a few clues trickled in. Then, in August, a Boy Scout troop discovered a shirt stuffed into a tiny creek, just a few miles south of where Pippin was last seen. Three weeks later I boarded a Chinook helicopter at dawn, along with twenty members of the Lewis and Clark County search-and-rescue team, the sheriff himself, three deputies, one ranger, one TV reporter, and a cadaver dog. Rosalie Pippin had posted on Facebook, "The sheriff asked us to ask any praying people to pray for him and the team 4 things: wisdom, discernment, guidance, and for A MIRACLE!"

We flew low beneath the rain clouds, meandered between the forested flanks of Moose Creek, then topped over a grassy ridge and saw it—the Chinese Wall—cresting overhead like a tsunami. We found the shirt within an hour and called for the dog, which arrived with her handler, a man with a potbelly and a gray walrus mustache. Heavy snow was falling. The dog sniffed the fabric without interest and lapped water from the stream. "If she'da got a scent of cadaver, she'da lay down, or sat," the handler said mournfully. A deputy extracted the shirt. It could have been there for years, having grown a pelt of green moss. By now 3 inches of snow covered the forest floor, wildflowers bending beneath the load. "That's what the good Lord sent," said Sheriff Dutton, "so we can know what Noah went through."

The next morning was sunny, and we broke into teams and combed the forest and boulder fields. "Thousands of hidey-holes out there," said someone. If Pippin were injured or hypothermic or starved—or suicidal—he could have crawled into any one of them and died. Then again, if he'd walked fifteen days debating whether or not life was worth living, this place—if anything—might have convinced him that it was. I belly-crawled into a cave and probed its corners with my flashlight. Maybe he was sitting on a beach in Zihuatanejo.

The foul weather prevented the searchers from reaching the spot where the trail left the wall, and ultimately the shirt could not be identified as Pippin's. Bones pulled from caves were animal.

In October, a few weeks before the search team could launch a second mission, the Pippins dropped a bombshell.

"We've asked the searchers to stand down," Mike told me. "We can't for the moment tell you anything more about it, which is the same thing we told the deputies. We're going to investigate it ourselves and find out if it's actually credible. We've got information that Noah may be alive."

~~~~~~

In April 2004, Noah Pippin and Charlie Company, First Battalion, Fifth Marines, arrived in Fallujah just days after insurgents ambushed four American contractors, mutilated and burned their bodies, and dangled them from the Euphrates Bridge. The marines fought a month of intense urban warfare. "It was gruesome," said Major David Denial, Pippin's platoon commander. "You'd kill people, and the dogs would come eat them at night."

By all accounts, Noah Pippin was a good marine. "He was very quiet and always could be relied on to get the job done," said Gunnery Sergeant Tracy Reddish, who years after retiring is still called Gunny Reddish by his men. Trying to piece together Pippin's life in LA and at Camp Pendleton, I'd flown to California to meet with Reddish and other members of his platoon. Whether charging an enemy position or scrubbing the toilet, Pippin never questioned an order. He was so averse to getting in trouble that when the men went out for beers in Oceanside in civvies, and were required to wear a flat-bottomed shirt or tuck their tails, Pippin did both.

Pippin's respect for rank approached meekness. One time a senior marine throttled Pippin with a leghold until his face was bright pink, and as the others hollered for Pippin to fight back, he gasped that he wouldn't strike a corporal. His buddies determined that at 220 pounds he resembled a huge panda, and called him Man Panda. When Pippin revealed a fanatical love for Imperials, the cinnamon candies in MREs, his nickname evolved to Manda, the Elite Imperial Guard.

Although his gentleness invited teasing, it also won respect and affection. Adam Padavic joined the Corps when he was just nineteen, a kid from a small town in Illinois who wanted to be a cop like his mentor, and he remembers Noah as one of the only senior marines who didn't scream at the rookies, or even raise his voice. "If you had a problem, you could go talk to him," said Andrew Chavez, another grunt from Charlie Company. "He treated us like a big brother, looking out for us. He'd notice if someone was getting upset, and he'd say, 'Calm down, it will be fine.'" Noah never drank, smoke, or chewed. In his free time at Pendleton, always struggling to maintain his weight, he would sometimes pack his gear and hike solo through the hills.

In February 2005, Pippin arrived for his second tour with Charlie 1/5, in Ramadi, another insurgent stronghold 77 miles west of Baghdad. The 215 men were housed in bunks at Camp Snake Pit, a long brown stucco barracks. Their mission was to drive convoys into the hostile city and capture or kill suspected terrorists. "Every house was considered unfriendly," said Reddish. "We went in with arms loaded, took over the house, made sure nobody was a threat, moved them all to one room, broke down as soon as possible, and got out of there."

Sometimes they found bad guys with guns and bombs, sometimes women and children huddled and wailing. Each day, Noah and his fellow marines loaded into Humvees and trucks and motored toward town, knowing that at any second they could be blown sky-high. Charlie Company would eventually hit thirty-eight improvised explosive devices. "Ramadi was like the Wild, Wild West," said Reddish. "There was a shoot-out damn near every day." The marines were required to haul the corpses of insurgents they had killed into vehicles for transport to a base, to be identified and then handed over to Iraqi authorities. "Noah was straight-faced," says Padavic. "He didn't share emotions. He didn't talk about killing, or how many he'd killed."

The marine whom Noah admired most was Matthew Trigo, who had proven himself an exceptional warrior in his first two tours. The letter of commendation for his Bronze Star reads like a Hollywood script. Trigo takes out three enemy vehicles with his Mk 19 automatic grenade launcher. Trigo rushes into gunfire and digs a position with his folding shovel, then decimates the enemy. Trigo loads a single round into his machine gun and from 750 yards kills the driver of a moving car. But Trigo takes no credit for running into gunfire to drag his brothers to safety. "They were lifted by the Holy Spirit," he told me. "I was just an ambassador. Best case: I save you. Worst case: I'm with my Father in Heaven." A wall of muscle with a kind face and thin-rimmed eyeglasses, Trigo is a master of nine martial arts disciplines and was something like Charlie Company's resident mystic. When he learned that Noah was estranged from his Christian upbringing, Trigo tried to coax him back into the flock.

"Bring on your Nietzsche," Trigo told Pippin. "Give it your best shot. I'm just a Neanderthal marine, but I've got truth and light on my side."

"You're my hero," Noah told Trigo. "I want to be like you."

"You can't be nice to me and then hard on yourself," said Trigo. Like Pippin's family, Trigo had noticed Noah's tendency to be self-critical. "I've lied, I've cheated. I kill men. I'm no better than you. Anything that's awesome about me is awesome about you."

Although most men in the platoon were not practicing Christians, Trigo led them in prayer. "Lord, unharden Noah's heart. No man can hear the prophecy and be unchanged. Intellect without love is educated barbarism." When I asked if his brother marines resented his preaching, Trigo seemed surprised.

"They love me," he said. "They love me."

Of all the war stories told by Pippin's fellow marines, none was more devastating than what happened on June 16, 2005. It was about 115 degrees, and Adam Padavic climbed aboard his Humvee, lead vehicle, rear right seat, same as always. He had carved his initials on the steel bench with his pocketknife. Erik Heldt was up in the turret. As the engines roared, John Maloney opened the door. Maloney was Charlie Company's veteran captain, and the men loved him. "The best man I ever knew in my life," said Reddish. He was what marines called a mustang—a grunt who'd risen to officer by proving himself. He wasn't some ROTC boy who arrived in Iraq with a textbook, thinking he could tell combat vets what to do. "The best CO we ever had," Padavic told me one day at his apartment in Los Angeles. "He really loved us."

That morning, Maloney sent Padavic to another rig. "I'm riding here today," he said.

They made enemy contact at the first house they stopped at. They were out of the vehicles, up on a rooftop, taking fire, returning it. Then back to the convoy to pick up the army engineers. On the way back to camp, there was an explosion. The men leaped from the vehicles and broke into a house, blasted through the windows, emptying their magazines into the streets, hot brass shells flying into their faces. "Fucking chaos," says Padavic. Suddenly Gunny Reddish appeared: "Where are the body bags?" Padavic didn't understand. Why did they need body bags for these guys? "It's not for them. Maloney's been hit." An IED had ripped open the fuel tank, the Humvee exploding and flipping in a storm of flame. When the fighting subsided, Reddish ordered his men away and brought in another platoon to hoist up the wreckage to find Heldt. He wanted his men to remember their brothers as they were in life.

As Padavic told me this story, he asked if I minded stepping outside with him so he could smoke. "I get kind of emotional," he said. We stood beneath the eucalyptus trees and hazy LA sunshine. He stubbed his cigarette and tossed the butt. "Cap Maloney was a big guy," he said, his voice cracking. He held his hands apart as if he were measuring a fish. "His body bag was only this big."

That afternoon, Camp Snake Pit was miserable. Maloney and Heldt were dead, and three others were critically burned. Gunny Reddish remembers Pippin and Padavic sitting on the porch, a look of shock and grief on their faces. Reddish didn't see the good in sitting around and moaning about it all day. What was done was done. They needed to take their minds off it. "Get your gear," he ordered. "We're going after the bad guys."

Noah Pippin was the first man on the truck.

As I waited to hear from the Pippins last fall about the mysterious development, I traveled around Montana tracing Noah's known whereabouts. Those who had seen him last were struck with a similar impression that he was saddled with a great emotional burden. I spoke with Bob Schall, who arrived at my Missoula home in jeans, a snap-button dress shirt, and a weathered Stetson. He recalled that after Pippin drained his coffee and walked off, Schall said to his friend, "That boy's got some problems." A few hours later, as the embers burned red, his friend turned to him and said, "You're right."

Schall figured the marine had been through a divorce or something like that, and was wandering the woods to clear his head. "That's what I did after my divorces," said Schall. "All of them!"

I drove to Hungry Horse from Missoula. It was a crisp fall day, cottonwoods bursting yellow on the banks of the river. At the Mini Golden Inns, Noah's last stop, the proprietor, Kodye VanSickle, showed me Room 59, where the aquamarine carpets and blond furnishings and framed watercolors delivered on the marquee's promise of Squeaky Clean Rooms. VanSickle was a delicate woman with gray hair, glasses, and sparkling eyes.

"He looked like he was carrying way too much," she told me. "His exterior being was silent, like he could not express it to anyone."

"What was on the interior?" I said.

"He was suffering," she said. "The kind you have to do alone. He was searching for that connection that feels whole. I saw a dark shadow over his being."

"Do you think he's alive?"

She paused as if communicating with the ether.

"I'm not feeling that at all." She cupped her breast. "I have a prayer heart—he's in there. He's one I wish hadn't gotten away."

She looked me in the eyes. "You were meant to be here, too." Ms. VanSickle placed a medallion in my palm. Saint Jude. "The saint of impossible causes," she told me. "You're going to need this."

From Hungry Horse I crossed the Rockies to Great Falls and looked up the Kerseys. "Not a day goes by when I don't think about him," Donelle told me as we sat in their living room more than a year after their encounter. "If I would have known that I was the last person to see him, maybe I could have convinced him to stay." Vern Kersey has had a recurring dream in which he is searching for Noah in the woods. Finally he comes upon a tiny ramshackle cabin. He pushes open the door. Hunched over a rickety table, eyes hollow and face drawn in emaciation, like a ghost, is Noah Pippin.

It wasn't until late October that Noah's parents filled me in about their new development. They had received a phone call from a man named Miguel who told them he had read about Noah's disappearance online. He said he had a niece who tended bar at the Loco Gringo in Tijuana. She had a boyfriend, a big American with a shaved head, who looked just like the pictures Miguel had seen of Noah. Miguel said he had a friend named Carlos from the National Guard who had helped buy the man a fake passport. Miguel wanted to know if it could be Noah, and if so, was it safe for his niece to be dating this man. Was he a killer? Rosalie said that her son was not dangerous. Miguel said he would call back.

A month later, a credit-card company called looking for Noah. Rosalie explained that he had been missing for more than a year. The agent said, "Well, someone's been using this card." The account had been opened at a department store in Iowa on August 15, 2010, two days before Noah arrived at his parents' house in Michigan. Someone had been making purchases with the card—and paying it off—as recently as March 2011. The Pippins asked to see the statements but, maddeningly, were told that only Noah himself could request information about his account.

The Pippins were cautious but elated. Regaining hope that Noah was alive, the family was determined to respect his privacy, which was why they decided to investigate the lead themselves instead of going to the police. Mike Pippin canceled his upcoming trip to canvass small towns in Montana and planned a visit to San Diego instead. For the first time in a year, the Pippins believed they were within reach of finding their son.

Noah Pippin returned from Iraq in 2007 to a nation that was largely indifferent. "America is not at war," said Gunny Reddish. "America is at the mall." When the war began in 2003, 74 percent of Americans believed it was worth fighting. By the time Noah returned, that number had dropped to 33 percent, where it has remained ever since. An Iraq vet can surmise that two of three people he encounters don't consider his sacrifice worth the trouble.

"You come back to this oblivion," says Reddish, "and people don't even care that you're in a bad way, that your friends had to be identified from a dog tag in their boots. They say, 'You did a great job. Now, how much money do you owe me this month?'"

A few weeks before his discharge, in March 2007, Noah visited home, and his parents threw him a twenty-seventh birthday party. Noah "has learned that he is more anxious than most in social situations and has a tendency toward paranoia and obsessive thinking," Rosalie wrote to a friend at the time. "Yesterday he described to Josiah that his 'demons' are beginning to come back (i.e., depression, anger, anxiety, etc.), and he lightly told Josiah it's time for him to leave."

"He looked war-weary, subdued, and overall just tired, like many vets I've seen since," wrote his friend Patrick McDonnell, who was preparing to deploy to Afghanistan. "It may have been a combination of his experiences overseas and the amount of growing up since we last saw one another, but I could tell at least a little part of my childhood friend wasn't there in his eyes anymore."

When Noah returned to Pendleton, his closest buddies had been discharged. "The marines are allowing him to stay in the barracks until April 21, but he does not know what he's going to do after that date," Rosalie wrote to a military support group. "Does anyone in your group have experience with how to help a son transition to civilian life?"

Noah left the Marine Corps with very little savings. After living in his car for six months, he was hired by the LAPD. His training salary didn't cover all the gear and uniforms, and the California National Guard was offering a hefty incentive. For a marine, the National Guard was a step down, but he needed the money. "I ended up joining the army (lol)," he wrote to marine Andrew Chavez, "and they gave me a $20,000 bonus in '07 for going into the National Guard (lol) as an infantryman."

While he waited for the payment, Noah lived in his car in the alleys near the police training center. With his military background, he was made a squad leader. But the honor only caused more anxiety; it was stressful enough to arrive an hour early to use the shower. The cadets teased him because sometimes he smelled like a homeless man. They didn't realize he actually was one.

Eventually, Noah rented a single bedroom in the back of an old house on the southern fringe of Koreatown, on a barred-window stretch of Crenshaw Boulevard, one of the city's busiest arteries. The landlord lived in front and spoke no English. Noah shared a bathroom and kitchen down the hall with some other cops. He furnished his room with an air mattress, a single chair, a television, and a small table for his laptop. There was no closet, and his few possessions were scattered in boxes on the floor. For the first year or so he ate out or ordered in, until his parents shipped him a Crock-Pot from the Sears catalog.

As a probationary officer, Noah was assigned to the crime-ridden Southeast District. Figueroa Street is dotted with storefront churches, payday-loan merchants, places to send money south of the border, and ratty motels. At night it's populated by streetwalkers and crack dealers.

Noah felt like he was arresting people for the same misdemeanors day in and day out, only to see them resurface a few days later. Instead of fixing a busted system, he was enabling it. Noah complained that some of the officers who trained him were lazy. They would respond to a call at the end of their shift, and if the senior officer didn't want to do the paperwork, he would tell the citizen to file it in person at the station. "Noah is a black-and-white guy," said his father, "but the LAPD was gray."

Although he expressed his unease to his family, Pippin's code of honor prevented him from publicly speaking ill of his fellow officers. "In Noah's background and way of thinking, he still owed loyalty to his peers no matter what they did wrong or how those things affected him," said his brother Caleb. "That's an idea and pressure that was placed on him mostly due to his military background."

Just a few months into his rookie year, Noah was called up by the National Guard to deploy to Kosovo, but he tore his ACL during a training exercise. After surgery, the army paid for a physical rehabilitation program in Los Angeles and gave him a desk job in a downtown skyscraper, in the security office of the Army

Corps of Engineers. His boss, Jeffrey Koontz, is an avuncular, bald-headed man who patrols his windowless cubicle in combat fatigues and fields phone calls by punching the speaker button and hollering *Sergeant Major!* When Pippin arrived for his first day on the job—also bald, also in fatigues—everyone joked that Sergeant Major had hired his own son.

"I'd be proud to have Noah as a son," says Koontz. He remembers Pippin as quiet, earnest, and unfailingly polite. "We had some great conversations," Koontz adds. "He was a really deep thinker, very analytical, not a typical cop."

Noah commuted in camo in his Corolla, up Crenshaw and across Wilshire. By parking in the five-story garage, it was possible for him to spend a day at work without ever going outside, or, for that matter, looking out a window. He arrived with his PT bag and worked out in the building's gym. Sergeant Major often invited Pippin to lunch, but Noah declined, typically eating from a brown bag by himself in the break room. He never talked about the war; Koontz never even knew he'd been in Iraq. A woman in the office found the stoic GI dreamy and would alter her route to linger at his desk, but he never so much as asked for her phone number.

Near the end of 2009, when Noah left the skyscraper, Sergeant Major offered him a permanent job. For several months he left follow-up messages, but Pippin never called back.

~~~~~~

Noah Pippin never sought treatment for, nor was he diagnosed with, post-traumatic stress disorder. He once told his parents that he was worried that any sort of medical treatment—even for the hearing loss he suffered—might rule out future jobs in the military or law enforcement. Nonetheless, Pippin's behavior after returning from Iraq appears to fit the symptoms, which often include the reexperiencing of combat, avoiding intimacy, and withdrawing from friends and family. Once during training for night-combat operations with the LAPD, in which he and his fellow cadets had to identify paper pop-ups as either threats (a man with a gun) or civilians (a woman with a baby), Pippin screamed *Contact front!* and in a barrage of cursing emptied his magazine at the target. In an exercise where cadets practiced arresting one another, Pippin discovered a gun on his "suspect" and knocked the handcuffed man face-first onto the ground. He was reprimanded but deemed fit to continue his training. I asked an LAPD spokesman if Officer Pippin had ever been evaluated for mental health issues, and he told me that such personnel records were confidential. Pippin's commander at the National Guard said that Pippin and all guardsmen were regularly evaluated for physical and mental health.

Diagnosed or not, the war has taken its toll on the men of Charlie 1/5. During my visit with Gunny Reddish, he told me that seven years after Ramadi he still gets phone calls, sometimes in the middle of the night, from young men—scared, drunk, about to do something stupid. He starts out gently, telling them to put down the bottle, take a deep breath, calm down. If that doesn't work, he reverts to drill sergeant, tells them to shut the fuck up right now or he's driving halfway up the state of California to put his boot in their ass.

Pippin never made such calls to Reddish or any of his other marines. Indeed, several living in the LA area had not even known that he was close by. Pippin told his mother that some of his marine buddies would get together, but because he'd gained so much weight after his injury, he was embarrassed to meet them. He became isolated. Noah did not keep in touch with his classmates from the academy, nor did he become close to officers from the Southeast Precinct.

When Pippin wasn't at work or the gym, he was at home, reading books, playing video games, and sinking deeper into his own mind. When I learned from his brother Josiah that Noah used the online moniker "benx6444," I searched and found a long record of his writings and activities—perhaps the most revealing history of a man who kept largely to himself. He logged hundreds of hours gaming, his favorites being Warhammer 40,000: Dawn of War (106 hours), Command and Conquer (89 hours), and Jagged Alliance (68 hours).

The site he apparently visited most was the Skeptics Guide to the Universe, a forum dedicated to "the paranormal, fringe science, and controversial claims from a scientific point of view." In the year leading up to his disappearance, Noah posted there 2,774 times. He indulged his passion for speculation and history and philosophy: "You wake up on a stretch of beach outside of Rome [in 10 BC]. How do you earn your living? What could you contribute? Build? Manufacture? What would be the easiest profession to take on/make to become rich?"

On a site dedicated to the Austrian economist Ludwig Von Mises, Noah split the sort of hairs generally reserved for graduate seminars:

Is there really a contradiction here between what Mises says about the impossibility of planning an economy due, in large part, to the unpredictable nature of human action and Mises's seeming implicit assertion that he has, according to the reviewer, "a tool for distinguishing one event from another, and for judging when they are the same."

In the Skeptics' forum, Noah showed increasing cynicism toward his profession. He quipped, "Cops = glorified janitors." In a thread offering the glib career advice "ROTC > Full Scholarship > Job > $$$$ > Live somewhere else > Shoot people," benx amended the final line to "Order other people to shoot people." To a young man seeking advice on love, benx replied, "It doesn't exist."

Pippin's online writings reveal a man slipping into the rabbit hole of his own mind. Instead of tackling the big questions, Pippin wove ever more complicated defenses of the smallest points. On GameSpot.com, he employed his rhetorical gifts to savage a review of a video game:

> Joe Dobson's whiny review of "Army of Two" isn't so much about the game as it is about his POLITICAL VIEWS on a subject and how he feels the game treats his political views. . . . Dobson can't handle someone else's perspective, or an interesting dialogue about the effectiveness of State Militarys [*sic*] vs Private ones. He's already made up his mind, and anyone attempting to even talk about this issue without his stamp of approval, or who isn't in lockstep with him, gets their game shut down. What a clown.

In November 2009, Pippin bought an expensive hunting rifle. Taking it to a shooting range was one of the few activities he remained passionate about. "It's so freakin' cool!" he wrote. "It's not like ordering a burger at McDonald's or buying furniture. When you walk into a firing range, you suddenly become aware that your fellow Man is there with you. It's kinda scary until you look left and right and see that . . . it's cool, ya know? You can trust each other."

He wrote that after mastering his rifle at the range, he might like to try hunting big game like bear, elk, and deer. Another poster mentioned that hunting black bear was illegal in Montana. Sometime thereafter, Pippin requested the hiking pamphlets for Yellowstone and the adjacent Gallatin National Forest. This was the closest link I found between Pippin and the Bob Marshall. But as for the rifle, instead of carrying it into the woods, Pippin left it in the basement of his parents' house.

~~~~~~

Miguel called again in October. He told the Pippins that Carlos's cousin, an illegal immigrant, and Noah were holed up at a cheap motel in El Cajon, a San Diego suburb. He said that Noah was holding a job in the States, crossing the border to see his girlfriend. Miguel said that one day, while the illegal roommate was at work, Noah invited his buddies over for a party. When the cousin returned, everything had been stolen. Since he was illegal, he couldn't call the police. He was a real hardworking guy, said Miguel, just trying to get ahead, to support his family back in Mexico, and it was a real shame that because of Noah, he'd lost everything.

The Pippins grew suspicious and asked Miguel for his phone number, but he declined. They asked if he had a Facebook page, and he said yes. They saw that it had been created that same day. The photo of Miguel was one easily available online. Feeling like they were in over their heads, the Pippins finally revealed their conversations to Detective Walsh, who told them without hesitation that the calls were part of a common scam used to shake down families of missing persons. "I see this kind of thing every day," he said. The phone calls from Miguel ceased.

Walsh also subpoenaed the credit-card records. He didn't give much credence to the theory that Pippin was alive and shopping. More likely, someone had found Noah's wallet and had been using the card. As it turned out, the hope offered by the credit-card agent was false; what appeared to be recent activity was actually just paperwork blips caused by the transfer of Noah's account from one bank to another.

Then, just as the case seemed to turn cold once again, another witness came forward. In October, Steven Pierce was driving near his home in Kalispell when he heard the story on the radio about the missing marine. By then, a year had passed since his hunting trip in the Bob. Noah—that biblical name—rang a bell. Pierce called Detective Walsh.

On the evening of September 12, 2010, three days before Noah had last been seen by the Kerseys, Pierce had hauled his trailer along the 64 miles of dirt road from Hungry Horse to the campground at Beaver Creek on the Spotted Bear River. He led the horses off the trailer and fed them some hay. He noticed the man at the adjacent site with no vehicle and said hello.

Pierce remembers the stranger as none too friendly. Pippin kept his back turned when Pierce started asking questions, and said curtly that he'd hiked in from Hungry Horse. Seeing the fatigues, Pierce asked if he was military, and Noah told him he was a vet.

"You been over in Iraq?"

"Got back a little while ago."

"I was in Vietnam," said Pierce, hoping to break the ice. "Navy."

Noah didn't answer.

"If you're going hiking in these parts, you need a gun," said Pierce. "Do you have one?"

"Yes, sir," he said. "Just a .38."

"That ain't much to stuff in the face of a grizzly when he's chewing on your foot."

"It's all I got."

"Where you from?"

"Southern California."

Pierce surveyed Noah's camp: a one-man bivy tent, a lightweight sleeping bag, a hunting knife, a small backpack, a plastic jug. It appeared to be all his worldly possessions. No provisions that Pierce could see.

"You're obviously not a hunter," said Pierce. "What are you doing out here, anyway?"

Pippin admitted that he'd had some financial problems. The only way to get out from under them, he said, had been to join the National Guard for the signing bonus—which he'd already spent—and now he was locked into more duty. He told the hunter he didn't want to go back to Iraq or Afghanistan. He was adamant about it.

This was a drastic break from what he had told everyone else. Like so much in the case of Noah Pippin, it just doesn't add up. If his financial problems were paramount, his parents, who had often encouraged him to finish college with the G.I. Bill, would have helped him make the transition. If his chief concern was avoiding a fourth tour, simply remaining in his Guard unit would have afforded him more than a year to figure out a solution. Maybe he felt that he had checkmated himself: By quitting his job, he had no choice but to redeploy, but now twelve days alone in the woods had brought the fatal clarity that he couldn't go back to combat, and neither could he face the shame of having failed to report.

Two things are clear. First, the date was September 12, a full two days after he was legally required to report for drill, a fact that surely weighed heavily on a marine who valued honor above all. The man who found sanctuary in the rules had, for the first time, broken them. Raised in black and white, saved or damned, he could not help but consider himself one of the defective. Second, as he grappled with these life-and-death decisions, he did so without the parents, brothers, and marines who loved him.

The two war veterans regarded one another at that campground picnic table.

"Are you AWOL right now?" said Pierce.

Noah wouldn't face him.

Pierce asked again.

"Yes, I'm AWOL."

"That's not good, son," said Pierce. "Marines don't do that shit. We don't cop out on our country."

Noah turned his back and said, "I'm going to bed now."

"There's bad weather coming," said Pierce. "You gonna be all right?"

"Yes, sir."

"You know the trails out here?"

"Yes, sir."

Pierce returned to his truck and brought Noah a couple of granola bars and an old map. When he set out on the trail in the morning, he didn't notice whether or not Pippin was still there.

~~~~~~

Where is Saint Jude when we need him? Kodye VanSickle at the Mini Golden Inns prays the novena to the patron saint of lost causes, of cases despaired of. As of February, Pippin's whereabouts were still a mystery. Beset by nightmares, Vern Kersey has volunteered himself for the next search mission, sure he could lead them to the right spot. Detective Walsh retired before solving the case, but during his final month as a police officer he went hunting, and of all the grounds he could have chosen, he picked the Spotted Bear River, where he retraced Noah's path; he saw a couple of bucks but didn't take a shot. Gunny Reddish is retired, too, and when he fields those midnight phone calls from his men, he's glad he spared them the horror of what lay beneath that incinerated wreck in Ramadi, a vision he's never been able to shake. When I left the Pippins in November, they prayed with me, asking for an end to this, hoping that if Noah is alive he might contact them. The war is officially over now, but it wanders our woods, haunts our dreams, and occupies our prayers.

On a Sunday afternoon in Los Angeles, back in October, I got a call from Matthew Trigo. I drove north three hours through the high desert and found him in a spacious home with a green lawn, kids on bikes, afternoon sunshine on the streets. While we talked in his backyard, the distant sun dropping slowly as the hours eased by, his three children crawled onto his lap and he twirled them with his Popeye arms as if they were kittens. Trigo told me he is on disability for his wounds, has trouble holding a job, and doesn't use the phone much. "I'm a believer in being completely present in the moment," he said. If a call distracts him from his children, he ignores it.

"I wish I was still there," he told me. "When you hear another friend is dead, you think: I should be there." I asked how he reconciled the demands of war with the tenets of his faith: *Thou shalt not kill* and *Turn the other cheek*. He spoke of the Old Testament warriors, of David slaying Goliath, of Samson destroying a thousand enemies with the jawbone of a donkey. "I'm a hypocrite and a sinner," said Trigo. "But we are redeemed by the blood of Christ."

Across this landscape of believers, Pippin's knell rings in biblical tones. His Father created a Garden, but Noah Pippin walked out of it, then found the fallen world impossible. While Trigo is able to navigate the jagged terrain between Camp Snake Pit and here, Pippin has not found his way home. Trigo told me that the last he heard from Noah was a few years back, when Trigo agreed to serve as a reference for the police job. He and Noah were messaging, Trigo's wife doing the actual typing, and Noah tapped in the same lines he used in Iraq. "You're my hero," Noah wrote. "I want to be like you."

"He was searching for peace," Trigo speculated, "and couldn't find it, so he went to the wilderness, where there is nothing to rebel against. You can't rebel against nature."

I asked Trigo if the police department had ever called him.

"No, they did not," he told me. "I was waiting for them. I had a lot of good things to say about him."

DEAD OF NIGHT

NED ZEMAN

~~~~~~

A brilliant American financier and his exotic wife build a lavish mansion in the jungles of Costa Rica, set up a wildlife preserve, and appear to slowly, steadily lose their minds. A spiral of handguns, angry locals, armed guards, uncut diamonds, abduction plots, and a bedroom blazing with 550 Tiffany lamps ends with a body and a compelling mystery: Did John Felix Bender die by his own hand? Or did Ann Bender kill him to escape their crumbling dream?

~~~~~~

The city of San José, Costa Rica, is a sprawling gray mess that doubles as the sex-tourism capital of Latin America.

Thanks to legalized prostitution, parts of downtown look like Disneyland for horny, middle-aged Australians. The urban center is a mix of shopping malls, semi-rises, and fast-food outlets that separate streets of grinding poverty from pockets of conspicuous wealth.

Rich expats gravitate to a suburban area called Escazú, because that's where the embassies are, and because misery loves company. It was there, in a high-security apartment complex for short-term diplomats, that I first met Ann Bender, Central America's most captivating accused murderess.

By this point—October 12, 2012—nearly three years had passed since the strange and bloody death of Ann's husband, John Felix Bender. John, forty-four when he died, was known on Wall Street as the troubled genius who'd quit the billionaire track without explanation in 2000 and retreated to a fortified compound in the Costa Rican jungle. His end came just after midnight on January 8, 2010, in the top-floor bedroom of a circular mansion that looked like something Colonel Kurtz would have imagined in his dreams. John was naked in the bed he shared with Ann, who was then thirty-nine. The cause of death was a single pistol shot to the back of the head.

The only witness to the shooting was Ann, who'd spent a dozen years as the yin to John's yang. Together they'd built the tropical Xanadu that surrounded the mansion: a 5,000-acre wildlife preserve built on and around the highest mountain in the most forbidding rain forest in Costa Rica. They nursed each other through a shared battle with manic depression, and together, thanks to a dicey blend of extreme isolation, mental health challenges, and conflicts with enemies real and imagined, the Benders had apparently gone mad.

On the night in question, Ann was found stroking her dead husband's hand while saying, "I tried to stop it, but I couldn't." She claimed John finally made good on his long history of suicidal behavior. But investigators came to doubt her—partly because of forensic evidence that didn't appear to match Ann's story. The day I met her, she was awaiting trial on a murder charge that could put her away for twenty-five years.

~~~~~~

At Ann's insistence, I was driven to our designated meeting place by her security chief and all-around fixer, Jose Pizarro, whose quiet warmth and casual style—close-cropped hair, mustache, polo shirt—did nothing to diminish his standing as a man to be obeyed. Having previously served as chief of Costa Rica's civilian security force, Pizarro, forty-five, couldn't drive 10 feet without a cop shouting *Generale!*, or *Don Pizarro!*

I complimented the tattoo on his arm. A cobra. "*Sí,*" he said. "I did it myself."

Pizarro's English was rudimentary, but his message was clear.

"This case is—how you say?—bullshit. Bullshit from motherfuckers, *sí?*"

Inside the building, Pizarro escorted me up to a two-bedroom unit. "Ann feels safe here," he said. "And she don't feel safe anywhere in Costa Rica."

Several questions sprang to mind. First: Costa Rica? Weren't we in the peaceable kingdom of ecolodges, zip-line tours, and romantic episodes of *The Bachelor*? No juntas, death squads, or drug cartels. No standing army. Nothing but democracy, beaches, and coffee, right?

Second: Was I heading to meet a human train wreck? Ann, during our brief e-mail correspondence—which had been initiated by her brother, who'd contacted me at the suggestion of a reporter I knew in Detroit—told me she was suffering from various physical ailments, among them Lyme disease and a potentially lethal blood clot situated just above her heart. Her afflictions and legal problems had caused her to be, by her own admission, a model of instability. There had been hospitalizations, talk of suicide, and anxious late-night e-mails hinting at dangers and conspiracies.

And then she walked in.

"First question," she said. "Can I hug you?"

She was a tiny thing—5-foot-3, 105 pounds, but in a sleek, elegant way. Black halter, black skirt, black suede boots; piercing brown eyes and unlined caramel skin; hair pulled back in a shiny ponytail. She displayed only one marker of ill health: an adhesive bandage, located just above her right clavicle, discreetly concealing a catheter that dripped small doses of morphine into her veins, to keep her pain and moods in check. "I'm not stoned," she said. "Trust me."

Despite her moods, which could be epic, Ann typically evinced a kind of cock-eyed pluck, a hummingbird baseline that stood in contrast to mania. Sometimes she seemed almost too sane for her own good, displaying pointillist recall of details perhaps best forgotten. Blood splatters and bank balances, pillow talk and court testimony: She held it all at her fingertips, literally.

"Make way for the bag lady," she said.

Ann was pushing a shopping cart stuffed with legal case files, transcripts, and research materials. "When I say 'I know,' I will be careful," she said. "If it's conjecture, I will say so. Otherwise, operate under the presumption that I have proof."

Ann's stockpile pertained to a trifecta of separate but related legal proceedings. Along with the murder rap, she was a suspected jewel smuggler. Police, while investigating John's death, had found millions of dollars' worth of "undocumented" gems inside the Bender mansion. Meanwhile, Ann was playing offense against a Costa Rican legal trustee she blamed for swindling her and John's fortune and sandbagging her to the point of indebted servitude.

The net effect: Her life was no longer her own. The Costa Rica criminal court had seized her passport and ordered her to show her face on a weekly basis. The trustee cited John's death as grounds to seize her purse strings. Now Ann lived on a bare-bones allowance covering little beyond monthly expenses, part of her medical care, and rent on this apartment.

For more than two years, Ann said, she tried to keep her story out of the news, lest she come off as the Ugly Americana in a country she still loved. "But enough," she said. "I didn't kill my husband, and I don't deserve this. That's why I made the very careful decision to tell you everything. I'm angry. And when I'm angry, I do a lot better than when I'm sad. Sad means passive. And that's exactly how the powers that be want me."

She launched into a complicated explication of a financial matter. Then, just as swiftly, she pumped the brakes.

"Too fast?" she asked

A little.

"Where should I start?"

The beginning.

She nodded and smiled. "John," she said.

~~~~~~

John Bender was brilliance descended from brilliance—the oldest of two sons born to Paul and Margie Bender. Paul, a noted legal scholar, held prominent posts in the Clinton administration's Justice Department and at two major law schools, Penn and Arizona State. Both parents say John's intelligence was evident very early.

"When I would take the kids grocery shopping, he'd be figuring out price per ounce," Margie says. "When he was in kindergarten, he'd say, 'Mom, you could get a better price if you bought a pound.'"

"His use of words was precocious," Paul says. "He didn't speak early. Then he started speaking in complete sentences. He never did anything until he was absolutely sure he could do it perfectly. He taught himself to read but didn't display the ability until kindergarten. He said if he'd done so earlier, he feared I would stop reading to him."

John won math competitions but lost his temper, typically with teachers or students who failed to question everything. The world's youngest individualist could play well with others, as long as they played his game; failing that he'd bolt, melt down, or both. He was a gifted percussionist who refused to audition and an A student who rejected Harvard because he hated the interview. "People were not John's favorite thing," Margie says. When he was in his early teens, John asked, "Mommy, is it all right if I *don't* have a birthday party?"

As a teenager, John spent his free time hanging around Penn's physics department, later enrolling as a student there. He was on track to a physics career until the summer of 1987, which he spent working at the Lawrence Livermore National Laboratory, a government-sponsored facility in Northern California that works with high-tech weapons. This was during the Reagan-era arms buildup; John concluded that most of his job opportunities in physics would involve "helping out with new ways to kill people."

His future was decided the day he visited a friend at the Philadelphia Stock Exchange, where he discovered options trading—a numbers game he could win or lose based solely on his talents. Almost immediately, he began buying options with his own money. He did well enough that friends staked him with funds to make a go of it.

John, then twenty-two, was built like a football player—6-foot-3, 250 pounds—and on the floor, with its shouters and showmen, fellow traders didn't know what to make of the shy young behemoth wearing medical scrubs instead of pants. "It was the *same* pair for a while," says Bernie Hirsh, one of John's former floormates. Another ex-trader, Jonathan Kaplan, pegged John as a wall-flower with dark shadings. "I definitely recall the social anxiety," Kaplan says. "He mostly was quiet, listening."

They both thought he was brilliant, and in time John came clean about the scrubs. "I wore them so everybody would think I was an idiot," he told Hirsh. "I wanted guys to trade with me."

At the heart of John's success was his embrace of game theory, a data-driven mode of strategic decision-making based on the anticipated actions of others. Ever the contrarian, he found anomalies in the probability theories most traders viewed as gospel. He used his predictive advantage to successfully bet against the conventional wisdom.

From 1992 to 1996, John's returns were through the roof. So it was only a matter of time before his hedge fund, Amber Arbitrage, attracted some big whales, among them the famed mogul George Soros. By the time John turned thirty-two, in 1996, he was on pace to become a billionaire by age forty.

~~~~~~

They met in March 1998, at a place called Golden Mountain Farm. The 100-acre spread was located in the lush countryside west of Charlottesville, Virginia. John had purchased the lot two years earlier, telling friends he needed to live "somewhere green."

Ann, then twenty-eight, was a new and exotic addition to rural Virginia. Her looks and style seemed more in keeping with her birthplace, Rio de Janeiro, where she was the second of two children born to Kenneth Patton III, an executive at Chase Manhattan who worked in Rio, and his wife, Gigi. "I wouldn't say I had a platinum spoon or a gold spoon in my mouth," Ann says. "Silver-plated, perhaps."

Her youth was marked by private schools, parties, and white-sand beaches. Then, in classic expat-brat fashion, Ann moved from Rio to Lisbon to London to New York. She earned a degree from Ithaca College, did a stint working at a fine-arts college in Baltimore, and experienced a kind of epiphany. "My mood swings and bipolarity had started ruling my existence," she says. "By the time I was twenty-two, I'd been pretty much always up and down, up and down. I don't think my move to Virginia was an incorrect one, but it was *definitely* something I did in a manic moment."

Ann arrived in Virginia scared, isolated, and frail. She made friends—including one who invited Ann over to meet her live-in ex-boyfriend, John Bender.

John was Ann's ideal specimen. He had massive shoulders and thighs the size of armadillos; his face, with its strong cheekbones and wide-set features, projected a quiet intensity that could play as aloofness or arrogance. Or both. Ann had always been "drawn to strong men, physically and mentally," says her mother.

"I like to feel safe," Ann says.

John, when he first met Ann, noticed her trembling hands right away. "Can I get you some water?" he asked.

"Oh, I'm just on an enormous dose of lithium," she said, in her unfiltered way. "I'm severely bipolar. So if I act strange, that's why."

John, equally unfiltered, volunteered that manic depression had colored his life, too, though to somewhat different effect. His depressions could be every bit as apocalyptic as Ann's. But where Ann never enjoyed the sparkly side of the condition, John's mania often fueled long periods of inspiration and productivity. He also suffered from obsessive-compulsive disorder, so it was no wonder he happily put in twenty-hour workdays.

Ann and John, during that first day, found too many commonalities between them to count. They shared family histories best described as "complicated." Mood disorders had brought havoc to both the Pattons and the Benders. Ann's parental conflicts were mostly related to that; John's were mostly tied to his father, who sometimes questioned John's impulsive choices.

Still, both sets of parents had warmly encouraged their children's passions for things like far-flung travel and wildlife. John, as a child, had always preferred the company of nonhumans. As an adult, he kept dozens of stray cats on his farm. When people asked why, he'd reply, "Because they don't talk."

John, who was treated for a mild aneurysm in 2000, told Ann that once he racked up enough money, he would get out of trading, sinking much of his fortune into a bigger, better version of the green idyll he enjoyed in Virginia. He told Ann he'd been scouting potential locations in Costa Rica and Brazil.

"I've already been to Brazil," she pointed out.

~~~~~~

The town of La Florida de Barú looms 2,200 feet above the Pacific, on the southwestern edge of Costa Rica—arguably the country's most undeveloped region. Prior to 1998, many of the one hundred or so people who lived there lacked electricity; most residents lived in weather-beaten farmhouses or tiny *cabinas* accessible only by narrow dirt roads that turned to slop during the rainy season.

To live there was to submit to the primacy of the rain forest: an area so vast (hundreds of square miles), so wild (deadly pit vipers, warring monkey tribes), and so damned out there that it remained impervious to the gringo land grabbers buying up the northern parts of the country. Nobody bought into this corner of Costa Rica. Not even Costa Ricans.

Then, in 1998, along came these two rich *yanquis* who dropped $10 million for 5,000 acres in the middle of the highland jungle. The land was composed of separate farms that produced a meager coffee crop and a few grazing areas for cattle. The main issue was accessibility, or lack thereof, thanks to the combination of rugged mountains and a massive escarpment that cut the place off from the world.

"Perfect," John said. "This is home."

Construction took four years, with an army of five-hundred-odd workers completing a vast compound that included four separate houses, a moat, and a helipad. The Benders gave it a name that they mistakenly thought was a species of local plant: Boracayan.

Admittedly, plopping a giant house into the rain forest doesn't sound like environmentalism, but the Benders mitigated that by making the structure ecofriendly, reforesting to undo the soil damage from coffee farming, and operating the place, first and foremost, as a refuge—the region's only large-scale private haven for endangered, abandoned, or injured animals.

Teams of armed rangers were hired to chase off poachers, who previously had used the land as a hunting ground for birds and animals whose meat fetched top dollar at local markets. Ann hired six full-time caretakers and brought in vets when needed. Virtually overnight, the preserve turned into a summer camp for monkeys, sloths, and parrots; every morning, in the foggy darkness before dawn, the Benders woke to the impatient squawks and stares of macaws dangling upside down from the ledge of their roof.

But the sight of sights was the main house, which sat atop the area's highest mountain, at roughly 2,500 feet. The interior structure took up 8,000 square feet. The total living area—the porches, sculpture garden, waterfall, reflecting pool stocked with tilapia, and more—approached 120,000 square feet.

The house benefited from Ann's light decorating touch and John's design masterstroke: no external walls. The only thing standing between the Benders and the elements was a series of roll-up storm doors. Whenever they were inside—cooking, taking a bath—they were outside. And whatever was outside came in, unabated: birds and lizards and insects, wind and fog. To lie in bed was to sleep in the clouds.

The master bedroom took up the entire top floor. Below, on the third floor, was an office space furnished with a large desk, a few chairs, and a computer. Despite John's "retirement," he was constitutionally unable to quit the game altogether. A satellite dish linked him to the outside world.

But every evening, just before sunset, John and Ann had a thing. They'd go to the second floor, which housed a chef's kitchen and a large dining area. They'd migrate out to a balcony that faced west. From there they could sometimes see all the way to Panama (on the left) and Nicaragua (to the right). And on the best nights, as they peered out over the Pacific, they would see an endless blue sea dotted by whales.

It was ideal. Then it all started going to hell.

~~~~~~

The troubles began in late April 2001, on a sleepy country road just outside La Florida. John and Ann were in their Ford F-350, on their way to buy seeds, when a car boxed them in. "John Bender!" the driver shouted. "You're coming with us!"

Two men aimed guns at John's head, ordered him out of the truck, and started forcing him toward their vehicle. During the confusion, the gunmen fired two warning shots, and one of the rounds sprayed up dirt near John's legs. Ann screamed. Suddenly, the assailants identified themselves as plainclothes police and arrested John. Hours later, in the local police station, a man John had never met handed him a summons and said, "John Bender, you've been served."

The summons was related to an ugly legal battle John was engaged in at the time. It involved a New York financial manager named Joel Silverman, who had invested seed money in Amber Arbitrage in the mid-nineties. In 2001, Silverman alleged that John had verbally promised him a 25 percent cut of the company's value, which by then ran in excess of $500 million.

Silverman tried to paint John as a tax mercenary who used foreign tax shelters to hide his money from both Silverman and the US government—an assertion that wasn't entirely inaccurate. John hated the IRS so much that he renounced his US citizenship when he and Ann moved to Costa Rica. He claimed that Silverman was behind the abduction, stating in a deposition that he had suffered "at the hands of Silverman's agents."

Meanwhile, the Benders became unpopular among the Costa Rican locals. Some were hunters tired of getting chased by men with guns; others were just pissed that they hadn't been hired to work at Boracayan.

A security expert was blunt, telling the Benders: "My advice to you is to get the hell out of here." After spending three months in Canada, the couple returned and hired security guards with paramilitary training.

Still, Ann couldn't quite shake her fear and agitation. This triggered a cycle of manic depression, a physical breakdown, and an emergency hysterectomy a few weeks after the incident with the gunmen. Ann, it turned out, had been four months pregnant.

A second crisis materialized one night in 2002, when guards exchanged gunshots with an armed intruder who was seen heading toward the house. After the intruder fled into the night, Ann spiraled downward. And when she crashed, John did, too. "He was very upset about Ann," says Brad Glassman, a Washington, DC, attorney who handled some of John's legal business. "And when things weren't working for John, he could go off the deep end. He got very manic, very out there."

Paranoia took hold. When John wasn't searching for cures to what ailed Ann, he was fortifying the home and buying weapons. At one point, they again fled the country, this time to New Zealand, for three and a half months. Again they were advised to cut their losses and move somewhere else. But no. "We chose Costa Rica," Ann says. "We were in love."

Their commitment was rewarded in 2003, when they sponsored and hosted a research team made up of botanists from the United States, Costa Rica, and Germany. In one week, the team discovered three new species of orchid on the preserve. One belonged to a particular genus, Gongora, known to be uniquely difficult to classify or understand. The team named this species *Gongora boracayanensis*.

By 2008, John and Ann's legal battles had been settled, and they had invested the bulk of their liquid assets—roughly $90 million—in a Costa Rica–based trust that promised several benefits. For starters, Costa Rica now rivaled the Caymans as a shelter for foreign wealth. More important, the trust insulated the Benders from future claims against their personal assets, including Boracayan. Legally, they were now mere servants of the trust, which would be administered by a local attorney John had come to respect. The trustee's name was Juan de Dios Alvarez.

~~~~~~

By the time John died, his closest neighbor was Paul Meyer, an American expat who owns a small tree farm in La Florida. Some nights, while driving through the area, Meyer would catch a good view of Boracayan. Mostly it was dark, he said, but the top floor of the main house—the master bedroom—would be glowing "like a clerestory window."

The glow came from one of Ann's design touches. She craved bright, colorful lights—the Benders collected Tiffany lamps—a desire that was especially strong during her dark periods, which were increasing in frequency and duration. John would do anything to improve her mood, which explained why, by 2010, the number of Tiffany lamps in their bedroom had reached 550.

Ann's health had taken a sharp turn for the worse. Now, on top of the Lyme disease and bipolar disorder, she was having trouble walking. John sent her to various specialists in San José, but nothing helped.

John started breaking down, too. Such was the extremity of his devotion to Ann, to *fixing* her, that he saw his failure as a failure of character. "He was always fanatical about trying to help Ann," says Pete Delisi, a stockbroker who was one of the few people John kept in touch with. "The abduction, her illness—he felt like he'd failed her."

That month, when Ann was off seeing a doctor, John sent her an e-mail in which he despaired about everything, from small health maladies to his larger mental condition:

I'm losing my fucking mind right now. First sick again and now this shit. Today is a total fucking nightmare and tomorrow will get worse. Just when I was feeling I could finally learn to be happy, now I get this and I want to be dead. I feel so fucking horrible. I want to kill everyone and then me. . . . I deserve to die.

Ann describes that period this way: "Every day, during the last six weeks, we would sit down and he would take all the medications we had and put them into piles and say, 'Okay, when am I gonna start taking the pills?' There would be these suicide dress rehearsals. And if I went along with them, we got through the day."

John no longer answered to anyone but Ann; anxious e-mails from his parents were ignored. Refuge employees hadn't seen him in weeks, except for one or two long-distance glimpses of "Don John" carrying Ann from room to room. "Gently," one of the guards recalls. "Like carrying a sick child."

John's life was playing out in an erstwhile dream home now patrolled by no fewer than nine armed guards who were forbidden even to enter it. His personal arsenal included two licensed Ruger pistols and two illegally acquired AK-47s.

Ann says John was convinced that the water in the area could cure her. He also set up his own treatment regimen: an unknown concoction administered daily by injection.

"He was psychotic," Ann says. "He started experimenting with me. He was injecting me with certain things. And I allowed this to happen." She shrugs. "Yeah, I *know*," she says. "But there was nothing non-intense about John's and my relationship."

The day Ann described the fatal shooting was our fifth together. We'd spent the previous four talking around the subject. She seemed like somebody trying to crawl out of the rabbit hole with a flashlight.

When zero hour arrived, on a muggy Thursday afternoon, her manner was one of resigned acquiescence. "Will it drive you berserk if I smoke?" she asked, pointing to a pack of Dunhills. It was the first time I'd seen her with a cigarette. She perched on the windowsill for ninety minutes, like a little bird, and took us back to sundown of January 7, 2010.

"After we did our sunset thing, we played *Fallout 3*," she said. The video game, which John played obsessively, is part of an action series whose central character roams a postapocalyptic wasteland in search of his missing father. "We would play for two or three hours. . . . When John said, 'I'm ready for bed,' I'd think, 'Okay, got through another day.' So we go upstairs to our bedroom on the fourth floor.

"John was talking. He was saying some things. I don't remember exactly what he was saying. . . . He had a routine ritual. He had to have his pillows arranged a particular way. I was already in bed. I was falling asleep, kind of in and out, and I heard him say something like, 'You don't know how it feels to wake up with your spouse half dead next to you.' I opened my eyes and I saw—and once one has seen it, you know what it is—those two little dots that are the sight of the gun. The glow. And I realized that he had one of the handguns in his hands. And he was lying back on the pillows. And he had the gun pointed at his face as he was talking.

"When I saw the gun I was stunned, and my immediate reaction was to get up on my knees and try to reach for it," she went on. "The gun was loaded and cocked. I reached for the gun with both hands, and I was up on my knees. And I *did* put my hands on the gun. And the gun slipped through my hands. And it went off."

Ann said she ran around to John's side of the bed, saw blood dripping to the floor, picked up a two-way radio to call for help, and turned on a light. "I think I was in shock, because I was running around—which, given the state I was in, I shouldn't have been able to do. But I remember I did, like, four laps around the bed as I was waiting for somebody to come up and help me. At this point, I already knew he was dead, because I'd heard that death rattle—that last breath."

At 12:15 a.m., a guard with an estate security team known as Imperial Park heard a gunshot echo from the upper part of the house. Then he heard a woman's voice crackle over his radio: "Post Five. Help! Help! Help!"

The guard, Moises Calderon, radioed his supervisor, Osvaldo Aguilar. Five frantic minutes elapsed before Ann and Aguilar were able to give Aguilar access to the secure private elevator. Once he reached the bedroom, Aguilar found Ann kneeling, splattered in blood, and stroking her dead husband's hand. Near her on the floor lay one of John's semiautomatic pistols: a 9x19mm Ruger P95.

Aguilar took Ann down to the second floor, where she popped a tranquilizer, sat at her laptop, and e-mailed her parents. Then she called her older brother, Ken Patton IV, at his home in Michigan. Ann's first words to him: "He finally did it."

From this point on witness accounts diverge. Ann's team of lawyers and support- ers describe a chaotic scene in which rubbernecking cops were texting snapshots to friends, swiping sunglasses and iPods, and grinning at her. Photos of the crime scene do show quite a crowd, but the prosecution insists everything was done by the book.

By eleven a.m., Ann was an hour inland, in a police station in the nearby city of San Isidro de General. There, she willingly gave investigators a witness statement and phoned Dr. Arturo Lizano, her psychiatrist in San José. "I need you to admit me," Ann said in a whisper. "My husband just shot himself."

That night at the hospital, both Lizano and Ann's attending physician, Dr. Hugo Villegas, were stunned by what they saw. "It was amazing how thin, pale, and weak she was," Lizano recalls. "She didn't have the strength to hold a cup of coffee."

She weighed about 80 pounds. The blood clot near her heart would require the installation of a permanent stent. Her skin was covered with open boils, welts, and infections. Most of the sores turned out to be needle marks from the injections John gave her.

"She was literally blank," Villegas says. "She had no recollection of what was going on, and she basically was unable to fathom what was going to happen tomor- row. She knew why she was in the hospital but was not aware of it. She knew, *Yes, my husband died.* But that was it—with no emotion whatsoever."

The status quo held for more than three months. Finally, Villegas says, "it started hitting her: *My husband died.* She became a lot clearer about what happened and what the consequences were. Of course, that generated its own levels of anx- iety and despair."

Gradually, Ann came out of it. She called Celine Bouchacourt, an old friend from Switzerland she hadn't seen since the 1990s. "John was her whole world," Bouch- acourt says. "Ann told me, 'I didn't forget about you. I didn't forget about other peo- ple. It was John. He wanted just me. And I felt that was what I had to give him.'"

Folie à deux. That was Dr. Lizano's assessment. John and Ann had dissolved into a state of shared psychosis. At a certain point, one person's delusions fed the oth- er's, and vice versa. Madness by osmosis.

When Ann finally walked out of the hospital after six months, she couldn't go back to Boracayan, which was now a ghost house. The police had confiscated nearly all the Benders' belongings. Beyond that, Ann's two attorneys, to insulate her from potential criminal charges, had filed a plea of *inimputado*, which basically means she couldn't be charged because of mental incapacity. At no point, it seemed, did her lawyers claim she was innocent.

Alarmed by this, Ann turned to the man who had hired the lawyers on her behalf: Juan Alvarez, John's handpicked trustee, who assured Ann that everything would be taken care of. He said the same thing right up until August 2011, when Ann was arrested and then charged with first-degree murder.

When this happened, Ann found herself at Alvarez's mercy. He severely restricted the flow of money to both Ann and the refuge, and security cutbacks allowed poachers to return. Alvarez justified his actions by pointing to a postnuptial agreement between John and Ann. The gist of it was that Ann had waived her right to John's property, and so Alvarez controlled everything on behalf of the refuge. Ann, however, believed that the postnuptial agreement was invalidated when they created the trust.

But then, in the months that followed, Ann caught a couple of breaks. One came in the person of Milton Jimenez, a former accountant at Alvarez's law firm. Jimenez was so distraught about Ann's plight that he quit his job and opened the firm's books to her. He alleged—both to me and in sworn court depositions—that Alvarez had bilked the trust for millions, which he used to finance a lavish lifestyle and grand real estate ventures, including a high-end equestrian center in northern Costa Rica. Alvarez had done so, Jimenez alleged, by exploiting the Benders' trust. "He believed that he was the sole heir and owner of the trust," Jimenez said in a deposition.

The second break came during a chance encounter with an attorney named Fabio Oconitrillo, who had just quit the biggest criminal-defense firm in San José and was looking to start his own practice. "I just have to ask you one question," Oconitrillo said when he spoke with Ann. "Did you at any point confess to shooting John?"

"No," she said. Oconitrillo told her to plead not guilty and started preparing a defense.

~~~~~~

Leading the case against Ann was an enigmatic, middle-aged county prosecutor named Luis Oses. Laconic and cagey, with a prominent forehead and close-set eyes,

Oses relished his street-fighter vibe. "There is very little I can talk about," he told me when we met in his office last October.

One thing he readily acknowledged: Ann had been under suspicion since the beginning. Within seventy-two hours of the shooting, Oses was reviewing forensic and police evaluations that cast doubt on her story. "One week after the death," Oses said, "we had sufficient evidence to consider it not a suicide but a murder."

According to the indictment, blood-pattern tests showed that the crime scene had been staged postmortem, forensic evidence indicated that the victim had been asleep when shot, and both the murder weapon and a spent shell casing had been found in incriminating locations. Firing a pistol nearly always leaves gun residue on the shooter's hand, and John's hands had tested negative for any trace.

But at the heart of the case was the question of why a suicidal man would somehow shoot himself in the *back* of his head. The entry wound was located to the right of John's cortex, in the right inferior occipital region of his brain—which means the bullet came from the back and right. John was left-handed. Ann slept to his right. Ergo.

The indictment offered no theory about motive, but in Costa Rica as in the United States, prosecutors are not required to establish one. Still, a failure to offer a motive tends to reduce the chance of a conviction, so it seemed likely they would come up with something.

Oses wouldn't discuss this with me, but his smile said plenty. "What I can tell you is that this case is basically divided," he said. "The murder litigation is taking place here. All the litigation concerning the precious stones that were found on the defendant's property—that case is being litigated in a separate court in San José."

And there it was. The prosecution's not-so-secret theory about motive was a noir classic: The lady wanted the jewels.

On the morning after John's death, investigators found more than three thousand gems inside the home: diamonds, rubies, opals. Some lay neatly arranged in custom-made display cases; others sat randomly on counters or were stuffed inside backpacks. According to prosecutors, most had been brought into the country illegally: no receipts, no duties paid.

Ann told me that everything had been legally acquired and that she was working on providing all the paperwork. But for the prosecution, an implied narrative began to form. The Wall Street bubble bursts in 2008. The Benders, facing liquidity problems, hit upon a cash business big on profits and short on tax oversight. But then the femme fatale kills her poor dupe to make off with the loot.

"That's me," Ann said sarcastically the day after I met Oses, "a criminal mastermind."

She showed me a series of photos that police took while cataloging the jewelry collection. The gems included a red diamond (which the Benders bought in a $2.2 million lot with other jewels) and boxes of opals and diamonds worth $8.5 million. "The reason I bring this up," Ann said, "is how do you make this work with this theory that I killed my husband to be able to run away?" She tapped the images. "This is $15 million," she said. "I *left* them. Right on the counter."

~~~~~~

The trial, conducted in Spanish, began on January 14, 2013, in the eggshell-blue courthouse that sits in the center of San Isidro. Team Ann had driven down from San José the previous afternoon, in a guarded caravan that included two of Ann's visiting relatives (her brother, Ken, and their grandmother, Ann Esworthy), her two closest friends (Celine Bouchacourt and Greg Fischer, a burly American she'd met in San José), and two friends of John's from the United States, Pete Delisi and Brad Glassman. John's parents, unable to attend, sent the court statements that were supportive of Ann.

"Until now I hadn't seen John or Ann in a decade," Delisi said.

"Same for all their friends," Glassman said.

Looking weak, Ann leaned on a cane as the group descended the steps of a sunken courtroom the size of a high school chemistry lab. Criminal trials in Costa Rica proceed much as they do in the United States. One big difference: Costa Rica eschews the jury system in favor of judicial tribunals composed of a chief justice and two associate judges. Verdicts need not be unanimous. The majority rules.

The chief judge in Ann's trial was José Luis Delgado, a square-jawed alpha male who presided with breezy authority. The two other judges scarcely said a word during the trial, which lasted six days and opened with a whiff of class warfare.

On one side was Fabio Oconitrillo, the immaculate private defender wearing an Italian-cut suit and flanked by an attractive young *paralegalista* carrying a zebra-skin bag and a white iPhone. Before them was a stack of case materials, neatly codified and color-coded.

Opposite them was Luis Oses, the lunchbucket civil servant wearing Dockers and a cheap dress shirt. Oses worked alone; on his table sat the single dog-eared case file he carried in an old backpack. While Oconitrillo addressed the court, he slumped in his chair, gazing blankly at points unknown.

Criminal defendants in Costa Rica are permitted to address the court during trial, and Ann spent more than an hour describing the life and death of her marriage. Her story was consistent with what she'd told me—except for the addition of one anecdote that served to illustrate the depths of John's self-destructiveness.

Two months before John died, Ann said, she'd thwarted his attempt to kill himself by jumping off their open-air elevator. This was news to me.

Ann, having waived her right to remain silent, submitted to questioning. But Oses seemed indifferent to the defendant; Ann, in turn, tended to supply one-word answers. Finally, they were interrupted by Judge Delgado, who asked Ann: "Did [John] give you reasons why he wanted to commit suicide?"

"He told me that he was not a good person, that he had failed to cure me," Ann replied. "He told me he was tired of living a very hard life with everything he was facing. And he also told me that he was scared that he could harm somebody and that he was sure I would be safer without him."

That night, with everybody eager to relax after a long day in court, Ann threw on a sparkly green dress and hosted a dinner at an outdoor restaurant specializing in chimichurri and sushi. The mood was reserved euphoria, thanks to a sense that the prosecution was weak. Someone reminded Oconitrillo of a moment earlier in the day when Oses had questioned the veracity of one of his own witnesses. "Just terrible," Oconitrillo said. "But don't tell him I said that."

The twice-divorced Oconitrillo was wearing a pink Izod polo shirt and tight jeans. His *paralegalista*, now dressed in evening wear, nodded obligingly while he reassured Ann about Judge Delgado. "I know how he works," Oconitrillo said. "If he'd been skeptical of your testimony, he would have thrown *fifty* questions at you."

The relief seemed to make Ann woozy. So in stepped her friend Greg, a former bodybuilder who handled her like a china doll. I was struck with the realization that the friend was actually the boyfriend. During all the time I'd spent with Ann, hashing over the deepest intimacies of her life, she'd never mentioned anything about a relationship. Instead, she described her life as being "almost always alone and isolated."

Late that night, I expressed bafflement to my translator, Ernesto, a San José hipster wearing oversize Prada glasses. "Accept that you can only know so much," he said.

~~~~~~

For the next three days, everything about the trial—the lawyering, the forensic work—seemed haphazard and baffling.

The best example was one of the prosecution's key witnesses, Dr. Gretchen Flores, a government pathologist who examined Ann after the shooting. Flores was there to prove that John couldn't have fired the fatal gunshot with his left hand. She made a compelling case, but only up to a point. Ann had repeatedly explained that, during the struggle for the gun, she'd jerked John's hands toward the right side of his head, at which point the gun discharged. Oconitrillo offered witnesses who testified that John handled guns ambidextrously. He asked the doctor if she'd factored this into her findings. "It would require research," Flores replied, "since that is a very different condition."

Meanwhile, evidence of John's self-destructiveness was everywhere. On the witness stand, Pete Delisi referenced three different times when John had confessed his suicidal urges, usually spurred by his inability to handle disappointment or failure. "Both my and his family knew his condition," Delisi said. "And we knew it was a matter of time until this moment would come."

At lunchtime I found Ernesto in the lobby having coffee with Oses. "The lady is going away for a very long time," Oses told Ernesto. When Ernesto challenged him, Oses smiled and said, "Just wait till Friday."

He placed a hand on Ernesto's shoulder. "I don't necessarily think the defendant is an evil woman," he said. "I think maybe it's possible to love someone too much."

On Friday, the last day of testimony, Oses began by recalling two experts he'd questioned earlier. The first was Luis Aguilar, an investigator for Costa Rica's top federal forensic unit. A placid giant, Aguilar served as ice to Oses's fire while they analyzed a series of grisly death-scene photographs. These were projected onto a large video screen. Ann couldn't look. One of John's friends nearly passed out.

There, on the left side of his bed, lay the nude, bloodstained body of John Bender. His head was tilted to the left. In the back of his head, on the right, was the fatal wound. His left wrist dangled off the left side of the bed. Beneath his left arm was a river of blood snaking down the side of the mattress. Beside the pool of blood on the floor lay John's pistol—a sight that made no sense given the location of the wound. We also saw images of the spent bullet casing, which lay *behind* the bed: closer to Ann's side than John's.

Next came Dr. Flores, the pathologist caught in the middle of the left-versus-right controversy. She, like Aguilar, contended that blood patterns on and around John's body were inconsistent with a self-inflicted gunshot. The same went for the positioning of John's body. "It shows no sign of struggling," Flores said, "and is consistent with what we characterize as a body in rest."

Finally, Flores discussed the significance of John's right hand, which was shown to be lying flat on a pillow tucked down by John's right waist. It was a given, she said, that John's vital functions had ceased the instant the bullet entered his brain. "It is very difficult, anatomically, to shoot in that position," Flores said. Even if John had done so, she said, his arm would have immediately fallen "*en estadio inert.*"

"Is it possible to shoot with the right hand and end with the position in which it was found?" Oses asked.

"In my experience," Flores said, "it is not possible."

Oses, during his two-hour closing argument, prowled and paced, staring straight at Ann. "She had the mental ability to turn the lights on," he said. "After that she called on her radio. Then she was able to unlock the elevator mechanism. She was also able to come downstairs and was even capable of turning on the computer and sending e-mails."

During the sixty-plus minutes before the authorities arrived at the scene, Oses said, Ann and her security team had plenty of time to wash her hands and move the gun. He held up the murder weapon and crouched, as if he were on the right side of the Benders' bed. "Our theory," Oses said, "is that Ms. Ann got close and, holding the gun sideways, fired at her husband."

He pulled the trigger. The click was loud enough to make Ann flinch. Then he gestured toward the back of the imaginary bed, where the shell casing was found.

He displayed the gun and said, "I have no approved gun permit and can, with no experience whatsoever, feed it and shoot it."

He cocked and pulled the trigger. Easily. Repeatedly.

Oses closed by reminding the court that the only Bender who tested positive for gunpowder residue was Ann. "The version of events given by Ms. Ann is false," he said. "It was Ms. Ann who shot the gun. That's why her clothes had gunpowder on them. And the elements of the crime scene prove that John Felix Bender did not shoot himself. Considering that she ended the life of her husband in what the penal code defines as a cruel manner, we ask for twenty-five years in prison."

Oconitrillo rose to Ann's defense. "There is not a single piece of criminalistics evidence from which we can conclude, 100 percent, that my client committed homicide," he began.

He tried to rebut many of the prosecutor's assertions. For one thing, there was ample evidence that both the crime scene and the body had been disturbed during the chaos that followed Bender's death. The crime-scene photos, it turned out, had been taken hours after investigators first found John's body. And of course Ann's clothes revealed traces of gunpowder—she'd been lying beside John when the gun went off.

"You don't kill your husband because 'Today I'm feeling bad,'" Oconitrillo said. "There is no motivation, and with no motivation there is no homicide. . . . Were they eccentric? Yes. It's not a crime. Were they millionaires? Not a crime, either. They lived in a four-story castle? Again, not a crime."

The final words came from Ann, who struggled to hold herself together as she blinked up at the tribunal. "I'm innocent," she said. "I did not kill John. Since this trial began, on Monday, is the first time in three years that I feel I have rights. It's been three years of hell. And I feel listened to and protected by the justice system. And I would like to thank you."

After she finished, Judge Delgado announced that the tribunal would wait until Monday to render its verdict.

On Monday, Team Ann reconvened outside the courtroom—only to be informed that the judges needed a few more hours. Everybody slouched back to the hotel to kill time in the lobby, too spooked and exhausted to manufacture small talk. While I feigned interest in e-mails, I felt a presence materialize beside me. It was Ann.

"Last night I was lying in bed," she said. "And I was thinking—What would I have done if I'd been in the prosecutor's position? I would have said, 'She's crazy, something set her off, and *boom!* She killed him in a fit of craziness.' But no. He goes for the whole enchilada. Which is really crazy."

Then, just as quickly, she was gone.

An hour later, at the courthouse, a line of spectators snaked through the lobby and out to the street. In court, Ann was a trembling mess as TV cameras trained on her face. Oses didn't show up, and Judge Delgado deferred to one of his colleagues, Francisco Sanchez. "Based on the evidence presented," Sanchez said, "we have unanimously decided the defendant is acquitted."

With good reason, I thought, the tribunal found the prosecution's case short on evidence, long on conjecture, and devoid of motive. The forensic analysis, Sanchez said, was based on a series of flawed or outright false assumptions.

But then, unbidden, Judge Delgado interrupted. "The tribunal does not count with certainty the criminal responsibility of the defendant," he said. "We found it possible that the defendant could have killed her husband, but also possible that it could have been a suicide. By not being certain, the tribunal found that the evidence is not conclusive as used by the DA."

If the caveat bothered Ann, she didn't show it. She was too busy hugging her team, ducking cameramen, fumbling for a cigarette, and getting the hell out of San Isidro.

Two hours later, at a roadside diner halfway to San José, I saw her for the last time. She was exhausted; her hands trembled.

"You okay?" I asked. She started to reply, but no words came out.

I left the next morning, relieved to see the drama end. Ann's counteroffensive against her trustee, Juan Alvarez, proceeded apace. Authorities had raided his office, and a judge had replaced him with an interim trustee who was tasked with determining how much money (if any) remained in the trust. Ann seemed to be headed for a better life, probably in Florida.

And yet.

Soon came news that the jewelry-smuggling case had gone from dormant to active. Also, on February 12, a Costa Rican TV news outlet reported that prosecutors were investigating whether Ann's trial was influenced by a past business deal between her attorney and one of the judges who acquitted her. In 2003, Oconitrillo had notarized the sale of a parcel of land to none other than Judge Delgado. In response, Oconitrillo said that a ten-year-old transaction in no way suggested the sort of "close friendship" forbidden by law. Delgado had no comment.

But the biggest twist came when prosecutors announced they would appeal the acquittal. In Costa Rica, prosecutors can complain to a higher court, which may either dismiss the appeal or order a new trial. Although the latter happens only rarely, Ann can't leave the country until the appeal plays out—a process that could take six months to a year.

On March 14, Ann sent me an e-mail that read, in part: "I've reached the point where I can't accept on a fundamental level what has happened. Everything I suspected has borne out to be true in the evidence. I can't sit here, a prisoner for an indefinite period of time, and not fight on all fronts. I'm willing to do anything to expedite ending this.

"The story is far from over," she concluded. "Nothing is over. Nothing."

BLOOD IN THE SAND

MATTHEW POWER

Each spring on Costa Rica's desolate Caribbean coast, endangered leatherback sea turtles come ashore at night to lay and hide their eggs. Poachers steal them for cash, and as our writer discovered on a harrowing reporting trip in 2013, they're willing to kill anyone who gets in their way.

It was only eight o'clock on the evening of May 30, 2013, but the beach was completely dark. The moon hadn't yet risen above Playa Moín, a 15-mile-long strand of mangrove and palm on Costa Rica's Caribbean coast. A two-door Suzuki 4x4 bumped along a rough track behind the beach. The port lights of Limón, the largest town on the coast, glowed 6 miles away on the horizon. There was no sound except the low roar of surf and the whine of the engine straining through drifts of sand.

Riding shotgun was Jairo Mora Sandoval, a twenty-six-year-old Costa Rican conservationist. With a flop of black hair and a scraggly beard, he wore dark clothes and a headlamp, which he used to spot leatherback sea turtle nests on the beach. Mora's friend Almudena, a twenty-six-year-old veterinarian from Spain, was behind the wheel. The other passengers were US citizens: Rachel, Katherine, and Grace, college students who had come to work at the Costa Rica Wildlife Sanctuary, a nonprofit animal-rescue center. Almudena was the resident vet, and the Americans were volunteers. By day they cared for the sanctuary's menagerie of sloths, monkeys, and birds. Working with Mora, though, meant taking the graveyard shift. He ran the sanctuary's program rescuing endangered leatherbacks, which haul their 700-plus-pound bodies onto Playa Moín each spring to lay eggs at night.

The beach's isolation made it both ideal and perilous as a nesting spot. The same blackness that attracted the turtles, which are disoriented by artificial light, provided cover for less-savory human activity. In recent years, the thinly populated Caribbean coast has become a haven for everything from petty theft to trafficking of Colombian cocaine and Jamaican marijuana. For decades, Playa Moín has been a destination for *hueveros*—literally, "egg men"—small-time poachers who plunder sea turtle nests and sell the eggs for a dollar each as an aphrodisiac. But as crime along the Caribbean coast has risen, so has organized egg poaching, which has helped decimate the leatherback population. By most estimates, fewer than 34,000 nesting females remain worldwide.

Since 2010, Mora had been living at the sanctuary and patrolling the beach for a nonprofit organization called the Wider Caribbean Sea Turtle Conservation Network, or *WIDECAST*. His strategy was to beat the *hueveros* to the punch by gathering eggs from freshly laid nests and spiriting them to a hatchery on the sanctuary grounds. This was dangerous work. Every poacher on Moín knew Mora, and confrontations were frequent; he once jumped out of a moving truck to tackle a *huevero*.

Rachel, Grace, and Almudena had accompanied Mora on foot patrols several times over the previous weeks. (Out of concern for their safety, all four women requested that their last names not be used.) They had encountered no trouble while moving slowly on foot, but they also hadn't found many unmolested nests. On this night, Mora had convinced Almudena to take her rental car. She was worried about the poachers, but she hadn't yet seen a leatherback, and Mora was persuasive. His passion was infectious, and a romance between the two had blossomed. Almudena was attracted by his boundless energy and commitment. Something about this beach gets in you, he told her.

The sand was too deep for the Suzuki, so Mora got out and walked toward the beach, disappearing in the night. Moín's primal darkness is essential to sea turtles. After hatching at night, the baby turtles navigate toward the brightest thing around: the whiteness of the breaking waves. Males spend their lives at sea, but females, guided by natal homing instincts, come ashore every two or three years to lay eggs, often to the same beaches where they hatched.

Around 10:30, Almudena got a call—Mora had found a leatherback. The women rushed to the beach, where they saw a huge female *baula* backfilling a nesting hole with its hind flippers. Mora stood nearby alongside several *hueveros*. One was instantly recognizable, a thirty-six-year-old man named Maximiliano Gutierrez. With his beard and long reddish-brown dreadlocks, "Guti" was a familiar presence on Moín.

Mora had forged a reluctant arrangement with Guti and a few other regular poachers: If they arrived at a nest simultaneously, they'd split the eggs. After measuring the turtle—it was nearly 6 feet long—Mora and Rachel took half the nest, about forty cue-ball-size eggs, and put them into a plastic bag. Then Guti wandered off, and the turtle pulled itself back toward the surf.

When they returned to the road, a police patrol pulled up. The cops warned Mora that they had run into some rough characters earlier that night, then drove off as Mora and the women headed south, toward the sanctuary, just 6 miles away. Soon they came upon a palm trunk laid across the narrow track—a trick the *hueveros* often played to mess with police patrols. Mora hopped out, hefting the log out of the way as Almudena drove past. Just as Mora put the log back, five men stepped out of the darkness. Bandannas covered their faces. They shouted at everyone to put their hands up and their heads down. Then they grabbed Mora.

"Dude, I'm from Moín!" he protested, but the men threw him to the ground.

Masked faces crowded into Almudena's window. The men demanded money, jewelry, phones, car keys. They pulled Almudena out and frisked her, and the Americans stayed in the car as the men rifled through it, snatching everything of value, including the turtle eggs. Almudena saw two of the men stuffing a limp Mora into the tiny cargo area. The four women were jammed into the backseat with a masked man sprawled on top of them. As the driver turned the Suzuki around, Almudena reached behind the seat and felt Mora slip his palm into hers. He squeezed hard.

The driver pulled off next to a shack in the jungle, and the men, claiming to be looking for cell phones, told the girls to lift their shirts and drop their pants. Mosquitoes swarmed them. After being frisked, Almudena caught a glimpse of two of the men driving off in the Suzuki. Mora was still in the trunk.

The four young women sat on logs behind the hut with two of their captors. The guys seemed young, not more than twenty, and were oddly talkative for criminals. They said they understood what the conservationists were trying to do, but they needed to feed their families. One said that Mora "didn't respect the rules of the beach."

The men announced that they were going to get some coconuts, walked away, and never came back. After an hour, the women decided to make a break for it. Huddled close together, they walked down to the beach and headed south toward the sanctuary. They were terrified and stunned, barely speaking and moving on autopilot. Two hours later they finally reached the gate but found no sign of Mora. Almudena started to sob. A caretaker called the police in Limón, and soon a line of vehicles raced north along the beach track. At 6:30 a.m. the police radio crackled. They had found Almudena's car, buried up to its axles in sand. There was a body beside it.

Mora was found naked and facedown on the beach, his hands bound behind him and a large gash on the back of his head. The official cause of death was asphyxiation; he'd aspirated sand deep into his lungs.

The news spread quickly. A chorus of tweets cast Mora as an environmental martyr akin to Chico Mendes, the Brazilian rain-forest activist who was assassinated in 1988. The BBC, the *New York Times,* and the *Washington Post* picked up the story. An online petition started by the nonprofit Sea Turtle Restoration Project called on Costa Rican president Laura Chinchilla for justice and gathered 120,000 signatures. Paul Watson, the founder of the Sea Shepherd Society and the star of *Whale Wars*, offered $30,000 to anyone who could identify the killers. "Jairo is no longer simply a murder statistic," Watson wrote. "He is now an icon."

There was a sense, too, that this killing would be bad for business. Long the self-styled ecotourism capital of the world, Costa Rica relies on international travelers for 10 percent of its GDP. "What would have happened if the young female North American volunteers were murdered?" wrote one hotel owner in an open e-mail to the country's ecotourism community. "Costa Rica would have a huge, long-lasting PR problem." Not long after, President Chinchilla took to Twitter to vow that there would be "no impunity" and that the killers would be caught.

That task fell to detectives from the Office of Judicial Investigation (OIJ), Costa Rica's equivalent of the FBI, and Limón's police department. The OIJ attempted to trace the victims' stolen cell phones, but the devices appeared to have been switched off and their SIM cards removed. Almudena, Grace, Katherine, and Rachel gave depositions before leaving the country, but it was clear that finding other witnesses would be a challenge.

Moín is backed by a scattering of run-down houses behind high walls. It's the kind of place where neighbors know one another's business but don't talk about it, especially to cops. The *hueveros* met OIJ investigators with silence. When detectives interviewed Guti, he was so drunk he could barely speak.

Not everyone kept quiet, though. Following the murder, Vanessa Lizano, the founder of the Costa Rica Wildlife Sanctuary, dedicated herself to fighting for her fallen colleague's legacy. I e-mailed her and asked if I could come visit, and she welcomed me.

I flew to San José two weeks after the killing, arriving at the sanctuary after dusk. Lizano, thirty-six, unlocked a high gate adorned with a brightly painted butterfly. "Welcome to Moín," she said in a theatrical voice, her auburn hair pulled back in a ponytail. The property covered about a dozen acres of rain forest and was dotted with animal pens. Paintings of Costa Rica's fauna adorned every surface. Lizano opened a pen and picked up a baby howler monkey, which wrapped its tail around her neck like a boa. "I keep expecting Jairo to just show up," she said. "I guess I haven't realized it yet."

Lizano had been running a modeling agency in San José in 2005 when she and her parents decided to open a butterfly farm near the beach. She leased a small piece of land and moved to Moín with her infant son, Federico, or "Fedé," her parents, and a three-toed sloth named Buda. They gradually transformed the farm into a sanctuary, acquiring rescued sloths and monkeys, a one-winged owl, and a pair of scarlet macaws seized from an imprisoned narcotrafficker. Fedé pulled baby armadillos around in his Tonka trucks and shared his bed with Buda.

Lizano operated the sanctuary with her mother, Marielos, and a rotation of international volunteers, who paid $100 a week for room and board—a common model for small-scale ecotourism in Costa Rica. The sanctuary was never a moneymaker, but Lizano loved working with the animals.

Then, one day in 2009, she discovered several dead leatherbacks on the beach that had been gutted for their egg sacs. "I went crazy," she says. She attended a sea turtle conservation training program in Gandoca, run by WIDECAST, a nonprofit that operates in forty-three countries. There she met Mora, who'd been working with WIDECAST since he was fifteen. Lizano arranged for the organization to operate a turtle program out of her sanctuary, and in 2010 Mora moved to Moín to help run it.

They soon developed something like a sibling rivalry. They'd psych themselves up by watching Whale Wars, then compete to see who could gather more nests. Normally a goofball and unabashed flirt, Mora turned gravely serious when on patrol. He loved the turtles deeply, but he seemed to love the fight for them even more. Lizano worried that his stubbornness may have made things worse on the night he was killed.

"Jairo wouldn't have gone without a fight," she said. "He was a very, very tough guy."

Lizano told me that her mission was now to realize Mora's vision of preserving Playa Moín as a national park. She had been advocating for the preserve to anyone who would listen—law enforcement, the government, the media. It was a frustrating campaign. The turtle program had been shut down in the wake of the killing, and poaching had continued. Meanwhile, Lizano seemed certain that people around Moín knew who the killers were, but she had little faith in the police. On the night of the murder, when Erick Calderón, Limón's chief of police, called to inform her that Mora had been killed, she screamed at him. Since 2010, Calderón had intermittently provided police escorts for the sanctuary's patrollers, and by

2013 he'd suspended them because of limited resources. Prior to the killings, Lizano and Mora had asked repeatedly for protection, to no avail. The murder, Lizano said, was Calderón's fault.

But there was plenty of recrimination to go around. The ecotourism community blamed Lizano and WIDECAST for putting volunteers at risk. The family of one of the Americans, Grace, had demanded that WIDECAST reimburse her for her stolen camera, phone, and sneakers. Lizano told me the accusations were unfair. "The volunteers knew what they were getting into," she said. "We would say, 'It's up to you if you want to go out.'"

Still, she was overwhelmed with guilt. "I know Jairo was scared, because I used to tease him," she said. "We'd make fun of each other for being afraid. We'd always kid around that we would die on the beach." She'd tell him that she wanted her ashes carried into the surf by a sea turtle. Mora was less sentimental. "He always said, 'You can do whatever, I really don't care. Just drink a lot. Throw a party.'"

We sat in the open-air kitchen, and Lizano held her head in her hands. "If you've got to blame somebody, blame me," she said. "I was the one who took Jairo and showed him the beach, and he fell in love."

~~~~~~

Mora was born in Gandoca, a tiny Caribbean town near the Panama border. He caught the wildlife bug early, from his grandfather, Jerónimo Matute, an environmentalist who helped found the Gandoca-Manzanillo Wildlife Refuge, a sea turtle nesting area. Jairo began releasing hatchlings at age six. Once he became a full-time WIDECAST employee, he sent much of his salary home every month to his mother, Fernanda, and completed high school through a correspondence program.

By 2010, Mora had moved to Moín, living in a tiny room over the sanctuary's kitchen. Some days, Mora and the volunteers—college students, mainly, from all over the world—counted poached nests or monitored the sanctuary's hatchery; some nights they'd go on patrol. Mora was clear about the risks involved, and some chose not to go, but others joined eagerly. It didn't seem that dangerous, especially in the early days, when the Limón police accompanied the patrols.

Still, there were tensions from the beginning. During nesting season, the *hueveros* squatted in shacks in the jungle. Most were desperately poor, many were addicts, and all considered Lizano and Mora competition. Lizano had no qualms about reporting poachers to the police.

A leatherback typically lays eighty fertilized eggs and covers them with about thirty yolkless ones. Poachers consider the yolkless eggs worthless and usually toss them aside. Lizano and Mora often placed those eggs on top of broken glass, causing a poacher to cut himself while digging for the good ones. Lizano even set volunteers to work smashing glass to carry in buckets to the beach. She sometimes found obscene notes scrawled in the sand. She'd write back: FUCK YOU.

Lizano got caught in shoot-outs between police and poachers at the beach four times, once having to duck for cover behind a leatherback. In April 2011, she was driving alone at night on Moín when she came across a tree blocking the road. Two men with machetes jumped out of the forest and ran toward her truck. She floored it in reverse down the dirt road, watching as the men with the machetes chased, their eyes full of hate.

In the spring of 2012, Calderón suspended the police escorts. Limón had the highest crime rate in Costa Rica, and the police chief was spread too thin trying to protect the city's human population, never mind the turtles. Mora and Lizano shifted to more-conciliatory tactics. They hired ten *hueveros* and paid each of them a salary of $300 per month, using money from the volunteers' fees. In return, the men would give up poaching and work on conservation. Guti was one of the first to sign on. The *hueveros* walked the beach with the volunteers, gathering nests and bringing them to the hatchery. It was a steep pay cut—an industrious *huevero* can make as much as $200 a night—so Lizano pushed the idea that the poachers could eventually work in the more-viable long game of ecotourism, guiding tourists to nesting sites. But the money for the project quickly ran out, and Lizano wasn't surprised when poaching increased soon after.

Around the same time, a menacing poaching gang showed up on Playa Moín. They seemed far more organized than the typical booze-addled *hueveros*. The group dropped men along the beach by van, using cell phones to warn each other of approaching police. They were led by a Nicaraguan named Felipe "Renco" Arauz, now thirty-eight, who had a long criminal history, including drug trafficking and kidnapping.

In April 2012, a group of men armed with AK-47s broke into the hatchery, tied up five volunteers, and beat a cousin of Mora's with their rifle butts. Then they stole all 1,500 of the eggs that had been collected that season. Mora, out patrolling the beach, returned to find the volunteers tied up. He went ballistic, punching the walls. Then he exacted vengeance, going on a frenzy of egg gathering, accompanied once again by armed police protection. Mora collected nineteen nests in three nights, completely replacing the eggs that had been stolen. But a few weeks later, Calderón once again suspended escorts, and no arrests were made.

A month after the hatchery raid, in May 2012, the dangers became too much even for Lizano. She was at a restaurant in downtown Limón when she spotted a man taking Fedé's photo with his cell phone. She recognized him as a *huevero* and confronted him angrily: "It's me you want. Leave the kid out of it." The man laughed at her. That was the final straw. She moved with Fedé back to San José, returning to Moín alone on weekends.

Mora remained, however, and when the 2013 season began in March, he returned to his patrols—mostly alone, but occasionally with volunteers. By this point, the volunteer program was entirely Mora's operation. The Americans, who arrived in April, knew there were risks. But according to Rachel, Mora never told her about the raid on the hatchery the year before. She entrusted her safety to him completely. "I had gone out numerous times with Jairo and never really felt in danger," she told me. "I knew he was there and wouldn't let anything happen to me."

But just a few weeks before his death, Mora told a newspaper reporter that threats were increasing and the police were ignoring WIDECAST's pleas for help. He called his mother, Fernanda, every night before he went on patrol, asking for her blessing. When Lizano saw Fernanda at Mora's funeral, she asked for her forgiveness.

"Sweetie," Fernanda replied, "Jairo wanted to be there. It was his thing."

Click-click.

The cop next to me, young and jumpy in the darkness, pulled his M4's slide back, racking a cartridge. As I crouched down, I saw two green dots floating—the glow-in-the-dark sights of a drawn 9mm. About 100 yards off, the police had spotted a couple of shadowy figures. *Hueveros.*

I was on patrol. Following Mora's killing, the sea turtle volunteer program had been suspended, but two of Mora's young protégés, Roger Sanchez and his girlfriend, Marjorie Balfodano, still walked the beach every night with police at their side. Sanchez, eighteen, and Balfodano, twenty, were both diminutive students, standing in bare feet with headlamps on. They weren't much to intimidate a poacher, but Sanchez was fearless. Before we set out, he told me with earnest bravado that he planned to patrol Moín for the rest of his life. When we saw the *hueveros*, we'd been walking for three hours alongside an escort of five officers from Limón's Fuerza Pública, kitted out with bulletproof vests, sidearms, and M4 carbines. Perhaps it was just a publicity stunt by Calderón, but it was a comforting one. We had encountered a dozen plundered nests, each one a shallow pit littered with broken shells. The *hueveros*, it seemed, were just steps ahead of us.

Then the cop on my right noticed two figures and pulled his gun. Three of the police told us to wait and confronted the two men. After several minutes we approached. The cops shone their flashlights on the poachers and made them turn out their pockets. One wore a knit cap, and the other had long reddish dreadlocks—Guti. They were both slurry with drink, and the cops seemed to be making a show of frisking them. The men had no contraband, so the cops let them stumble off along the beach.

After a while the radio crackled. Another police truck had found two nesting leatherbacks. We rushed to the spot. In the darkness, a hump the size of an over-turned kiddie pool slowly shifted in the sand. The *baula*'s great watery eyes looked sidelong toward the sea as it excavated a nest in the beach with back flippers as dexterous as socked hands. With each labored effort, it delicately lifted a tiny scoop of sand and cupped it to the edge of the hole. Sanchez held a plastic bag in antici-pation, ready for her to drop her clutch.

Then Guti's drunken companion stumbled up to us, knelt beside Sanchez, and offered a boozy disquisition on sea turtle biology. The cops ignored him, and the spooked animal heaved forward, dragging her bulk away without laying any eggs. A few more heaves and the foaming waves broke over the turtle's ridged carapace.

The night wasn't a complete loss, though. A short distance away, the second leatherback had laid its nest. Soon a second patrol truck pulled up and handed Sanchez a bag of sixty eggs. We hitched a ride back to the sanctuary and a wooden shed packed with Styrofoam coolers. Sanchez opened one, sifted beach sand into the bottom, then began placing the eggs inside. I noticed that a pen had been stuck into one of the coolers. Next to it, a set of stylized initials was scratched into the Styrofoam: JMS. Altogether, there were perhaps one thousand eggs in the coolers. Almost all of them had been gathered by Mora.

~~~~~~

A couple of days later, I went to see Erick Calderón at the police headquarters in Limón. With his small build and boyish face, he seemed an unlikely enforcer, and he'd clearly been affected by the pressure the killing had brought on his depart-ment. Since the murder, Calderón said, the police had patrolled Moín every night. "I want to make the beach a safer place, control poaching of eggs, and educate the population so the demand isn't there," he said. But it was unclear how long he could sustain the effort. He said that only a dedicated ecological police force would make a lasting impact. They'd need a permanent outpost on Moín, a dozen officers supplied with 4x4s and night-vision goggles.

Then Calderón insisted that Mora's murder was an anomaly and that Costa Rica was "not a violent society"—an assertion belied by the fact that the previous afternoon, a shoot-out between rival gangs had happened just a few blocks from the station. He seemed ashamed that the murder had happened on his watch—that Lizano had screamed at him. "I know Jairo was a good guy," he told me.

That afternoon I met up with Lizano's father, Bernie. His means of processing his sorrow had been to turn himself into a pro bono private investigator. A former tuna fisherman, Bernie was sixty-five, with a full head of white hair and a pronounced limp from an old boating accident. As we drove around Limón, he seemed to know everyone's racket, from the drug kingpins behind razor-wire-topped fences to a guy on a corner selling drinks from a cooler. "He keeps the turtle eggs in his truck," Bernie whispered conspiratorially. At one house he stopped to chat with a shirtless, heavily tattooed man. The guy offered his condolences, then said, "Let me know if you need any maintenance work done." As Bernie pulled away he chuckled: "Maintenance. That guy's a hit man."

We drove to a squat concrete building with dark-tinted windows on the edge of town—the office of the OIJ. After Bernie and I passed through a metal detector, one of the case's detectives, tall and athletic, with a 9mm holstered in his jeans, agreed to speak with me anonymously. He said that OIJ investigators in Limón were the busiest in the country due to drug-related crime. I asked whether he thought the killers were traffickers, and he shook his head wearily. "If they were narcos, it would have been a disaster," he said. "Every one of them would have been killed."

Like Calderón, he promised that Mora would not be a mere statistic. He insisted that they were closing in on serious leads. Walking out, Bernie told me he had spoken in private with the detective, to whom he'd been feeding every scrap of information he'd gotten. "He told me, 'We are very close to getting them, but we don't want them to know because they'll get away.'"

Bernie's PI trail led back to Moín, where he had tracked down a potential witness—a man who lived near the beach. The man had been the first to find Mora early on the morning of May 31. He walked Bernie to the spot where he'd found the body. As he described it, there were signs of a struggle from the footprints around the car. It looked to him like Mora had escaped his captors and dashed down the beach. Another set of tracks seemed to show a body being dragged back to the vehicle.

Bernie had begged the man for some clue, mentioning Paul Watson's reward, which had now swelled to $56,000. "He said, 'No, no, I don't need the money. It's not that I don't need it, it's just that they did something very bad.'" If he talked, he was sure that he and his family would be killed.

~~~~~~

On July 31, the OIJ conducted a predawn raid, called Operation *Baula*, at several houses around Limón. Dozens of armed agents arrested six men, including Felipe

Arauz, the thirty-eight-year-old Nicaraguan immigrant suspected of being the ringleader of the violent *hueveros*. A seventh man was caught ten days later. The suspects were Darwin and Donald Salmón Meléndez, William Delgado Loaiza, Héctor Cash Lopez, Enrique Centeno Rivas, and Bryan Quesada Cubillo. While Lizano knew of the alleged killers, she was relieved that she hadn't worked with them. "Thank God none were my poachers," she said.

Detectives from the OIJ had been talking to informants and quietly tracking Mora's stolen cell phone. According to court documents, one of the suspects, Quesada, twenty, had continued to use it, sending incriminating texts. One read: "We dragged him on the beach behind Felipe's car and you know it."

To Lizano, the motive was clearly revenge, but the authorities cast the crime as "a simple robbery and assault." They also laid blame on Mora and Lizano's failed attempt to hire poachers for conservation. An OIJ spokesman claimed that the program had bred resentment among *hueveros*. The accusation infuriated Lizano. "They're just looking for a scapegoat," she said.

Lizano thought that the authorities were deflecting blame. It turned out that on the night of the murder, a police patrol had encountered several of the suspects— they were the same men the cops had warned Mora about. A few hours later the gang lay in wait. Whether or not they intended to kill Mora will be argued at the trial later this spring.

Even so, the arrests haven't brought much closure to those closest to Mora. Almudena, back in Madrid, was deeply depressed when I reached her. "Jairo is dead," she said. "For me there is no justice." The only positive outcome, as she saw it, would be for a preserved beach. "In ten years, there have to be turtles at Moín," she said. "If not, this has happened for nothing."

Lizano, meanwhile, redoubled her efforts to protect Moín. Any legislative change to preserve the beach is far off, and the turtles now face an additional threat—a massive container-port development project that a Dutch conglomerate hopes to build nearby. Still, Lizano told me, "I really believe it has to continue. I can't stop and let the poachers win. For me it's not an option."

In July, Lizano brought Fedé back to Moín. She woke him up one morning before sunrise, and together with a group of volunteers they walked to the beach. The night before, at the sanctuary, the first turtle hatchlings had broken up through the sand in their Styrofoam-cooler nests. Lizano showed Fedé how to lift the tiny flapping things out and set them gently on the sand. The people stood back and watched as the turtles inched down the beach, making their way toward the breaking waves and an uncertain future.

UP ON COVE MOUNTAIN

EARL SWIFT

~~~~~~

In September 1990, a brutal double murder on the Appalachian Trail shocked the nation and left haunting questions about violence and motive. Our writer was hiking the route and knew the victims. Twenty-five years later, he went back to the woods of Pennsylvania, searching for answers to a crime that still haunts travelers on America's most popular through-hiking trail.

~~~~~~

It is a quiet, restorative place, this clearing high on a Pennsylvania ridge. Ferns and wildflowers carpet its floor. Sassafras and tulip trees, tall oak and hickory stand tight at its sides, their leaves hissing in breezes that sweep from the valley below.

Cloistered from civilization by a steep 900-foot climb over loose and jutting rock, the glade goes unseen by most everyone but a straggle of hikers on the Appalachian Trail (AT), the 2,180-mile footpath carved into the roofs of fourteen Eastern states.

Those travelers have rested here for more than half a century. At the clearing's edge stands an open-faced shelter of heavy timber, one of 260 huts built roughly a day's walk apart on the AT's wriggling, roller-coaster course from Maine to Georgia. It's tall and airy and skylit, with a deep porch, two tiers of wooden bunks, and a picnic table.

A few feet away stood the ancient log lean-to it replaced. When I visited this past spring, saplings and tangled brier so colonized the old shelter's footprint that I might have missed it, had I not slept there myself. Twenty-five summers ago, I pulled into what was called the Thelma Marks shelter, near the halfway point of a southbound through-hike. I met a stranger in the old lean-to, talked with him under its low roof as we fired up our stoves and cooked dinner.

Eight nights later, a southbound couple I'd befriended early in my hike followed me into Thelma Marks. They met a stranger there, too.

What he did to them left wounds that didn't close as neatly as that fading rectangle in the forest floor. It prompted outdoorsmen and trail officials to rethink conventional wisdom long held dear: that safety lies in numbers, that the wilds offer escape from senseless violence, and that when trouble does visit, it's always near some nexus with civilization—a road, a park, the fringe of a town.

And it reverberates still, all these years later, because what befell Geoff Hood and Molly LaRue at the Thelma Marks shelter is a cautionary tale without lesson.

Then as now, this clearing was a lovely place.

And near as anyone can tell, they did everything right.

It's no surprise, what with the millions who use the path each year, that the AT had seen violence before the early morning of September 13, 1990. Five of its hikers had been killed in four attacks, the earliest in May 1974, the most recent in May 1988.

Those crimes shared traits with what transpired at Thelma Marks. Two of the four attacks were aimed at couples. Three came at trailside shelters. All were ghastly.

Still, none drew the attention, or generated the angst, of the incident here. Perhaps it was because Thelma Marks fell within range of news media in New York, Philadelphia, Baltimore, and Washington, DC, and because it involved not only a crime but a mountain manhunt that lasted a week. Perhaps the shelter's remoteness—far greater than that of past trouble—played into our big-city uneasiness about what lurks in the woods at night.

Maybe it was the sheer savagery of the act. Or the questions that lingered when the man responsible would not say why he shot Geoff three times or why he tied Molly's hands behind her back and looped the rope around her neck. Why he raped her. Why he stabbed her eight times in the neck, throat, and back.

"It probably took me a good fifteen years to just process," says Karen Lutz, then and now the top staffer in the Mid-Atlantic Region for the Appalachian Trail Conservancy (ATC).

"I was up at the shelter. It was very real. It was very fresh. It was god-awful."

Or maybe what set this sad affair apart were the victims, who combined competence, wholesomeness, and smarts.

"This might have to do with my age, but I find I get more emotional about it now," says former Perry County, Pennsylvania, prosecutor R. Scott Cramer, who tried the case in 1991. "I get choked up thinking about Molly and Geoff.

"These were good kids. They were going to make a difference. All the indicators suggested that. And to have their lives snuffed out at that age—it's a tragedy beyond words."

They'd met in Salina, Kansas, where both worked for a church-sponsored outfit that took at-risk youngsters into the backcountry to salve their troubles with adventure. At twenty-six, Geoff was a friendly, contemplative Tennessean, even-tempered and patient. Molly, a year younger, was a sunny, energetic artist who in high school had won a national contest to design a 1984 US postage stamp.

They shared a love for kids and the outdoors. Geoff had rock-climbed in Colorado and taught climbing at New Mexico's Philmont Scout Ranch. Molly had tackled two Outward Bound courses and spent a year providing wilderness therapy to kids in the Arizona desert.

They ventured onto the AT, as many do, at an unsettled juncture in their lives: They'd learned that, come May, they'd be laid off, and a six-month hike seemed a good way to decide what to do next. "We got a phone call from her one day," Molly's father, Jim LaRue, recalls. "She said, 'You know I've always wanted to do the Appalachian Trail, and I have a friend here who wants to do it, too. Do you want to know something about the friend?'

"I said, 'Yes, I would.'

"She said, 'Well, he's a male.'

"I said, 'Are you announcing a relationship?'

"And she said, 'Yes, I am.'"

By then she and Geoff were close to inseparable. "I love you forever, I like you for always," he wrote in April, when he was off in the backcountry. "As long as I'm living my ALL you will be." She cashed in her savings to finance their trip, which they'd start in Maine, as only one in ten through-hikers do.

And so, on June 4, 1990, having climbed the day before to the AT's northern terminus on the peak of mile-high Mount Katahdin, they set off on their long walk—and found it surprisingly arduous. "We reminded one another before we started this ordeal that there would be tough days: Days we would ask ourselves, 'Why are we doing this?'" Molly admitted early on, in a journal they shared. "Well, we had one of those days." Geoff's next entry whimpered: "Our bodies have had almost as much as they can take."

But they also wrote in the logbooks left in shelters, which, in the days before cell phones, were the most reliable means for through-hikers to connect. Reading those entries made it obvious to all in their wake that they were enjoying themselves immensely.

Which is how I first made their acquaintance, in a poem Molly left in a Maine lean-to and signed with her trail name, Nalgene.

> *Last evening I whispered "I think there're less bugs."*
> *This morning, BRING ON THE SLUGS.*
> *Through the roof of our tent I see their familiar sludge*
> *The stuff that resembles butterscotch fudge.*
> *Squish between my toes in my sandal*
> *Yuck! This is something I just can't handle.*

I read this a few days south of Katahdin, which I'd climbed twelve days behind them. I was stinking, blistered, and covered in mosquito bites. My pack weighed nearly half as much as I did, and every pound hurt. Blackflies kamikaze'd into my eyes and mouth. I missed my girlfriend.

My first reaction was: How can this Nalgene person be so obnoxiously *happy*?

~~~~~~

Eleven days into my hike, I stumbled out of the woods and into Monson, Maine, where I met Greg Hammer, an army vet in his late twenties whose Virginia home was just a short distance from mine. Greg, trail name Animal, was easygoing and smart, and together we pushed into the windswept mountains of western Maine.

Along the way, the hikers ahead of us came into focus, none more so than Nalgene and her partner, who called himself Clevis. They left upbeat log entries at every shelter. They thanked the volunteers who maintained the trail. They gave shout-outs to other hikers, including one named Skip "Muskratt" Richards, whom they'd met in Monson. They were self-deprecating, funny, kind.

And they were slow. By the time I left Monson, I'd gained three days on them, and I was no speedster. At the New Hampshire line I'd picked up a week. As Molly predicted in one log entry: "If you're behind us you will pass us."

Their glacial pace was no accident. They were stopping to take pictures, to study plants, turtles, and salamanders, to bake bread. Animal and I resolved to catch them. We sped over the high, wild Presidential Range and down the 2,000-foot Webster Cliffs, setting up camp at the bottom two nights behind Geoff and Molly. Shortly after midnight, as I snored in my tent and Greg slept in his bivy sack, we were startled awake by a concussive thud: a rotted tree had toppled into the four-foot space between us, coming within inches of my head.

We eyed the near miss by flashlight, awed by the almost surgical precision with which fate had spared us—and unnerved that life or death could turn on such blind, stupid luck.

Our rendezvous came on Friday, July 20, at the Jeffers Brook shelter near Glencliff, New Hampshire, after we'd crossed an above-tree-line peak in a crashing thunderstorm. As I exchanged handshakes with Clevis and Nalgene, I told them that I felt like we'd already met. First impressions: Molly—blond and dimpled, quick to smile, solidly built but obviously fit. Spirited. Funny. A blue-haired troll doll dangled from her backpack. Geoff—bearded, beetle-browed, and thin, with a smoky, high-pitched Tennessee drawl. I noticed that he carried one of the best packs around at the time, a mammoth green Gregory, and that both of them handled their gear with an expert nonchalance.

Our conversation was halted by the approach of a short, bearded man in a baggy black suit and large-brimmed hat, staggering under a pack that towered high over his head. Without a hello, he demanded that he be given the shelter's east wall, where Greg had already set up. He huffed, impatient, when Greg didn't jump to clear the space.

Irritated, Greg told the newcomer, whose name was Rubin, that he'd have to make do with the shelter's middle. He unpacked, muttering, as our conversation resumed. Molly, Geoff, and I talked about Salina, where I'd interviewed for a job once. Greg chatted with two section hikers, Elizabeth and Chris, who'd been traveling with them for days.

Rubin interrupted. Why had I chosen my model of backpack, he wanted to know. He had heard it was bad. It's worked just fine, I told him. Oh, you think it's fine? Yes, I said, I think it's fine. Well, if you think it's fine, why have I heard it's a bad pack?

And so on, whenever he opened his mouth, which he did a lot: to my everlasting regret, I devoted far more space in my journal to Rubin than to Geoff and Molly. With the sun setting, he yanked six Old Milwaukee tallboys from his pack and chugged them in quick succession. He crunched the empties into makeshift candleholders. As the rest of us crawled into our bags, he began to celebrate the Sabbath.

In what seemed a trance, he chanted, wailed, and danced in the middle of the shelter for one hour, then two. Then beyond two. At 9:30, Greg stopped him: "Are you almost through?" Rubin nodded, then went right back to it. Shortly after ten, when he'd paused to wolf down some bread, I told him he'd have to stop. "These people are trying to sleep," I said, nodding toward the others. "There's got to be a way you can pray to yourself."

Rubin brushed me off. "They're probably sleeping right through it."

From the darkness of the shelter's west wall, Molly yelled, "*I'm* not sleeping through it!" A chorus backed her up.

~~~~~~

Morning came. Rubin needed no coffee to get up to speed. Throughout his babble, Geoff and Molly—who wrote in their journal that they'd "had a very poor night's sleep due to the noise pollution"—treated him with quiet tolerance, never rising to his bait, just letting him be.

Still, they beat us out of camp. We caught up with them that afternoon as they took a break at a road crossing, chatting about the strange night we'd shared and our relief that Rubin was northbound. Greg and I pushed on but reunited with the other four southbounders that evening at a Dartmouth Outing Club bunkhouse. Geoff had hitched to a store for beer, and we all sat around the house's kitchen table, drinking and talking, late into the evening—about their layoffs, their plans for grad school after reaching Georgia, and, not least, Rubin.

The next morning, we all took a 2-mile detour to a restaurant for the hiker's special: six pancakes, four pieces of sausage, coffee, and juice, for $5. We lingered, talking and laughing, long after we'd gorged ourselves. Back outside we split up: Greg and I decided to hike an old section of the AT, while the others backtracked to the rerouted trail.

We watched as they hitched a ride from a pickup and, waving from its bed, motored off for the trail crossing. We expected to reunite with them that night. But we covered close to 16 miles that day, far more than they did. We didn't see them again.

~~~~~~

A few days later, we caught up with Muskrat at Vermont's Happy Hill shelter. We'd followed his register entries from Maine, and he proved an affable companion, at ease in the woods after working at fish camps close to the Canadian border.

Near Manchester Center, Vermont, both Muskrat and Animal pulled ahead of me, and no matter how far or fast I hiked, I couldn't catch up; they seemed to stay a shelter ahead through the rest of New England, until, after a hell-for-leather sprint, I managed to catch Muskrat just inside New York State. I hiked with him for several days, lost him near the New Jersey border, caught him again near Palmerton, Pennsylvania, lost him again. Greg left notes in shelter logs asking where I was, but he stayed just ahead of me.

Meanwhile, Geoff and Molly enjoyed late starts and lunch breaks that stretched into overnights. I left hellos to them in logbook entries, and sometimes, I learned much later, they replied. By the time I reached central Pennsylvania, they trailed me by eight days.

A thousand miles south of Katahdin, I crossed the Susquehanna River and walked into the old ferry town of Duncannon, Pennsylvania, following the trail's white blazes on telephone poles up High Street past churches, a hardware store, and simple, sturdy houses on well-tended lawns. The next day, I sweated 4 steep and rocky miles up Cove Mountain to the Thelma Marks shelter.

Another southbounder was already there: Marcus Macaluso, aka Granola, of Kennett Square, Pennsylvania, a long-haired, deep-thinking Grateful Dead fan, eighteen years old, who carried bongos in his pack and left clever register entries that I'd enjoyed for weeks. We wound up talking past eleven p.m.

Both of us slept late and lounged at Thelma Marks, drinking coffee, until close to noon. Any hopes for respectable mileage already shot, we settled for an easy 7-mile stroll to the Darlington shelter.

At this point a chase was under way. Three southbounders—Brian "Biff" Bowen and his wife, Cindi, of Amherst, Virginia, along with Gene "Flat Feet" Butcher, a retired soldier I'd camped with in Vermont—were trying to catch Geoff and Molly, who were trying to catch up with Muskrat, who was now just behind me. I was still trying to catch up with Greg, who had left word in Darlington's register that he planned to end his hike in Harpers Ferry, West Virginia, a few days to the south. "Hope to see you before I get off," he wrote.

~~~~~~

That same day—September 5, 1990—a thirty-eight-year-old farmhand left his cabin on a South Carolina tobacco spread, caught a ride to the nearest Greyhound depot, and bought a one-way ticket north. He was a short, stocky man, considered smart and hardworking by his bosses. They'd also remember him as rootless, quiet to the point of secrecy, and prone to lengthy, unexplained absences. The shack he left behind was piled with garbage and empty beer cans.

A day later he stepped off a bus in Winchester, Virginia, and embarked on a zigzag course of hitched rides—west to Romney, West Virginia, north into Maryland, northeast to Gettysburg, Pennsylvania—until, six days after leaving the farm, he walked into a library in East Berlin, Pennsylvania, halfway between Gettysburg and York, looking for hiking maps. A librarian suggested he try the York branch, wrote directions, and asked that he sign the guest book. He put down *Casey Horn*.

His name was really Paul David Crews, and he was a suspect in a murder. Four years earlier, on July 3, 1986, a woman had offered him a ride home from a bar in Bartow, Florida. She was later found naked and nearly decapitated on an abandoned railroad bed. Not long after, according to law-enforcement records, Crews had turned up at his older brother's place in Polkville, North Carolina, driving the woman's bloodied Oldsmobile. With the law closing in, his brother gave him a lift into the country, and he took off running. The police recovered the car, along with Crews's knife and bloody clothes, but found no sign of him.

Since then he'd laid low, avoiding attention and revealing little of his past, which had been troubled from the start. Abandoned in childhood, he was adopted at age eight by a couple in Burlington, North Carolina, but he ran away frequently. He joined the marines in 1972 and married in January 1973. Became a father the following month. Attempted suicide, went AWOL, and got discharged from the corps. Divorced in 1974. Bounced around.

In 1977, he turned up in southern Indiana, where he worked a string of dead-end jobs and met his second wife. One morning he crawled into bed behind her and held a bayonet to her throat. They divorced, too.

He wandered back to Florida, where he picked oranges each spring until the homicide in Bartow—a crime he was formally charged with on July 7, 1986. So the police thought Crews might have killed before. And now, late on the afternoon of September 11, 1990, he found his way to the Appalachian Trail.

At the time, the AT followed 16 miles of paved road through Pennsylvania's Cumberland Valley—a shadeless hike, hard on the feet. The trail's caretakers had worked for years to reroute the footpath into forest they had acquired piecemeal. On this afternoon, the ATC's Karen Lutz was surveying one such property when she noticed a bearded man plodding up the road behind her.

She was a stone's throw from the Pennsylvania Turnpike and figured him for a hitcher between rides, a drifter. No chance he was a hiker: he wore a flannel shirt, jeans, and combat boots, had a small rucksack on his back, and carried two bright red gym bags, each emblazoned with the Marlboro logo. He kept his head down as he trudged past, headed north toward US 11.

Two hours later, Lutz drove north on the trail, following its blazes through several turns. Well north of 11, she encountered the stranger again. So he *was* hiking, she realized. He wasn't far from the spot where the AT veered from the road and into the trees. If he hustled, he might make the Darlington shelter, little more than 3 miles away.

Lutz drove on, unnerved. Something about the man—his filthiness, his clothes, his joyless progress—filled her with dread. She didn't know that the stranger carried a long-barreled .22 caliber revolver, a box of fifty bullets, and a double-edged knife nearly 9 inches long. She didn't know he was among Florida's most wanted fugitives. Even so, Lutz, herself a 1978 through-hiker, decided that Darlington was a place she most sincerely did not want to be.

For years she would be haunted by that moment, by "tremendous guilt over the fact that I had seen him, and that I had sensed an evil aura coming off him.

"I know that sounds wacko, but that's exactly what I felt," she says. "And I didn't do anything."

Earlier that day, Geoff and Molly had broken camp at the tiny, squalid Peters Mountain shelter north of the Susquehanna River. They were almost halfway through their hike now, and ambitious days came comfortably, though they didn't make them a habit. They continued to dawdle through meals. They lounged on any rock with a view. They even paused to do some counseling. "We reached the Allentown shelter for breakfast," Geoff wrote on September 6. "There we met Paul, whom we talked with quite a while. He is a fifteen-year-old who was kicked out of his house. We talked about some different ideas for him to try."

Along the 11 miles to Duncannon, they encountered a section hiker, Mark "Doc" Glazerow of Owings Mills, Maryland, who joined them at a pizza parlor in town. His companions were still eating when Glazerow announced that he had more hiking to do, wished them luck, and groaned his way up to Thelma Marks.

Geoff and Molly walked two blocks to the Doyle Hotel, the crumbling fossil of a once-grand inn. In 1990 as now, its bar served wonderful burgers and cheap draft beer, but even at $11 a night, the twenty-three peeling, spider-infested rooms upstairs were only so much of a bargain. They shared just three baths.

Still, those rooms had mattresses. The hikers unpacked their gear and called their parents, discussing their planned reunion in Harpers Ferry to celebrate making it halfway. Better bring soap and brushes, Geoff told his mother, so that we can scrub the smell out of our packs. Glenda Hood promised to bring two pumpkin pies, his favorite.

One more thing, Geoff said—we have something to tell you when we all get together. "There's always been a lot of speculation about what that was going to be," his younger sister, Marla Hood, says. She thinks they planned to announce their engagement.

That night, while feasting on shrimp and mushrooms, the couple signed the Doyle's register, countering a previous hiker's claim that he was the last of 1990's southbounders.

"Hey Greenhorn you most certainly are *not* the last entry of the season," Geoff wrote. "As you can't read this we'll tell you when we catch you! As we hear it we're about mid-slip of the southbounders moving down—oops getting food on the book. Good food too; time to go—Clevis & Nalgene."

In the morning—Wednesday, September 12, 1990—they met Molly's elderly great-aunt and two other relatives on the town square, then accompanied them to lunch at a nearby truck stop. Afterward, they picked up mail, stopped at a small grocery, and, at 3:45 p.m., followed the trail into the woods and up Cove Mountain.

The climb over lichen-flaked stone and loose scree ended at Hawk Rock, a promontory offering a sweeping vista of the town, rivers, and rolling farmland below. From there they faced an easy 2 miles of ridgetop to Thelma Marks— which waited, dark and droopy, its back to the AT, at the bottom of a steep 500-foot side trail.

Geoff and Molly likely arrived there sometime after five p.m. The graffiti-carved plank floor slept four or five comfortably, eight in a pinch. They would have had plenty of room to unroll their sleeping gear and spread out a bit.

Sunset came at 7:22 p.m., but the shelter was hunched against the mountain's eastern flank, in the shade of the ridgetop.

Night fell fast.

Geoff and Molly most likely died between five and seven the next morning. Little else about the event is certain. Were they in trouble from the moment they met Crews? Unknown. Were they attacked as they slept? Unclear. Did they have a conversation with him? The killer's own words, to others he met in the days that followed, suggest they talked and that he stole their story along with their gear: He said he'd started hiking in Maine around the first of June and was trying to catch up with Muskratt.

Jerry Philpott, the Duncannon lawyer who represented Crews at his 1991 trial, says he believes the couple reached the shelter first. "They were settling down for the night," he says. "It was summer—it would have been pretty light. He came upon the scene, and something happened.

"This is a brain on cocaine and a quart of Jim Beam," Philpott says of Crews. "He would take a quart of Jim Beam and a cigarette pack full of powder cocaine, and that's how he would hike."

Crews shared little information with him, Philpott says. "He never wanted to talk about this incident, or any of his alleged murderous incidents."

Indeed, Crews offered only monosyllabic responses to police, said next to nothing in court, and has described to no one, as far as is known, why things took such a horrible turn at Thelma Marks. He did not respond to several interview requests for this story.

Bob Howell, a Pennsylvania state police investigator at the center of the inquiry, offers a straightforward take. "He went on the trail looking for an opportunity," he says. "Bingo. That's it, as far as I'm concerned."

Jim LaRue's explanation is almost as cut-and-dried. "He happened to fall on these two kids and I'm sure saw Molly as a rape prospect.

"Molly was a strong girl," he says. "I wish she had had the strength to overcome him, and even if she had had to kill him, that would have been all right with me— just to protect herself and maybe save Geoff. But that's not the way it played out."

This much is known: Later in the day on September 13, Crews returned to the trail and hiked north into Duncannon without his red gym bags. Now he wore a big green Gregory.

He hitched a ride east to Interstate 81 and got at least one ride south before rejoining the trail in the next county, far from Thelma Marks. He walked south from there, assuming the guise of a through-hiker.

At the same time, the trio of southbounders chasing Geoff and Molly walked into Duncannon. Gene "Flat Feet" Butcher decided not to dally and hiked up Cove Mountain shortly after Crews had descended the same path. Peering down the steep mountainside toward the invisible Thelma Marks shelter, Butcher decided not to stop in and hiked on to Darlington. There he found the shelter littered with trash—including an empty red gym bag, a discarded bus ticket, and a library note written to someone named Casey Horn.

~~~~~~

Back in town, Biff and Cindi Bowen retrieved a mail drop and stuffed themselves on pizza, ice cream, and beer. It was close to five p.m. when they started climbing, and about six when they reached the turnoff.

Cindi, an elementary school teacher, and Biff, a jeweler, knew they were close on Geoff and Molly's heels. They planned to celebrate Biff's upcoming birthday at Thelma Marks, and were excited that they might do so with a couple they'd followed for nearly three months. "We knew they were good people," Cindi says, "because we'd been reading their entries."

But they slowed as they approached the lean-to's rear. The clearing was dead quiet. An hour later they were back in Duncannon, phoning the state police.

That night, detectives who'd never set foot on the trail struggled for three hours to reach Thelma Marks. "I think most of the conversation was curse words," recalls Pennsylvania state trooper Bill Link. "We were in dress shoes. It was dark." The crime scene unfolded piece by piece in the beams of their flashlights. Geoff was lying in a back corner, his head on a makeshift pillow. "At first glance," Link wrote in his report, "one would be led to believe that the subject was asleep."

"At the other side of the lean-to," he wrote, "the body of the female was observed laying facedown in a pool of blood."

It took another four hours to maneuver a pair of all-terrain vehicles up the mountainside on an old logging road, troopers chopping down trees to clear the way, so that the bodies and evidence could be removed.

After that the investigation proceeded rapidly. From Karen Lutz, they learned of the stranger with the red gym bags. They found one such bag at Thelma Marks, the other at Darlington. The library note Flat Feet had discovered gave them a name.

Glenda Hood, at home in Signal Mountain, Tennessee, switched on the radio the morning of September 14, just in time to hear a news report that two hikers had been murdered near Duncannon. Geoff had called from there three days before.

She knew her son was careful. In the past, when they had discussed someone meeting a bad end in the outdoors, he'd told her, "He either didn't know what he was doing, or he wasn't doing what he knew he should be."

Just the same, she phoned Jim LaRue, up in Shaker Heights, Ohio, and told him what she'd heard. He burst into tears. "I was sure it was them," he says. "I just knew." He saw Molly's mother, Connie, pull into the driveway with a load of groceries. He walked out and told her, "I think this is going to be the longest day of our lives."

It was, and the days that followed were not much better. The families arranged for memorial services while police searched for the killer. Geoff was laid to rest near his home in Tennessee, in a plot overlooking Signal Mountain. Molly's body was transported to a funeral home outside Cleveland, where the LaRues found her on a mat, covered with a sheet. The funeral director told them, "I thought you might like to hold her."

Jim, Connie, and their son, Mark, three years older than Molly, dropped to the floor and wrapped their arms around her. "It was one of the most wonderful gifts," Jim says. "She looked like she was asleep. It reminded me of when she was little and scared and couldn't sleep, and going into her room to give her a hug."

I was still on the trail, hiking in Virginia's Shenandoah National Park, when a pair of day-hikers told me a couple had been killed on the trail up in Pennsylvania five days before. A phone call home gave me their names.

Granola had pulled ahead of me, and I lay alone in a shelter that night, stunned and scared. I'd never known a murder victim. Until then I'd been a typical suburban American who figured that violence usually came by invitation. I'd hear of a crime and do a little calculus to separate myself from the victim: *I* wouldn't hang around a crack house. No way would *I* walk that street at three in the morning.

This time the math didn't work. I couldn't claim to know Geoff and Molly well, but they seemed far savvier in the woods than I was. They were traveling as a pair, too, which was considered common sense. They were certainly more patient than me, and far better equipped to defuse trouble. And they were so damn nice, even to Rubin.

If chaos could find them, I realized, it could find anyone. The senseless happened. The universe had no plan. Their deaths seemed a terrible accident of time and geography. Biff Bowen had the same frightened thought: "Had we hiked a little faster, it might have been us."

Granola and I reunited a couple of days later. In Waynesboro, Virginia, we ran into an older southbounder, George Phipps, whom we'd camped with in Maryland. The killings dominated our conversation.

"Some of Geoff and Molly's register entries impressed me so much, I wrote them down," George told us. He flipped through his trail journal, started reading.

Last evening I whispered "I think there're less bugs."
This morning, BRING ON THE SLUGS.

When we had that conversation, Crews was in the custody of federal park rangers in Harpers Ferry, having been captured a few hours before as he walked a bridge across the Potomac. A hiker who'd embarked on a freelance search for the killer recognized Geoff's pack on his back and sounded the alarm.

Crews was jailed, pending trial. Lawmen in Pennsylvania began putting together their case.

The families grieved. Glenda Hood, a pediatric nurse, threw herself into caring for ailing children. Connie LaRue, also a nurse, volunteered at a hospice on the shore of Lake Erie. The women talked often. They became close.

Jim LaRue found comfort in an idea offered by one of Molly's college friends—that Molly, ever artistic, was now adding her touch to each evening's sunset. "From that day forward," he says, "there's not a day that goes by that I don't see a spectacular sunset and think: Ah, Molly's at work."

Strange as it sounds, the fact that family and friends were thrust into the unexpected role of defending the Appalachian Trail might have helped them cope. "We kept getting comments like, 'Well, do you feel the trail is too dangerous to use?' and 'Should it be shut down?'" Jim says. "That's when Molly's voice would come up and tell me, 'If you ever let my death be an excuse for anything happening to the trail, I'll never forgive you.'

"Mol was where she wanted to be, doing what she wanted to do, caring about what she wanted to care about, having fun, and meeting and enjoying so many people," he says. "To die doing something you love is not the worst thing in this life. There are no guarantees."

Glenda Hood climbed Cove Mountain on the first Mother's Day after the murders. The trail was abloom in wildflowers—jack-in-the-pulpits, native columbine—which almost seemed a message, a gift, from Geoff and Molly. She ventured into the clearing.

"I expected it to be a dark, sinister place, and it wasn't," she says. "The sun was coming down through the trees, and it was a peaceful place, despite what had happened there.

"I consider that Geoff and Molly were murdered in God's cathedral," she says. "If someone were murdered in God's cathedral, then murder could be committed anyplace."

~~~~~~

Testimony in the trial started three days after Glenda's hike, on May 15, 1991. The state presented 60 witnesses and 158 pieces of evidence that spun an inescapable web around Crews: He'd been arrested wearing Geoff's pack, boots, and wristwatch, and he was carrying both murder weapons. He'd left his own gear at the scene, some of which was traced back to the tobacco farm in South Carolina. DNA linked him to Molly's rape. He was convicted and sentenced to death by lethal injection.

I was in the courtroom. Unable to shake the confusion I'd felt upon learning of the deaths, nagged by a need for explanation, I'd begged off work to return to Pennsylvania. The proceedings offered only roundabout, unsatisfying clues as to why the killings had happened. During the trial's penalty phase, a psychiatrist appearing for the defense testified that Crews had a personality disorder and that his consumption of whiskey and cocaine had triggered "organic aggressive syndrome." The doctor described the condition as "a short period of time after taking cocaine, maybe an hour or two, when a person can become violent." That was as much explanation as we got.

But the trial was not without its rewards. Hikers were on hand to testify, and others, like me, had simply shown up. Some of us formed lasting bonds with Geoff's and Molly's families. So it was that when Biff and Cindi finished their hike that summer—having avoided shelters every night—Glenda Hood picked them up at the trail's southern terminus at Springer Mountain, Georgia.

And in June 1992, when Geoff's sister, Marla, set out to finish the couple's hike, I went along for her first week. We started south from Boiling Springs, Pennsylvania, our pace modest in the Geoff and Molly tradition, reaching Pine Grove Furnace State Park, near the trail's midpoint, on our second day out. We ate lunch at the top of a fire tower and shared a shelter with a pile of northbounders on day three, visited an emergency room when Marla pulled a knee on day four, and reached the Maryland line on day six.

Others joined Marla after me—Kansas friends, a couple of hikers the ATC had lined up, and the ATC's chief spokesman, Brian King—before an infected blister forced Marla off the trail in Virginia.

~~~~~~

Ten years later, in September 2000, I learned from Karen Lutz that the Thelma Marks shelter was to be replaced. I drove to Duncannon, slept at the Doyle, then swore my way uphill to the clearing. Lutz was already there, watching a crew from the Mountain Club of Maryland finish the new shelter, which was built of beams from a century-old barn. We stood together under a tall sassafras tree, songbirds chatty in its branches, and eyed the careworn and mouse-infested Thelma Marks for the last time.

"This event really seemed to mark the end of the trail's innocence," Lutz told me. In the years after the killings, hikers were more apt to bring pepper spray along with their freeze-dried meals, and to take dogs along. The ATC had become far more sensitive to reports of disquieting conduct on the trail, and quicker to intervene. Earlier in the year, the organization had even published a 176-page handbook called *Trail Safe: Averting Threatening Human Behavior in the Outdoors.*

"This week is always a tough one," Lutz said. "There's a certain quality of the light this time of the year, and the temperatures suddenly get cooler and the humidity drops off, and it all comes right back."

Not long after, the crew removed the old shelter's corrugated metal roof, dismantled its log walls, and sawed them up. They burned the wood in a bonfire, scattered the rock foundation. It was an exorcism as much as a demolition. When they finished, nothing remained of the old hut but a bald patch in the forest floor, not even its name. They called the new place the Cove Mountain shelter.

The forest got busy reclaiming the footprint.

~~~~~~

Fifteen years have grayed the new shelter's wood. It blends comfortably, unobtrusively, into its setting, has become one with the surrounding timber.

Those same years saw Connie LaRue fall ill with cancer and spend her final days in the hospice where she volunteered. She awoke from a dream near the end to report that she'd seen Molly waiting for her. Glenda Hood held her hand shortly before she died in July 2006.

Glenda continues to grieve not only Geoff, but also the future he might have had with Molly. It's a loss she emphasized at a December 2006 hearing where Crews's death sentence was replaced with life in prison without parole. "That day half my future was taken from me," she told Crews. "I have missed his wedding to Molly. I have missed seeing them share their lives together. I have missed their children, who would be my grandchildren."

Biff and Cindi Bowen have divorced, but their son, Mason, took on the trail in 2010. Like his parents, he was a southbounder. Flat Feet met him at Springer Mountain.

Karen Lutz has achieved an uneasy peace. "There isn't a week that goes by that I don't think of that, twenty-five years later," she says, adding: "It's better than it used to be—it's no longer every minute, or every hour."

Jim LaRue has lost Connie, whom he'd known since both were five. But he later found Barbara, who'd lost her husband. They live in a home on rolling woodland that they share with school groups exploring the natural world. "I want to spend my time caring about things my daughter cared about. I think that's how I can best honor her memory," he says. "If she knew I was wallowing in grief, she would kick my ass. She would say, 'If you love me, get over it. Get over it, Jimmy.'"

His statement to Crews at that 2006 hearing reflected, he thinks, what Molly would have wanted. "Paul, I am here today to offer forgiveness for what you have done," he told his daughter's killer—at which point, he says, Crews locked eyes with him and held the connection. "I wish that you and I can now find peace.

"Molly had decided to devote her life to working with troubled children, like you certainly were," he told him. "Paul, I think it would be great if you could pick up where Molly left off, starting with yourself. Help the Mollys of this world learn who you are, and try to enlist the help of other inmates to help in this effort. You are a gold mine of critical information that needs to be unearthed.

"Peace be with you, brother," he said in conclusion. "Peace be with you."

This past spring, I climbed again to the clearing. In the quarter-century since my first visit there, through-hiking had mushroomed in popularity: In 1990, the ATC recorded more than 230 completed end-to-end treks, just 8 of them southbound; last year, the total had grown to 961. Though a few well-publicized homicides have occurred on trails or parklands near the AT since Geoff's and Molly's deaths, just one—the unsolved 2011 killing of an Indiana hiker, Scott "Stonewall" Lilly, near a shelter in Amherst County, Virginia—has claimed someone actually walking the path.

My visit got me thinking of my 158 days and nights on the AT, the people I'd met, the friends I'd made, and when I got home I phoned Animal to revisit our adventures together. It had been twenty-one years since I'd last seen him, when I'd attended his wedding. He has a pair of teenage sons now. He's also a Southern Baptist minister.

We read our trail journals aloud, laughed over our descriptions of Rubin, then turned to the subject of Geoff and Molly. Greg was confident that what had happened to them was part of a divine architecture, that the world's sin, its evil, is no accident—that everything is "part of God's sovereignty."

Including his own hike. When he left Katahdin, he said, he had not been a good Baptist—which would explain all that beer he drank with me. But he took a step toward the righteous path late in his hike, he told me, and he could remember the night it happened: Wednesday, August 28, 1990, at the Thelma Marks shelter.

He reached the hut two weeks before Geoff and Molly. He was alone there. A storm rumbled in the distance as he pulled a Bible from his pack, along with his journal. "The lack of direction in my life was due to my leaving God," he wrote, "but He loves me and I feel a new strength. I pray that I can retain this and use it in my life."

A few minutes later, the weather hit. The wind rose to a sustained yowl, shredded the treetops, racked the old lean-to, seemed to be swelling toward a terrible end. Then it fell quiet. "I thought a tornado was on the way," Greg wrote. "I was really scared, but you have to keep the faith."

The next morning, he stepped out of the shelter and into the clearing. Sunshine splayed through the trees to dance at his feet. Birds trilled. The air smelled fresh, and all about him the woods seemed renewed. And he recognized the place as a little piece of paradise.

WHAT KILLED
THE BEAR LADY?

BRANDON SNEED

For twenty-eight years, Kay Grayson lived side by side with wild black bears in North Carolina's swampy coastal forests, hand-feeding them, defending them against poachers, and letting them into her home. When she went missing in 2015, the only thing the investigators could find were her clean-picked bones. And that's just the start of the mystery.

When Kay Grayson called her bears, she liked to sing: "It's okay, it's okay." It was part of a show she put on for people. Six feet tall, with white hair and the lean body and graceful movement of a dancer, she would walk into a clearing near her trailer in the North Carolina woods, hold out her long arms, and turn her palms to the sky. Then, in a loving voice, she would sing.

Visitors would hear grunts and huffs and the rustle of big creatures moving through brush. And then, out from the forest, black bears would lumber toward her. She called them by name. Munchka. Susan. Highway 64. Betty Sue. David. "Stand up," she would tell them, and they'd stand, and then she'd feed them peanuts out of her hand.

Kay and her bears lived in the middle of some 5,000 acres of swampy forest, thick with muck peat and goldenseal and pine trees, in Tyrrell County, in northeastern North Carolina. She called her land Bearsong, and locals called her the Bear Lady. It was a nickname of admiration or mockery or hatred, depending on who spoke it. No matter the tone, Kay embraced it. "I am woman," she once wrote. "A seeker of truth, peace, and sense of fair play, a lover of all things beautiful, be they created by nature or mankind."

For twenty-eight years, she lived in trailers off a rutted dirt road near the Alligator River Marina in Columbia, a tiny town of around nine hundred. She had no running water or electricity, and used a five-gallon bucket for a toilet, even in her sixties. The only signs of humanity for miles in any direction were power lines and the occasional small, rough path. "It's a place for wild things," county sheriff Darryl Liverman says.

In early January 2015, Kay's friend Shiron Pledger dropped a meal at Kay's gate. When it was still there several days later, Pledger reported her missing. On January 27, two Tyrrell County deputies walked into the Bearsong woods with the emergency management coordinator and a canine handler, who brought a dog to catch Kay's scent.

They hiked a half-mile down the muddy, waterlogged road before they found a maroon coat, a black turtleneck, and, in the middle of the path, a plastic grocery bag containing unopened batteries, socks, cigarettes, and Tylenol. Farther back in the trees, across a ditch nearly overflowing from recent downpours, they saw more clothing. They made a bridge out of fallen trees, climbed across, and found a pair of black ski pants, a slipper, and a gray tank top. Over the next hour, they also found a small piece of flesh with some long, white hair attached and multiple bones, all of them picked clean.

Then, on a knoll formed by the roots of a fallen cypress tree, they found a human skull: skin gone, brain rotting. The smell made them gag.

Liverman told a news reporter that bears had eaten Kay, and the story went viral via Gawker, Fox News, *People*, the *Daily Mail*, and dozens of other outlets. Reactions ranged from sympathy to admiration to judgment toward yet another human who had tried and failed to become one with the wild. "She should have known better," wrote one reader on People.com. "Bears are apex predators and even if they seem tame, AREN'T." Still, Kay's cause of death remains as much a mystery as her life. The official autopsy is filed as incomplete, the medical examiner refuses to comment, and local theories abound as to how she died and how she lived. Though the people of Tyrrell County are one of the state's smallest, poorest populations, they have big, rich imaginations: She had been a high-end prostitute working for the Washington, DC, elite. Or the queenpin of a Miami drug operation. Maybe someone wanted her dead. Or maybe she faked her death and fled.

Liverman thought he might find some answers when he tracked down Susan Clippinger—Kay's niece—in Kissimmee, Florida. But when he did, Susan said that much of what he thought he knew about Kay was wrong. For example, she wasn't sixty-seven, like the death certificate said. She was seventy-three. Her real name wasn't Kay Grayson, either. It was Karen Gray.

She was beautiful when she was young. In pictures that Susan has of Karen Gray in her twenties and thirties, she's glamorous and alluring, outfitted in expensive dresses, jewelry, and furs, hair always just right, even at the pool.

Her childhood is murky—her parents are dead, and her brother, Susan's father, wouldn't talk to me. (They didn't get along.) Born into a middle-class family in Pittsburgh in 1941, she spent her teenage years in Florida, where she cut class and chased guys.

After high school, Karen lived an itinerant life, city to city, man to man. "I always left when the relationship ended. It seemed to heal the pain quicker in new surroundings," she wrote in one of many letters she sent to Susan over the years. (She was a prolific letter writer and kept frenetic notes about her life on yellow legal pads.) "Just wish I could find a strong EQUAL in a man."

She spent her twenties in Las Vegas, where she always said she was a showgirl. But many believe that's not all she was—some friends think she was a high-end call girl. Whatever she did, she could afford a new Lincoln Continental, and pictures from her Vegas days in the sixties show her on the arms of much older, clearly wealthy men with whom she traveled—to Miami, Tijuana, Acapulco. "If you had money, she didn't mind hanging around. It's just the way she wanted to live," says Susan. "She always said, 'If you want to see the world, go get it.'"

In 1965, she married a businessman named Leo Busch in Nevada. But Susan says Karen hated marriage: "She woke up one day about six months in and said, 'This is it?' And then she was gone."

In the seventies, she dated a man named Gordon Griffith and helped him run Horseman's Park, a dude ranch near San Diego. At the end of the decade, she moved to Fairfax, Virginia, near Washington, and trained attack dogs. After that, during the first half of the eighties, she lived in South Florida, selling boats, organizing semiprofessional sailing races, and living on a boat with a yacht broker named Gary Causey. She even had a brief, illustrious sailing career: In 1985, she entered the now-defunct TransAt, an 800-plus-mile yacht race from Daytona Beach to Bermuda, and won her class—the first female captain to do so.

That summer she got a call from Albert Brick, a seventy-something lawyer from DC. Brick owned 1,400 acres of land in Tyrrell County, along a stretch of Highway 64 running in and out of Manteo, a cozy town on the Outer Banks, and he wanted Kay to help him sell or develop it. When Kay visited in February 1986, she found an enormous forest of pines and oaks, thick and raw, bordered by unpolluted canals that helped drain the area into the Alligator River. "I was greatly impressed by its natural beauty and serenity," she wrote. "Immediately I foresaw a place to be explored." Kay signed a contract agreeing to develop the land in exchange for a percentage of the profits.

Later that year, Kay left Causey and moved into a barge turned houseboat docked on the Little Alligator River, which ran along the northern edge of Brick's land. Brick bought 800 more acres, including Old South Shore Road, a muddy former logging path traversable only by four-wheel drive until Kay had it rebuilt. They planned to make money from logging and by developing an ecofriendly marina resort along the river.

Kay met her first bear one night soon after she arrived. She came home and there he was, sitting on her mattress, eating a sweet roll. She shrieked and ran, and the bear did the same, limping as he went. When she went back inside, she found his muddy paw prints on her mirror.

The bear came back the next day, looking starved. In the daylight, Kay saw a wounded creature in need of help, skin stretched thin against his ribs, a bullet hole in his thigh, and a dislocated hip, like he had been hit by a car. "It's okay," she said. She fed him that first day, fed him again when he returned, and then kept feeding him every day after that.

Eventually, she named him: Highway 64. In time his wound healed, though his hip never quite did; the bear limped for the rest of his days. She never cleaned his paw prints off her mirror. "Get a bear, you'll never want a dog again," she told friends.

Soon that first bear became two, then four, then a half-dozen. Angel. Travis. Rusty. Judson.

That's when Kay began to call the land Bearsong. She frequented the Dare County library in Manteo to learn how they lived and how to live with them. They were black bears, ranging from a couple hundred pounds to 500 or more. Though populations were perilously low in the mid-1900s, by the mid-1990s they had rebounded, in part due to successful management policies and habitat protection: Approximately 10,000 bears roamed 20,000 square miles along North Carolina's coast. Kay convinced local store owners to give her day-old goods (or retrieved them from dumpsters), filling her truck until she could carry no more, feeding the bears bread, pies, and rolls in addition to peanuts and dog food.

Everyone—friends, the sheriff, wildlife officers—told her to stop. Shiron Pledger, one of Kay's closest friends, says, "I told her all the time, if something happened to her and they got hungry enough, they would eat her. She'd say, 'Those bears aren't gonna hurt me. They love me.'"

In Kay's home videos from the time, the bears do seem to love her, interacting like 500-pound puppies. They try to climb into her trailer, until she reprimands them—"Back!"—and they duck their heads, tuck their ears, and slink away. In one scene, she calls Highway 64 over and holds up her hand, and he goes from all fours to his hind legs, towering over her in obedience. In another, she hands him an apple pie, which he sniffs and tosses aside, grunting for the pastry in her other hand. "Picky!" she says.

In a sweet voice, Kay details various bears' lives and lineages. "This is Legs Two," she says about a bear sniffing her camera, his big snout right on the lens. "Father of the cubs. He's a generation behind Highway 64 and Munchka, taught by them. Let's go see the cubs." She shows a few cubs relaxing in the trees like monkeys. She cuts to the mother, who sits right beside her. "Raven," Kay says. "*Rayyy-ven.*" Raven is calm as can be. "She would be a half-sister to Munchka. Same mother, different father."

When guardrails went up on the highway, the bears struggled to get across, so Kay taught them to jump over. When the bears suffered wounds from wrestling or fighting—or from hunters' bullets or arrows—Kay gave them penicillin that she got from a veterinarian in town. Some nights, Kay even let them sleep with her. The Bear Lady, Mother of Bears.

By the early nineties, Kay was caring for roughly twenty bears. In her presence they seemed happy. But danger was always present. One day, on a hike with a bear Kay called Mykee, she heard gunshots, as she often did. Mykee heard it, too. "The look in his eyes asked me if the guns we heard on the land and nearby were shooting at him or me," she wrote. "I told him, 'They are shooting at both of us, but we are going to change that.'"

Bears in Tyrrell County can be hunted for one week in mid-November and two weeks in mid-December. "It's a big time of year. Bear hunters everywhere," says Sergeant Mark Cagle of the North Carolina Wildlife Resources Commission. "And it's a big shot in the arm for the economy." Hunters need a hunting license (residents pay $20, others $80), a big-game permit ($13 or $80), and a bear permit ($225 for nonresidents). "All the restaurants and hotels are full," Cagle says. "People with single-wide trailers rent them out to the bear hunters for a grand a week."

In 2014, a total of 1,867 bears were killed in a thirty-seven-county area with a population of roughly 12,500. Each hunter is allowed a single bear per season. But one group of men, whom Kay called the Bear-Killing Bunch (BKB), killed many more; some of them were later charged (though never convicted) for hunting out of season and in off-limits sanctuaries, following a 2007 investigation. The BKB was led by a man I'll call Crockett, whose actions in this story were gleaned from publicly available records. He once spent fourteen months in prison after shooting a man right in front of a deputy. Now in his fifties, he's 6-foot-1 and 290 pounds, with thick shoulders, a scruffy face, and big paws for hands. Crockett is something of a bear-hunting legend in Tyrrell Country. "He was addicted to hunting bears," says Cagle, who has a picture of Crockett poking a caged bear with a stick. Cagle said that Crockett loved every part of hunting: the camaraderie, the tracking, and the killing. He even figured out a way to make money on it, by selling bear-hunting dogs, which can go for several thousand dollars each when fully trained.

Kay began to think that the bears came to her to get away from Crockett, which made him her natural enemy. The hunters ran their dogs almost constantly, disrupting the bears' feeding and sleeping patterns. Kay discovered that the men were even using Old South Shore Road—Brick's logging road—to get in and out of the thousands of acres of otherwise-inaccessible forest surrounding her.

Though she posted NO HUNTING and PRIVATE PROPERTY signs all around her land, the BKB kept driving their trucks down the road, usually with dogs, and often, according to investigators, with 55-gallon barrels of peanut butter, bubble gum, and crushed peppermint candy—illegal bear bait.

When she saw any of the poachers, she'd race to the Alligator River Marina and call the sheriff and wildlife officers. But by the time they arrived—and they often didn't—the men would be long gone.

Wildlife officers wrote Crockett tickets, but many of his activities went unchecked. Kay consulted a local lawyer, but he did nothing except say that she should prepare to defend herself. "I noticed the fear in his voice and eyes and purchased a gun," Kay later wrote. "Living alone on the land, I now realized my life could be in serious danger."

Albert Brick dismissed her concerns about the BKB. "I suppose you will have to live with that," he wrote to her. He said the same when a historic wet period from 1988 to 1989—which included Hurricane Hugo—left the land and road so badly mucked that Kay's contractors refused to continue logging. That wasn't all that stalled development plans, either. Brick constantly wavered between developing, logging, and selling the land, and he torpedoed investment deals by asking for outlandish sums of money, as much as $50,000 per acre. (One investor told Kay that the land was worth $300 per acre.) In April 1991, he terminated his contract with Kay, leaving her with next to nothing. She sued him for $2 million and 18 acres surrounding her home on Old South Shore Road. The lawsuit dragged on for more than two years. Even after Brick died, in June 1993, his estate battled on, until September 1994, when the court awarded Kay $20,000 and 937 acres, including Old South Shore Road. But the settlement did nothing to stop Crockett and the BKB.

With little help from law enforcement, Kay decided to get the public on her side. She produced a newsletter and sold home videos to fans. The films show bears rolling on the ground and wrestling with one another, cubs climbing skinny trees until they bend to the ground. "Out here, they've barely been making it to two or three years, it seems like," she says. "Maybe it's time we started killing the killers. I'm just kidding. Of course."

Kay entertained print and television reporters, even though she hated being on camera. By the late nineties, she no longer had any teeth but refused to wear dentures, one friend told me, because she heard that bears interpret the display of teeth as a sign of aggression.

Fans sent piles of letters and donations; most of the money was used to buy food for the bears. Despite the outpouring of compassion, the hunters continued poaching in the area. Kay locked the Old South Shore Road gate; the BKB cut her locks and chains. She hauled felled trees into their path; they took her to court. In 2003, a local judge ruled that Kay and the hunters had to share Old South Shore Road, which had been purchased by two of Crockett's friends—John Jackson and John Reeves—after Brick's estate failed to transfer the title to that section of land to Kay. He also made the hunters give her a key to their gate lock. As soon as she got it, though, she replaced the lock with one of hers. The judge sentenced her to thirty days in jail for contempt of court.

"They think they got me," Kay told Susan, "but I got three square meals a day for a month. That's nothing."

Once Kay had served her jail time, she went to the Alligator River Marina, where new pictures hung on the wall—pictures of smiling men and women posing with dead bears. Kay's bears. Hunters knew that most mornings they came from the woods on one side of the highway to get to Kay's land, and they'd lain in wait. Among the photos, she recognized a bear she hadn't seen in a while: Highway 64. The hunter who pulled the trigger, a wildlife officer, had known him by his limp.

Kay screamed and raged until deputies came and carried her away.

~~~~~~

After jail and the death of most of her bears, Kay's hold on reality began to slip. She made daily trips to Manteo to get supplies at the Piggly Wiggly and chat with her friend, Maureen Daigle, a cashier there. She did laundry at the neighboring Laundromat and ate Chinese food or Subway.

She still had a little gang of bears, but she became convinced of vast conspiracies among hunters and lawyers and law enforcement, all parties she believed were out to make money off the animals. Environmentalists' helicopters were coming to harm them. Brief closures of the Alligator River bridge were part of an elaborate plot against her. Her living conditions deteriorated. Out in the woods, she accumulated four trailers, buying new ones when the old ones grew too decrepit or collapsed under a fallen tree. And she clipped articles about people doing terrible things to animals and nature, hoarding the horrors of the world in milk crates.

She began brandishing a machete, and anyone using the road without permission—even friends—faced her wrath. Deputies and wildlife officers had to escort the BKB into the woods, sometimes to hunt legally, sometimes to access the public land beyond Kay's property. She took blurry pictures of them on disposable cameras and wrote down their interactions. In 2005, she sued Jackson and Reeves for $7 million, without a lawyer. *"Pro Se Defendo,"* she wrote in a letter. Defend yourself! The lawsuit went nowhere.

When she needed money, she sold pieces of her land—though she had strict requirements: ecofriendly homes only, no hunting, no dogs.

Kay constantly called wildlife officer Mark Cagle, who began overseeing several counties, including Tyrrell, after he was promoted to sergeant in 2006. Cagle was different from his predecessors. He sympathized with Kay. He, too, planned to take to the woods when he retired, albeit with his wife and indoor plumbing. Whenever he saw her name on the caller ID, he'd think, It's Kay—better get on the road. Even if he expected to find nothing, Cagle went. "Just to make her feel good," he says. "She could be a fanatic, and a little overprotective, and everybody thought she was crazy. But she was a person, just like me and you. To me she was always nice, friendly, easy to get along with."

Cagle was also sick of the poaching. He'd heard about Crockett since the late nineties, when Cagle worked a few counties away. So, in the spring of 2007, Cagle assembled a team of local officers. As his investigation proceeded, he brought in the Bureau of Alcohol, Tobacco, Firearms, and Explosives, since it was illegal for Crockett, a felon, to use guns at all. Cagle woke at three a.m. for a month to sneak in and out of the woods to do surveillance on Crockett's bait sites. He found dozens of bear skeletons. According to Cagle, many of them were in the section of the county just north of Kay's land.

Four hundred hours of overtime later, Cagle arrested Crockett and charged him with at least fifty hunting violations, including killing bears out of season, baiting bears, and killing bears over bait. Some of the BKB even gave evidence against him.

But those were misdemeanors, which rarely receive significant judgment, so prosecutors ignored the hunting charges and focused on the felony gun charges. Crockett was convicted in 2008. He spent six and a half years in federal prison. Jackson and Reeves sold their land to an environmental group (Kay "wasn't worth the aggravation," Jackson told me), and that was the last of Kay's fight with hunters.

After decades of such battles, Kay struggled to accept the peace. She almost got arrested again after pulling a machete and a pistol on an environmentalist trying to scout woodpeckers. She grew ever more volatile with her friends, appearing uninvited in their living rooms on cold nights. She demanded money. Once, while sitting in her friend Tracy's car at the Bearsong gate, Tracy's dog wouldn't stop barking, and Kay said, "Shut him up or I'll slit his throat."

Then there was Susan. For years she had sent Kay money, several thousand dollars in all. Kay paid some of it back but just as often asked for more. During the recession in 2009, Susan said no and Kay erupted. They barely spoke after that.

Kay's final years were painful. She'd always been slender, but she became sickly and skinny. She burned her foot while boiling water and refused to see a doctor, resulting in a persistent limp, like Highway 64.

She would sit in a plastic chair beside her gate, watching traffic, making sure nobody so much as thought about using her road. Friends stopped to chat, and Kay's bears lumbered out to say hello. "Get back in there!" she'd snap, sending the bears slinking back into the woods. With her pale skin and white hair, and often wearing a white nightgown, she started to look like a ghost.

Shiron Pledger urged Kay to apply for government assistance, saying she would qualify for food stamps and probably housing.

"You're crazy to stay back there," Pledger told her.

"I've been doing it all my life. I can keep on doing it," she said.

Pledger told me, "She'd say God told her that was what she was supposed to do. After all the dancing, all the partying, all the—well, you know, that sort of lifestyle. She said that God wanted her to take care of the bears."

Pledger invited Kay to her family's house for Thanksgiving dinner every year, but Kay always said no, that she'd rather spend her holidays with the bears. Even so, Pledger occasionally cooked fresh meals and left them in plastic bags at the Old South Shore Road gate. "I felt like she needed a friend," she says. "If I were in the same situation, I would want somebody to befriend me." Pledger dropped the meals off on her way into town for work, and Kay would always pick them up by the time Pledger drove home. Until, in January 2015, she didn't.

~~~~~~

Investigators spent three days in the Bearsong woods, packing Kay's bones and fragments into plastic bags. As they gathered her remains, they found bear scat containing fragments of human bone, along with enough of a skeleton for the medical examiner to piece together a six-foot-tall woman with no teeth.

They also examined Kay's run-down mobile homes. Her primary trailer, located in a clearing off Old South Shore Road, was trashed. Bears had busted through the door and clawed at the cabinets and walls. Paw prints smeared the mirror and windows.

Some of the damage surely happened after her death, but investigators weren't certain how much; the place seemed barely habitable. There were holes in the floors covered by loose boards. In one room, there were so many papers, photographs, and videotapes piled in milk crates and loose stacks that investigators couldn't see the floor.

But how Kay died never became clear. Under cause of death, her death certificate simply says, "Cannot be identified."

Despite theories to the contrary, investigators have ruled out the idea that Kay's bears killed her. The medical examiner found no trauma to her bones indicating an attack. There were several bags of dog food in her trailers, suggesting that the bears were being fed at the time of Kay's death. County emergency coordinator Wesley Hopkins told me that if hungry bears had attacked her, he would have found a big pool of blood.

Some of her friends think she could have been murdered, since police never found her cell phone, cash, or guns. Still, the sheriff said there were no signs of foul play.

Investigators' prevailing theory is that Kay died from a medical condition. The winter was harsh. Kay had been spending days in her trailer hunkered down under piles of blankets—some even say with an older bear named Betty Sue. Her skin was turning gray, which could suggest emphysema, pneumonia, or a pending heart attack. The fact that her outerwear was found untorn could also suggest hypothermia, which sometimes makes victims feel like they're burning up.

Hopkins told me that Kay probably collapsed while walking back to her home. He said it's even possible that the bears carried her into the woods, thinking they were protecting her.

True or not, that's a nice way to think of Kay's end, her bears spiriting her body away into the wild. After half a lifetime of strife, she deserved some peace.

There is some evidence that she may have found it in her last days. Though she still hoarded copies of articles, they weren't all about bears or people hurting the world anymore. Some were about people like Mark Cagle, people doing good.

That final year—to Pledger's shock—Kay actually went to Thanksgiving. When Pledger last saw her in January, a few days before she went missing, Kay was still talking about it. "One of the best times I've had in my whole life," she said.

Kay continued to make occasional calls to Cagle out of concern for her bears, but her last one was different. It came in late December, just after bear season, a couple of weeks before her death. As always, Cagle saw who was calling and readied himself for the road.

But no, this time Kay just wanted to say thank you. The wild things were having a restful winter.

"We're okay," she said. "We're okay."

A SHOT IN THE NIGHT

CAROLINE ALEXANDER

At an all-girl's camp in the mountains of Tennessee, a group of men, drunken and rowdy, begin rowing toward the lakeside cabins of the oldest campers just past midnight. One girl runs to summon the camp director, who grabs her gun. Two shots are fired into the darkness. A few minutes later a man is dead, and the lives of a dozen teenagers are forever altered.

Miss Katie's camp was set in the Tennessee Mountains on the edge of a forest-ringed lake, the water of which, as I remember it, was even on the sunniest days an impenetrable blue-black.

The camp did not deal in half measures. We were committed by our parents to Miss Katie's care for two solid months every summer, a period that was undiluted by interference from the outside world. We were forbidden to receive packages or even telephone calls from home. Too frequent association with one's own relatives in camp was discouraged, it being understood that one was there to make new friends. My sister and I always took a circuitous route through the back trails when we set out to visit each other.

Being English, my sister and I were unfamiliar with the institution of summer camp—indeed, the word "camp" for our family, as for most Europeans, held only sinister connotations. As it turned out, however, Miss Katie's was an ideal place to spend the summer. Most of camp life was lived outdoors under warm and brilliant skies, although occasionally thunderstorms descended over the mountains, driving us inside.

Miss Katie was a woman of marked importance in the state, by virtue of both her family connections and her immense personal wealth. Her face had great character, reminiscent of the unlovely but engaging countenances that challenge one's gaze in seventeenth-century Flemish portraits—vibrant, canny, and down-to-earth. She was solid and rather square in build, and extremely fit. Although nearly sixty in the year I first went to camp, she could, through all the summers I knew her, hold her own with most of the campers in a game of tennis. Indeed, on Visitors' Days she might challenge the odd father who had wandered too close to the tennis court and, if the unfortunate man were rash enough to accept, essentially unman him before the eyes of her young charges. It was said that in the early days, she used to sit up all night on her trailer steps, guarding the camp, a shotgun across her knees. She dressed always in open-necked shirts with cotton slacks and canvas shoes. Her long iron-gray hair may have been her one vanity: Usually she wore it knotted in a no-nonsense bun, but on special camp occasions she let it stream down over her shoulders.

In its superficial structure Miss Katie's camp was like many others, revolving around a daily schedule of classes in all the usual summer skills—canoeing, swimming, riding, crafts, and so forth. But underneath this benign veneer lay a tough interior core. Our small cabins were spartan affairs of gaping split-log timbers, which, it was said, had been built in the 1940s by German prisoners of war. Once a week we were taken in a cattle truck down the dirt mountain roads to yet more remote places in the woods, to the shores of other unfrequented lakes, where we were left for the night and following day, expected to fend for ourselves in the way of building fires, picking berries, preparing food, and, finally, when the cold night dew began to fall, rolling ourselves up in cotton sleeping bags under the open skies. As campers we were expected not merely to pull our weight on the long hikes in the mountains or to rein in the essentially unbroken horses on trail rides; we were expected to enjoy doing so. A "sorry attitude" was not acceptable.

"Now isn't that too bad?" Miss Katie would say scathingly in the assembly after meals. "I got a phone call from someone's mama asking me why her little girl had written to say that she was so stiff in her old joints from taking a little walk in our beautiful mountains. Isn't it too bad that, with all the fun things we all are doing, someone had to make her mama so unhappy?"

It was not weakness that was contemptible in Miss Katie's eyes, but passivity, and the survival skills we were so vigorously taught were meant to enable us to engage at every level in the physical world—lakes were to be swum in, mountains to be explored, starry nights to be passed in the open. But while every aspect of the camp experience seemed to have been geared specifically to fostering a sense of self-reliance, the campers themselves came for the most part from extremely wealthy, conservative Southern families whose widest ambitions for their little girls centered on their marriage prospects. And it was not Miss Katie's purpose to undermine these expectations. She herself was married and had daughters and granddaughters who had been to camp, although she left her husband behind in Nashville every summer. Only by extrapolating from both Miss Katie's feminine convictions and the apparently contradictory aims of her camp did one acquire a picture of the kind of woman a camp girl was ideally meant to become: a woman who could listen to her husband's story of his fishing trip with the secret knowledge that she would have known how to clean and gut his catch and how to build a fire—in the rain, if necessary—on which to cook it.

The level of athletic ability was extraordinarily high at Miss Katie's camp. State tennis champions, competitive swimmers, experienced show jumpers—this was the kind of talent the camp fostered. In virtually all sports a girl's ranking was to a great extent dependent upon the chance ability of the other campers for that particular year. The lone exception was in riflery, which was dominated every year by Amy Slatkin. To say that Amy was a marksman was not the same thing as asserting that Allison Southey was the best rider we had ever had in camp. Amy's skill was absolute: A regulation target can, after only, only be a regulation target. Fifty feet must, at any time and place, be 50 feet. And a .22 caliber rifle is always a .22 caliber rifle. Under the standards observed by the National Rifle Association, Amy Slatkin was a Marksman First Class.

Amy was a lanky Texan girl with short, straight, sandy-colored hair who walked with a long, bouncing gait. Like most of the younger campers, I regarded her with awe, and in my eyes the fact that she came from Texas gave her an additional cachet— Texas representing a wild, alien, masculine world that I felt I would almost certainly never visit. Her happy-go-lucky nature and irreverent wit made her immensely popular, and she was one of the most idolized girls at camp. I also recognized, however, that by the standards of the conservative South she must have been something of a misfit. She was an athletic, handsome girl, rather than conventionally "pretty," and I found it difficult to imagine her assuming the adult roles that would shortly be expected of her. But here she was on home territory. One sensed that she regarded camp not as a summer interlude, but as her real life, around which the events of the outside world and other seasons revolved as background distractions.

It was camp tradition that one shared one's skills, and the oldest girls usually helped out with the instruction of one sport or another. From age fourteen, Amy Slatkin was put in charge of the rifle range, which was located at the end of a long woodland trail to the north of camp. I often passed her as she loped along to target practice in the morning. At the range, Amy struck me as cool, focused, serious, and in dealing with other campers, extremely cautious. Clearly, Miss Katie's faith in her was not misplaced. Her concentration when she shot was legendary. For several years she had owned her own rifle, a mahogany-butted Winchester, which was kept with the camp guns under lock and key in the general office, where she returned it every evening.

To say that there were no males in the camp would be to overlook Mr. Stuart, the caretaker, who lived year-round with his wife and two sons in a little cabin near the entrance. There were many local people like them, generally living on the opposite side of the lake, but the Stuarts were the only ones the campers had real contact with, and we called them "hillbillies."

Of medium height and build, with a pasty complexion, Mr. Stuart wore heavy blue overalls and a green-and-white-striped railroad hat. He roamed about the grounds, usually on foot or, if he needed to carry tools or supplies with him, in his misshapen dark-green pickup truck. In my early years at camp, his sons trailed along as he made his rounds. In late years, Mr. Stuart himself personally undertook only the most important jobs, content to leave the odd chores to the attention of his sons. In my memories, they are only shadow presences, appearing unobtrusively at the stables, the docks, the cabins, or wherever there was work to be done. A camper might greet Mr. Stuart out of general respect for a recognizably older person, but the sons fell into no known category of human being. Certainly the fact that they were men in an all-girls' camp was not acknowledged: On Miss Katie's terrain men were inconsequential, and in the outside world a man was, by definition, someone like your father or—amounting to much the same thing—someone you might hope to marry.

Only once that I know of did the Stuart boys elicit recognition of their sex, and then only by mistake. One July afternoon, during rest hour, the Stuart boys went down to the swimming dock to repair a water-eaten timber and blundered onto a handful of girls from the senior camp who were sunbathing topless. The subsequent report had it that most of the girls rolled over onto their stomachs but that two or three were caught sitting up. The Stuart boys each gave a quick up-and-down glance and abruptly left. After so many years, my memory of important details is hazy, and I cannot be sure of the chronology of events; but I am certain that Amy Slatkin was on the dock that afternoon—and based on what I felt I knew about her, I could well imagine that such a public undressing would have been a bitter humiliation.

I am reasonably sure that the incident occurred soon thereafter. It is even possible that it happened that very night.

The senior camp at Miss Katie's was strictly off-limits to all but fifteen- and sixteen-year-olds. A long, root-knotted path led from the volleyball court, threading in and out of trees before eventually dead-ending at three secluded cabins. There were no other buildings anywhere around to distract from this unspoiled corner of the lake.

On that night, only the oldest girls were left in this solitary part of the camp, the others having gone on an overnight cookout to Hatcher Mountain. The girls turned off the lights around eleven. It was just after midnight when they first heard the sound of male voices coming from the lake. From inside their cabin, they couldn't quite distinguish the voices, which seemed to be bouncing back and forth across the face of the water. After a whispered conference, the girls decided to go outside. As they were reluctant to give away their positions by using the flashlights that several of them had in hand, they could do nothing more than stand as quietly as possible among the sycamore trees at the edge of the lake and listen. The sounds soon sorted themselves out, and the girls were able to establish that a number of young men with "hillbilly voices" were making their way across the lake, aiming specifically for the senior camp, which they had evidently known would be more than half-deserted on this particular night. The girls could tell that the men had been drinking and could hear their crude comments and rough laughter as clearly as the wake-up bell.

Robin Courtney, who was the fastest runner, was sent to tell Miss Katie, while the other girls remained on the edge of the lake. Robin's knocking drew Miss Katie out onto her porch in her pajamas, her long gray hair reaching down to the middle of her back, and they set off together in the little golf cart that Miss Katie used when she had to make long runs. It is entirely characteristic of her that she did not at this point call either Mr. Stuart or the police of the nearest town. In her eyes, no situation was an emergency until she declared it to be one, and she couldn't know that until she encountered it herself. She did, however, take the precaution of stopping by the office and taking from the racks the first rifle that came to hand, which as it happened was Amy Slatkin's mahogany-butted Winchester.

She found the girls standing in their thin nightgowns, just as Robin had left them. No one made a move back toward the cabin, which seemed suddenly to offer less protection than the wide and intricate woods. Reflecting on this event from the distance of years, I realize now that no one ever actually articulated what it was that the men might have intended. But even as a child without knowledge of such unspoken details, I knew that their mere presence in Miss Katie's lake represented a violent transgression, that a line between the camp and the outside community had been crossed—and that Miss Katie herself, standing under the trees looking into the indistinguishable blackness of sky and water, was right to believe that anything was possible.

It was not as strange as it might seem that she resisted calling out a warning. What effect, after all, could she have expected the voice of one old lady to make on those determined men? What is odd, however, is that she did not shoulder the gun she had taken the trouble to bring, but instead saw fit to hand it to Amy Slatkin—as if a blind shot into the air could be fired only by the camp's best marksman.

Amy took her familiar rifle, adjusted her stance, raised the gun to her shoulder, and fired high into the trees. A sudden silence immediately followed, then sounds of floundering and splashing, and the girls realized with some shock that the men were not in boats as they had assumed. The voices fell away, and only soft, surreptitious plops could be heard from the water. Amy again raised her gun to her shoulder without changing her stance and fired a second, somewhat lower shot.

Instantly screams were heard from the water. A man's voice called out in terror not to shoot again. The cries continued and then gave way to pleas for help. The girls darted along the shore, wading into the shallows, calling to the man to raise a hand. The erratic beams of their flashlights swept back and forth, merely batting at the immense black union of lake and night. But who could say how those frantic skidding beams appeared from the water? The men could be heard thrashing about distractedly, while the voice of their stricken friend bubbled more and more feebly from the water until at last it sank for good. Only at this point did it dawn on the other men that the girls had been searching the lake to help, not to hunt them down. Safe with this realization, they began to curse them while beating a slow retreat to the opposite shore.

Given Miss Katie's importance in the community, it was no small matter when, early the next morning, she summoned the sheriff, who came out with his men to drag the lake. None but the oldest girls who witnessed the incident were allowed near the water, but I was told that the sheriff's operation was watched from the bridge by a sullen crowd from town. The body was eventually recovered, and after being identified by the sheriff as that of a young man who had lived on the opposite side of the lake, it was hastily wrapped in a sheet and whisked away in the back of the sheriff's truck.

The sheriff, in his report to Miss Katie, said that the young men had come out on a dare with the intention of scaring the girls. As was typical of the local boys, none of them could really swim, and they had come across the lake in inner tubes, one of which it seemed had suddenly—and, as it turned out, fatally—deflated. The sheriff declined to speculate as to why this might have happened, saying only that the dead man had injured his back some months earlier and had worn a brace until very recently. "This boy here," the sheriff said, "had been sick for some while, and

I guess he bit off more than he could chew. That shot must have scared him so that his strength just wore out."

In camp this was the final word on the incident. To my knowledge the deflated tube was never found, nor did I ever hear any reports about an inquest. Only one detail snagged in my mind over the intervening years, hinting that other parties, outside of the camp, may have perceived the situation differently. The sheriff, in turning to leave, had warned Miss Katie that everyone connected with the camp should stay away from town "for some while." And in deference to his advice, the Catholic campers, who usually went to mass at the local church, stayed behind that Sunday.

The event caused a mild ripple among the campers but was not discussed as much as one might have expected. Everyone instinctively assumed Miss Katie's own unruffled, back-to-business attitude. It was, as Miss Katie would say, "just one of those things." Still, I was later surprised to discover that no story of the incident was handed down, and when I made a visit to camp years later, I found that it had sunk without a trace.

~~~~~~

At camp, the rifle range consisted of a simple lean-to with a wooden floor and a corrugated metal roof that looked down a green forest tunnel, carved from trees, to the target stands. Before going to camp I had never seen a gun, let alone handled one, and riflery was for me a revelation. Once a deer wandered out of the trees directly into my line out of sight, and I lowered my gun and watched, entranced. My mind made no connection between the deer standing timidly in the sunlight and the loaded gun in my hand, and it did not occur to me until a week or so afterward that at that moment I had possessed the power to kill. I later wondered whether, if I had been a better shot, I would have known immediately. But target shooting was for me a purely meditative art, akin to Zen, a cathartic ritual that entailed clearing one's mind of all extraneous thought so as to concentrate on the sole objective at hand—the firing of a perfect bullet into the center of a target.

For many years I considered target shooting as something exclusively associated with camp, and had I not found myself one year doomed to spend an entire summer in Texas, I doubt I would have turned to it again. But perhaps because I associated Texas with guns, and perhaps, too, because the best marksman I had known had come from there, I decided to take up pistol shooting during this sojourn. The range I found was divided into shoot cubicles with hard cement floors that looked down a track of sun-scorched grass buzzing with the relentless song of grasshoppers—a far cry from my sylvan gallery at Miss Katie's. Yet even here I found in the ritual of performance the same tranquility I had known at camp.

This ritual begins in the isolation of one's booth: The shooter assumes his familiar stance, often drawing chalk marks around his feet to ensure that his position will not change. He breathes deeply and relaxes before raising his arm several times to verify that it falls naturally in alignment with the target. Every shooter has his own preference for laying out ammunition—five bullets stood on end, or laid in a row, or loaded into an extra magazine. The method does not matter, as long as it never varies. One's faith in the system should be so absolute that it is enacted without thought. Finally, the shooter grasps his pistol as if shaking hands with it. He raises the gun, concentrating all attention on the front sight while slowly and evenly squeezing the trigger. One's concentration should be so intense that the shot, when it is fired, comes as a surprise. The final element of this ritual is the "shot analysis," in which the marksman, preferably while the gun is still raised, mentally calls the shot—notes to himself the exact location of the bullet on the target, by virtue of his last memory of the crucial front sight.

The range was run by a local gun club that made an effort to provide first-rate coaches along with the range supervisors. One of these was an ex-marine sergeant who had a flattop, little eyes, and a mouth full of very large, square teeth. The coach was less concerned with technique than with the follow-through. "Call your shots!" he would say. "Know where that bullet went! Go down and score your targets. I'm not going to monitor you—how you score is between God and your conscience." He told us we should perform twenty push-ups a day on our fingertips to develop our grips and trigger fingers, a suggestion he followed with a demonstration. After each round he would stride down the range and make comments on every target. He greeted the women with a supportive, fatherly squeeze of the shoulders: "So, what have we got here? Say! Is this yours? That's not so bad!" I never heard what he said to the men, but from across the range I saw that his face became furrowed and serious and that he stood with his arms folded across his chest, nodding gravely and occasionally making complicated gestures with his hands.

I had quickly reached that uncomfortable gray zone of competence that can be broadly labeled "above average," and showed no sign of improving. The fact that there was no fault to be found with my stance, my grip, how I raised my arm, or even how I squeezed the trigger only made my situation all the more dire, for it indicated that my problem lay not with mechanics, but with a fundamental misunderstanding of the sport.

One afternoon, toward the end of practice, an expert marksman who had won almost every shooting honor of any note, including an Olympic medal, walked over to my booth. He said he had been watching me and volunteered that he saw my problem. "You're looking at the target," he said. "You shouldn't even see it." He then demonstrated the impossibility of focusing simultaneously on a near object—the front of the sight—and the far-off target. "It's one or the other, but you can't look at both."

In fact, he wasn't telling me anything I hadn't heard before, but for the first time the significance of what was being said sank into my consciousness. Seeing that he had genuinely caught my attention, he became confidential.

"Do you know how I prepare for a big competition?" he asked. "In a darkened room. I don't need a target." He tapped his temple. "The target's in my head."

~~~~~~

One summer, years later, I drove to the mountains of Tennessee to revisit Miss Katie's camp. I was amazed to discover that the vast, foreboding blue-black lake was in fact so unremarkable. From the swim dock, the forest on that once-distant shore seemed only one long dive away. There were fewer trees in the camp itself. I had remembered the cabins as being set within the most grudging of forest clearings, but in fact there were broad, brown patches of beaten earth around them. I was especially struck by the size and youth of the campers: They were, after all, only little girls. It may be, then, that my memory, so unreliable in these essentials, has led me to attribute to Amy Slatkin skills that she did not possess. But if she was the marksman that I took her for, then at some point in her life—either on the edge of the black lake, or years afterward, perhaps, in her comfortable Dallas home, late at night when her husband and children were in bed—at some point in her life, she would have called that second shot.

STRANGE
PHENOMENA

FOOT. LOOSE.

CHRISTOPHER SOLOMON

In the late 2000s, something strange was happening in the coastal waters near Vancouver, British Columbia. Detached human feet—seven of them, neatly wrapped in running shoes—had been found washed up on beaches or floating next to piers. The Mounties weren't talking, but locals had plenty of theories. Our writer just hoped they were wrong about the flesh-eating lobsters and the rural loner with all the knives.

AND A CHILD SHALL LEAD THEM

When you're dealing with a tale of intrigue and suspicion in which nothing wants to be what it seems, the best place to start is at the beginning, before everything about the Mystery of the Feet got complicated. Before the dogged reporter and her theory of the Smiley Face Killers. Before the funeral feast of the submerged pig and the ravenous lobsters. And way before my afternoon with a knife-wielding man named Mountain Mike. Before all this, there is only the bucolic image of a little girl on a beach, looking for shells.

It's August 20, 2007. The girl and her family are on a sailing trip in British Columbia. They toss anchor at uninhabited Jedediah Island, 50 miles northwest of Vancouver. It's high summer, but the day is moody with drizzle, the cedars dark and foreboding above the pretty curl of cove.

The girl finds four sneakers on the sand. She lines them up, chooses one. It's a Campus-brand shoe, a righty, white with blue mesh, size 12. She unties the laces, tugging at a sandy sock within.

And, right then, out plops the Start of Everything. Because inside the sock is a human foot. Over the next fifteen months, six more feet, also clad in socks and sneakers, will wash ashore at six different places on the puzzle of islands in the Georgia Strait, between Vancouver and Vancouver Island, and in the nearby Fraser River delta.

At first the feet are all men's feet, all right feet. Then a woman's foot appears. Then a left foot. Four of the feet match: one pair of women's feet, one pair of men's. That's seven feet, bow-tied in seaweed, that were once attached to a total of five bodies—bodies that don't turn up.

The media arrive by helicopter and boat and do what the media do best: go apeshit. Reporters deliver fevered sound bites and write punny headlines ("Investigators Seek Leg-Up in Mystery Feet Case"), and for a few news cycles in early 2008, the whole world widens its eyes and scratches its head. Even the United News of Bangladesh clucks at the odd and tragic goings-on up there in British Columbia.

In Vancouver, at the HQ of the Royal Canadian Mounted Police, the authorities know little and say less, and they do it in that grumpy, pinch-lipped way that makes people wonder what they aren't being told. In November 2008, Corporal Annie Linteau, a Mountie spokeswoman, tells me over the phone that they aren't even close to coming up with an explanation. But that, she says, is mainly because there's no reason to think anything fishy is going on.

Seriously? Yes, Linteau says, pointing out that there were no saw marks on the bones, no evidence of foul play. Without that, what do seven feet amount to, really, other than ghoulish serendipity?

By the time I head out from New York for a personal look-see, in early 2009, detectives haven't solved the mystery, but they haven't given up. The Major Crimes Unit is trying to put names to the feet by tracking down DNA from relatives of fifty-seven high-probability men on B.C.'s missing-persons rolls. (At press time, only one foot, the first, had been identified: It belonged to a missing man whom the authorities won't name, in deference to his family.) But even this gumshoe work might not crack the case. As Corporal Linteau tells me when we meet in person—inside a windowless briefing room, where she flips through pictures of empty shoes set against rulers, like grim flash cards—the search is limited to people known to be unaccounted for.

And so, as I head for the water-licked fringes of Greater Vancouver, the mystery is still as open-ended as a drinking straw.

TABLOID JUICINESS 1,
CANADIAN COOLHEADEDNESS 0

One foot on a beach might've only made a splash in the local *Alberni Valley Times*. But six days after the first foot was found, on a Sunday afternoon in late August 2007, Vancouver couple George Baugh and his wife, Michèle Géris, went hiking on Gabriola Island, about 40 miles south of Jedediah Island and across the Georgia Strait from Vancouver.

"We were on a trail that obviously hadn't been used for a while—ferns were all grown up over it," George is telling me. It's February, and we're sitting inside a cafe in downtown Vancouver. He says he and Michèle were walking single file, Michèle in the lead, when suddenly she stopped and said, "Look, there's a foot."

This is why I especially wanted to talk to George and Michèle. It's not just that they found a foot (though that helps); it's that, in all the newspaper accounts, the couple seemed so sensible. And that's what a story about severed feet cries out for, isn't it? Grounding? Credibility?

George is a slim, fifty-two-year-old wine importer whose entire presence whispers Canadian civility. He's wearing a forest-green turtleneck and a tight, gray-flecked Caesar haircut. When Michèle came across the shoe, a Reebok runner sitting a couple of yards off the trail at the base of a madrona tree, they both kept walking—at first. It was just a sneaker in the woods, after all; maybe it had been carried up from the beach by a dog. But then they went back, because something bothered them about that shoe. It looked so . . . full.

George poked it with Michèle's hiking stick. He saw "something white, not dried out at all, sort of greasy-looking" nesting inside a fringe of frayed white sock. He called 911: no reception. Michèle suggested that they knock on the doors of homes near the path—homes that just happened to be sitting on an isolated country lane called Stalker Road.

George: "I said, 'No, we're not going to knock at any houses. These guys could be involved.'"

Now, here in the cafe, he's talking, with characteristic thoughtfulness, about how humans crave patterns. It's how we make sense of things, he says. That day on Gabriola, as they sat waiting for the Mounties to arrive, he pulled a newspaper out of a rural mailbox. "Then we read about the Jedediah foot, which was the first one," he says. "I thought, 'I think we've found the other foot! We've solved the mystery.'"

But the mystery was just getting started. In February 2008, workers clearing brush on Valdes Island, just south of Gabriola, found Foot Number Three. It was another righty! Another runner! Another size 12! (Well, actually, size 11. But . . . close enough!)

And this—well, this was when things sorta went nuts.

NOIR BY NORTHWEST

Oddity breeds speculation. Deny the people a quick answer to strange doings and they'll gladly make up a story to fill in the gaps.

They're victims of the 2004 Asian tsunami.

They're part of the rising body count in VanCity's mushrooming war of gang-bangers.

Somewhere in there was the mouse peep of another story, perhaps a truer story—that these were just distraught people who took a long walk off a short pier, or the unfound victims of some half-forgotten plane crash. Conspiracy abhors a vacuum.

And, of course, there was always that other possibility.

A couple of years ago, a sociologist named James DeFronzo ran the numbers. The northwestern United States, he found, has more serial killers per capita than anywhere else in the nation.

Argue the reason, but this land of Most Livable Cities—Portland! Seattle!—breeds killers the way Texas sires halfbacks. The Want-Ad Killer. The Box Car Killer. Ted Bundy. The Green River Killer, who likely murdered more than forty-eight women around Seattle in the eighties and nineties before getting nabbed in 2001. Long before that, in the 1910s, there was Dr. Linda Hazzard, in Olalla, Washington, whose cure for patients consisted of frequent enemas and a few teaspoons of asparagus broth a day. She killed at least forty people at her "sanitarium," Wilderness Heights. The locals called it Starvation Heights.

Like the apple maggot and *American Idol*, some unfortunate things don't stop at the border. Perhaps you've heard of Robert Pickton, B.C.'s shame? For several years, starting in the nineties, he brought prostitutes from Vancouver's heroin-plagued Downtown Eastside to his pig farm outside the city. There, he threw wild parties at his Piggy Palace Good Times Society and killed perhaps forty-nine women, grinding some of them up to feed the pigs and serving pork chops to visitors. Before Pickton, there was the "Boozing Barber," Gilbert Paul Jordan, who killed at least seven Vancouver prostitutes. Farther north, between Prince Rupert and Prince George, as many as nineteen women are missing along the so-called Highway of Tears.

There's a reason *The X-Files* was filmed in Vancouver and not Phoenix. Call it Northwest noir. It has its own hallmarks: winter's sooty, daylong dusk; the look of neon bleeding into the gutters; the way people sometimes head into the mountains and simply disappear. For all its deep-green beauty, the Northwest has more than enough mist and mystery to give a body chicken-skin.

So, for people up here, when three feet appeared, it wasn't much of a leap to imagine the worst. The Reebok Ripper? Sure, why not? After all, as the poet said, we have been acquainted with the night.

SOMEHOW, EVEN A STREET SIGN GIVES ME THE WILLIES

The feet kept coming in 2008. After Foot Three was found in February, Four, a woman's New Balance, washed up in May, just south of Vancouver on Kirkland Island, in the Fraser River delta. In June, Five came ashore downstream, on the rural farming enclave of Westham Island, at the dock of married fishermen Mike and Sharon Bennett. Was the tide sweeping the feet upriver from the same spot? I wondered. What could savvy watermen like the Bennetts tell me?

Driving out to Westham Island in midwinter makes you think of that Annie Dillard line about the Northwest: "It was not quite raining, but everything was wet." Moss on roofs. Ducks floating in drowned berry fields. All this can put you in a dark and darty-eyed state of mind if you're on an errand to talk about severed feet. It doesn't help that the sign guiding me to the water's edge reads SAVAGE ROAD (NO EXIT).

When I first called Mike, he'd said, "It's sure been an odd one around here, because I know two of the other people who found feet. Now that's weird, eh?" Yes, I agreed, that was weird. Obviously, we had a shared sensibility; he told me to drop on by when I got to town.

Now Mike is walking into his kitchen from outside, where he's been readying the family herring boat for the season. He's a strong-looking guy, buzz-cut. Out of the gate, he'd like to share some thoughts about the Mounties' working theory that all these feet are a coincidence—just so much cosmic buckshot. "They're trying to make it look like a freak random thing," he says. "But that's just complete bullshit."

So what's his take? "I would say they all came from up the river," he says. "In fact, I'm sure of it. We found ours during the freshet time of year." The freshet, he explains, is when the spring snowmelt down the Fraser is so big that nothing gets upriver by wind or tide.

"This is one of the great rivers of the world," Mike continues, proud to live on its banks. After coursing nearly 900 miles through the Rockies and the Cariboos and the Coast Range, B.C.'s longest river ends here in a spraddle of channels and rich black mud, but not before it drains a Utah-size piece of provincial real estate. O Fraser, Drainpipe of the Canadian West! That foot could've come from anywhere! (Except downstream, is Mike's point.)

Mike and Sharon's foot showed up on June 16, 2008. "It was in the morning," he recalls, "coffee time." On a gorgeous late-spring day, they took their joe and headed out to see a friend whose boat was tied up at the end of their dock. As they walked out, they saw a runner floating sole side up. "There's a sneaker for you," Sharon joked. "That's not good," Mike replied, sounding serious. "It's a low floater."

This one was inside a Nike, size 11, the first lefty. Eventually police would match it up with Foot Three.

Long after it was bagged and tagged, the foot kept bothering Mike and Sharon. "The sock was in perfect shape," Mike says. "And . . . ah!" he adds, as if he nearly forgot, "The shoe had what appeared to be a bloodstain on the tongue."

Wait—a bloodstain? The police never mentioned a bloodstain. Mike gives me this look, like, Now you know.

Everybody I talk to has a pet solution to the feet mystery, but Mike offers one I haven't heard yet: the Container Theory. "My thought was, if somebody killed a bunch of guys and put their bodies in a container, and after a couple of years the container popped open, the shoes would be the only thing that came up."

He adds, "It could be a car gone over a bank, when I said 'a container.'"

"So it's not necessarily nefarious?"

"But remember the blood on the tongue," he says, chiding me.

Bloody footwear, "containers" stuffed with bodies—my head is spinning. Sharon agrees to walk me down to where they found the foot. By the water, a skiff dangles from a winch. A gull cries overhead. Sharon stands on the dock and jabs a cigarette at the green, glassy water. Back at the house, she told me that finding the foot had left her with an ugly feeling. "I cried a little bit," she said. "And after I lifted the foot, I couldn't wash my hand enough."

Now, standing here, I feel foolish and selfish. What did I expect to gain by making her walk down to the dock? Behind us, the late-afternoon sky is exploding, pink cotton-candy clouds edged with gold adrift on the mirrored water. It's ridiculously peaceful.

Sharon says, "We had a friend who drowned a few years ago, on the Fraser. And that was the first thing we thought of when we found it. That it was him."

And suddenly I understand: Crying is an entirely appropriate reaction to finding a foot floating outside your peaceful island home.

THIS PORTION NOT SPONSORED BY THE GREATER VANCOUVER TOURISM BUREAU

The Big Picture. That's what this tale lacks. Context. Perspective. A frame, to show how the puzzle pieces fit together. But the police won't—or can't—say much about it. Who else knows the shape of things?

Sandra Thomas.

Nobody writes as often or as well about missing British Columbians as Sandra, a pleasant bulldog of a reporter for the twice-a-week, 140,000-circulation *Vancouver Courier*. Sandra is fifty, a heavy-breasted woman with a recent islands tan and red nails as perfect as Chiclets. When I drop by her house, she admits that, for a while, she didn't think much about the feet. She remembers the day she started to care, though. "It was after Bryan Braumberger went missing. It will be two years this June."

On the evening of June 1, 2007, Braumberger, a seventeen-year-old from the Vancouver suburb of Burnaby, left a friend's house. His car was found not far from his home the next day, unlocked, lights on. "He just vanished," says Sandra.

A few months later, around the time the first foot turned up, a young guy named John Kahler disappeared. Then Derek Kelly. Then Kellen McElwee. "It was after Kellen went missing in March that I really started to think," Sandra says. Her research led to a shocking discovery: Not just a few but dozens of men had gone missing in southwestern B.C. in the previous four years. Even if you took away the ones who had any reason at all to disappear—the tweakers, the drug mules, the psychically ravaged—you still had, Sandra wrote, "twenty-two healthy, apparently happy men from southwestern B.C. who have simply vanished."

No way, you're thinking. This is Vancouver. Olympic City! And you'd be right—up to a point. From some angles, the place really is Emerald City, with its green-glass high-rises ringed by mountains that wear a geisha face of fresh powder, the air smelling of all good things—earth and mountains and salt water. But shift your gaze a little, or pick up a newspaper, and your perspective changes. You read about seven young people shot in the past six days. You see the shuffling knots of junkies and whores at Hastings and Main. You find out that young men are vanishing like cigarette smoke. Even paradise has its underbelly.

And it's not just Vancouver. All of B.C. has a missing-persons problem. Since 1950, more than one in five people who've gone missing in Canada have disappeared here, even though the province is home to just 13 percent of the population. That adds up to more than 2,400 people gone as of August 2009. By rough comparison, Kentucky, with the same population, is looking for 515.

For decades, you could rightly blame it on B.C.'s role as North America's break-water. Charlie was last seen hauling in his nets? Okay, sad, but at least we know how he died. Yet today hardly anybody disappears by falling off his Chris-Craft. Other things are making them go away—and in much greater numbers during this decade than ever before. Nobody knows why.

Back at Sandra's dining-room table, I'm feeling dizzy. Again. Every puzzle piece I pick up fractures into smaller pieces. Through the sliding-glass door, I can see her backyard, and above that the sky, which is white, or maybe smudged with the first bits of a front—a sky waiting for color.

"But where do the feet fit in, Sandra?" I ask.

She smooths the newspaper stories on the table and says that, once she began writing about the missing men, "I started wondering if there's a con-nection between the three of them—the feet, the missing men, and the Smiley Face Killers."

According to two former NYPD detectives, Kevin Gannon and Anthony Duarte, there's a loose-knit gang of murderers at work across North America. They've killed thirty-five or more healthy, college-age men over the past decade or so, and they've gotten away with it by making the deaths look like drowning acci-dents. Graffiti'd smiley faces have been found at the alleged crime scenes.

Or so the detectives claim. Most law-enforcement officials aren't convinced. There's simply not much evidence that these deaths are attributable to anything but the sad confluence of young men, booze, and deep water. Still, Duarte and Gannon have hawked their theory on outlets from the *Today* show to CNN, and Sandra has pondered in the *Courier* whether the Smiley Face Killers have anything to do with the feet or with Vancouver's missing men. So far, the feet don't match any of the absent locals, and the Mounties are dismissive. But Sandra's point is, Who knows?

She raps a fingernail on the table. "The day after my first story came out," she says, "a foot was found near the Massey Tunnel. And again on June 16, after I was on the radio discussing the missing men, another foot washed up."

Wait, is she saying there was a message from the killer?

"I'm sure it's coincidental," she says. "But, still, it's creepy."

THINGS YOU LEARN BEACHCOMBING WITH THE FUZZ

Many statistical problems have one piece of data that doesn't seem to fit. For B.C. police, it was a black Everest hiking shoe that washed up almost exactly one year after the first foot appeared. The trouble with Foot Six? It was found on

Washington State's Olympic Peninsula, a good 100 miles southwest of Vancouver, on the Strait of Juan de Fuca. Could it be related? Was a copycat at work?

On the scene that foggy afternoon was Detective Sergeant Lyman Moores, of the Clallam County sheriff's office, who just now is steering his black Ford Excursion toward the beach where the foot was discovered. If there's a dress code somewhere for middle-aged detectives, Moores got the memo. He has the bald crown, the mustache, the thick-soled black loafers. A Styrofoam cup of bad filling-station coffee balances on a knee of his prune-colored wash-and-wear pants. With his non-steering hand, he gestures his way through an overview of what he and his detectives have learned about that shoe.

Only 252 size 11's of that model were made, Moores says. "They were all sold in Canada."

Aha! So the foot came from Canada! I mean, it had to. Right?

Well, maybe. But it could have been bought there and worn down here. Moores knows he needs more evidence before reaching any conclusion.

He pulls over at the rusting gate of an old seaside camp, the Silver King Resort, and we follow the seashore smell of clams to a small bay lined with skipping stones. By the steps to the water, some wit has written *Footloose Beach* on a piece of driftwood. Not 50 yards away, Moores points out where he found the foot. He toes a thick mulch of tide wrack with a black loafer.

"The wind'll often come from the north, and this is what happens," he says. "The day we found the shoe, the wind had been blowing real hard from the north. There's no doubt in my mind that what's out in the strait is gonna wash up here." So, given this, he says, maybe the foot did come from up in Canada.

That all makes sense, but I ask Moores a slightly broader question: What the hell is going on?

He answers with a detective's caution. "My mind's wide-open that it could be a combination of things," he says. "Did a plane crash that we don't know about? Was this something related to a sports team? Because they were all wearing athletic shoes . . ."

A cop doesn't become a detective without being good at what he does, which means being suspicious. "I can't help thinking, being a cop, that someone's trying to dispose of bodies," he says. "I remember a few years ago, there was a mortician down south who was burying them in his backyard." And what about that other guy, who was supposed to be burying people's cremated ashes at sea but instead stacked them in a storage locker?

Yeah, what about those guys? Surely they could have imitators?

"It's just too much of a coincidence," Moores says, squinting out toward the strait, where Canada lurks in the mist.

A PLEASANT STROLL WITH A
KNIFE-WIELDING STRANGER

Water is the common denominator to this mystery. Water embraces these islands. It carried the feet to shore. I've got to get closer to the water to get closer to the answer. But how?

Then Mountain Mike calls back. Mountain Mike, who found Foot Four and who's called Mountain Mike, he says, "because I can survive just about anywhere." Which includes, apparently, an island in the Fraser River, alone, with only his dog, Sophie, for company.

The town of Ladner is a sloughy place south of Vancouver where farmland, sea, and suburb meet—and where Mountain Mike comes in sometimes for a beer. "Ask him how many knives he's carrying!" the boys at Speed's Pub said when I went there looking for him. (One guessed five.) Now, as Mountain Mike motors toward me up the dead harbor, I can hear their laughter again, and I think, Uh-oh. Because now that I see Mountain Mike, he sure looks like he might be the One, with his crazy Taliban beard crawling up his face to meet his low-tugged camo hat, and his feral caterpillar eyebrows wrestling atop his nose.

A ginger dog bounds off the skiff to sniff my boots. "She's the one that found the foot," Mountain Mike says. Not much of a retriever, he says. Won't touch dead things. She's left-handed, he adds. A real rat killer.

This seems like a lot of information. And very little. So I just nod and climb aboard.

As we head out of the slough, I take stock: I'm deepening my knowledge of missing and possibly murdered and dismembered citizens by heading out alone with a disheveled, knife-wielding stranger who looks and smells like a Sergio Leone villain.

But it's too late to turn back, so I decide to enjoy the morning sun, which is making the waters as bright as hammered sheeting, empty and beautiful. I comment on the river's beauty. Mountain Mike corrects me. There's crap all over the place, he says, pointing out a log off the port bow. Run into one of those babies at full speed and you can forget about it. Mike's fifty-seven, a lifelong fisherman, and he's helped fish out his share of watermen's bodies over the years.

We cross Ladner Reach, tie up at Kirkland Island, and hop onto an ATV. Mountain Mike is the caretaker of four islands clumped in the Fraser's south arm, a private bird-hunting preserve. While he drives, he talks about fishing, about birds, about trees. He pretty much talks the whole time.

The ATV rounds the northeastern tip of the island; the main channel of the Fraser, which bounds Kirkland Island's north side, swings into view. It's a good half-mile from our shore to the river's far shore, home to the city of Richmond. "They found the other foot right across the way there," he says, pointing at a distant riprapped shore. Foot Seven, he means—the last one found, and the one that matched Mountain Mike's Foot Four. It was picked up last November by a local politician's wife.

At a break in the trees, I stare hard at the Fraser's wind-scuffed water. Mountain Mike is right. It looks peaceful, but it's not, at all. The water is full of flotsam—a deadhead nodding in a wave, a branch reaching up. Maybe the clue I'm supposed to absorb is that the bodies didn't necessarily come down the Fraser. They could've come *from* the Fraser.

I'm still a bit jumpy when we stop at a beach strewn with logs and matted canary grass. Here, Mountain Mike says, is where he stepped right on top of a woman's New Balance while out on one of his regular island walks. Sophie just kept staring at it, then back at him, then back at the shoe. "After the third time," he says, "I knew this was something out of the ordinary."

A coyote was following them that day, picking up the rats Sophie killed. I can't leave it here, Mountain Mike thought. He found a 5-gallon bucket. Then he carried the foot all the way back across the island and rowed to town. For two hours, it was just the three of them: Mountain Mike, Sophie, and the foot.

After that, he says, Sophie changed for a long time. Wouldn't let people get near her. "She was really subdued. I don't know how they know." I look at Sophie, worrying a stick on the beach. She seems better.

The foot rattled Mountain Mike, too, more than he thought it would. "It took me from May till September to come walk on these beaches," he says. He's sitting on a driftwood log facing me now, smoking a hand-rolled cigarette. "I mean, you've found it, but you can't put the rest of it together. It's like when you get a craving for a chocolate bar, and you're in the middle of nowhere, and you don't have one, and there's like . . . a hole."

I look at the man across from me. I don't see a knife-wielding loner anymore but one of the most thoughtful people I've met in a long time. I think that Mountain Mike is a good symbol for this entire Mystery of the Feet. He seems to be one thing in the imagination, but in reality he's something else entirely. And nothing to be frightened of.

WHAT THE PIG KNOWS

Why does a loose foot, or seven, skeez us out so badly? Why can't we shrug it off, let it sink back down and disappear, accepting the question mark?

Sinking is on my mind as I head up to see Gail Anderson. Gail is a renowned forensic entomologist who told me that, lately, her research has involved sinking dead pigs to the seafloor and watching what eats them.

This I really want to see.

Inside her office at Simon Fraser University, where she works in the School of Criminology, she presses some buttons on her computer and, through the magic of technology, we're 300 feet below the waters of Vancouver Island's Saanich Inlet. I watch as spot prawns mince across a pig carcass on delicate spot-prawn stilt legs. A squat lobster tears roughly at a jowl. I daydream about how delicious free-range, pork-fed lobster must taste. Anderson interrupts to say that, in three weeks, crabs and shrimp can reduce a 50-pound pig to a skeleton.

These experiments are showing Anderson what can happen to a body that, say, a bad guy sinks to the seafloor. But they're also a lesson in what nature can do on its own. And this is the point she wants to make when I ask about the feet: Nature can do weird-seeming stuff.

"Often, when we've found a body in the water, it looks like the guy has been through a terrible fight," she says. "His knuckles can be all ripped up. His face can be ripped off. Your first thought is, My God, this guy's been through a helluva beating." But that appearance can be caused by waves cheese-gratering the body against the bottom, she says.

Fair enough, you say. But if there's an answer for everything, why were the finds always feet? Well, our hands and feet are like kites, attached only by a few tendons. Underwater, they flap around and come off pretty easily when body tissues break down. Hands would dissolve and be eaten. Rubber-soled shoes would be natural flotation devices, and they would float sole up, protecting what's inside from gulls.

So why haven't we seen so much of this before? Well, in times past, leather and canvas shoes would disintegrate. Now the shoes survive.

Yeah, but this is seven freakin' feet. That doesn't sound a little odd to you?

Anderson shrugs as if to say, No, maybe it's not so odd after all. "I've spoken to a colleague in New Zealand who said, 'Oh, we get fifteen feet in runners every year.'"

"How many times have you seen a shoe along a beach?" she asks. "How many times have you seen shoes hanging on telephone wires? Did anyone ever look in those?"

IN WHICH WE ACHIEVE CLOSURE— OR SOMETHING LIKE IT

I think I understand what Anderson is telling me: We are blind. We stumble through our world every day, unseeing, uncurious. Maybe we're just trying to keep it together and get the kids to soccer practice. We don't have time to look inside shoes on the beach. Then something happens. We look. And suddenly we see feet everywhere. And so we keep yearning to connect the dots. Even when we know that sometimes a foot is just a foot.

During one of my last afternoons in B.C., I meander in my rental car back to Westham Island. I turn onto a one-lane road that runs atop a dike over the Fraser, and I peer down, fascinated by the flotsam.

Ahead, an empty, wrecked shack slumps into the river. Time has flaked its fake red-brick siding. Driftwood shoals against its walls. And everywhere in the drain-clog-hair-mess of the scene there are reminders of a big river's appetite for junk: Quaker State bottles. A cooler. A crushed Bud can. A frayed bight of rope, coiled in the cattails like a serpent.

Then—look! Right in the shack's window! A shoe! A boot! Okay, actually sort of a low-cut boot thingy! Black, rubber. Sitting up on the shack's glassless wooden windowsill! My heart pole-vaults into my throat. I want to show somebody, but no one is around on this winter-bleak island. Somewhere, a dog barks. A boat's motor purls in the glassy channel.

It's definitely a man's boot. About a size 11, it looks like from here. And now I can see that the shack really isn't empty. Past the boot, where the underfed afternoon light hits the inside wall, something has been spray-painted that from up here looks an awful lot like—is it? Could it be?—a smiley face.

My scalp crinkles electrically. My eardrums are pounding like a timpani. Then I'm heading down the embankment, laughing and terrified, to where the boot waits for me in the window as peacefully as a still life in its weathered frame.

THE KILLER IN THE POOL

TIM ZIMMERMANN

~~~~~~

In 2010, when a 12,000-pound orca named Tilikum dragged his SeaWorld trainer into the pool and drowned her, it was the third time the big killer whale had been involved in a death. Many observers wondered why the animal was still working. But some experts, knowing the psychological toll of a life spent in captivity, have posed a darker question: Was it human error, or can a killer whale choose to kill? This story led to the critically acclaimed documentary Blackfish—and widespread changes for an industry built on turning wild creatures into mass entertainment.

~~~~~~

To work closely with a killer whale in a marine park requires experience, intuition, athleticism, and a whole lot of dramatic flair. Few people were better at it than top SeaWorld trainer Dawn Brancheau, who, at forty, was blonde, vivacious, and literally the poster girl for the marine park in Orlando, Florida, appearing on billboards around the city. She decided she wanted to work with killer whales at the age of nine, during a family trip to SeaWorld, and loved animals so much that as an adult she used to throw birthday parties for her two chocolate Labs.

This past February 24, Brancheau was working the Dine with Shamu show, featuring SeaWorld's largest killer whale, a 6-ton, 22-foot male known as "Tili" (short for Tilikum). Dine with Shamu takes place in a faux-rock-lined, 1.6-million-gallon pool that has an open-air cafe wrapped around one side. The families snacking on the lunch buffet that Wednesday were getting an eyeful. Brancheau bounced around on the deck of the pool, wearing a black-and-white wetsuit that echoed Tilikum's coloration, as she worked him through a few of the many "behaviors" he had learned during his nearly twenty-seven years as a marine-park denizen. The audience chuckled at the sight of one of the ocean's top predators performing like a circus animal.

The show ended around 1:30 p.m. As the audience started to file out, Brancheau fed Tilikum some herring (he eats up to 200 pounds a day), doused him a few times with a bucket (killer whales love all sorts of stimulation), and moved over to a shallow ledge built into the side of the pool. There, she lay down in a few inches of water, talking to him and stroking him, conducting what's known as a "relationship session." Tilikum floated inert in the pool alongside her, his nose almost touching her shoulder. Brancheau was smiling, her long ponytail flaring out behind her.

One level down, a group of families gathered before the huge glass windows of the underwater viewing area. A trainer shouted up that they were ready for Tilikum. That was Brancheau's signal to instruct the orca to dive down and swim directly up to the glass for a custom photo op. It's an awesome sight when 6 tons of Tili come gliding out of the blue. But that day, instead of waiting for his cue and behaving the way decades of daily training in captivity had conditioned him to, Tilikum did something unexpected. Jan Topoleski, thirty-two, a trainer who was acting as a safety spotter for Brancheau, told investigators that Tilikum took Brancheau's drifting hair into his mouth. Brancheau tried to pull it free, but Tilikum yanked her into the pool. In an instant, a classic tableau of a trainer bonding with a marine mammal became a life-threatening emergency.

Topoleski hit the pool's siren. A "Signal 500" was broadcast over the SeaWorld radio net, calling for a water rescue at G pool. Staff raced to the scene. "It was scary," Dutch tourist Susanne De Wit, thirty-three, told investigators. "He was very wild." SeaWorld staff slapped the water surface, signaling Tilikum to leave her. The whale ignored the command. Trainers hurried to drop a weighted net into the water to try and separate Tilikum from Brancheau or herd him through two adjoining pools and into a small medical pool that had a lifting floor. There he could be raised out of the water and controlled.

Eyewitness accounts and the sheriff's investigative report make it clear that Brancheau fought hard. She was a strong swimmer, a dedicated workout enthusiast who ran marathons. But she weighed just 123 pounds and was no match for a 12,000-pound killer whale. She managed to break free and swim toward the surface, but Tilikum slammed into her. She tried again. This time he grabbed her. Her water shoes came off and floated to the surface. "He started pushing her with his nose like she was a toy," said Paula Gillespie, one of the visitors at the underwater window. SeaWorld employees urgently ushered guests away. "Will she be okay?" one asked.

Tilikum kept dragging Brancheau through the water, shaking her violently. Finally—now holding Brancheau by her arm—he was guided onto the medical lift. The floor was quickly raised. Even now, Tilikum refused to give her up. Trainers were forced to pry his jaws open. When they pulled Brancheau free, part of her arm came off in his mouth. Brancheau's colleagues carried her to the pool deck and cut her wetsuit away. She had no heartbeat. The paramedics went to work, attaching a defibrillator, but it was obvious she was gone. A sheet was pulled over her body. Tilikum, who'd been involved in two marine-park deaths in the past, had killed her.

"Every safety protocol that we have failed," SeaWorld director of animal training Kelly Flaherty Clark told me a month after the incident, her voice still tight with emotion. "That's why we don't have our friend anymore, and that's why we are taking a step back."

Dawn Brancheau's death was a tragedy for her family and for SeaWorld, which had never lost a trainer before. Letters of sympathy poured in, many with pictures of Brancheau and the grinning kids she'd spent time with after shows. The incident was a shock to Americans accustomed to thinking of Shamu as a lovable national icon, with an extensive line of plush dolls and a relentlessly cheerful Twitter account. The news media went into full frenzy, chasing Brancheau's family and flying helicopters over Shamu Stadium. Congress piled on with a call for hearings on marine mammals at entertainment parks, and the Occupational Safety and Health Administration (OSHA) opened an investigation. It was the most intense national killer whale mania since 1996, when Keiko, the star of *Free Willy*, was rescued from a shabby marine park in Mexico City in an attempt to return him to the sea. Killer whales have never been known to attack a human in the wild, and everyone wanted to know one thing: Why did Dawn Brancheau die?

~~~~~~

Killer whales have been starring at marine parks since 1965. There are 42 alive in parks around the world today—SeaWorld owns 26 of them—and over the years more than 130 have died in captivity. Until the 1960s, no one really thought about putting a killer whale in an aquarium, much less in a show. The public knew little about them beyond the fact that they sounded dangerous. (Killer whales, or orcas, are the largest members of the dolphin family.) Fishermen tended to blast them with rifle fire if they came near salmon and herring stocks.

But Ted Griffin helped change all that. A young impresario who owned the Seattle Marine Aquarium, Griffin had long been obsessed with the idea of swimming with a killer whale. In June 1965, he got word of a 22-footer tangled in a fisherman's nets off Namu, British Columbia. Griffin bought the 8,000-pound animal for $8,000. He towed the orca, which he named Namu, 450 miles back to Seattle in a custom-made floating pen. Namu's family pod—twenty to twenty-five orcas—followed most of the way. Griffin was surprised by how gentle and intelligent Namu was. Before long he was riding on the orca's back, and by September tens of thousands of people had come to see the spectacle of the man and his orca buddy. The story of their "friendship" was eventually chronicled in the pages of *National Geographic* and in the 1966 movie *Namu, the Killer Whale*. The orca entertainment industry was born.

Namu was often heard calling to other orcas from his pen in the sea, and he died within a year from an intestinal infection, probably brought on by a nearby sewage outflow. Griffin was devastated. But his partner at the aquarium, Don Goldsberry, was a blunt, hard-driving man who could see that there was still a business in killer whales. He and Griffin had already turned their energies to capturing orcas in the Puget Sound area and selling them to marine parks. Goldsberry first built a harpoon gun, firing it by accident through his garage door and denting his car. Eventually, he and Griffin settled on the technique of locating orca pods from the air, driving them into coves with boats and seal bombs (underwater explosives used by fishermen to keep seals away from their catch), and throwing a wall of net across their escape path. Goldsberry and Griffin would then choose the orcas they wanted and let the remaining ones go. They preferred adolescents, particularly the smaller females, which were easier to handle and transport.

In October 1965, Goldsberry and Griffin trapped 15 killer whales in Carr Inlet, near Tacoma. One died during the hunt. Another—a 14-foot female that weighed 2,000 pounds—was captured and named Shamu (for She-Namu). In December, a fast-growing marine park in San Diego, called SeaWorld, acquired Shamu and flew her to California. Goldsberry says he and Griffin were paid $70,000. It was the start of a billion-dollar franchise.

Over the next decade, around 300 killer whales were netted off the Pacific Northwest coast, and 51 were sold to marine parks across the globe, in Japan, Australia, the Netherlands, France, and elsewhere. Goldsberry, who became SeaWorld's lead "collector" until he retired in the late 1980s, caught 252 of them, sold 29, and inadvertently killed 9 with his nets. In August 1970, concerned about backlash, Goldsberry weighted some dead orcas down with anchors and dumped them in deep water. When they were dragged up on a Whidbey Island beach by a trawling fisherman, the public started to understand the sometimes brutal reality of the "orca gold rush."

In 1972, the Marine Mammal Protection Act prohibited the taking of marine mammals in US waters, but SeaWorld continued to receive killer whale capture permits under an educational-display exclusion. In March 1976, Goldsberry pushed his luck and the limits of public opinion. He sighted a group of killer whales in the waters just off Olympia, Washington's, state capital. In full view of boaters—and just as the state legislature was meeting to consider creating a Puget Sound killer whale sanctuary—he used seal bombs and boats to chase six orcas into his nets at Budd Inlet. Ralph Munro, an aide to Governor Dan Evans, was out on a small sailboat that day and remembers the sight. "It was gruesome as they closed the net. You could hear the whales screaming," Munro recalls. "Goldsberry kept dropping explosives to drive the whales back into the net."

The State of Washington filed a lawsuit, contending that Goldsberry and Sea-World had violated permits that required humane capture, and as the heat and publicity built, SeaWorld agreed to release the Budd Inlet killer whales and to stop taking orcas from Washington waters. With the Puget Sound hunting grounds closing, Goldsberry flew around the world looking for other good capture sites. He settled on Iceland, where killer whales were plentiful. By October 1976, Sea-World's first Icelandic orca had been captured.

Over the next few years, Goldsberry spent freely to help create the infrastructure to net and transport whales out of Iceland. In November 1983, in the cold, rough waters off Berufjördur, Icelander Helgi Jonasson drew a large purse-seine net around a group of killer whales. Three young animals—two males and a female—were captured and transported to the Hafnarfjördur Marine Zoo, near Reykjavík.

There they were placed in a concrete holding tank. The smaller male, who was about two years old and just shy of 11.5 feet, would remain there for almost a year, awaiting transfer to a marine park. In the pool, he could either cruise slowly in circles or lie still on the surface. He could hear no ocean sounds, only the mechanical rush of filtration. Finally, in late 1984, the young orca was shipped to Sealand of the Pacific, a marine park just outside Victoria, on British Columbia's Vancouver Island. He was given a name to go with his new life: Tilikum, which means "friend" in Chinook.

Sealand, situated at Oak Bay Marina, was a wholly alien world for a wild orca. Its performance pool—about 100 feet by 50 feet, and 35 feet deep—was created by suspending mesh netting from the floating docks. The pool was open to the marina water, and thus to any bilge oil or sewage pumped into it by boaters. Marina traffic and motors created a cacophony of artificial underwater background noise, obscuring the natural sounds Tilikum had known in the wild. In the fourteen years before his arrival, seven orcas had died under Sealand's care. Their average survival time was just shy of three and a half years.

At Sealand, Tilikum joined two female killer whales, Haida and Nootka, who were sorting out the social pecking order. (Orca society is dominated by females.) That meant conflict and tooth raking for all three orcas, and even after Haida established herself as dominant, both females continued to push the young Tilikum around. The stress was worse at night. Sealand's owner, a local entrepreneur named Robert Wright who'd captured his share of Pacific Northwest killer whales in the early 1970s, worried that someone might cut the net to free his orcas, or that they might chew through it themselves. So at 5:30 p.m., after the shows were over, the orcas were moved into a small metal-sided pool that was 26 feet in diameter and less than 20 feet deep. The trainers referred to it as "the module," and the orcas were left in it for the next fourteen and a half hours.

According to Eric Walters, who was a trainer at Sealand from 1987 to 1989, while working toward a bachelor's degree in marine biology at the University of Victoria, the module was so tight that the orcas had difficulty avoiding conflict, and their skin would get scratches and cuts from rubbing against the sides. About once a week, Walters says, one or more of the orcas would simply refuse to swim into the module and would have to be left in the performance pool overnight.

The orca show was performed every hour on the hour, eight times a day, seven days a week. Both Nootka and Tilikum had stomach ulcers, which had to be treated with medication. Sometimes Nootka's ulcers were so bad she had blood in her stool.

Walters was interested in the science of training and was encouraged when Sealand brought in Bruce Stephens, a former SeaWorld head trainer, to make recommendations to improve Sealand's practices. Stephens gave each trainer a handbook, which warned, "If you fail to provide your animals with the excitement they need, you may be certain they will create the excitement themselves." He emphasized that killer whales needed constant change to keep them engaged and responsive, and made a series of recommendations for new learning sessions and playtime for Sealand's orcas. But within a month, Walters told me, Sealand was back to its usual routines. "They basically ran it like you would run McDonald's," he says. "It just can't be good for an animal that is so intelligent to do the same thing every day." (Wright still runs a marina at Oak Bay but declined to speak to *Outside*.)

As Stephens had warned, bored killer whales look to make their own fun. If any unusual object ended up in the water, Haida, Nootka, and Tilikum would race for it and play keep-away with the trainers. Once the orcas took something, they were determined to hang on to it. Walters worried about what might happen if one of the trainers—who worked in rubber boots on a painted fiberglass deck—fell into the pool. Many marine parks try to defuse the danger with desensitization training that teaches the killer whales to stay calm and ignore anyone who falls in. The training might start with just a foot in the water (the orca is conditioned to ignore it), but ultimately requires gradually easing an entire person into the pool. According to Steve Huxter, who was the head of animal training and care at the time, desensitization was a catch-22. After thinking about it carefully, "Bob [Wright] was not willing to take that risk."

Each whale had a distinctive personality. Tilikum was youthful, energetic, and eager to learn. "Tilikum was our favorite," says Eric Walters. "He was the one we all really liked to work with."

Nootka, with her health issues, was the most unpredictable. According to Walters, Nootka pulled a trainer into the water. (He quickly yanked her out.) Twice she tried to bite down on Walters's hands. Not even the audience was safe. A blind woman was once brought onto the stage to pat Nootka's tongue. Nootka bit her, too.

Frustrated, Walters quit in May 1989. A year later, he wrote a letter to the Canadian Federation of Humane Societies, to share with participants at a conference on whales in captivity. In it, he detailed Sealand's treatment of its marine mammals and the safety concerns he had. In closing, he wrote, "I feel that sooner or later someone is going to get seriously hurt."

On February 20, 1991, Sealand had just wrapped up an afternoon killer whale show. Keltie Byrne, a twenty-year-old marine-biology student and part-time trainer, was starting to tidy up when she misstepped and fell halfway into the pool. As she struggled to get out, one of the killer whales grabbed her and pulled her into the water. A competitive swimmer, Byrne was no match for three orcas used to treating any unusual object as a toy. "They never had a plaything in the pool that was so interactive," says Huxter. "They just got incredibly excited and stimulated." Huxter and the other trainers issued recall commands and threw food in the water. They tried maneuvering a life ring close enough for Byrne to grab, but the orcas kept her away from it. In the chaos and dark water, it was hard to see which killer whale had her at any one time. Twice, she surfaced and screamed. After about ten minutes, she popped up a third time for an instant but made no noise. She had drowned.

Bryne was the first trainer ever killed by orcas at a marine park. It took Sealand employees two hours to recover her body from Nootka, Haida, and Tilikum. They had stripped off all of her clothes save one boot, and she had bruises from bites across her skin. "It was just a tragic accident," Al Bolz, Sealand's manager, told reporters at the time. "I just can't explain it."

Paul Spong, seventy-one, director of OrcaLab, in British Columbia—which studies orcas in the wild—did part-time research at Sealand before Tilikum arrived.

He is not so befuddled. "If you pen killer whales in a small steel tank, you are imposing an extreme level of sensory deprivation on them," he says. "Humans who are subjected to those same conditions become mentally disturbed."

Byrne's death led to a coroner's inquest, which recommended a series of safety improvements at Sealand. The park responded, but according to Huxter, "the wind came out of [Wright's] sails for the business." In the fall of 1991, Sealand contacted SeaWorld to ask if it would like to buy Nootka, Haida, and Tilikum. Sealand closed in 1992.

~~~~~~

If you want to try to get an inkling of what captivity means for a killer whale, you first have to understand what their lives are like in the wild. For that, there's no one better than marine biologist Ken Balcomb, sixty-nine, who has spent thirty-four years tracking and observing killer whales off the coast of Washington State.

In early May, I meet Balcomb in his cluttered yard on San Juan Island. He's trying to find the source of a leak on his Boston Whaler. His wood-framed house, which also serves as headquarters for his Center for Whale Research, sits perched atop the rocky shores of the Haro Strait, a popular orca hangout; Balcomb says he sees them about eighty days a year from his deck. Inside, there's gear all over the place—spotting scopes, cameras, tool kits—from a recent expedition to California. In the middle of it all, on a table, sits an enormous killer whale skull that he picked up in Japan in 1975, when he was a flier and oceanographic specialist for the US Navy.

Balcomb, of medium build, with a ruddy, sunbaked face and a salt-and-pepper beard, has been carefully photographing, cataloging, and observing the Puget Sound orcas—also known as the Southern Residents—since he was contracted by the National Marine Fisheries Service in 1976 to assess the impact of the marine-park captures. Many people assumed there were hundreds of orcas around Puget Sound. After identifying each individual killer whale by its markings, Balcomb found that there were just seventy left.

Since then, he's become the Southern Residents' scientific godfather, noting every birth and death, and plotting family connections. The population, he says, is now at eighty-five orcas, but he won't know for sure until they show up this summer. Talking on his sunporch, Balcomb stresses that one of the most important things to know about killer whales like Tilikum is that, in the wild, they live in complex and highly social family pods of twenty to fifty animals. The pods are organized around the females. The matriarch is usually the oldest female (some live to be eighty years old, or more), who has a wealth of experience and knowledge about where food can be found. Within the pod, mothers are at the center of smaller family groups. Males, who can live to be fifty or sixty, stay with their mothers their entire lives, and often die not long after she does. According to Balcomb, separation is not a minor issue.

The Southern Resident population is made up of three distinct pods. Each pod might travel some 75 miles a day, following the salmon, and vocalizing almost constantly to keep the entire group updated on who's where, and whether there are fish around. Killer whales are highly intelligent. They coordinate in the hunt, share food freely, and will help an injured or ill member of the pod stay on the surface to breathe. Most striking is the sophistication of their dialect. Each family group within a pod uses the same vocalizations, or vocabulary, and there are also shared vocalizations between pods. Balcomb says he can usually tell which pod is about to turn up simply by the sounds he hears through a hydrophone.

The social and genetic connections that bind orcas in the wild are intense. There's breeding between the Puget Sound pods. Sometimes they'll all come together at once and go through a distinctive greeting ceremony before mixing. But they will have absolutely nothing to do with the genetically distinct, transient killer whales that sometimes pass through their waters. (Transients travel in much smaller groups over vast distances and mostly feed on marine mammals instead of fish.) "When you get born into the family, you are always in the family. You don't have a house or a home that is your location," says Balcomb. "The group is your home, and your whole identity is with your group." Aggression between members of a pod almost never occurs in the wild, he adds.

Puget Sound is small enough that Balcomb used to run into Goldsberry from time to time. Despite their differences, the two men would talk killer whales, drink Crown Royal, and trade stories. Today, Goldsberry, seventy-six, lives about 100 miles away, in a small, ground-level condo near Sea-Tac Airport. His only water view is of a man-made lake, and when I go to see him he's busy drilling a walrus tusk that's been made into a cribbage board. Goldsberry has a square head, with close-cropped white hair. His health is fragile, and he has an oxygen tube clipped to his nose. But he still has the beefy arms of a waterman, and he appears unmoved by the controversy of his hunting days. "We showed the world that killer whales were good animals and all of a sudden people said, 'Hey, leave these animals alone,'" he says, sipping a mug of vodka and ice. "I had to make a living."

Goldsberry has mostly kept his mouth shut about his work for SeaWorld and doesn't much like talking to reporters. "I'm only speaking with you because those idiots out there, mainly the politicians, want to release all the killer whales," he growls. "You might as well put a gun to the whales' heads." He spends the next couple of hours telling me about his cowboy days in the orca business: how he helped build the global trade, how he kept one step ahead of Greenpeace and activists, and how he battled the media, dropping one TV newsman's camera into the water, asking, "I wonder if this floats?"

Goldsberry says he always got the resources he needed to keep the killer whales coming, and developed relationships with other marine parks around the world, which would often hold killer whales for him, many of which would eventually end up at SeaWorld. (Balcomb calls it Goldsberry's "whale laundry.") "I would go into SeaWorld and say, 'I need a quarter of a million' or 'a half-million dollars,' and they put it in my suitcase," he says with a grin. "It was good, catching animals. It was exciting. I was the best in the world. There is no question about it."

Asked about Goldsberry's work for SeaWorld, Fred Jacobs, vice president of communications, denies that killer whales were laundered. "Any killer whale that entered our collection from another facility did so in full accordance with their export and our import laws," he says. "We have imported whales that were collected by other institutions, but they were not collected on our behalf and held for us."

Goldsberry's last great haul of wild orcas came in October 1978, when he caught six off Iceland. (Five ended up in SeaWorld parks.) He continued to collect all sorts of other animals for SeaWorld for the next decade. When Goldsberry and SeaWorld finally parted ways, in the late 1980s, Goldsberry says he was offered $100,000 to keep quiet about his work for two years. He happily took it. SeaWorld's Jacobs explains that Goldsberry's relationship with SeaWorld occurred under prior ownership. "I have no way of knowing if this is true or not," he says.

Whatever his methods, Goldsberry had helped SeaWorld turn killer whales into killer profits. The company currently has parks in Orlando, San Diego, and San Antonio, which are visited by more than twelve million people annually. Most of those visitors, paying up to $78 each for an entrance ticket, come to see killer whales. Last year, Anheuser-Busch InBev sold SeaWorld's marine parks—and seven amusement parks housed with SeaWorld under the Busch Entertainment umbrella—to private-equity giant the Blackstone Group. The purchase price was reported to be $2.7 billion.

One of the keys to SeaWorld's success was its ability to move away from controversial wild orca captures to captive births in its marine parks. The first captive birth that produced a surviving calf took place at SeaWorld Orlando in 1985. Since then, SeaWorld has relied mostly on captive breeding to stock its parks with killer whales, even mastering the art of artificial insemination. "Early in the morning, the animal-care crew would take hot-water-filled cow vaginas and masturbate the males in the back tanks," says John Hall, a former scientist at SeaWorld. "It was pretty interesting to walk by."

Tilikum's sudden availability in 1991 was a boon to the captive breeding program. While preparing to transfer Haida, Nootka, and Tilikum, SeaWorld, one of only a few facilities with the expertise to care for them, discovered that Tilikum had already impregnated Haida and Nootka. A sexually mature male, even one involved in a dangerous incident, was a welcome addition. "It was not the only reason [SeaWorld] had interest, but definitely a part of the decision," says Mark Simmons, who worked as a trainer at SeaWorld from 1987 to 1996, and was part of a team sent to Sealand to manage Tilikum's transfer. Media reports at the time pegged Tilikum's price at $1 million.

~~~~~~

If Sealand was like a McDonald's, SeaWorld Orlando was like a five-star restaurant, with 220 acres of custom marine habitats, thrill rides, eateries, and a 400-foot Sky Tower. There were seven different killer whale pools, including the enormous Shamu show pool, and 7 million gallons of continuously filtered salt water kept at an orca-friendly 52 to 55 degrees. There was regular, world-class veterinary care. Even the orcas' food was a custom blend, made up of restaurant-quality herring, capelin, and salmon.

The big question for SeaWorld was whether to teach Tilikum to perform with trainers in the pool. Called "water work," it has long been the most thrilling element of the Shamu shows. In contrast to Sealand's repetitive food-for-work equation, SeaWorld's training strategy was finely honed and based on intense variation. Daily activities were constantly altered, and the orcas were given a variety of rewards—sometimes food, sometimes stimulation (backrubs, hose-downs, toys, or ice), and sometimes nothing. "Variability makes the animals more flexible about what the outcome is and keeps them interested," says Thad Lacinak, who was SeaWorld's vice president and corporate curator for animal training when Tilikum arrived, and who left in 2008 to found Precision Behavior, a consulting firm for zoos and other animal facilities.

Lacinak believed that Keltie Byrne had died because Sealand's killer whales had never been trained to accept humans in the water. So when she fell in, they treated her like any other surprise object. Lacinak had confidence that Tilikum could be trained for Shamu-show water work. But he and SeaWorld's top management also knew that when it comes to killer whales (or any wild animal), there are no guarantees. Normally, SeaWorld begins training in-water interaction when its killer whales are 1,000 pounds or less, but Tilikum was by now a very large bull. Plus Tilikum had been involved in a death. "If something did happen, you would look like a fool," Lacinak says. "It was too risky, and from a liability standpoint it was decided not to do [water work]."

Some of the trainers at least wanted to desensitize Tilikum in case someone fell in. "There were several of us that pushed for water de-sense training. You don't run from the storm; you harness the wind," says Mark Simmons, who left SeaWorld in 1996 to earn a business degree and later cofounded Ocean Embassy, which consults on conservation and marine parks. "We wanted to make humans in the water so commonplace that it didn't elicit any response. And if that had been done, it would be very unlikely that we'd be having this conversation today."

But SeaWorld faced the same vexing catch-22 that had given Sealand pause. SeaWorld's head trainer, Flaherty Clark, says that it's impossible to prove or disprove what might have happened if Tilikum had been desensitized. "It's easy for former trainers to frame that as a hypothetical," she says, "but we viewed water work with him—and all the conditioning that might have permitted it to be effected safely— as simply too great a risk."

Instead, SeaWorld focused on creating roles for Tilikum that showcased his size and power when no trainers were in the water. The sight of him rocketing into the air awed the crowds. One of his specialties was inundating the front rows—the "splash zone"—with a tidal wave pushed up by his enormous flukes. "He's a crowd-pleasing, showstopping, wonderful, wonderful wild animal," says Flaherty Clark.

Keeping Tilikum from water work made sense for another reason: As long as SeaWorld had been putting trainers in the water with killer whales, trainers had been getting worked over by them. Since the 1960s, there have been more than forty documented incidents at marine parks around the world. In 1971, the first Shamu went wild on a bikini-wearing secretary from SeaWorld, who was pulled screaming from the pool. For every incident the public was aware of (the ones that occurred in front of audiences or that put trainers in the hospital), there were many more behind the scenes. John Jett was a trainer at SeaWorld in the 1990s. He left to pursue a PhD in natural resource management in 1995, having grown disillusioned with the reality of keeping large, intelligent animals in captivity. He says that getting nicked, and sometimes hammered, was just part of the price of living the killer whale dream: "There were so many incidents. If you show fear or go home hurt, you might be put on the bench." Flaherty Clark says SeaWorld gives trainers wide latitude: "The safety of our trainers and animals is paramount. Our trainers are empowered to alter any show or session plan if they have even the slightest concern."

In 1987 alone, SeaWorld San Diego experienced three incidents that hospitalized trainers with everything from fractured vertebrae to a smashed pelvis.

Jonathan Smith was one of them. In March, during a show, he was grabbed by two killer whales that slammed him on the bottom of the 32-foot-deep pool five times before he finally escaped. "One more dunk for me and I would have gone out," he says. "They let me go. If they didn't want to let me go, it would have been over." Smith was left with a ruptured kidney, a lacerated liver, and broken ribs. In response to these serious injuries, as well as other incidents, SeaWorld shook up its management team, pulled trainers from the water, and reassessed its safety protocols. After a number of changes (including making sure that only very experienced trainers worked with killer whales), trainers were allowed back in the pools.

Despite the modifications, in 2006 another serious incident took place at Sea-World San Diego, when head trainer Kenneth Peters was attacked by a killer whale called Kasatka. Kasatka grabbed Peters and repeatedly held him below the surface of the pool for up to a minute. He came close to drowning, and Kasatka joined Tilikum and a couple of other unruly SeaWorld orcas on the "no water work" blacklist.

Following the Peters incident, OSHA opened an investigation. After digging into the inner workings of SeaWorld's killer whale shows, OSHA issued a report in 2007 that warned, "The contributing factors to the accident, in the simplest of terms, is that swimming with captive orcas is inherently dangerous, and if someone hasn't been killed already, it is only a matter of time before it does happen." SeaWorld challenged the report as filled with errors, and OSHA agreed to withdraw it.

In late March 2010, a month after Brancheau's death, I visit Orlando's SeaWorld park for the first time. I pause for an instant to take in the sheer enormity of the place, with its hundreds of diversions, but there is just one thing I really want to see: a killer whale show. I thread my way through families and packs of ecstatic kids. Shamu Stadium, SeaWorld's colossal amphitheater, looms before me.

The current Shamu show is called "Believe," and Dawn Brancheau was one of the stars. Music, video, and killer whales are wrapped around the story of a kid who paddles out to bond with a wild orca and is inspired to become a trainer. Every element is intimately choreographed, with whales exploding into the air and onscreen in perfect synchronicity. Even though Brancheau's death has prompted SeaWorld to temporarily reinvent "Believe" without trainers in the water, it is still absolutely mesmerizing. The show builds to a climactic finale with a pack of orcas lining up and using their flukes to sweep a tidal wave of water onto the shrieking and willing inhabitants of the splash zone.

After the show, I sit down with Brad Andrews in front of the underwater view-ing area of G pool. Two killer whales are amusing a crowd of people who probably have no idea of the scene the same windows revealed a month earlier. Andrews is SeaWorld's chief zoological officer, and he's been with the park since 1986. He explains that while part of the goal is entertainment, SeaWorld's aim is to use the shows to educate and inspire visitors, as a way to help conserve the environment and support wildlife.

There's a lot of criticism that flies back and forth between SeaWorld and the hard-marine-science community, but there's no question that SeaWorld's close contact with killer whales over the course of decades has contributed to the world's knowledge of them. "The gestation of killer whales was never known to researchers in the wild. It was always assumed it was like a dolphin, twelve months," Andrews says. "Then we found out it's seventeen to eighteen months. We supplied an answer to a part of their puzzle."

The advances SeaWorld has made in veterinary care have also paid off when it comes to rescuing stranded or sick marine animals, and SeaWorld's state-of-the-art breeding techniques could be useful in trying to preserve marine mammal pop-ulations on the brink of extinction, such as the vaquita porpoise in the Sea of Cortez. SeaWorld also nurtures multiple partnerships with leading conservation nonprofits, from the World Wildlife Fund to the Nature Conservancy. "Every year we spend $3 million to $4 million on research and conservation programs outside our park and another $1.5 million on rescuing stranded animals," Andrews says.

Head trainer Kelly Flaherty Clark still has faith in the benefits of SeaWorld's mission in the wake of Brancheau's death. One of her mantras, known around the park as "Kellyisms," is "Do the right thing." As we sit together in the stands of Shamu Stadium, "Believe" looks like pure family fun. But for the trainers, the shows are the product of countless hours of hard work and practice. They know there are risks. "These are not dogs," Flaherty Clark says. "Every day you walk into your job, you are walking into a potentially dangerous situation. You never forget that. You can't afford to forget that."

SeaWorld doesn't forget, and conducts safety and rescue training once a month. Among other things, trainers are taught to go limp if they are grabbed, so the whales will lose interest. The killer whales are taught to keep their mouths closed while swimming, and desensitized so they stay calm and circle the perimeter of the pool if someone accidentally falls in. They learn emergency recall signals—transmitted via a tone box and hand slaps—and are trained to swim to a pool exit gate if a net is dropped in. Scuba gear is always nearby. SeaWorld's intensive regime helped its trainers interact with killer whales more than two million times without a death. But when a killer whale breaks from its training, all bets are off.

It's hard to know exactly what triggers an incident. It could be boredom, a desire to play, the pent-up frustration of confinement, a rough night in the tank with the other orcas, the pain of an ulcer, or maybe even hormonal cycling. Whatever the motivation, some trainers believe that killer whales are acutely aware of what they're doing. "I've seen animals put trainers in their mouths and know exactly what the breaking point of a rib cage is. And how long to hold a trainer on the bottom," says Jeffrey Ventre, who was a trainer at SeaWorld Orlando from 1987 until 1995, when he was let go for giving a killer whale a birthday kiss, in which he stuck his head into an orca's mouth.

If you're a killer whale in a marine park, there's probably no better place than SeaWorld. Yet no matter how nice the facility, there's stress associated with being a big mammal in a relatively small pool. Starting at Sealand, Tilikum had developed the habit of grinding his teeth against metal pool gates. Many of his teeth were so worn and broken that SeaWorld vets decided to drill some of them so they could be regularly irrigated with antiseptic solution. And once again, he had to deal with the stress of hostile females, particularly a dominant orca called Katina. "Tili was a good guy that got beat down by the women," says Ventre, now a doctor in New Orleans. "So there are a lot of reasons he might be unhappy."

John Jett, who was a team leader for Tilikum, says he sometimes would suffer a beatdown bad enough to rake up his skin and bloody him and would have to be held out of shows until he healed. Jett had a term for the blood left streaming in the water: "skywriting." After a good thrashing from the other orcas, Jett says, Tilikum might be "off" for days, "splitting" from his trainer to swim at high speed around the pool, acting agitated around the females, or opening his eyes wide and emitting distress vocals if asked to get into a vulnerable position (like rolling over on his back). "It's extremely sad if you think about being in Tili's situation," says Jett. "The poor guy just has no place to run."

SeaWorld's Fred Jacobs denies that Tilikum was ever held out of shows due to injuries from other orcas. "Injuries as part of the expression of social dominance are rare and almost never serious," he says. "We manage Tilikum's social interaction on a daily basis."

In 1999, Tilikum reminded the world that, at least when it came to humans, he could be a very dangerous animal. Early on the morning of July 6, Michael Dougherty, a physical trainer at SeaWorld, arrived at his office near the underwater viewing area of G pool. He glanced through the viewing glass and saw Tilikum staring back, with what appeared to be two human feet hanging down his side. There was a nude body draped across Tilikum's back. It wasn't moving. As in the Brancheau incident, Tilikum was herded onto the medical lift in order for SeaWorld staff to retrieve the body. Rigor mortis had already set in. It was a young male, and again the coroner's and sheriff's reports are telling. He had puncture wounds and multiple abrasions on his face.

The victim was Daniel Dukes, a twenty-seven-year-old with a reddish-blond ponytail, a scraggly beard and mustache, and a big red "D" tattooed above his left nipple. Four days earlier, he'd been released from the Indian River County Jail after being booked for retail theft. On July 5, he apparently hid at SeaWorld past closing or sneaked in after hours. At some point during the night, he stripped down to his swim trunks, placed his clothes in a neat pile, and jumped into the pool. Perhaps he was simply crazy, or suicidal. Perhaps he believed in the myth of a friendly Shamu.

The coroner determined the cause of death to be drowning. There were no cameras or witnesses, so it's not known if Tilikum held him under or hypothermia did him in. But it's clear Tilikum worked Dukes over. The coroner found abrasions and contusions—both premortem and postmortem—all over his head and body, and puncture wounds on his left leg. His testicles had been ripped open. Divers had to go to the bottom of the pool to retrieve little pieces of his body. SeaWorld ramped up its security, posting a twenty-four-hour watch at Shamu Stadium. Keltie Byrne had not been an aberration.

~~~~~~

If anyone was going to take care around Tilikum, it was Dawn Brancheau. She was one of SeaWorld's best, and completely dedicated to the animals and her job. (She even met her husband, Scott, in the SeaWorld cafeteria.) She had worked at SeaWorld Orlando since 1994, spending two years working with otters and sea lions before graduating to work with the killer whales. She was fun and selfless, volunteering at a local animal shelter, and often keeping everything from stray ducks and chickens to rabbits and small birds at her home.

Over time, Brancheau had become one of SeaWorld's most trusted trainers, one of the dozen or so authorized to work with Tilikum. "Dawn showed prowess from the minute she set foot here. There's not one of us who wouldn't say that she was one of the best," says Flaherty Clark. Brancheau knew the risks and accepted them: "You can't put yourself in the water unless you trust them and they trust you," she once told a reporter.

Perhaps she trusted Tilikum too much. Thad Lacinak, the former VP of animal training at SeaWorld, thinks so. He says Brancheau was an exemplary trainer, one of the best he'd ever seen in the water. Still, Lacinak thinks Brancheau made a mistake lying down so close to Tilikum's mouth and letting her hair drift in the water alongside him. "She never should have put herself in that vulnerable a position," he says. "One of the things we always talked about at SeaWorld was you never want to get totally comfortable with any animal."

Former trainer Mark Simmons has been involved in deconstructing previous SeaWorld incidents between trainers and killer whales and was a friend of Brancheau's. He also thinks Brancheau's vulnerable position and hair (which he says she was growing long so she could give it to cancer patients for wigs) were the key factors that led to her being pulled into the pool. "Tilikum has never had an aggressive disposition," he says. "This was not the first time Dawn had laid down next to Tili in that position, but it was the first time her hair was that long and contacted Tili." Simmons believes Tilikum reacted to this "novel stimuli" by taking it in his mouth. When Brancheau tried to tug it free, as spotter Jan Topoleski described, Tilikum suddenly had a tempting game of tug-of-war, which he was bound to win. (After Brancheau's death, SeaWorld's long-standing policy that long hair be kept in a ponytail was revised to mandate that it be kept in a bun.)

At least two witnesses, however, told investigators they saw Tilikum grab Brancheau by the arm or shoulder, which would suggest a more-intentional act. Asked how certain he was that Tilikum pulled Brancheau in by her hair, SeaWorld's Fred Jacobs responds, "Witness accounts support that conclusion, and we have no reason to doubt it."

The second critical question is: Why did Tilikum get so violent once Brancheau was in the water? The coroner cataloged a fractured neck, a broken jaw, and a dislocated elbow and knee. A chunk of skin and hair was ripped from her scalp and recovered from a pool. "When a 12,000-pound animal gets its hands on 'the cookie jar' and responds with the excited burst of energy common in such situations, it can have tragic consequences," Simmons says. "Once the alarm was sounded and emergency net procedures were initiated, Tilikum's behavior became agitated. This is what appears to the untrained observer to [constitute] an 'attack.'"

Whether the emergency response increased Tilikum's agitation or not, once Brancheau was in the water, her fate was up to a killer whale that hadn't become accustomed to humans in the pool. "He got her down and that was it—she wasn't getting out," says former trainer Jonathan Smith. "I truly believe that they are smart enough to detect and know what they are doing. He's going to know she is trying to get to the surface." Former trainer Ventre agrees. "If they let you out, it's because they decide to," he says. "We don't know for sure what motivated Tilikum. But there's no doubt that he knew exactly what he was doing. He killed her."

SeaWorld says it is conducting the most exhaustive review in its history. At press time, the review was not complete, and OSHA's report is not expected until late summer. For the moment, SeaWorld is not taking any chances. No trainers are performing in the water with orcas, and all direct human contact with Tilikum has ceased. "We used to interact very closely with Tilikum, but now maintain a safe distance," Flaherty Clark wrote on the SeaWorld blog in March. Where Tilikum once got regular rubdowns and close contact during cleanings and other husbandry, now he's hosed down instead of hand-massaged, and his teeth are cleaned with an extension pole. His isolation has only increased, opening a wider debate about the future of killer whale entertainment.

After Brancheau's death, Jean-Michel Cousteau, president of the Ocean Futures Society, made a videotaped statement in which he said, "Maybe we as a species have outgrown the need to keep such wild, enormous, complex, intelligent, and free-ranging animals in captivity, where their behavior is not only unnatural; it can become pathological," he said. "Maybe we have learned all we can from keeping them captive."

Cousteau raises a profound point. But regardless of how this incident affects orca captivity, Tilikum's fate is likely sealed, despite calls for his release back into the wild. *Free Willy*'s Keiko underwent extensive retraining before being released into the seas off Iceland, and appears to have foraged for food on his own. But he never reintegrated with a pod. A little over a year later, after swimming to Norway, he died, likely from pneumonia. Ken Balcomb still believes that most marine-park orcas can be taught what they need to know to be returned to the wild. (No real effort was made to find Keiko's family, Balcomb says, which is a key to success.) But even he rules Tilikum out. "Tilikum is basically psychotic," he told me as we looked out over Haro Strait in May. "He has been maintained in a situation where I think he is psychologically unrecoverable in terms of being a wild whale."

There is one other option. "We have proposed to Blackstone Group a sea-pen retirement," says Naomi Rose, a marine-mammal scientist at the Humane Society International. "Tilikum needs more space, more stimulation to distract him. Living as he is, with minimum human contact in a small concrete tank, is untenable."

SeaWorld's Fred Jacobs dismisses the idea. In addition to citing worries about the impact of taking him out of the social environment he is now accustomed to, and potential threats to his health from pollution and disease, Jacobs says, "All the animals at SeaWorld allow people a really rare privilege to come into contact with these extraordinary animals and learn something about them, and maybe when they leave SeaWorld, carry that respect forward into their lives. Tilikum is a really important part of that."

Whether or not Tilikum ever performs again, he's still SeaWorld's most prolific breeder. He's sired thirteen viable calves, with two more on the way this summer. Most likely, he will finish his life as he's mostly lived it, in a marine park.

He's nearly thirty, and only one male in captivity, who is still alive, is known to have lived past that age.

Three thousand miles away, Balcomb often sees a pod of killer whales easing their way through the wilderness of water that is his Haro Strait backyard. They swim with purpose and coordination, huffing spumes of mist into the salty, spruce-scented air. The group is known as L Pod, and one, a big male designated L78, was born just a few years after Tilikum. Balcomb has been tracking L78 for more than two decades. He knows that his mother—born around 1960—and his brother are always close by. He knows that L78 ranges as far south as California with his pod, in search of salmon.

L78's dorsal fin stands proud and straight as a knife, with none of Tilikum's marine-park flop. He hunts when he's hungry, mates with the females who offer themselves, and whistles to the extended family that is always nearby. He cares nothing for humans and is all but oblivious to their presence when they paddle out in kayaks to marvel as he swims. He knows nothing of the life of Tilikum or the artificial world humans have manufactured for him. But Tilikum, before twenty-six years in marine parks, once knew L78's life, once knew what it was like to swim the ocean alongside his mother and family. And perhaps, just perhaps, that also helps explain why Dawn Brancheau died.

CONSUMED

GRAYSON SCHAFFER

~~~~~~

At just thirty-two, South African Hendrik Coetzee was already a legend in the world of expedition kayaking. But in 2007, he decided to call it a career after a decade of first descents on the wildest rivers in Africa—and he wanted to go out with a last hurrah: an ambitious exploration of the Congo and its tributaries. The river's most feared predator had a different ending in store.

~~~~~~

The lone African explorer drags his kayak ashore and begins to collect firewood from around the little beach on the left bank of the White Nile. It's April 10, 2007, and the day's descent of some of the continent's most powerful rapids has worn him to exhaustion. But he can't sleep. Not without fire. He's also careful not to stray beyond the jungle's green curtain—this is Uganda's Murchison Falls National Park, after all, home to the world's densest populations of hippopotamus and Nile crocodile, one an extremely territorial 4,500-pound vegetarian with six-inch dagger tusks, and the other, a voracious 12-foot-long opportunist.

The explorer is Johannes Hendrik Coetzee, thirty-two years old, 5-foot-11, with a thick build and a receding hairline shaved to skin. He's a former South African Defence Force medic and a giant in the world of whitewater exploration, having organized and led a historic source-to-sea descent of the Nile in 2004. Though he's charismatic and charming, the kind of guy who changes the gravity in any room he enters, he now prefers to travel alone. Four elite teams have descended Murchison's two-day section of Class V water before now, and Coetzee was on three of them. But nobody had ever tried it solo before this trip.

Now he sparks his fire in the quickening equatorial dusk, a lonely prick of light in a nearly 1,500-square-mile "chunk of untamed African savanna bisected by the mighty river Nile," as the park's literature proclaims. Below him, the river drops ferociously over a roughly 30-mile stretch before abruptly reaching the unrunnable 140-foot Murchison Falls itself, at the edge of the Rift Valley escarpment. The only humans this deep in the park are the rebels of the Lord's Resistance Army, which controls the right bank of the river and has, since 1987, been attempting to replace the Ugandan government with a strict Christian theocracy.

Hendri, as he's called, is an obsessive chronicler of his adventures. He takes mental notes that he'll later type into his laptop journal.

Across the river, a big storm that's filling the sky is approaching. It's still far off, and I sit and watch the lightning until it reaches me.

Barefoot as always, he feels vulnerable, but not afraid.

I ask myself, Are you ready to die? I give it some serious thought. I believe I am. I look back on my life, and I feel satisfied.

He slides inside his bivy bag and falls asleep.

During the night I am aware of the rain at times, of water inside the bivy. I'm a sitting snack for anything that likes meat, but I never fully wake until I feel the approach of dawn.

Coetzee unzips his bag, packs his boat, and slips back into the barreling 20-foot standing waves and terminal ledge holes. His Fluid-brand creekboat is 7 feet, 3 inches of plastic sealed with a neoprene skirt that locks over the cockpit rim and snugs around his rib cage. Coetzee balances through the tumult of 80-degree water in part with forward momentum, like a skier, but mostly by heaving his 195-pound frame, forehead tucked behind his leading elbow, into wall after wall of unrelenting chaos.

Then calm—but not safety. The eddies and banks are as dangerous as the rapids.

The river is so narrow that I have to worry about the flat dogs on both banks.

The "flat dogs" are the crocodiles. Statistically, hippos may be the most dangerous animals in Africa, known to bite a man in half as the penalty for trespassing. But they can be summoned to the surface with a loud slap of the paddle and then avoided. Crocodiles are stealthy and indiscriminate, charging fearlessly at anything resembling a meal with only their eyes above the water. On Coetzee's 2004 Nile expedition, one launched itself out of the water at a crew member sitting on board a raft before the team hammered it back with paddle blows.

And so it is this time.

I felt it before I saw it. A croc had managed to sneak within 50 feet of me. It was already time for plan B: throw a decoy. I had kept my helmet on my deck for just such an emergency, hoping that I wouldn't have to test this flimsy theory. Mid-stroke I lob the helmet. A few seconds later I look back; the croc is still coming hard, but at least it's a race. From my experience it seems that crocs have a short sprint speed. It gave up the chase shortly thereafter and swam toward my helmet.

Two hours later, Coetzee reaches the pool above the massive falls. He dodges a pod of hippos and climbs up the left bank to safety. His best friend and mentor, Peter Meredith, is there waiting for him high on a hill overlooking the river.

Coetzee is glad to be done, but he'll later write that he felt no relief. In the larger sense, he hoped that this audacious solo would cure him of his obsession with huge risks. But even as he peels off his gear, the itch is returning. Coming down off his "missions," as he calls them, Coetzee's restlessness and uncertainty have begun veering into depression. "For me it's not so much the bad times as the in-between times that are hard to stomach," he would later write to a friend, "when my life seems like a compromise not worth making."

He'll be back on the water again soon.

~~~~~~

The British colonial towns of Victoria Falls, Zimbabwe (population 36,000), and Livingstone, Zambia (population 110,000), straddle the Zambezi River, where it plunges some 350 feet over Victoria Falls and makes two nearly 180-degree cutbacks through a legendary Class V gorge. In the 1990s, the two cities formed a transnational tourism hub that rivaled adrenaline hot spots like Interlaken, Switzerland, and Queenstown, New Zealand. The gorge featured outfitters for bungee jumping, heli-tours, skydiving, and, most prominently, the world's most coveted stretch of guided whitewater. South African Peter Meredith had just started as the rafting manager for Safari Par Excellence in 1997 when twenty-one-year-old Hendri Coetzee, fresh out of a year in the army, arrived looking for adventure.

"A friend came to me and said, 'I've just met this awesome guy. You should come meet him,'" says Meredith, now forty-two, and on an extended spiritual quest in India. "Let's grab him, and we'll do a sundowner on top of the gorge," the friend said.

Coetzee, who'd landed a job as operations manager at a helicopter sightseeing outfit shortly after arriving on the Zambezi, projected an infectious energy. He listened carefully and spoke clearly, fully engaging Meredith, who'd also served in the military. "There was an intensity about him," says Meredith. "Confidence shone in his eyes, and he had an easy and intelligent sense of humor." Coetzee, like Meredith, played chess and sought out pop philosophy books like Robert Pirsig's *Zen and the Art of Motorcycle Maintenance* and the eccentric novels of Tom Robbins. "In a half-hour I'd offered him a job," says Meredith, "despite the fact that he'd never been on a river in his life. It was unheard of. Generally, you'd never hire someone for a Grade V river until he had at least five years' guiding experience." Meredith's boss took a bit of convincing but ultimately relented. A month later, Coetzee was calling strokes for clients on one of the world's most difficult commercial rafting runs. It was like walking into Everest Base Camp having never worn crampons and suddenly guiding people to the summit.

He was also learning to kayak. "We taught him to roll in a swimming pool and then put him in the river," says Meredith. Another South African, Steve Fisher, thirty-eight, a top pro, recalls Coetzee as an extraordinarily aggressive novice. He'd found the thing he was truly good at—and he attacked it. Whitewater kayaking at an elite level requires extreme athleticism and an ability to keep both fear and risk in check. Early on, it was only this last skill that seemed to elude Coetzee.

"He was a bit too eager," says Meredith. "He was really talented, but I had to hold him back." On one commercial trip, while the rest of the guides and clients portaged the rafts along the bank of a Class VI rapid called Number 9, Coetzee, without telling anyone, ran it in his kayak. "He barely made it through and thought he was the bee's knees," says Meredith. "He had more balls than brains at that stage. I told him that if he did it again, he was going to get fired."

According to Coetzee's mother, Marie Nieman, her son had always been both fearless and attention-hungry. Coetzee was born in 1975 in the small town of Ottosdal, in South Africa's North West province, two years after his sister, Charlene. In seventh grade, underdeveloped for a twelve-year-old and suffering from a rash, he pinned a photo of himself to the school notice board along with a note: LOOKING FOR GIRLS—ANY GIRLS—BETWEEN THE AGES OF 10 AND 14. "He had all this stuff all over his face," says Nieman. "It was just a terrible photo."

Coetzee's father, Henk, was a major and an intelligence officer in the South African Special Forces, stationed along what's now the Namibian border with Angola. During the South African Border War, the family lived in the town of Oshakati, where they came under artillery fire from Soviet-backed Angolan forces on at least one occasion. In the manuscript of his unpublished memoir, Coetzee recalled the strange thrill of the bombardments.

When the explosions began I would crawl . . . under the bed, as instructed. My young ears delighted by the adventure of it all. This way I got to fight in the war just like my dad.

In 1986, Henk moved the family to Pretoria in time for Coetzee to start high school, which he found boring except for drama classes and theater productions. Shortly after he graduated, in 1993, Coetzee's parents divorced, partly because of the emotional toll of Henk's military service. "The war definitely changed [Henk]," says Charlene. "He'd seen things that nobody should see."

Nieman remarried about a year later, adding to the immediate family two stepbrothers and a stepsister, all close to Coetzee's age. Coetzee took off, spending a year on a kibbutz in Israel, then came back and ripped around on his motorcycle for a while before Henk helped him land a job with a tourist outfitter deep in the Namibian desert that took clients into the villages of primitive tribes. Henk made the long drive to the desert with his son in the fall of 1995, and, when Coetzee returned, encouraged him to join the military. Later, father and son drifted apart, though they never lost touch, and Coetzee would come to think of the Namibian experience as the beginning of his manhood.

Coetzee established himself on the Zambezi in 1997 and 1998, and during his time off used the cachet of his experience on the river to land jobs as a raft guide and safety kayaker in whitewater meccas like Norway and West Virginia. "He was simply not interested in making lots of money," says Celliers Kruger, the owner of South Africa's Fluid Kayaks, one of Coetzee's two sponsors. "He didn't even take all of the free boats he was allowed according to his agreement with me. He owned very little apart from books and a laptop."

In late 1999, after hearing stories of an epic stretch of whitewater on the upper reaches of the Nile that was bigger than anything anybody was kayaking at the time, Coetzee made his way to Jinja, Uganda (population 87,000), at the outlet of Lake Victoria. There, the Nile slides over a series of channelized cataracts that produce some of the world's biggest warm-water rapids.

A couple of rafting outfits had set up shop in Jinja, and Coetzee called Peter Meredith, who was still on the Zambezi. "He said, 'We need to guide in Uganda,'" says Meredith, who showed up two weeks later.

Coetzee and Meredith spent two years working for a company called Adrift. Along with other well-known South African paddlers, like Steve Fisher, who arrived in 2002, and Dale Jardine, they gave the area a reputation as kayaking's North Shore—the ultimate proving ground for both freestyle paddlers, who were developing new aerial maneuvers on the Nile's outsize standing waves, and river runners, who charged into roiling Class V drops. Coetzee claimed first descents on some of the more-difficult rapids, including one called Dead Dutchman, and a forbidding series of recirculating ledges on the right side of Itanda Falls. "I still don't run the right side of Itanda," says Fisher. When top American pros like Rush Sturges, Tyler Bradt, and Brad Ludden came to town, it was often Coetzee who showed them the ropes.

The Nile high season ran from May to August, and when it was over Coetzee would pick up and head to the next swelling river, or just go on walkabout. During one break, around 2001, he stole away to Mombasa, Kenya, and began a solo trek south along the empty coast, carrying a small backpack, intending to walk 1,500 miles home to South Africa.

About two weeks into the journey, he stumbled upon a remote coastal lodge in what is now Tanzania's Saadani National Park. Among the guests was Jonathan Yevin, a magazine writer and a popularizer of luggageless travel. "This dude just wandered off the beach," Yevin recalls. By then, Coetzee had walked 200 miles. Yevin invited him to dinner with the lodge's owner, Costa Coucoulis, who couldn't believe that Coetzee had simply appeared out of the wilderness. "We sat at the staff table, and Costa opened this special bottle of wine," says Yevin, who would correspond with the explorer for years. The next morning, Coetzee walked back into the bush.

The Rock Garden is a sprawling strobe-and-gel-lit outdoor nightclub attached to the posh Speke Hotel, on Nile Avenue, in the center of the Ugandan capital of Kampala. It's the sort of place where locals and expats sweat into the early morning, dancing to American music from the eighties. Coetzee and his Jinja paddling friends frequently made the hour-long drive to Kampala to let loose. It was on one of these excursions, in late 2002, that Coetzee first met Juliana Buhring. At the time, the encounter must have looked like just another hookup to Coetzee's friends, but it was the beginning of a surreal courtship between two people on a similar search for meaning.

As Coetzee would later describe it in detail, Buhring, a striking then-twenty-one-year-old German national living in Kampala, was standing with her back to the Rock Garden's VIP bar. Coetzee, who'd taken ecstasy that night, lingered at the edge of the shadows, nursing a Red Bull and vodka. Their eyes met and Coetzee held her gaze. They walked toward each other until their faces were only inches apart.

"You can't keep your eyes off me," said Buhring.

"And you are just dying to kiss me," Coetzee replied. She took his hand and led him into one of the dark corners of the club.

"We were like two magnets," Buhring says. At last call, rather than ruin "the perfection of the moment" by asking for each other's phone numbers, they simply parted ways.

They crossed paths again, by chance, at a New Year's Eve house party in Kampala that same year. "He walked straight up to me and kissed me," says Buhring. "We had sex in the carport."

After that, they saw each other from time to time, and Coetzee took Buhring on a commercial raft trip down the Nile. "We were always like two wanderers, and whenever we passed it was like no words were ever spoken and we were together in that moment," says Buhring. "It was only later that we actually started to talk about why that was."

Meanwhile, Buhring was keeping a secret, leading what she describes as a double life. She'd been born into the notorious Children of God cult and endured a torturous upbringing, forced into sex acts with the group's elders and with other children, and sent into the streets to beg for money. Buhring, who traveled through thirty-five countries while with the group, says she "was just in the process of leaving the cult" when she met Coetzee. Later, in 2007, Buhring and two of her sisters, Celeste and Kristina Jones, recounted the abuse they'd suffered in their best-selling memoir, *Not Without My Sister*. "I've always managed to separate my life in the cult and my life outside it," says Buhring. "I was never a believer."

She and Coetzee kept up their itinerant romance until 2004, when Buhring finally broke away from the Children of God. After that they lost touch, and in 2006 Buhring left Kampala for good. But while they were apart, Buhring maintains, "We knew what each other was thinking, even across time and space."

In early 2004, Coetzee set off on the most prominent expedition of his career, a four-and-a-half-month source-to-sea rafting trip down the Nile with Peter Meredith. The adventure was the first in a string of increasingly bold projects that would define the rest of his life.

Coetzee and Meredith had spent the better part of the previous year organizing the trip and convincing the Sudanese government, as well as its enemy, the Sudanese People's Liberation Army, that allowing paddlers to cross through a war zone would be an act of peace.

Meredith and Coetzee met up with four other expedition members on Lake Victoria and set off onto the outflowing White Nile. The most challenging aspect of the journey turned out to be internal politics. The team included a cameraman; a doctor; a South African oarsman and mechanic named Frazer "Bingo" Small, who co-owned Jinja-based outfitter Nile River Explorers; and Kiwi expat Natalie McComb, an overland tourist-truck driver and logistics whiz whom Coetzee knew from Jinja. Coetzee and Small were almost immediately at war with each other.

"Hendri was the most experienced on the water but maybe needed more experience organizing people," says Small.

"Hendri was the youngest," adds McComb, "but he was insistent on being the leader, to such a degree that he was not taking advice from his elders."

Though Coetzee came across as brash to his teammates, he was aware that he was a big part of the problem, and later reflected on his shortcomings in his journal.

> My untested idea of leadership consisted of letting the team decide, until I thought they were wrong. If their being wrong threatened, in my opinion, the safety or objectives of the expedition, I then overruled them. I figured that as leader they would then follow me. Turns out I knew little about leadership and even less about my group.

When the rafts reached Sudan, Small "bailed," according to Meredith. Small now downplays the conflict and says he had plans to meet his family in Cairo. Either way, tensions eased and the friendships mended.

~~~~~~

Despite the arrangements with the government and SPLA leaders, who were observing a cease-fire at the time, the expedition suffered a close call with a government gunboat in the flatwater of Sudan. To limit their time in the area and avoid detection, the team floated twenty-four hours a day and didn't use any lights at night. The gunboat, which could have easily mistaken them for rebels, happened upon them in the dark.

"We tried to be quiet and hoped they wouldn't notice us," says Meredith, who didn't know whose side the boat was on. "But they did. We heard rifles cocking in pitch dark. We could see them, because they had lights, but they couldn't tell who we were." The soldiers never attacked.

In the end, only Meredith and Coetzee completed all 4,130 miles from Lake Victoria to the Mediterranean. (McComb was with them at the end, but she'd skipped the Murchison Falls section.) They finished a few weeks after a less-ambitious but better-publicized source-to-sea expedition down the 3,200-mile Blue Nile, led by American Pasquale Scaturro, and were largely ignored by the media. The little coverage they did receive focused on the controversy caused by Coetzee's billing of the trip as the "first-ever source-to-sea Nile expedition." The claim was quickly contested by supporters of American John Goddard, who in 1951, along with two Frenchmen, had traced the course of the river using cloth-shelled folding kayaks. Goddard, now in his mid-eighties and living in Los Angeles, had published a story about the adventure in the May 1955 issue of *National Geographic*, which Coetzee discounted due to Goddard's 125-mile portage along the Murchison Falls area.

"We were forbidden by the Ugandan authorities," says Goddard, citing the kind of bureaucratic block that remains a major obstacle to explorers in Africa. "Their bottom line was: We don't have the resources to look for your bodies." During the trip, he shot a 13.5-foot crocodile with a borrowed gun. In one of the *National Geographic* photos, Goddard is wearing the reptile's severed head like a helmet, his smiling face, tongue stuck out, encircled by the jaws.

Coetzee eventually recognized the audacity of Goddard's journey and came to see him as a kindred spirit from another generation. He reached out over e-mail to set the record straight. "I have given the Nile issue a lot of thought over the years and have concluded that I was wrong," he wrote Goddard in 2009. "If someone comes along and does the few rapids I missed, will it then make him the first? You deserve the title of first descent." Like so many other people Coetzee met through circumstance, Goddard became a friend and stayed in touch.

Coetzee's Nile conquest, which was featured in a 2005 *National Geographic* documentary film called *The Longest River*, was the kind of résumé piece that could have made him into a river-running celebrity who gets paid to travel the world. But the infighting and first-descent controversy had soured him on big-time expeditions. Rather than step into the spotlight, he shrank from it.

~~~~~~

Coetzee's next adventure was a turn inward. While continuing to live in Jinja, he completed a degree in psychology through a distance-learning program at the University of South Africa in 2007, and began considering a PhD thesis that would explore the link between the euphoric states he was experiencing on the river and similar feelings described by the devout.

"It is now clear to me that these peak experiences are gateways to something bigger and more powerful," he wrote to one professor, "though I hesitate to use the word God."

"Hendri and I were always looking for answers," says Meredith, "which was probably one of the things that helped forge our bond. His adventures became a tool for exploring himself as much as the rivers."

It was during this period of reflection that Coetzee started running the more-dangerous rapids around Jinja alone, often at dusk. Other paddlers wondered whether he had a death wish. After his solo Murchison Falls run in 2007, Coetzee's mother had repeatedly encouraged him to settle down. Instead he set his sights on an unprecedented solo descent of the Congo and its tributaries, calling on John Goddard, who'd paddled the river shortly after descending the Nile, for advice.

Beginning in the spring of 2009, with little more than his kayaking gear and a change of clothes, Coetzee spent five months paddling an enormous section of the Congo, the world's second-largest river by volume. The trip, which he funded himself for $4,000, was everything he'd hoped for—"the mission of my life," he later wrote—but it began in frustration as he waited for his shipped kayak for six weeks in Kisangani, the third-largest city in the Democratic Republic of the Congo (DRC), some 1,300 miles up the river. As always, it was this "in-between time" that caused him the most anxiety. He would later describe his feeling to friends in an e-mail: "The amount of self-doubt, loneliness, hopelessness I felt sitting around day after day in a hotel room watching my money float away. The only thing that saved me was writing."

When he finally got on the water, he was exalted by both the rapids and the wilderness. "Nights were spent on sandy beaches with a campfire surrounded by jungle, water, and sky," he wrote. "The Congo has the worst reputation in Africa, but I think that's unjustified. It's the heart of Africa, but it's not the heart of darkness."

Coetzee was told by locals that the long stretch of flatwater down to Kinshasa was inhabited by the Ngombe tribe, alleged cannibals who had reportedly killed and eaten two Belgian canoeists in 1989. To avoid the danger, he boarded a commercial commodities barge for the three-week voyage downstream. Each night, when the barge tied up along the bank, Coetzee would slide his kayak into the river and paddle in the darkness to maintain his fitness.

After a few nights without trouble, he was floating about 400 yards upstream from the barge when he heard a piercing scream. It was a war cry. In the moonlight he saw six dugout canoes, each roughly 20 feet long and powered by four standing Ngombe tribesmen holding long wooden blades like stand-up paddleboarders. He recounted the incident in his memoir:

> *Screaming angrily they charge at an angle that will cut me off from the barge. In perfect unison the men bend double, throwing their body weight onto long thick paddles. The distance between us is closing fast.*

Coetzee realized he couldn't outpaddle the canoes, so he charged them like a running back, breaking their line. The paddlers simply spun about on their boats and began chasing him down as he raced back to the barge. Coetzee screamed for help from the passengers on the barge's deck, who'd just finished their evening church service. As the dugouts closed in, the men closest to him swung their long blades within inches of his head. Several blows thudded heavily against his stern. Soon the canoes overtook Coetzee, and a tribesman lassoed him from 6 feet away with a nylon rope. He was caught.

"*Kimya, kimya!*" he yelled, using the Swahili word for "calm." The men stopped swinging at him but tied another length of rope to the rear grab loop on his kayak and began towing him upstream.

"Sir, I have friends on the boat. I want to go back to them!" Coetzee shouted, this time in English. When one turned and yelled something at him, Coetzee rubbed his thumb and first two fingers together, making the universal sign for money.

The canoes stopped. One man stood over him, bending down, screaming unintelligibly, spittle flying, while a pregnant woman in another boat egged the man on. The hesitation was enough, though. In the distance, perhaps 300 yards away, shouts came from the barge as it steamed toward them, spotlights blazing.

When the barge arrived, a boy on board reached over and attempted to untie Coetzee's bonds before being slapped away by a warrior. Finally, the two sides reached an agreement. Coetzee was untied, and barge passengers pulled him aboard, kayak and all.

Coetzee later asked what the tribesmen had been demanding. A passenger told him, "They were saying, 'This is our white guy.' They were going to eat you." For the remaining two weeks of the barge trip, Coetzee stayed on board.

And yet somehow Coetzee still hadn't faced the most daunting part of his expedition. Unlike most rivers, which go flat near the sea, beyond Kinshasa the Congo drops more than 900 feet in its last 300 miles. Livingstone Falls and the Lower Congo Rapids produce 20-foot-wide whirlpools and exploding boils. The water is unnavigable in a large vessel, but a kayaker can bounce through.

Before setting off on this final stretch, Coetzee wrote a letter to his mother and left it with American scientists working in Kinshasa, with instructions for it to be mailed if he disappeared. Then he pushed off into a series of rapids hundreds of times more powerful than the biggest sections of the Colorado River through the Grand Canyon.

Coetzee came off the Congo drained and lonely. Instead of filling him with insight, the epic trip had left him empty. In September 2009, as if she knew what he was feeling, Buhring sent him a Facebook friend request from England after being out of contact for five years.

"We started up exactly where we left off," she says. Their long-distance connection quickly grew intense. Through e-mails, texts, and Skype video chats, they found common ground in existential dilemmas and a passion for literature. In one note, Buhring compared Coetzee to the warrior figure in Brazilian novelist Paulo Coelho's *The Fifth Mountain*, who "suffers at indifference and becomes desperate with loneliness. After all this has passed, he licks his wounds and begins everything anew." Coetzee shared passages from Nietzsche and the Holocaust survivor Viktor Frankl, who believed in finding meaning through extreme suffering. "Hendri always thought there was nobody else like him," says Buhring, "but we were the same."

Coetzee was staggered to learn of Buhring's past through her book, and he asked her for advice on a memoir he'd begun writing. She picked at his armor, forcing him to explain his increasingly dark thoughts. "I would be lying if I said I have never thought of suicide," he responded. "I do not fear death. I don't think I will ever take my life in any conventional way. . . . [G]oing on an expedition never to come back is, however, another matter." He also explained the paradox of the hyper-social solo paddler. "I am always alone," he wrote. "Even in crowds of people I consider friends, I watch myself and them like a spectator. . . . Almost everybody bores me."

Within three months of reconnecting, though they still hadn't seen each other again in person, Buhring and Coetzee began to imagine a future together. Coetzee told her about Peter Meredith's transformation after meeting a woman he truly loved. "What they have is the real deal," he wrote. "It gives me hope, that happy endings are possible."

"Hendri didn't believe in marriage," says Buhring. "Neither of us do. But he wanted a companion to grow old with. He had this fantasy of being seventy, lounging around reading the paper and me playing with his toes." Still, despite making almost daily contact with Buhring throughout the spring of 2010, Coetzee never told anyone about his feelings for her. More seriously than ever before, he contemplated retiring from exploration and launching an adventure inner-tube tour company in Jinja.

That July, he received an e-mail from American kayaker Ben Stookesberry with the subject line "Congo 2." Stookesberry, a thirty-two-year-old Californian, and Chris Korbulic, twenty-four, of Gold Hill, Oregon, two of the world's most talented expedition paddlers, were quietly planning to run the tributaries of the upper Congo River that Coetzee had skipped the previous year. There was only one person qualified to lead them. "He had the keys to the Congo," says Stookesberry. "I approached him with a great deal of respect."

Coetzee didn't take the bait at first, writing back, "My focus has shifted a bit in the last year. I don't have any plans for epics, but I would be happy to help you with advice or contacts."

Coetzee quickly suggested a detailed itinerary. They'd start out in Uganda, warming up on the same section of the White Nile through Murchison Falls National Park that Coetzee had paddled solo in 2007. The rest of the plan included the Ruzizi River, which forms the boundary between the DRC, on the west, and Rwanda, on the east, with a string of Class V rapids that would be popular with expert paddlers were it not the front line of a smoldering war. After that, they'd take a water-taxi ride across Lake Tanganyika, home of Gustave, the 20-foot male Nile crocodile that has achieved mythic status as the killer of some three hundred people, and put in on the outflowing Lukuga River.

But as Coetzee pored over the trip's details for several days, he found himself organizing an expedition he didn't want to miss. Suddenly he was offering his service as a paid guide. "I would love to paddle with you as much as this role affords me, and 'guiding' when needed," he wrote to Stookesberry.

A few weeks later, Coetzee wrote to Buhring about his plans. "He made it clear that this was going to be the last expedition," she says. In October, Coetzee purchased a piece of property on the Nile. Soon after, Buhring bought an open-ended ticket to Uganda for New Year's Eve, though she never really believed Coetzee was done with his adventures. "It's like he knew his time was short and he had to fit one more in."

~~~~~~

To be a kayaker in Africa is to be constantly warned that the rivers are too dangerous—too many lethal rapids, too many angry hippos, too many hungry crocodiles.

Like John Goddard and others before them, Coetzee, Stookesberry, and Korbulic had simply come to terms with the risks.

The new team did, however, have one serious misunderstanding of the small rivers that feed the upper Congo. The general rule in Africa is that alpha predators are still no match for men with guns, meaning that crocodiles and other monsters are at their most menacing in protected areas, where they can't be shot. For this reason, the team took particular care in Murchison Falls National Park, which is notorious for its aggressive animals. But on the Lukuga River, which is sporadically settled, "wildlife was never really one of our primary concerns," says Stookesberry.

What the team didn't realize was that years of bloody skirmishes in the region had likely boosted the Lukuga's crocodile population. Many of the bodies of the estimated 5.4 million killed during fifteen years of fighting have been dumped into rivers, where the reptiles developed a taste for human flesh and grew to enormous sizes relative to the waterways.

The expedition, which was sponsored by outdoor-clothing maker Eddie Bauer and covered regularly by this magazine's website, was to last two months, from the end of October through Christmas. The team had contacted the nonprofit International Rescue Committee (IRC), which helps refugees rebuild in war-torn countries, for help with logistics. In return, they'd report back on the status of remote villages. Whether or not the paddlers had official permission from the Congolese government to run some of the rivers remains a bit fuzzy.

They began the trip in late October. After two weeks on the White Nile and a week exploring the Rwenzori Mountains, they crossed overland by minivan into the DRC at Goma, bribing the border guards with an extra $850 to accept the visas they'd already paid $550 for at the Congolese embassy back in Uganda. Their access point into the Ruzizi was at a hydroelectric dam just below the city of Bukavu. The Rwandan soldier who stopped them as they drove up to the dam briefly considered the colorful kayaks strapped to the roof and their outlandish request—to run rapids that must have looked to him like certain death—and turned them away. They appealed to a number of government officials without success. Still, in a posting on the blog he'd created for the trip, Coetzee seemed undeterred. River exploration in central Africa was always going to involve some bending of protocol, and the line was looking as blurry as ever:

> With a new dam proposed and the area likely to remain on a political knife's edge, we realized that this might be the last chance anyone gets. That, and we really, really wanted to. . . . Desire overtook common sense again.

They scouted the lower gorges on rented motorbikes and made a plan to evade the guard at the dam and slip into the rapids. As they locked their spray decks into place and pushed off from the bank, they noticed people at the power station watching them. Coetzee filed another post reflecting on the moment.

> *I was surprised at how easily we decided to run the first drop and then see what happened. . . . My mind was spinning with the decision, the repercussions, and the consequences, but strangely, inside it felt right.*
> *So we went.*

After completing the Ruzizi without incident, the paddlers spent the night of December 5 at an IRC guesthouse in Kalemie before putting in on the Lukuga. They drank Tanzanian *waragi*—local moonshine—and Coetzee smoked cigarettes while he regaled the two Americans with some of his father's hairier stories from the war in Angola.

"He revered his father," says Stookesberry. "He told us the adventures that we were getting into, and even what he had gotten into in southern Sudan, were nothing compared to what his father had faced."

Stookesberry and Korbulic went to bed, but Coetzee stayed up. In Italy, Juliana Buhring "had a weird feeling" and logged into Skype, even though Coetzee had told her he'd be completely out of contact. "He was there waiting for me," says Buhring.

In an hour-long text chat, they typed out their plans to reconnect on New Year's Eve in Uganda, where Coetzee would pick Buhring up at the airport in Kampala.

Hendri: The energy between us is going to be something to behold . . .

Juliana: Hell, I can feel you halfway across the world . . .

Hendri: If ever there was incentive to survive a mission.

Juliana: Please come back in one piece. I need all of you . . .

Hendri: And you shall have it . . .

Juliana: Safe journey, my river god.

Late on the first day on the Lukuga, Korbulic spotted a 12-foot croc on the bank—bigger than anything they'd seen thus far on the trip. Coetzee quickly grouped the team together and laid out the protocol. They'd have to stay tight and pay attention to the banks. If anybody saw a croc, they'd accelerate as a group and try to outrun it before it got too close.

That night, the team stayed downriver of the village of Niemba, where they'd asked locals how the IRC could help them. Clean water and education were the first answers, but then, says Stookesberry, "a small fellow looked us straight in the eye and said that they still had a major problem, and that's crocodiles." Over the past twenty years, 125 people had been taken from the area.

It took the team two more days to complete the rapids.

On the clear, sunny afternoon of December 7, the river reached a hard 90-degree left-hand turn they'd seen on Google Earth. Stookesberry lagged behind after that last rapid, and then noticed Coetzee signaling him forward. Korbulic had just seen three or four small crocs—"3-foot little guys"—slip into the water, so they grouped up and paddled hard. Stookesberry was leading on the left, Coetzee in the middle and slightly behind, and Korbulic on the right. "We were so close that Chris had to pay attention to Hendri in order to avoid clinking paddles," says Stookesberry.

They were about 250 yards farther on, in a channel less than 200 feet wide, when Korbulic caught a flash of motion in his peripheral vision, off the left side of Coetzee's stern and directly behind Stookesberry. He turned and saw a gaping pair of jaws arcing cleanly out of the water and toward Coetzee's body.

"Hendri yelled, 'Oh my God!'" recalls Stookesberry. "I thought it was a joke. It was the intonation—it wasn't a scream; it wasn't desperate; it was this weird statement of fact, of reality. I turned and saw this massive fucking crocodile—bigger than anything we'd seen—and I didn't understand how something that big could have come out of that river without us having any inkling."

The croc locked onto Coetzee's left shoulder and pulled him under. "The kayak was all turmoil," says Stookesberry. "It was impossible to tell what was happening below. Chris was about two feet away, and I was about four feet back. Before we could even react, the kayak almost completely submerged. When it came back up, it rocked slightly to reveal an empty cockpit. "It didn't seem real," says Korbulic. "We paddled for our lives."

Unlike the surface-swimming crocs that the paddlers were accustomed to, this one had attacked from the depths, rising silently like a trout, then striking specifically at the human form. The entire episode lasted ten seconds, and they never caught another glimpse of either Coetzee or the croc, which, based on the approximate length of its head, was at least 15 feet long. A croc of that size, some

2,000 pounds, would have taken Coetzee to the bottom of the river, life jacket and all, and rolled him there until he drowned. He'd likely have lost consciousness in the first few seconds as the beast clamped down on his chest and neck with 5,000 pounds of pressure per square inch.

"Once we saw the croc, it was . . ." Here Stookesberry nearly breaks down in the retelling. "God, I lost all hope in that instant."

The two paddlers raced downstream for a mile, into the village of Kabeya Maji, where the locals initially ran from the frantic white men who'd suddenly appeared out of the river in helmets and thick vests. Stookesberry and Korbulic begged desperately for a motorboat to take them back upstream to look for Coetzee. They explained—using broken French, their arms extended in the universal sign for crocodile jaws—that their friend had been taken. But Kabeya Maji has no boats. The locals had given up on water travel after seven of them had been snatched overboard by crocodiles since 2006.

Twenty minutes later, with the entire village of several hundred people amassed on a bridge over the Lukuga, Coetzee's boat and paddle floated into view. His water bottles and kit were still neatly tucked into the center beam, and neither the boat nor the paddle showed any marks. It was as though he had been plucked from it by the hand of God.

~~~~~~

In Italy, less than twenty-four hours later, Buhring logged on to Facebook and noticed something about Coetzee in her news feed—"some kind of tribute." She checked his blog, and condolences had been posted as comments on the page. "I asked one of his friends, 'What the fuck happened to Hendri?'" she recalls. The friend sent her a link to a news report. "Then I went to pieces. I stayed in my house for two days and cried. For the first week I held out hope that he would come crawling out of the river somewhere."

On the 31st, as planned, Buhring flew to Kampala's Entebbe airport. After clearing customs, she entered the mob of drivers and porters, tears hidden behind dark glasses, and hired a taxi to Jinja. "Although I knew it was ridiculous," says Buhring, "I still looked for Hendri's face among the crowd waiting outside."

Pete Meredith and his wife, Leyla, had also come back to Uganda. He'd decided to carry on Coetzee's business, Zen Tubing, and settle in Jinja.

Stookesberry and Korbulic faced a tribunal in the Congo investigating the incident before being allowed to leave the country. They spent a week in Jinja with Coetzee's friends before returning to the States.

Coetzee's remains were never recovered. On January 7, Meredith, Buhring, Korbulic, Nieman, and around two hundred of Coetzee's friends gathered in Jinja for a memorial. They placed written messages to him in a wooden raft, then set it ablaze and floated it into Itanda Falls.

Before he left for his last trip, Coetzee had e-mailed the three-hundred-page manuscript of his memoir to Buhring, Meredith, and several others. He also left behind thousands of pages' worth of private journals, blog entries, essays, e-mails, Facebook posts, and chat logs. Taken as a whole, these documents portray a man who never did overcome his compulsion to pursue life by risking death. But in one passage, written shortly after his solo down the Murchison Falls, he appeared to understand it.

I need to believe that there is more to this world than what we know. I need to believe there is magic out there. I cannot believe these things blindly, though, and maybe that is why I had to do this mission—to prove to myself that we can do things which are bigger than ourselves. I needed to walk through a minefield to feel protected.

THE VANISHING

BOB FRIEL

~~~~~~

In the stunning and remote wilderness along northern British Columbia's Highway 16, at least eighteen women—by some estimates, many more—have gone missing over the past four decades. After years of investigation, authorities still don't know if it's the work of a serial killer or multiple offenders. Our writer drove deep into the darkness to find some disturbing answers.

~~~~~~

For generations, the young people of Vanderhoof, British Columbia, have raced through the night down Blackwater Road, their four-wheel-drives kicking up gravel as they spin onto a rutted track scraped through the evergreen woods surrounding Hogsback Lake. By day, this small park is a peaceful spot for a picnic, a paddle, or setting off to hike a stretch of nearby Telegraph Trail. After dark, Hogsback's shoreline offers a great place to throw a party.

On Friday, May 27, 2011, Madison Scott, twenty, threaded her hand-me-down 1991 F150 between fir trees and parked in a grassy clearing at the edge of the lake. With long ginger hair, green eyes, a big smile, and a spray of freckles across her pierced nose, Maddy radiated life. A 2009 graduate of Vanderhoof's Nechako Valley Secondary School, she stood a sturdy 5-foot-4 and 170 pounds, and had played ice hockey and rugby.

Growing up in Vanderhoof, a small (pop. 4,800) mill town punched square on the sawdust belt of this rugged Canadian province, Maddy was a real northern B.C. girl. She'd dress up for a dance but was also comfortable atop a horse, dirt bike, or snowmobile. She could handle a socket wrench, and had recently begun an apprenticeship as a mechanic in her father's shop.

Maddy's softer side showed a passion for photography. She focused her camera on birds, flowers, friends, and, especially, her younger sister. During one long exposure, an uncharacteristically serious-faced Maddy posed on a bleak snow-covered field. She set off the flash, then walked out of the frame, leaving a haunting image of her body dissolving into the night. In the winter of 2010, one of her cousins commented on the photo on Facebook, saying, "I don't like ghost stuff." Maddy responded, "Haha, you're a baby!!"

The day Maddy drove to Hogsback Lake, a windy front had blown itself out by early morning, but it remained unseasonably cool and overcast, never breaking 50 degrees. The forecast called for it to drop into the low 40s that night. Still, Maddy planned on camping at the lake with one of her girlfriends after the party. She climbed down from her truck and staked out her two-tone blue nylon tent. Then, dressed in a black T-shirt and capri jeans, she joined the fun.

The clearing filled with about fifty people, all from the Vanderhoof area, a mix of eighteen- to twenty-five-year-olds, with a few oldsters mingled in. No one who attended wants to publicly say what went on, partywise. In general, folks say it was what happens whenever young people gather in the woods at night—the same thing their parents had done when they, too, hung out at Hogsback Lake decades before.

The party rolled deep into the morning. Maddy's girlfriend reportedly went home early after hurting her knee, but Maddy decided to stay and camp alone. The latest anyone admits to seeing her was around three a.m.

All the next day, Saturday, Maddy's truck and tent sat in the middle of the park's most trampled spot. On Saturday night, there was an even bigger gathering at the same clearing, with as many as 150 people partying all around Maddy's campsite. No one, though, says they saw her.

Well-known in the small town, Maddy had dozens of friends and a large extended family that owned part of a local lumber mill and Vanderhoof's grocery store, Scott Foods. She was also an experienced camper who'd been to Hogsback many times. Still, by Sunday morning, when not one of her friends or family had heard from her since the party, Maddy's parents, Eldon and Dawn Scott, drove out to the lake. They found her truck, tent, and purse intact, but no Maddy. They immediately called the Vanderhoof detachment of the Royal Canadian Mounted Police (RCMP).

When the Mounties arrived, they didn't see any sign of a struggle, a flat tire, or any other reason Maddy would have ditched her truck, or any bear or cougar tracks. Maddy's keys and iPhone were gone. It looked as if she'd simply walked off or gotten into another vehicle. However, with the Scotts prominent in the community, and Maddy known as a responsible, hardworking kid, there was no hemming and hawing about whether this was a legitimate missing-person case.

"Something was obviously amiss," says RCMP sergeant Rob Vermeulen. The local police called in search-and-rescue teams from Vanderhoof, the small neighboring communities of Fort St. James and Burns Lake, and northern B.C.'s largest city, Prince George (pop. 80,000), an hour east on Highway 16. They also quickly looped in B.C.'s North District Major Crime Unit.

But Madison Scott had disappeared into the night.

One young woman from a close community gone missing is heartbreaking enough. Go a little wider on the map, though, and Vanderhoof becomes just another of a series of tragic waypoints along a slice of northern B.C. where there are dozens of unsolved cases of women and girls who've vanished or been murdered, going back four decades. The only link between many of the cases remains proximity to Highway 16, a road now infamously known as the Highway of Tears.

Sixteen's less ominous alias is the Yellowhead Highway, a 1,700-mile road from Winnipeg to Prince Rupert named in honor of Pierre Bostonais, a blond Métis mountain man who blazed the route west across the Rockies in the early nineteenth century. B.C.'s strand of the Yellowhead is a ruggedly beautiful run from the Alberta provincial line to the Pacific coast. The lonely 450-mile stretch from Prince George to the port of Prince Rupert is the portion that has earned the Tears epithet.

The road has barely left Prince George—ranked Canada's most dangerous city two years running for its epidemic of drug and gang violence—when the first MOOSE CROSSING sign appears. It's a fitting symbol of the duality of this part of B.C., where a fragment of urban affliction butts up against spectacular scenery, where clear-cuts mark the edges of some of North America's last wild places, where Alaska-bound $500,000 motor homes stream past struggling First Nations villages and small mill towns.

Put the murders and the missing out of mind and Highway 16 serves as a mainline adventure artery connecting jumping-off points for exploring the B.C. wilderness. A stuffed grizzly waves a glass-eyed welcome from the chamber of commerce in the small town of Houston, while a salmon statue marks excellent steelhead country—the highway rarely wanders far from good casting its entire length. Smithereens, the 5,400 residents of alpine-themed Smithers, live beside—and bike, ski, and climb—the startling bulk of 7,648-foot Hudson Bay Mountain, which towers above the highway. After breaching the Coast Mountains, the road stops at Prince Rupert, where boats carry fishermen to halibut and salmon grounds, whale watchers to humpbacks, and bear lovers to the Khutzeymateen Grizzly Sanctuary.

Drive Highway 16 long enough and you'll feel its fickle personality. The two-lane gray-top demands your attention. Past the town of Terrace, it begins to wrap around the mountains, and you learn to hug the edges of sharp, often rain-slicked turns where top-heavy lumber trucks threaten to spill into your lane.

Towns like Vanderhoof are relatively upscale bumps along the highway, though it, too, has been dragged up and down northern B.C.'s boom-and-bust cycles. The settlements are strung far apart, and the road slows as it passes through each one. Some of the isolated First Nations villages are little more than smatterings of mobile homes, handmade log cabins, and cinder-block motels. The farther west you drive, the tougher things look.

"We're in the 75 to 85 percent range of unemployment in these villages," says Mark Starlund, chief counsel of the Gitanyow, a First Nations band long known for their skill at carving cedar totems. "There are a lot of unemployed and under-employed. A family might live on $1,000 a month in social assistance. That's brutal, Third World poverty."

A few minutes from any of the towns or settlements and you're in vast forest. Convenient for anyone trying to dump a body, skid roads slash through every sizable patch of trees near the highway, especially east of the mountains. It's often left to hikers or hunters to stumble upon a victim's remains.

Billboards on 16 warning KILLER ON THE LOOSE! are constant reminders of the missing. The disappearances along the highway and two of its desolate tributaries, Highways 97 and 5, date back to 1969, when twenty-six-year-old Gloria Moody was found murdered near Williams Lake. There have been clusters of disappearances each decade since, but it's difficult to get a handle on the actual number of victims.

In testimony to B.C.'s Missing Women Commission of Inquiry—formed in 2010, mainly to investigate why it took law enforcement so long to catch Willie "the Pig Farmer" Pickton, a serial killer who preyed on Vancouver women from 1995 through 2001—First Nations bands and local community groups claimed that as many as forty-three women have been killed or gone missing along Highway 16. In 2005, the RCMP created a special unit called E-Pana (*E* is the RCMP designation for all things British Columbian, and *Pana* is an Inuit god who caretakes souls in a frozen underworld before reincarnation) to examine some of the disappearances, and to determine whether another serial killer was at work. Its investigators eventually sorted through hundreds of unsolved murders, missing women, and sexual assaults in B.C. over the past four decades and found that eighteen cases shared enough similarities to be possibly linked.

The number of cases E-Pana took on was limited by certain criteria. Investigators considered adding a case only if the victim was female, had been involved in a high-risk activity, such as hitchhiking or the sex trade, and had disappeared or been found murdered within a mile of Highways 16, 97, or 5. Nine of E-Pana's victims are aboriginal, and nine are Caucasian. They range in age from twelve to thirty-three; twelve of them are under the age of twenty.

Then, in 2009, the *Vancouver Sun* used similar criteria but widened the search beyond a 1-mile limit to come up with thirty-one cases of missing women in the general area, all of them similar enough to be potentially linked.

Thumbing a ride is one of the major risk factors for women who end up on the Highway 16 lists. Caution-yellow billboards insist GIRLS DON'T HITCHHIKE ON THE HIGHWAY OF TEARS. But they do. "What scares me," says Starlund, "is that you can drive this highway today and still see young girls hitchhiking even when they know what's going on. But it's not like they can ask, 'Mom, can I borrow your car?' because Mom's so poor she doesn't have a car." Two women from Mark Starlund's Gitanyow band are on E-Pana's list of eighteen.

The idea of getting regular public transportation running between the communities comes up every time there's a study group or public meeting. "We started the Kitwancool bus on welfare day so people can get to Terrace to cash their checks," says Starlund. "Some other villages do that same kind of thing, but that's just a couple of times a month." The rest of the time, there might be no other option than hitching if these girls want to get someplace.

There are other Tears cases where the girls were doing nothing riskier than riding their bikes, walking, or hanging out with friends near the highway that runs through their small town—like twelve-year-old Monica Jack, who was plucked off her bike near Nicola Lake in 1978. Her remains were discovered seventeen years later on a logging road.

No new cases have been added to E-Pana's list since 2006, but that doesn't mean the region's murders and disappearances have ended. Between October 2009 and September 2010, three Prince George women went missing. Two were found murdered. One has yet to be recovered, though RCMP officials—who created another special unit, called E-Prelude, to investigate these cases—say they have evidence that she was killed.

And then, most recently, there's Maddy Scott, who was at a party with friends. Because she disappeared some 10 miles from the highway and wasn't involved in anything considered high-risk, Maddy isn't on E-Pana's Highway of Tears list. "There is nothing to indicate at this time that Maddy's disappearance is connected to the ongoing E-Pana investigations," says RCMP constable Lesley Smith, the spokeswoman for North District Major Crime.

But for the people living in the small communities along 16, all the chilling tales start to run together.

~~~~~~

When North District Major Crime, the RCMP unit that handles the most serious cases in that part of the province, took charge of Maddy Scott's file, a dozen investigators poured into Vanderhoof and began working the case from a crime angle—doing forensics and interviewing potential witnesses—at the same time the search was still ramping up.

Bloodhounds strained to latch on to Maddy's scent. Aircraft mounted with infrared cameras probed the bush. Boats towed underwater cameras and side-scan sonar arrays through Hogsback Lake; divers searched its silty bottom. Even the Canadian Rangers—local detachments of the army—joined in the effort. Within a day, 150 volunteers had shown up to help.

On May 31, 2011, four days after Maddy's disappearance, the RCMP suspended the search. The volunteers, however, kept looking. On June 21, Maddy's parents offered a $15,000 reward, which they eventually raised to $25,000. (It has since been raised again, to $50,000.) In a September 1 statement, the Scotts asked those with any information to come forward, and thanked the tight-knit community. "We have always loved living here," they said, "and it is often in a time of crisis that you truly see the network of support that exists in an area that we are proud to call home." But the days and weeks dragged on, with no results. At press time, eleven months after she went missing, there was still no sign of Maddy.

The RCMP's E-Pana hasn't made much progress on its cases, either. The special unit has grown to a team of fifty people with an annual budget of $6 million, and investigators have come up with thousands of persons of interest. E-Pana began doing background checks and profiles on more than two thousand possible suspects. Then it cast an even wider net, over an additional five thousand persons of interest. The project received 1,006 tips in 2010 alone, and has made 16,000-plus inquiries since its creation in 2005.

Though the unit's spokeswoman, RCMP corporal Annie Linteau, says they are pleased with the progress to date, there have been no arrests, and no files have been closed. "Homicides and missing persons investigations are complex," Linteau explained in an e-mail. "We don't think we will be able to say whether there is a serial killer at play until we have been successful in solving or charging in all eighteen of the files, or the majority. At this point, evidence gathered in these cases has yet to lead us to believe that a single person is responsible, although we are very much alive to the possibility."

Linteau said that each investigation had undergone numerous reviews to determine whether evidence could be forensically retested using new technology. "In many of these cases, the women were not reported missing for a long time, so there were few if any clues other than the body. In others, there is still no body. And many of the murders happened before the current advances in DNA testing. We've been able to obtain DNA from old samples of clothing and tissue."

Occasionally, there have been artist renderings and vehicle descriptions of last-seen-withs. There have been murder confessions that later proved false. There's a man, Leland "Chug" Switzer—now in jail for killing his brother—who the RCMP feels is somehow connected to twenty-five-year-old Nicole Hoar's disappearance in 2002. Hoar, who'd spent a season planting trees for Prince George–based Celtic Reforestation, was waiting at a gas station on Highway 16, looking for a ride west to Smithers, where she was going to visit her sister. She hasn't been seen since. Switzer's property has been searched, but he's never been charged.

Truck drivers carrying cargo to and from the port of Prince Rupert have long been mentioned as possible suspects in the highway murders, but none have ever been arrested. Then in April 2011 came a harrowing story from a twenty-year-old woman who stopped near Highway 97 and Kamloops to help a unibrowed, bushy-bearded man who'd flagged her down. He tried to force her into his 1992 Dakota pickup, but fortunately she punted his nuts up into his throat and escaped. She gave a good description of the hairy guy and his truck, but like all the other leads, it has yet to prompt any arrests.

The RCMP did have a recent break in a murder case unrelated to E-Pana. On Saturday night, November 27, 2010, a young Mountie saw a black GMC Sierra pickup come skidding out of one of the Vanderhoof area's innumerable old logging tracks. The constable lit up the truck and pulled it over. A wildlife cop was called to investigate and trudged up the logging road. His flashlight illuminated the body of fifteen-year-old Vanderhoof resident Loren Leslie, a tenth grader at Nechako Valley Secondary School.

"She told her mother she was going out to get coffee with a girlfriend," says Loren's father, Doug Leslie. "Later that day, she texted a friend to say she was going for a ride with this Cody guy, and that's the last anyone heard from her."

The truck's driver, twenty-one-year-old Cody Legebokoff, was raised just up the road from Vanderhoof in Fort St. James, and his and Loren Leslie's grandparents had grown up together in the nearby town of Fort Fraser. Loren and Cody were allegedly also Facebook friends.

Then, on October 17, 2011, nearly one year after Legebokoff was arrested for Loren's murder, the RCMP's E-Prelude unit investigating the 2009–2010 disappearances of the three Prince George women charged him with those killings. If the charges are proved, Legebokoff was both a ruthless monster, cruising the dark alleys of Prince George in his black pickup looking for random victims, and the snowboarding small-town boy next door who asked a young family friend to go for a ride and then killed her.

Legebokoff, who goes on trial this year for the four first-degree murders, was already in custody when Maddy Scott disappeared. And the RCMP says it has no evidence linking him to any of the crimes on E-Pana's list. That leaves the residents of northern B.C. facing three unnerving possibilities: There is still a serial killer out there, maybe more than one; the other murders were committed by different men who likely still live among them; or they are losing their daughters to a combination of both. It's hard to figure which alternative is more frightening.

~~~~~~

The RCMP investigations have no shortage of critics. "They've got all this money and these resources and spent two years inputting all this information into their super-computer," says Ray Michalko, an RCMP constable turned private investigator. "When it didn't spit out the name of a killer, they said, 'Uh-oh, what do we do now?'"

I met Michalko one morning at an east side Vancouver coffeehouse. At 6-foot-2, 240 pounds, with arms that take up more than his share of the table, Michalko, sixty-four, still looks like he could handle himself in the Manitoba mining-town bar brawls where he cut his teeth as a Mountie. Michalko left the force after he was transferred to Vancouver, where they expect their cops to be more refined. "If somebody in Manitoba told you to fuck off," he says, "you flattened him, and there was no flap. Here, it was a lot different."

Along with missing the two-fisted form of frontier justice, Michalko says he grew weary of what he calls the RCMP's "dysfunctional bureaucracy." He's spent the past fourteen years working as a PI. In late 2005, while he was sitting in his home near Vancouver, a news story came on about Tamara Chipman, another young woman gone missing from Highway 16.

"I'm bitching to my wife that even I could solve this case, that the RCMP haven't done bugger all! And she said, 'Well, instead of just talking, why don't you try to do something about it!'"

Michalko's wife shares a home office with her husband, and he soon had a wall covered with pin maps, case notes, and head shots of dead women. "She recently asked me to take those photos down," he says.

Without access to the RCMP's state-of-the-art Violent Crime Linkage Analysis System software or its warehouse full of files on the highway murders, Michalko still thought he had an edge. "I know from experience that the Natives do not like the RCMP," he says. "They just don't trust them or the government. That bad blood goes all the way back to the residential schools and to when Canada outlawed the potlatch, which was the Natives' way of ensuring that every family in the band had enough to live on. Now in those communities there's a lot of misery."

Claims of institutional racism within the RCMP toward members of the First Nations are often brought up in discussions of the highway murders. According to the Native Women's Association of Canada, in 2010 the country's average clearance rate for homicides was 84 percent, while for indigenous women it was 53 percent. It falls below even that dismal average in B.C., where only 51 percent of the murders of Native women are ever cleared. (The RCMP's Annie Linteau says that each case, regardless of the victim's ethnicity, is thoroughly investigated.)

Michalko thought the key to solving the cases was old-fashioned, door-knocking police work in local villages. And for such a big, pasty white guy, Michalko has always had a good relationship with Canada's aboriginals. "They're good people," he says. "A lot of them have drug and alcohol problems, and they drive me crazy sometimes, but I really like them. I think I must have been one of them in a past life."

Limited to working nights, weekends, and whatever spare hours he had, Michalko jump-started his Highway of Tears investigation by putting ads in small-town newspapers along the Yellowhead. "I just said, 'If you know anything about the missing or murdered girls, call me. . . .' And the phone started ringing."

Michalko says that his first big break came in March 2008, when he found someone who claimed to be a witness to the murder of sixteen-year-old Ramona Wilson on the outskirts of Smithers. He immediately brought that person to the RCMP. "Problem was," he says, "their theory was that this girl had been done by a serial killer. My witness blew that idea out of the water, and they didn't like that. I talked to the witness a couple of weeks later, and while the RCMP did talk to the guy he identified as the killer, to my knowledge no one followed up again. So I wrote the RCMP and told them that if they had no objection, I was going to continue investigating. They wrote back telling me that not only was I *not* going to work on that case, but I wasn't working on any other case, or they'd charge me with obstruction of justice."

Michalko's involvement caught the attention of the local press. "The RCMP's attitude toward me was the best thing that could have happened," Michalko says. "Now the First Nations people up there were certain I wasn't one of the RCMP boys." (The RCMP eventually backed off and said it welcomes input from citizens and follows up on all leads. Meanwhile, Linteau says she can't comment on the Wilson investigation because it's ongoing.)

Most recently, Michalko has been working with Claudia Williams to find out what happened to her younger sister, Alberta, one of the E-Pana eighteen, who disappeared on August 25, 1989. The sisters, members of the Gitanyow band, had gone to a Prince Rupert hot spot called Bogey's Cabaret to celebrate the end of the summer salmon season, which they'd spent working together at a nearby cannery. After last call, Alberta asked her sister to accompany her and some friends to a party. Claudia looked away to talk to someone for a few minutes. When she turned back, the whole group, including her sister, was gone. That was the last time she saw Alberta. A month later, hikers found her body off Highway 16.

Claudia says that Alberta knew everyone she was last seen with. Still, almost twenty-three years later, the murder remains unsolved. "Every one of those people are covering up, and that's going to break down," says Claudia, now fifty-two, who was thirty at the time, four years older than her sister. She has been keeping the investigation alive, badgering the RCMP, soliciting information through social networks and old-fashioned flyers, and hiring Michalko, who's charging her a fee of one Canadian loonie.

All along, Michalko has theorized that most of the highway murders were not committed by a serial killer but had happened under horrifically mundane circumstances: the bad uncle, the boyfriend from hell, the date rape or domestic-abuse case that went from bad to worse. Still, all the hours and all the tips have yet to lead to an arrest. "I can't tell you how many times I've said, 'Okay, this is it, I give up,'" says Michalko, who estimates he's worked forty hours a month on the Highway of Tears cases since taking them on six years ago. "Within a day or two of that, though, my phone rings and, Hey, this is good information! I'm still convinced I'm going to solve one of these, but I thought it would be easier."

On the drive back from Prince Rupert to Prince George, I stop again in Vanderhoof. Down Blackwater Road on a night with no party, Hogsback Lake lies so still I can hear the kisses as fish rise to the surface to feed.

The Scott family has spent many nights camping out at the lake, returning again and again to the woods where Maddy was last seen. Volunteers continue to expand the search area; they've now covered hundreds of miles. Calls come in from psychics around the world.

The idea that someone from this little town that people say has always been such a wonderful place to live might be keeping a dark secret haunts locals. How can somebody just disappear like that from a group of people she knew? Somebody knows. Why aren't they saying something?

"For investigators," says the RCMP's Rob Vermeulen, "it's frustrating any time you know there's information out there that could help but hasn't gotten to you yet. We continue to appeal to people who, for whatever reason, haven't passed on that information to please get that to us."

In another of the area's terrible turns, Vanderhoof local Fribjon Bjornson went missing early this year. A father of two young children, twenty-eight-year-old "Frib" had recently hired on at a logging camp in Fort St. James. According to his mother, Eileen, Frib was friends with Maddy Scott and had been very troubled over her disappearance. A couple of weeks after he vanished in mid-January, police received a tip that led them to partial human remains in a neighborhood on the nearby Nak'azdli reservation. They identified them as Frib's by his dental records. The rest of his body has not been found.

No charges have been laid in Bjornson's murder, and the RCMP and Eileen say there is no connection between his case and Maddy's. But in this small rural community that has seen three of its young people murdered or gone missing, and another from a nearby town charged as a serial killer—all within fourteen months—the lack of answers only feeds the sense of dread.

Today, some neighbors are looking sideways at each other. Some families find themselves treated as outcasts because their sons were at the party with Maddy and have come under suspicion. Wild rumors circulate about human trafficking, dungeonlike bunkers on rural properties near Hogsback Lake, and the involvement of local drug dealers. Vanderhoof mayor Gerry Thiessen says this has always been a place that pulls together through hard times, but even he describes the pain as "gut-wrenching." It's twisting the little town into knots.

As I drove out of Vanderhoof after ten on a rainy night, the small pool of light cast by the Scott Foods shopping center quickly faded as I headed east on Highway 16. At the edge of town, my headlights picked out a face in the blackness along the side of the road. I was so surprised that it took me a moment to realize it belonged to a woman in dark clothes, hitchhiking. I was already too far past her to stop and back up, so as soon as I could, I made a U-turn. I wanted to pick her up, ask what the hell was worth the risk, and then make sure she got there safely. By the time I made it back to the spot where she'd been standing—within sight of a big billboard asking for help finding Maddy Scott—she was climbing into a black pickup.

CATCH ME IF YOU CAN

DEAN KING

~~~~~~

When Robert Wood Jr. disappeared in a densely forested Virginia park in 2011, searchers faced the challenge of a lifetime. The eight-year-old boy was autistic and nonverbal, and from his perspective the largest manhunt in state history probably looked like something else: the ultimate game of hide-and-seek.

~~~~~~

A ball of fire with twinkling blue eyes, Robert Arthur Wood Jr. is a 4-foot-6, 70-pound eight-year-old who loves to swing. His doting grandmother, Norma Jean Williams, calls him Bud, and he gives as good as he gets when he and his brother, Ryan, a year younger, scrap over a toy. Robert can see and hear fine, but he can't talk, swim, sit still for a movie, or use the bathroom by himself, because he is also severely autistic.

Ryan, a dark-haired version of Robert and also autistic, but less so, hugs and kisses his brother. Robert is not as affectionate. He is prone to repetitive motions, like hitting himself over and over with an empty plastic soft-drink bottle. But most of all he enjoys swinging. If you let him, he'll do it until his hands blister and the skin on the back of his legs rubs raw. Even then he keeps swinging.

Robert and Ryan are both in constant motion, jumping, rocking, and pounding things. Like many children with autism, they are fearless. As a toddler, Robert liked to climb on top of the television and the refrigerator. He also likes to wander—or, as behavioral specialists call it, "to elope." At Walmart, Robert's mother, Barbara Locker, still puts him in the shopping cart. If you don't hold him by the hand or by his shirt, he might run off.

That's exactly what happened on October 23, 2011, a warm Sunday afternoon. After lunch, the boys' father, Robert Wood Sr., thirty-four, known as Robbie, and his girlfriend (Wood and Locker have been separated for six years) took Robert and Ryan for a walk at the rarely visited 80-acre North Anna Battlefield Park, in Virginia's Hanover County, fifteen minutes from the boys' home in Ruther Glen. This was no ordinary walk in the park. The hilly green thickets of central Virginia, where Grant vied with Lee in an epic battle for nearby Richmond, are prickly and hardscrabble, with skin-ripping greenbrier and blackberry bushes, not to mention coyotes and bobcats. In this land of rivers, ravines, swamps, mosquitoes, and water moccasins, the Union general soon discovered, inhospitality was endemic.

Within the park, narrow paths tunnel through dense woods. A warren of Confederate breastworks leads to a bluff—with no guardrails—that plummets 90 feet. Below, the North Anna River rumbles through the boulders and Class III rapids of Falls Hole. Nothing separates the park's other boundaries from a massive open Martin Marietta gravel quarry, with its clatter of industrial dump trucks, bulldozers, and freight trains and roar of controlled explosions. It's a fantasy-land for any boy, autistic or not.

At around 2:30 p.m., while the group was resting after a mile-long walk, Robert ran down a spur trail. Somehow both his father, an avid Civil War–relics hunter, and his father's girlfriend missed seeing him take off. Wearing a red long-sleeved shirt, blue pants, and blue tennis shoes, Robert would not have been difficult to spot. Yet he vanished.

Within five minutes of Robert's disappearance, according to Wood and his girlfriend, they had placed a call to 911 for help. Within an hour, the Hanover sheriff's department was searching the area with two canine teams. Hanover Hounds, a local tracking organization, arrived with two more teams.

Because of his autism, Robert probably didn't know that he was lost. If he heard people coming through the woods, he might well have taken cover from them, thinking it was a game of hide-and-seek. Or he might not have wanted to be found by a stranger, even one calling out his name. This made efforts to locate him extremely difficult, and it's how Robert managed to elude what would soon become one of the largest search-and-rescue operations in Virginia history.

~~~~~~

When he disappeared that day, Robert began an unlikely adventure that placed him at the center of the newest concern in the search-and-rescue (SAR) world: lost autistic children. Why autistic kids have the tendency to run off is not known, but the urge is strong in half of all children diagnosed with the disorder.

A neurological condition present from early childhood, autism is characterized by difficulty communicating and forming relationships, as well as cognitive abnormalities. The condition is measured on a spectrum, from high-functioning to low-functioning, from those with Asperger's syndrome—associated with above-average intellectual ability, impaired social skills, and restrictive, repetitive patterns of interest and activity—to the 40 percent who, like Robert, are nonverbal. The Centers for Disease Control and Prevention reports a staggering increase in the number of autistic children in recent years. In 2008, 1 out of every 178 children had some form of autism. By early 2012, that number had risen to 1 in 88. Little is known about the sudden upsurge of cases, but researchers at the National Institutes of Health believe that a genetic predisposition to the disorder may be exacerbated by an unknown environmental component. The condition affects five times as many boys (1 in 54) as girls (1 in 252).

Unable to filter out distractions and easily overstimulated, autistic kids don't like noisy environments or group settings. "Usually, when we see a child wander off, bolt, or elope, they are on the severe side of the spectrum," says Lori McIlwain, mother of a twelve-year-old autistic boy, Connor, and executive director of the Boston-based National Autism Association. She helped found the organization in 2003 to advocate for policy change in medical care for those with autism. Connor has run off nine times from three different schools. "Autistic kids can't tell us, 'Hey, the sunlight is bothering me,' or 'I saw a pool I want to check out,' or 'There's a swing I want to see.'"

McIlwain estimates that 40 percent of children with autism will go missing at some point in their lives.

It was the case of nine-year-old Logan Mitcheltree that alerted McIlwain to the budding crisis. In December 2004, at five p.m. on a Saturday, the 4-foot-tall, 55-pound boy with reddish-blond hair and dark brown eyes slipped out of his home in South Williamson, Pennsylvania. For two days, firefighters, forest rangers, state troopers, civil air pilots, police, and hundreds of volunteers searched around the clock. A snow squall hit, and the temperature plunged to 15 degrees. Logan, who was wearing a long-sleeved shirt, blue jeans, and slippers and was carrying a knapsack, died of hypothermia a mile and a half from his home. He was headed up a nearby mountain, probably attracted by the flashing lights of a radio tower.

Since September 2011, McIlwain says, 143 cases of missing autistic children have been reported around the world. Circumstances vary widely. In February 2012, outside Melbourne, Australia, seven-year-old Ryan Pham, who had disappeared overnight, was found naked and shivering in the reeds, about to wade into the swift Kororoit Creek. In April, thirteen-year-old Ross Harrison bolted from his home on West 182nd Street in the Bronx and rode New York City subways for three days while his parents, friends, and the authorities searched for him. Two riders eventually found him late at night on a J train in Brooklyn.

Once Robert Wood was off and running, he was quickly lost, too. Dashing up and over trenches, through thickets of mountain laurel and briars, he caught spiderwebs in the face and picked up ticks and chiggers as he ran. The forest floor was littered with large trees, branches, and piles of deadfall caused by recent hurricanes and tropical storms. Robert likely moved from one thing that provoked his curiosity to the next—boulders to climb, trees to examine, the allure of a train-whistle blast. If it weren't for the profusion of copperheads, black snakes, and corn snakes, it would have been the ideal place to play paintball or hide-and-seek.

Over the age of four, normal children recognize that they are lost and will look for their parents. Their spatial maps are flawed, but they will devise strategies to get found. "The biggest difference," according to SAR expert Robert Koester, is that nonautistic kids are "a lot less likely to be evasive. Once they get hungry or cold, they will call out to searchers."

But Robert doesn't feel pain the way normal children do. He could sprain an ankle or suffer cold and dampness without complaint. The pangs of hunger wouldn't make him cry. He'd harbor no fear of the dark or the bogeyman and wouldn't dread solitude, so he wouldn't get panicky at dusk.

He is also in possession of a healthy dose of determination. One educator called him "a very tough kid," "a very resilient kid," and "resourceful, in his own way."

～～

Robert's father and his girlfriend had been sitting on a bench in the park at observation deck number seven when Robert bolted. The north-facing bench looks out on a ravine up which a futile Union assault had been made on May 24, 1864. A sign describing the battle, and the kindnesses rendered to a fatally shot Union officer afterward, is entitled SAVE YOURSELF IF YOU CAN.

From there the police dogs had tracked the boy going toward the river. Like many autistic children, Robert is obsessed with water. Autistic kids can be hypersensitive to certain stimuli, and some experts believe that water is soothing to them. Though Robert can't swim, he thinks he can. According to the National Autism Association, from 2009 to 2011, 90 percent of the deaths of missing autistic kids were by drowning. The river would remain an area of major concern throughout the search.

Typically, after a 911 call is received for a missing person, police officers report to the scene and evaluate the situation for foul play and other factors. When a minor is involved, any adults associated with the child, including parents, are routinely assessed as to whether they should be considered suspects. The reporting officer usually has discretion to initiate a search.

Robbie Wood, an unemployed maintenance worker, has weekend visitation rights with his sons, and they'd stayed with him the night before. The day after the trip to the park, he was due in court. He had been summoned by a judge in Caroline County, where the boys and their mother live, for failure to pay child support amounting to $6,698.01. Locker was seeking a court order and possible jail time to get him to pay up. But while the family has its troubles, authorities ruled out either parent as a suspect and quickly initiated a search for Robert.

Once a person is officially declared missing, often it is a combination of police officers, fire department personnel, and other specialized units who conduct the search. Decisions are made as to which resources to tap, usually SAR units—dive teams, technical teams, dog-tracking teams—sourced from local and regional emergency services. State police specialists, including air support, are the next level.

Half of all searches are concluded within three hours and ten minutes—an overdue hiker, having sprained her ankle, finally surfaces, or a hunter emerges from the woods after a prolonged search for a lost hound. Within twelve hours, 81 percent of all lost-person cases are wrapped up, and 93 percent of the time the case is closed within twenty-four hours.

As the hours passed without any sign of Robert, Hanover County authorities called in more and more support from neighboring Caroline and Henrico Counties, Virginia State Police, and local search organizations. They issued a reverse 911, using computers to send a message about the lost boy to all the landlines in the area. Neighbors started searching their yards and beyond.

Norma Jean Williams, Robert's maternal grandmother, a dialysis technician who lives next door to Locker and the boys and often cares for Robert and Ryan, found out on Monday morning, while she was at work, that Robert was missing. One of her coworkers had heard about it on the radio.

A salt-of-the-earth Baptist whose family has beaten a living out of the land in Ruther Glen for three generations, Williams, fifty-eight, jumped into her 2003 Dodge Dakota quad-cab pickup—she has a backseat for Robert and Ryan—and drove to Battlefield Park. A deputy sheriff stopped her at the entrance. No one was being allowed in; the park was being treated as a crime scene. She parked her truck outside, as near as she could to the entrance.

Locker had found out the evening before, when she received a phone call from Wood. Late that night, a sheriff and a dog tracker came by her home to pick up some of Robert's clothes and toys to use as scent articles for the dogs. Locker stayed with her mother by the truck during the day and left in time to bring Ryan home from school. Because Williams, Locker, and Wood were emotionally distraught and the park terrain was strenuous, authorities declined to have them participate in the search. (Williams and Locker talked to me for this story. I also spoke with Robbie's father, Roger, but was unable to reach Robbie, who, Roger told me, had been hospitalized with kidney failure.)

As Monday afternoon wore on, the area around Williams's red pickup looked like Armageddon. County- and state-police dog teams deployed in the woods and nearby fields. Tactical dive teams headed for the river. Helicopters thundered overhead, sometimes only 500 feet or lower, using infrared cameras designed to detect heat through smoke, fog, or haze. Because autistic children are often drawn to bright objects and certain noises, fire trucks twirled their lights and ran backup sirens, audible across hundreds of acres, hoping to attract Robert. With the same goal in mind, searchers hung glow sticks in the trees. They also put out water and blankets for him.

Williams hung glow sticks, too, and she refused to leave until the boy had been found. She slept in her truck.

~~~~~~

Monitoring from the sidelines, Billy Chrimes, deputy SAR coordinator for the Virginia Department of Emergency Management (VDEM), kept abreast of the search from his home in Roanoke. Chrimes, a thirty-six-year-old search-and-rescue training specialist, helped build Virginia's SAR system, one of the nation's best. But there are strict protocols and codes of behavior in the field. Representing a state agency, Chrimes had to be invited in by local authorities before he could help. "There are 134 localities in Virginia," he says, "and 134 different ways to do things. Some of them call to alert us the minute they know someone is missing and call us again within a few hours to bring resources." But after twenty-four hours, the state still hadn't been called.

Nevertheless, Chrimes and his colleagues spent Monday night preparing and planning their version of the search, sectoring off a map of the area and parsing the first forty tasks to be accomplished if they were called. Finally, Chrimes decided to seek an invitation to help. At two a.m. on Tuesday, he got out of bed after two hours of sleep. As he prepared for the three-and-a-half-hour drive east to Battlefield Park, his mind churned. Originally from Wise County, in the southwestern reaches of the state, Chrimes had gone on his first rescue operation at the age of five, with his father, a firefighter and EMT, to save an injured caver. When he was thirteen, he started working for the volunteer rescue squad. Chrimes never played high school sports. On weekends, when a call came in, he either was already at the station or would speed the quarter-mile there on his bike—and often be the first person to arrive. He skipped college to work in the Coast Guard in Alaska and at jobs as a deputy sheriff and fire department captain.

In the fall of 2008, Chrimes began to overhaul the training for Virginia's 700-plus volunteer system, a corps of dog handlers, visual trackers, cavers, case analysts, and other search experts. He's currently rewriting the state's SAR training manual, which VDEM will share across the country and internationally. He sometimes operates for weeks on end out of his Ford F350 four-door long-bed pickup, which doubles as a mobile command center. He hauls around all sorts of rescue gear—ropes, litters, an SAT phone, a dozen two-way radios, a laser printer for producing topo maps, and a PowerPoint projector for briefing searchers. He handles more than a hundred SAR operations a year for people who need help—ranging from campers, climbers, and boaters to natural-disaster and crime victims to autistic children and elderly people suffering from dementia.

The search for Robert had become statewide news. Tuesday morning, Chrimes showed up at the Hanover County sheriff's department command center and requested a meeting with Sheriff David Hines. A high-profile search can become a turf war, and Chrimes wanted to avoid that. He sat and waited three hours—watching silently as the overwhelmed deputies and their staff tried to process and deploy hundreds of untrained "emergent" volunteers—before making his pitch to two majors.

By noon on Tuesday, the first ground-pounders—as emergent volunteers are known to SAR veterans—were in the field, and Sheriff Hines gladly ceded search-operations management to Chrimes, though he would still maintain his own base at Battlefield Park. Chrimes set up shop in a public-safety building at the nearby Kings Dominion amusement park, where he'd deal with the processing and deployment of volunteers and manage the state's resources.

"Given the circumstances," says Chrimes, a blunt, optimistic country boy, "I felt like we were going to find him the first night."

Chrimes had modern technology, dogs, choppers, and thousands of searchers—including equestrian, kayak, and rappelling teams—at his fingertips. He also had Professor Rescue, the man who revolutionized the field of search-and-rescue, to lean on.

Charlottesville, Virginia–based Robert Koester had joined the Appalachian Search and Rescue Conference in 1981. He is a VDEM incident commander and a former president of the Virginia Search and Rescue Council. He has conducted SAR operations and research for NASA, the US Coast Guard, the National Park Service, and FEMA. Over the past two decades, the forty-nine-year-old self-avowed "numbers guy" has almost single-handedly codified the search-and-rescue world by collecting SAR cases and feeding them into his international incident database. Published in 2008, Koester's handbook, *Lost Person Behavior: A Search and Rescue*

Guide on Where to Look—For Land, Air and Water, is regarded as the field bible. Using the book's forty categories to create a lost-person profile, a searcher can better predict whether a victim is alive and, if so, where to find him or her.

According to Koester's book, where lost hikers are concerned, 97 percent of those found on the first day are recovered alive, while just 49 percent located on the fourth day are. Although it varies by terrain and climate, about 25 percent are found within a mile of where they were last known to be, 50 percent within 2 miles, 75 percent within 4 miles, and 95 percent within 12 miles. Half of all hikers are found within 100 yards of a trail or road. Similar data can be found for cavers, climbers, horseback riders, hunters, mountaineers, mountain bikers, runners, skiers, snowboarders, snowshoers, snowmobilers, and ATV riders. There are also statistical breakdowns of children, organized by age, and sections on people with dementia, mental illness, and autism.

Koester's stats told searchers that 50 percent of autistic kids in temperate environments are found within 1 mile of their last known location, and 75 percent are found within 2.3 miles; that even in the wilderness, 45 percent are found inside structures and 20 percent on roads; and that 50 percent are found within 15 yards of a linear feature—a river, railroad, trail, or road—and 75 percent within 22 yards. "That gives you a model that sort of looks like spaghetti thrown against a plate," Koester says with a wry chuckle. Nonetheless, it is a searcher's road map.

Despite identifiable tendencies, autistic kids are considered highly unpredictable. As the saying goes in the field, "When you meet one autistic person, you meet one autistic person." The bottom line for Robert's profile was troubling. The model went out only forty-eight hours, at which point there was only a 56 percent chance of finding him alive.

It would have seemed even worse if it hadn't been for a remarkable case eighteen months earlier in the Florida swamplands north of Orlando. There, eleven-year-old Nadia Bloom, who suffers from ADD, anxiety, and Asperger's syndrome, wandered off from home and was lost for four days. She slept in an "itchy" bush the first night, managed to evade snakes and alligators, and ate spongy plants until a rescuer found her, dehydrated but otherwise okay. How did she spend her time? She took photographs, many of sunlight flashing hotly off water.

~~~~~~

By 2:30 p.m. on Tuesday, Robert had been missing for forty-eight hours. At home he took medication to help him sleep on a normal schedule. "He would wake up at three a.m. and start playing like it was the middle of the day," Locker told me. In the wild he might be semi-nocturnal, roaming for several hours and then sleeping for several, making him harder to locate, since he would be hunkered down for at least part of the daytime, when he'd be easiest to spot if he were moving around.

Based on their research and experience, Chrimes and Koester figured they still had some time to find Robert, as long as he hadn't gone to the river and the relatively mild weather didn't take a turn for the worse. Temperatures were dropping into the 40s at night, and the forecast called for rain and colder weather later in the week.

Thirst was much more of a threat to Robert than hunger. People can go weeks without eating, but dehydration will start to weaken and disorient them within forty-eight hours. There were plenty of streams to slake Robert's thirst, but no one could be sure he would know to drink from them.

Chrimes, Koester, and two others analyzed data and factored in various likely scenarios—Robert had initially gone down to the river or over to the cliffs, or he had wandered outside the park. They circled areas of special interest on the map, giving various chunks of real estate priority in the search, especially the nearby quarry, which would be searched repeatedly by ground and dog teams. "There is a methodology," says Chrimes. "It's all about putting resources in the right place at the right time."

If Robert had not gone to the river and drowned, then, given the searches that had already gone on, he was probably either hiding from them or on the move, or both.

In the field, searchers need to nail down the initial planning point (IPP), which is either the place last seen (PLS) or the last known position (LKP)—say, where a lost person's wallet was found or where his car turned up. "If you don't get your IPP right, you're going to have problems," Koester says.

Chrimes had already dispatched Rob Speiden, who runs his own man-tracking and land-navigation school in Christiansburg, Virginia, and is one of the nation's top visual trackers, to GPS-map the PLS and LKP. Hanover sheriff's department canine handler Matt Crist, the first man in on Sunday, showed Speiden where his dog had tracked Robert and where Wood said he had last seen him, on the park's observation deck number seven. As he wandered off, Robert had dragged a walking stick he'd picked up in the woods. Crist found scuff marks in the path. This LKP indicated the direction of travel: northeasterly toward deck number eight, some 50 yards away.

Then Crist led Speiden to some footprints that had been found about a half-mile east of the PLS, on a sandy bank about 10 feet above the river. Robert and Ryan had been wearing the same kind of Nike shoes. Speiden knelt down and took measurements. They were the right size. Ryan's shoe, which they had a cell-phone image of, had small half-inch square patterns, but this track was scored with bars and flex grooves. The match was negative.

Tuesday evening, Koester helped brief some seventy-five core SAR volunteers in the public-safety building. At 11:30, he called it a night. He was flying to Winnipeg, Manitoba, the next morning to speak at an SAR conference on searches for autistic children. He had worked with Chrimes long enough that he could read him. "He was under a lot of stress," Koester says, pointing out that Chrimes was struggling under the weight of so many emergent volunteers. "Things weren't going the way they normally go."

At 1:30 Wednesday morning, a glimmer of hope came. As a member of the mounted search team combed an area about half a mile northwest of the PLS, he heard a strange noise in the woods. It was brief and inscrutable, but it sounded human to him, like someone yelling out. Then nothing. The searcher investigated but saw no sign of the boy.

During a three a.m. debriefing, the command team turned to the Internet and listened to the sounds of various indigenous nocturnal animals—raccoons, opossums, owls—to see if the searcher could identify a match. He couldn't.

Was it possible that Robert was still alive? "I've seen a lot of searches where they give up after two or three days," Koester says. "That always makes me cringe. Search-and-rescue is about everybody coming together to find the person—and not giving up."

When it comes to a lost child, communities will rally in astounding numbers, making great sacrifices of time and resources. Wednesday morning, people began registering at the Kings Dominion volunteer center before daybreak—at least those who came through official channels. Search teams would report well-meaning neighbors combing the grounds and the river on everything from ATVs to horseback to paddleboards. The first official teams headed into the woods at eight a.m. In all, 940 volunteers would be deployed that day. This was a blessing and a curse.

"A lot of times, they bring local knowledge and know things that don't appear on a map," says Koester. But it's remarkably easy to miss what you're looking for. Koester calls it *screening*—the eye stops at the outer layer of foliage and doesn't register what's beyond the screen door. "Searchers are looking for a full-blown human being," he says. "If the subject is hiding, they might see part of a shoe or a patch of flesh, and subconsciously it doesn't register. They don't recognize that's what they're looking for."

For Chrimes, the volunteers presented a massive logistical challenge. The extra traffic tramples footprints and contaminates the scent pools that tracking dogs are trained to find. Then there are safety issues in tramping off-trail through the woods: ticks, snakes, tricky slopes, hazardous water crossings, and tree limbs that can poke eyes. Volunteers have to be screened for fitness and gear. Some show up in sandals. Others become exhausted and need medical treatment for fatigue.

There was a benefit to the numbers, though. "We were able to search a monumental area," says Chrimes, who over time extended the perimeter several miles in every direction.

All day Wednesday, hundreds of volunteers conducted seventy-four search missions, some over the same ground twice, tackling a 22-square-mile area north and south of Verdon Road, which contains the entrances to both the park and the quarry. Searchers walked in grids for miles through thick, swampy woods, many carrying treats and toys for the boy and squeezing empty plastic bottles, making a crinkling noise Robert was known to like. They fanned out in long lines, combing woodlands and harvested cornfields. They paced through rows of soybeans, climbed over Civil War trenches, and crawled under farmhouse porches. One searcher fell and had to be treated for a sprained knee.

Many of the volunteers worked in emergency services or were themselves parents of autistic children. A Pennsylvania Turnpike worker came for two days. His eleven-year-old son is autistic and had once evaded the watching eyes of four adults at the beach. The boy had taken off in a flash, zipping through the sand so fast that it took the adults an hour to run him down. A Dallas businessman, also the father of an autistic child, skipped his return flight after a meeting in Richmond, visited a Walmart for blue jeans and boots, and joined the line.

"I have two autistic kids, so it hit really close to home for me," volunteer Tammy Rogers of nearby Powhatan County told the *Richmond Times-Dispatch*. "As a mother you ache. This is the best medicine, just to get out here."

Another volunteer, Donald Turbin, forty-seven, from Chesterfield County, is a father of four and has an autistic cousin. "Soon as I heard about it, something told me to go help," he says. "We went through thicket after thicket, stuff so dense you almost needed a hunting dog. And some swamp, too, with knee-deep water and lots of bugs. It was worth every step as long as that boy got out of there fine."

"I was worried about copperheads," says volunteer Rodney Clifton, sixty-five, a retired glazier. "A black snake will run from you. A copperhead will bite you." Clifton showed up underdressed, in shorts and a short-sleeved shirt, and scratched up his arms and legs, but that didn't matter to him. "My grandchildren, I worry so much about them," he says. "If something happened to them, I hope someone would go out and hunt for them."

Two o'clock Wednesday afternoon marked the seventy-second hour that Robert had been missing. Chrimes believed that, if he hadn't drowned, he was playing hide-and-seek, and playing it well. He thought the boy was mobile, meaning that the areas they swept could be considered clean for only a short time. After every sector search, team leaders reported in and graded the effort.

"The way to picture it is if there were one hundred milk bottles in your sector. Given the number of searchers, the time of day, weather conditions, and other factors, how many would you have found?" Chrimes says.

Rappelling teams descended the steep bluffs to the North Anna River, searching for clues—or a body. A helicopter-assisted state-trooper dive team was taken in hard hats to the center of the Martin Marietta quarry, where it searched along the surface edges of pits that plummeted 75 feet to dark pools of water.

"We were seeing nothing," Chrimes says. "We weren't finding any clues to follow up on." But Chrimes is no quitter. In 2000, he saved the life of a teenage hiker who had been missing in snow and freezing rain for eight hours on the Appalachian Trail, near the Dragon's Tooth rock pinnacle on Virginia's 3,000-foot Cove Mountain. Severely hypothermic and unconscious when found just off the trail, the teenager was nearly given up for dead by other rescuers. But Chrimes determined that he still had a pulse. He and another rescuer stripped off the boy's wet clothes and their own and did body-to-body warming. The boy was talking and coherent as they carried him off the mountain wrapped in their jackets.

Early Wednesday evening there was another glimmer of hope. Independent tracker Scott Forbes's Dutch shepherd, Da Wu ("big warrior" in Mandarin), found a human scent. Dogs play a major role in any wilderness SAR mission. Robert's was no different. "Dogs are huge in that one dog can cover what a team of half a dozen searchers can cover," says Chrimes, noting that humans shed 40,000 cells a second. "What the dog is doing is finding the most abundant thing we leave behind. They don't have to lay eyes on the person."

Da Wu is trained to find cadavers but can also follow living scents. However, on Wednesday evening he was frequently thrown off by some other smell. Then Forbes saw something he didn't like. A bold coyote was paralleling him and Da Wu in the shadows. "The boy would be easy opportunity for a pack of coyotes," Forbes recalls. An awful thought crossed his mind: Maybe they took him and buried him somewhere. Even the veteran searchers were beginning to get spooked—and to think the unthinkable.

By ten o'clock Wednesday night, Chrimes was spent. He had not had more than a catnap at his post since Monday evening. At a nearby Best Western, which had generously provided free rooms for the searchers, he took a hot shower and collapsed into bed.

On Thursday morning the mood turned darker. At around eleven a.m., an explosion shook the ground under Norma Jean Williams's truck. The Martin Marietta quarry, part of the nation's second-largest producer of construction aggregates, had delayed a scheduled blast next to Battlefield Park for as long as it could. Quarry officials said they had searched the area twice that day and needed to go ahead with the detonation. Then volunteer Rodney Clifton, who uses a pacemaker and had shown up for another four-hour search, suffered a massive heart attack at the end of his shift. (A quick-moving medical student would revive him.)

Later that day, searchers learned Williams's special nickname for Robert. They swept the area close to the PLS once again, calling out for Bud. At around 8:30 that evening, two of the state's top trackers, Randall Burleson and Mark Gleason, from Appalachian Professional Tracking Group, heard something near the PLS that made the hair stand up on the backs of their necks. It was human-sounding: a high, guttural noise—*bepp, bepp*—coming from the woods. They looked at each other and called out Robert's nickname again. They heard the same noise, but fainter. "Hey, Bud, let's go see Daddy," they called. "Let's get something to eat." No response. The searchers thrashed into the bushes. They found nothing, but were sure that they had been within yards of Robert.

Chrimes responded with everything he had: canine teams and searchers with night-vision goggles and thermal-imaging cameras. They scoured the area for four and a half hours. At one a.m. they gave up. If it was Robert, he had pulled another amazing vanishing act.

That night, as predicted, it started to rain and it got colder. Williams had to turn on the heat in her truck. Each night she had parked it in a slightly different place, shining the lights into the woods at a new angle, hoping in vain that they would attract Robert. It was her fourth night in her cramped Dodge, and her nerves, her body, and her will were shot. "I gave up hope," she says. "I cursed the Lord. I told him he wasn't any God to children."

By nine a.m. on Friday, 350 trained workers were in the field. At this point, Forbes says, "I was thinking it was much more likely we were doing a recovery than a rescue."

That afternoon, local authorities finally let Robert's father, Locker, and Williams into the park. They drove Williams in on an ATV because she does not get around well. The three hurried down the paths calling out "Robert" and "Bud." There was no answer. For Robert to be found alive at this point was going to take a miracle.

That's exactly what happened in the case of Nadia Bloom, the eleven-year-old autistic girl lost in the swamps north of Orlando for four days. A man named James King, a member of the church Nadia attended, had a dream. In it he saw the girl sitting on a log in the swamp. God told him to "follow the sunrise."

"He directed my path," King later told *Good Morning America*. "I would be praying and calling out Scripture, and at one point I called out 'Nadia,' and I heard 'What?'"

Could lightning strike twice?

A Richmond-area man, who would insist upon remaining anonymous, said he was reading the newspaper Friday morning over breakfast with his wife when he saw that the temperature was about to drop and that it was going to rain. He told his wife he wanted to go look for the boy. On the way, he stopped at a store to buy a coat, gloves, and a hat.

The man drove to the volunteer processing center to join the search. But he was too late for that day's training session and was turned away. Instead, he drove himself to the search area, parked, and followed his instincts. They led him to Misty Morning Lane, a dusty road beside the Martin Marietta quarry. Somehow he evaded the quarry guards, who at other times had been posted at entries to the property. Chrimes's searchers saw the man in the new coat. They left him alone.

Less than a mile from where Robert had last been seen, the man walked between an agricultural field and the quarry. At some point, he either climbed a wire fence posted with NO TRESPASSING signs and two strands of barbed wire strung across the top, or he found one of two openings where the fence had been breached by fallen trees. He then pushed his way through scrub brush and onto the backfill from the quarry, scrambling over soft gray earth toward a vast, deep quarry pit. He scanned the pocked, gravel-piled, eroded quarry moonscape. There, near a sheer chasm, in a deep, wet gully, he saw a figure lying on its left side, tucked into the fetal position.

Barbara Locker was with her friend Carolyn Coutts, in Coutts's RV, where she had gone to get coffee. Coutts got a phone call and told Locker that Robert had been found. "The look on her face and the screech she let out," Coutts told a *Richmond Times-Dispatch* reporter, "that was worth every second of every minute we were there."

When Williams saw a sheriff's car speed up and then heard the news from a plainclothes detective that Robert had been found, she dropped to her knees. "I thought he was going to tell me he was dead," Williams says. When she found out that her grandson was alive and was being flown to Richmond for treatment, she said, "I've got to get to the hospital."

The man in the new coat had found Robert, still dressed in all of his clothes except his shoes. The boy was cold and scared. His hands and feet were purple and swollen. He had been mauled by insects and spiders and inhabited by chiggers and ticks. His body was covered in dirt, bruises, and scratches, and his head was skinned up. But he was alert and breathing without trouble. The man took off his new hat—a stocking cap—and put it on the boy's head. He slipped his new gloves over the boy's bloated hands and wrapped him in the new coat. He gave Robert some water, which he gulped down. Then he called 911.

"I don't think Robert would have lasted one more day," his grandmother later said.

News spread among the searchers. Word went around summoning all the volunteers back to their base stations. There they learned that Robert had been found. There were hugs and tears and shouts of joy.

Several men, including a firefighter and Sheriff Hines, had formed a chain and passed the boy up out of the gully to where others stood with a litter. "Bud, Grandmother loves you. She misses you," one of them told Robert. Shortly after two p.m., Robert was airlifted in fair condition to Virginia Commonwealth University Medical Center Children's Hospital by a Virginia state-police helicopter. By that evening, his condition was upgraded to good. At some point, he had eaten something that had torn his esophagus, probably a stick, but the abrasion would heal itself.

As soon as the man called in his find, the sheriff's department sealed off the area. Neither press nor other searchers were allowed in.

Like James King, the man who found Robert wanted no credit for finding him. Instead, he issued a statement through the Hanover sheriff's department: "I was guided by the Holy Spirit," he said. "To take any recognition for finding Robert would take credit away from God."

Despite repeated efforts by me and others, the man has never been identified, and he has never spoken publicly. The Hanover sheriff's department refuses to forward him a message. Few if any questioned the story in the tsunami of praise that came for the humble man.

Norma Jean Williams tried several times to learn his identity through the sheriff's office. "They said they would deliver a message," Williams says. "But they never would tell me who he was."

~~~~~~

How had Robert beaten the odds and, for five days, evaded multiple searches of the area that he was ultimately found in? There are rumors that a quarry employee actually found Robert, but Martin Marietta officials aren't talking. Nor is the

Hanover County sheriff's department, which refused my request to discuss the search with its officers, other than a spokesperson.

The expert searchers want to know, too. "Our hounds checked this man's steps," says Forbes. His story checked out. "We tried to backtrack on the boy but could not find a scent," he says. "A dozen dogs on the ground . . . I'm still baffled by it."

The only explanation is that anytime Robert heard someone nearby, he ran and hid. And he was damn good at it.

Chrimes and Koester are taking it in stride. "I'm a gut-instinct kind of guy," Chrimes says. "In this case, someone listened to his gut and happened to be in the right place at the right time." He adds, "Everything Robert did fell into the file of what would be expected of him. The area where he was found was searched anywhere from six to ten times."

Koester agrees. "It didn't strike me as a particularly unusual outcome," he told me. "It ultimately fit the model well. Being evasive fit the model well. His survivability doesn't actually surprise me all that much. Lost people last longer than the general public thinks they will. There's a big difference between being uncomfortable and being dead."

Robert is alive and well, living at home with his mother and grandmother and going to school. He still can't tell us where he was all that time or what he was doing. He and Ryan now wear miniature transmitters on snug vinyl straps around their ankles, acquired for them through Project Lifesaver, a program that helps those suffering from Alzheimer's, dementia, or autism, and through the Caroline County sheriff's department. The transmitters send out a signal for up to a mile and can be tracked by law enforcement.

But Robert has also changed.

"You can touch him now. You can hold him," says Williams. "Before, he would never let you. When I say, 'Give me a kiss,' he gives me a kiss. And he doesn't run off like he did before. He would run out in the field or toward the road. Now, if he runs, he runs to the front door to go inside or to the door of my truck."

Robert's time in the woods might change things for other autistic kids, too. "Robert's case brought it to a national level," says Lori McIlwain of the National Autism Association. "Law enforcement is now asking more about autism. And it showed that you shouldn't give up too easily. These children can be found. We would hate for our kids to be left out there."

Sometimes it just takes a little luck—or a divine act. "I don't dismiss the religious side," Koester says. "A few protracted searches for a child with autism had very similar outcomes, where somebody had divine guidance and just went somewhere and looked."

CLIFFHANGER

PETER FRICK-WRIGHT

On New Year's Day in 1985, Eastern Air Lines Flight 980 was carrying twenty-nine passengers and a hell of a lot of contraband when it crashed into the side of a 21,112-foot mountain in Bolivia. For decades conspiracy theories abounded as the wreckage remained inaccessible, the bodies unrecovered, the black box missing. When two friends from Boston contacted our writer about organizing a high-altitude expedition to search for the remains, we gladly signed on for the quest. We had no idea they'd blow the case wide open.

By the time it crashed, Eastern Air Lines Flight 980 would have been just about ready to land. Beverage carts stowed, seat backs upright, tray tables locked. The twenty-nine people on board would have just heard the engines change pitch and felt the nose dip slightly, seat belts tugging at their stomachs.

One imagines a focused cockpit. Pilot Larry Campbell was responsible for the safety of everyone on the flight, and this was just his second landing in the Bolivian city of La Paz. Copilot Ken Rhodes was a straightforward military man. No foolishness, especially when descending through a mountain valley in bad weather. Sitting behind both, flight engineer Mark Bird was a retired fighter jock. In the Air Force, he was known for buzzing the tower and other high jinks, but he'd joined Miami-based Eastern only a few months before, and during a tricky approach in the middle of a thunderstorm would not have been the moment to chime in.

On January 1, 1985, the mostly empty Boeing 727 was headed from Asunción, Paraguay, to Miami, with stopovers in Bolivia and Ecuador. Landing in La Paz was always difficult. Ground controllers there had no radar, and what navigational equipment they did have was spotty, so they relied on the cockpit crew to track their own position.

At 13,325 feet, El Alto International, which serves La Paz, is the highest international airport in the world. The air is so thin that planes land at 200 miles per hour because they would fall out of the sky at the usual 140. Air brakes find less purchase here, so the runway is more than twice the normal length. The airport is so high that, as the plane dropped toward La Paz, the pilots would have worn oxygen masks until they reached the gate, per FAA regulations. Passengers would have felt the altitude's effects as the cabin depressurized: increased heart rate, deeper breaths, fuzzy thoughts.

The last anyone heard from the jet was at 8:38 p.m. Eastern time. According to ground controllers, the flight was about 30 miles from the airport and cruising on track at roughly 20,000 feet. It was cleared to descend to 18,000 feet when it plowed straight into a mountain.

Mount Illimani, a 21,122-foot mass of rocks and glaciers rising from the eastern edge of Bolivia's Altiplano region, towers over La Paz. The Andean mountain is so textured by ridgelines, high peaks, and shadows that, viewed from the city, it seems to move and change shape throughout the day.

Flight 980 hit nose first on the back side of Illimani, just below the summit. It probably cartwheeled forward, the fuselage bursting and splattering across the mountain like a dry snowball hitting a tree. Nearby villagers said it shook the whole valley. The airport's radio registered only a single click.

It took a full day to locate the wreckage. Once the Bolivian air force saw it on the peak, it mobilized a team to get to the crash site, but a storm had dumped several feet of snow, and avalanches turned them back. The Bolivian team was soon followed by representatives of the US embassy in La Paz and those from the National Transportation Safety Board (NTSB) and the Airline Pilots Association (ALPA), the two organizations responsible for investigating crashes by US airlines. But none of them were acclimatized enough to do any climbing. The agencies asked to borrow a high-altitude helicopter from Peru, but Bolivia wouldn't allow it inside the country.

"The Bolivian government did not want the world to know that the Peruvians had a better helicopter than they did," says Bud Leppard, chairman of the ALPA Accident Analysis Board, who departed for La Paz immediately after hearing about the crash. Eventually permission was granted, and Leppard devised a plan to reach the crash site by jumping off the helicopter as it flew above the ground at 21,000 feet, then skiing down to the plane. Better judgment prevailed when he realized that the chopper couldn't hover at that altitude.

Sikorsky Aircraft shipped an experimental high-altitude helicopter to Bolivia that could drop Leppard off at the crash site, but the mechanics sent to reassemble it were so altitude-sick upon landing in La Paz that several days passed before they could do any work. When they did get it flying, bad weather at the summit kept everyone in the chopper.

One Bolivian climber, Bernardo Guarachi, apparently made it up to the wreckage on foot two days after the crash but then said almost nothing about his findings. When the Bolivian government filed an official—but inconclusive—crash report a year later, Guarachi wasn't named in it. It was unclear who'd sent him in the first place.

Two months after the crash, in March 1985, a private expedition of Bolivian alpinists commissioned by Ray Valdes, an Eastern flight engineer who would have been on board if he hadn't swapped shifts, successfully navigated the treacherous mix of rock and ice. The small team encountered wreckage and luggage, but they couldn't locate the plane's black box. Stranger than that, no one found any bodies at the crash site. Or blood.

Another private expedition went up in July 1985, followed by NTSB investigators in October, but neither was able to spend more than a single day at the crash site.

In all, at least five expeditions have climbed Illimani in search of the wreckage over the past thirty years. None of them found any bodies or flight recorders, nor could anybody establish what brought down the plane. Officially, it was designated a "controlled flight into terrain," which means it couldn't be blamed on a bird strike or an engine malfunction or hijackers. The NTSB ultimately filed its own report to supplement the Bolivian one, but it came to the same flat conclusion: The plane was destroyed because it ran into a mountain.

As time passed, however, details emerged that invited speculation among South American journalists, the families of the victims, and anyone else still following the story. The flight crashed because of an equipment malfunction; no, the crew was new to the route and flying in bad weather; no, the Paraguayan mafia blew it up because the country's richest man was on board; no, Eastern Air Lines was running drugs; no, it was an attempted political assassination—someone took down the flight to get at the US ambassador to Paraguay, Arthur Davis, who was supposed to be aboard but changed his plans at the last minute.

The thing is, even the more-outlandish theories had some ring of truth. Five members of Paraguay's prominent Matalón family, who built an empire selling home appliances, were on the flight. The wife of the US ambassador to Paraguay—Marian Davis, who had continued on without her husband—died in the crash. In 1986, a criminal indictment against twenty-two Eastern baggage handlers revealed that, for three years, the airline had indeed been used to deliver weekly shipments of 300 pounds of cocaine from South America to Miami. (Eastern declared bankruptcy in 1989, and dissolved in 1991.)

So the mystery deepened. Theories festered and grew. Where were the flight recorders? Where were the bodies?

One of the more-comprehensive explanations came from George Jehn, a former Eastern pilot who published a 2014 book about the crash called *Final Destination: Disaster*. In it he theorizes that a bomb went off, depressurized the plane, and sucked all the bodies out of the cabin. Then he speculates that either Eastern or the NTSB hired Bernardo Guarachi to get rid of the flight recorders as a way of halting further inquiry into the crash, for fear that a full investigation would have revealed that the airline was running drugs for President Ronald Reagan. It's a convoluted plot, too far-fetched to take seriously, but seductive as hell to those looking to explain the inexplicable.

"Not one body, not one body part, no bloodstains. Why not?" Jehn said when we spoke in May. "It's the single greatest aviation mystery of the twentieth century."

But the case of Flight 980 is about as cold as they come. Any remaining clues have been locked in the ice of a Bolivian glacier for decades. Trying to solve it would combine the dangers of high-altitude mountaineering with the long odds of treasure hunting—a losing hand almost every time. So here's another question worth asking: What sort of foolhardy seeker suddenly takes an interest in a thirty-year-old plane crash?

~~~~~~

Dan Futrell is an affable, loud, heart-on-his-sleeve kind of guy. Impulsive. Persistent. In college he was the Gonzaga bulldog mascot at basketball games, dancing and making costumed mischief during time-outs. After graduating in 2007, he served two tours in Iraq. He completed Army Ranger School but decided to move on to civilian life. Now thirty-three, he manages people and spreadsheets for an Internet company in Boston, where he lives.

To say that he misses the physical challenge of soldiering is an understatement, but that's his preface when you ask him what kicked off his interest in the crash. Since leaving the army, he's made a habit of regularly scheduling sufferfests—he once took aim at all seven peaks in New England named after presidents and bagged them in one day. A little more than a year ago, he stumbled across a Wikipedia list of unrecovered flight recorders. Next to Eastern Air Lines Flight 980, the article listed "inaccessible terrain" as the reason the flight recorders had never been found.

"Challenge accepted," he wrote on his blog.

Isaac Stoner, Dan's roommate, was the first to hear his let's-go-find-it sales pitch. Though they've known each other only two years, they act and argue like brothers. But where Dan has dark hair, weary eyes, and an expressive face with many angles, Isaac has the blond hair and classically handsome features of a small-market news anchor. Dan is spontaneous and emotional; Isaac is calm and analytical. After the army, Dan attended grad school at Harvard; Isaac worked in biotech and then went to MIT.

Finding the box sounded pretty good to Isaac. And it took priority over their other screwball ideas, like running a marathon in a suit or attempting to set the world record in the pieathlon, a 3.14-mile race in which you eat a whole pie.

Most people still tracking this plane crash have deeply personal, often tragic reasons to care about it but very little capacity for travel and risk. Dan and Isaac had no reason but the adventure. They had no sponsorships, benefactors, or Kickstarter funding—just a crazy plan, a bit of money in the bank, and two weeks' vacation.

The first step was to divvy up the responsibilities. Dan was in charge of learning about the crash and its history, figuring out where to start searching, and blogging about the trip. Isaac researched the altitude, weather, skills they'd need to learn, and contingencies if things didn't go smoothly—in short, he was tasked with keeping them alive.

They embarked on a five-month training plan that consisted of running stairs at the Harvard football stadium and sleeping in a Hypoxico altitude-simulation tent. Four weeks before wheels up, a friend of a friend sent me a link to their blog and relayed that they'd be happy to have me along. Two days later, I was on the phone ordering my own altitude tent.

Our primary search area was not the crash site itself, but a roughly 1-square-mile patch of glacial moraine 3,000 feet below it. Flight 980 hit a saddle on the south side of Illimani, near the top, and for the past thirty-one years plane parts have been sliding down the mountain in icefalls, plunging over a cliff, and then slowly grinding downhill toward a glacier at the bottom.

The Bolivian summer and fall of 2016 (the Northern Hemisphere's winter and spring) had been warm and rainy, and we were told that the glacier had melted far up the mountain. The moraine—and the wreckage—was more exposed than ever. We planned to spend four days searching the debris field at about 16,000 feet, then another searching the original crash site at 19,600 feet.

Which is how we find ourselves standing amid a heap of rental gear in a climbing shop in La Paz, three days after leaving the United States. Off to one side, I'm nauseous and dizzy from climbing a single flight of stairs. We're at 13,000 feet, but to me it feels like the summit of Everest. Isaac says it looks like I got hit by a large bus. He says he got hit by a smaller one.

Meanwhile, our climbing guide, Robert Rauch, has fallen asleep in his camping chair. Fifty-nine years old, born in Germany but living in Bolivia for the past twenty years, Robert has pioneered more than a hundred routes in the country, including three on Illimani's south side. His house has an entire room devoted to equipment for different kinds of pull-ups. He does not own a couch. Dan calls him "the most interesting guide in the world."

Rauch had taken an interest in the crash as well. He'd traveled through the debris field while scouting routes on Illimani and thought that a concerted, methodical search of the area might turn up the recorders and bodies. "The whole area will lie in front of us like a Google map," he'd written in an e-mail.

A few minutes later, our expedition's cook, Jose Lazo, shows up. He's Aymara— one of Bolivia's indigenous peoples—and he and Robert are soon telling stories about the time Jose was chased by a bear, the time Robert was chased by a condor, the time an angry mob chased the two of them out of Jose's village and they fled 300 miles in seven days, crossing jungles and alligator-infested rivers to get back to La Paz. Dan calls him "the most interesting cook in the world."

Back in the store, Isaac is trying to convince Dan to rent warmer snow pants; Dan is rolling his eyes. Robert is down to his skivvies, having dropped trou in the middle of the shop to rub his sore left knee with an herbal balm he bought on the street.

I'm still feeling queasy, resting on a box of something or other, when a climber with a man bun sits next to me and says that a week of wind sprints before we start will help me adapt to the altitude.

"When do you leave?" he asks.

"Tomorrow morning."

~~~~~~

To get to Mount Illimani, we tie our bags to the roof of a rented Land Cruiser and tell the driver to head south from La Paz, following the Irpavi River all the way down to 3,000 feet, where the air feels soupy and rich and our pulses finally find the low side of 70. I feel remarkably better. Then we cross the river and drive to 12,000.

At least it's a rest day. Our only responsibility is riding in a car and then unloading our overstuffed backpacks and duffel bags at Mesa Khala, an abandoned tungsten mine at 15,400 feet that's a forty-five-minute hike from the lower debris field. As we drive up the other side of the steep valley, past an active uranium mine, we round a corner and see 50 yards of impassable rock blocking the road.

"What if we just drive faster?" Dan says.

We're still 2 miles and about 3,000 vertical feet below our base camp at Mesa Khala, and we're going to have to hike it. So much for the rest day.

Dan and Robert walk to the uranium mine and return ten minutes later.

"*Cinco* porters-o," Dan tells us, exhausting his knowledge of Spanish. "They'll carry our shit-o. Up the mountain-o."

This is great news, except we packed like we were driving all the way to base camp, so even five porters won't be enough. "This is how Livingstone traveled," Isaac says, surveying the explosion of gear as we hastily jettison nonessential items—candy, notebooks, an extra stove, more candy—to send back in the 4x4.

The ascent doesn't kill us, but it tries. Jose sets the route, and it turns out that Aymara-style climbing consists of walking straight up the fall line. By the halfway point, I'm resting every few steps.

Four hours later, we've covered the 2 miles to Mesa Khala. Setting up camp among the ruins, we find plane parts that locals must have brought to the mine from the debris field. Scrutinizing and discussing each one in detail, we're transfixed, as if this random piece of aluminum tubing or that tiny drive shaft or the mechanism from an inflatable life vest might shed light on what brought down the aircraft.

The next morning, we hike to the steep glacial moraine that marks the edge of the debris field and find more parts on the ridge. It's exciting. This is exactly what Dan and Isaac spent five months imagining a Bolivian mystery adventure would be like—scattered clues leading to a search area laid out in front of them like a Google map.

In fact, it was only recently that this trip went from being a simple treasure hunt to something heavier, a story about tangible grief and unexplainable loss. Only recently did they meet Stacey Greer.

~~~~~~

Greer has a few very specific memories of her dad, flight engineer Mark Bird. Talking on his radio. Eskimo kisses. The two of them snuggling in his recliner. She was three years old when the plane crashed.

"My mom didn't really talk about it a lot," Greer told me when I called her at her home in Fort Benning, Georgia, a few weeks before we left for Bolivia. "She just said that he had been in a plane crash. As a kid, your imagination runs wild. You always ask yourself, Why couldn't he just jump out of the plane? Crazy stuff like that."

She didn't fully understand what had happened until she watched the video of his memorial service as a teenager.

"It was just my dad's flight helmet and a picture of him. It clicked," she said. "There was no casket. There was no body."

In the past few years, Greer, now thirty-four, has started questioning the official narrative that the crash site was too difficult and dangerous to reach. She read George Jehn's book and contacted him by e-mail; he sent her a link to Dan and Isaac's blog. A former army nurse who met her husband in Iraq, she forged a quick connection with Dan, who was also in the army and raised by a single parent.

But where Dan carefully avoids any mention of conspiracy, favoring a more-straightforward interpretation of the crash, Greer seems to have embraced the idea.

"It's the only plane crash that has never been properly investigated by the NTSB," she said. "And then a few years later, Eastern goes under."

In total, Flight 980 carried nineteen passengers and ten crew. Eight were Americans, five of whom worked for Eastern, and seven were Paraguayans, five of whom were part of the Matalón family. There were also nine Korean passengers and five Chilean flight attendants.

With seating for 189 passengers, the crash could have been far more deadly, and Greer never heard from any of the other families. To her it felt like everything was immediately swept under the rug. The missing bodies aren't so much a mystery as a sign that the general public stopped caring.

"People need closure," she said. "Imagine one of your family members on the mountain for years, and their body has been frozen over and over and over again."

***

Robert finds the first body part. It's a femur, roughly 14 inches long, and so dry that it's almost mummified. You can see skin, muscle, and fat still attached.

"That's pretty gruesome," Dan says. "It just sheared right off in the crash."

Encased in ice for more than a quarter-century, the bone likely spent several years sliding down the mountain from the crash site, several seconds falling over a 3,000-foot cliff, and—judging by the milky white marrow still visible inside the bone and its location at the base of a rapidly melting glacier—perhaps only months in the sun before being found by us. It's one p.m. on our first day of searching.

"Shall we say some words?" Isaac asks.

Sure, but no one can really think of anything.

"Shall we bury it?" Dan says.

They dig a small grave, stacking rocks as a marker. Not long after, we find another bone—probably a tibia. Then, a few feet away, cervical vertebrae with frayed nerves still visible down the spinal column.

As we search, the temperature swings wildly between T-shirt weather in the sun and down-jacket weather in the shade. Every hour or so, a massive block of ice—possibly carrying more plane parts—drops off the saddle and roars toward us before disintegrating into a sugary white cloud.

Our plan was to walk a precise and thorough grid. But the search area is longer and thinner than we anticipated, a lifeless alpine moraine filled with boulder gardens and ice fields, walled off on three sides by vertical rock. Sixty-foot-tall glacier fragments and 10-foot-deep canyons force us off our pattern. So instead we spend the morning scrambling between pieces of wreckage on our own, congregating whenever anyone finds something interesting.

This happens quite a bit. There are plane parts everywhere. First we discover pieces of fuselage and a jet engine, then wiring and toggle switches and seat belts and children's shoes. Then Robert finds a black plastic box.

"That's a black box," Isaac says when Robert holds it up. "Not *the* black box."

We see an astonishing number of contraband crocodile- and snakeskins, which were probably being smuggled to Miami to be made into black-market goods like shoes and handbags.

Dan gets on the radio to tell us that he found a roll of magnetic tape. "This is either from one of the black boxes," he says, "or it has a great 1985 movie on it."

Isaac and Dan also both find a few chunks of orange metal, which is exciting because—despite the name—flight recorders are painted international orange to help investigators locate them. But the pieces seem too trashed to have come from supposedly indestructible boxes.

Most planes carry two flight recorders: the cockpit voice recorder, which documents conversation among the pilots and the engineer, and the flight-data recorder, which notes the status of the plane's mechanical systems several times per second.

Current specifications require that a flight recorder's metal case be capable of withstanding temperatures of 2,000 degrees, underwater depths of 20,000 feet, and impacts up to 3,400 times the force of gravity. To hit these marks, the outer shell is made from a blend of titanium and steel. It also must have an underwater locator beacon that emits a ping for thirty days.

These standards weren't so rigorous and uniform in 1985, and we couldn't nail down which type of recorders were on Flight 980, in part because the airline has been shuttered for twenty-seven years. Most of Eastern's planes used a model of flight recorder manufactured by Fairchild that recorded via magnetic tape. But not all of them. So aside from the color, we aren't really sure what the black box will look like.

Dan is adamant that the orange metal pieces are part of the flight recorders—but they're aluminum, not titanium or steel. The metal must be a piece of something else on the plane; the tape could just be a home video, stashed in luggage. It feels like our discoveries have only prompted more questions: What happened on all those other expeditions? Why didn't they find any body parts? And could you believe all those snakeskins?

~~~~~~

In La Paz, the theories surrounding Flight 980 have less to do with missing bodies and cover-ups and more with the dubious rumor that Enrique Matalón—then the richest man in Paraguay—supposedly carried $20 million on board in a duffel bag.

In 2006, a Bolivian climbing guide named Roberto Gomez got wind that plane parts were turning up in the glacier below the crash site. If the wreckage was turning up, he thought there might also be a bag of money. Gomez and his team spent three days searching the glacier.

"The strangest thing we found was lizard skins," Gomez says when we meet in his office in La Paz. "But it was a really sad scene, because we found a lot of children's clothes, and many pictures."

As Gomez tells his story, it's clear that the Bolivian and American versions of this mystery diverge fairly quickly. The only place they overlap is at the beginning, when Bernardo Guarachi made it to the crash site and then clammed up about what he saw there.

In his book, George Jehn has a lot of questions for Guarachi. "Was he paid? If so, who paid him?" he writes. "What was his specific mission? What did he discover? Did he take pictures? Did he see or recover the recorders? Why didn't the NTSB demand answers to these important questions?"

Oddly, though, Jehn never actually attempted to find Guarachi, even though he's a fairly prominent climbing guide in Bolivia and is open to being interviewed when I contact him.

Born in Bolivia but raised in Chile, Guarachi returned to La Paz to look for work when he was nineteen. After being taken in by a more-experienced guide in Bolivia, he went to Germany for formal training as a mountaineer and came home looking to make his name. He introduced himself at various organizations and said he was available if they ever needed help in the mountains.

He tells me that a man named Royce Fichte from the US embassy contacted him after a Bolivian plane spotted the wreckage of Flight 980 the day after the crash. They met at the airport on short notice—Guarachi didn't even have time to grab a camera—and took a helicopter toward the mountain. By the time they arrived at Puente Roto, a base camp on the west side, there were already teams assembling from the Red Cross and the Bolivian military.

The team stayed there that night, and the next day Guarachi and two assistants climbed to the crash site while Fichte stayed behind. Partway up, someone on the radio told them to turn around—he wasn't sure who it was—but Guarachi insisted, and finally got permission to keep going. After climbing to the saddle beyond the summit, he could tell they were getting close from the overpowering smell of jet fuel, but he couldn't see the plane. It was only during a tiny break in the weather that he caught a glimpse and hiked over.

There was wreckage scattered everywhere. The team found open suitcases, papers from the cockpit, crocodile skins, and shoes. Fichte had described where the flight recorders should be, but everything was a mess.

"When you went to the crash site, did you see body parts?" I ask him.

"No bodies," he says. "Not even a finger. But there was blood. The plane hit the mountain dead-on. Everything disintegrated."

They slept at the crash site and the next day got word that they would be resupplied from the air and possibly joined by another investigator, who would drop out of a high-altitude helicopter on skis—probably Bud Leppard. But during test runs, the maneuvers were deemed too dangerous, and the supplies never came. Guarachi and his team had to descend.

On the way back down, they saw footprints at their previous camp. They had been followed, but whoever it was didn't continue to the crash site. They just stopped at the camp and left.

"I don't think their intention was to rescue us or see what happened to the plane," Guarachi says. "They were monitoring us."

At base camp, Guarachi's team was detained by the Bolivian military, separated, and taken to three different tents.

"They searched us all," Guarachi says. "My backpack, even our clothing. They got us naked."

He told them that all he'd found were plane parts and snakeskins. They were taken by helicopter to the airport and interrogated again. The official Bolivian crash report states that there were no bodies or blood, but Guarachi says that's because he was too scared to talk about what he saw.

"One of the men threatened me," Guarachi says. "He said, 'Careful telling anyone about this. I will ruin you.'"

We start higher on the search field the next day, marching with purpose toward the glacier. Yesterday it felt like the plane parts were in better shape the higher we climbed, so we start by searching the melting ice itself. Soon we're finding wheels, pistons, switches, hydraulics, another engine, life jackets, an oxygen tank, cables, alligator skins, and tangled clusters of wires.

Dan and Robert find a piece of metal lodged in ice, chip it out, and then decide not to do that again—there's not enough oxygen up here to swing a pickax around. By midmorning we're all thoroughly exhausted, and the novelty of new plane parts has worn off. Back at camp, it felt sort of miraculous to discover wreckage on a mountain, like each piece deserved our attention. But here, in the newly melted ice, there's an almost comical number of parts.

"I think something happened here," Isaac deadpans.

"Maybe a plane crash of some kind?" Dan responds.

You can hardly sit and rest without finding something aviation-related in the rocks at your feet. Jose and Robert find a pilot's jacket half buried in the glacier and start digging it out. Twenty minutes later, I find the cabin's altimeter.

On the way back to our packs for lunch, Isaac spots a lump of green cloth tied off with thick white yarn and begins to unwrap it.

"I hope it's not a body part," Isaac says, embracing the gallows humor that has become a mainstay of the trip. "No body, no body, no body . . ."

I point out that it's more likely to be cocaine.

"Cocaine!" Isaac says, comically hopeful. "Cocaine, cocaine, cocaine!"

It isn't cocaine. It's a brick of papers in a ziplock bag. And a 1985 Baltimore Orioles schedule. And a plastic toy. And some crayons. And pages from a diary?

Oh. No way. This belongs to Judith Kelly.

~~~~~~

In July 1985, Judith Kelly made the second private expedition to the crash site. Her husband, William Kelly, had been director of the Peace Corps in Paraguay and was on Flight 980, headed back to the United States. When the NTSB's immediate response was stymied by weather and logistics, Kelly began preparing for her own trip.

She devoted three months to getting in shape, took a mountaineering course in Alaska, and then went to Bolivia. Kelly declined to be interviewed for this article, but she told her story to George Jehn. In his book, Jehn describes how she met with NTSB investigator Jack Young, who died in 2005. Young reportedly told her to move on and put the loss behind her.

"Perhaps you could say that to someone with a broken arm or leg," she told Jehn. "But not a broken heart."

Kelly took a few weeks to acclimatize in Bolivia before hiring Bernardo Guarachi to take her up the mountain. They arrived at the wreckage on July 5, and Kelly spent a day reading letters she had written to her husband since the crash. She had also collected letters from the families of other victims. When she was done, she wrapped the package and buried it in the snow, where it began the same slow descent as the plane parts.

Back home, Kelly lobbied Eastern to conduct a more-thorough investigation. She'd reached the crash site without any problems, she argued, so there was no reason not to send another team. When that failed, she appeared on the *Today* show and said the same thing.

A few days later, the NTSB announced an expedition, which embarked in October 1985, after the Bolivian winter, with logistical support from the Bolivian Red Cross. According to a report by lead investigator Gregory Feith, the mission was nearly its own disaster. It describes how, on the first night, porters delivered their supplies to the wrong base camp. When the two parties did connect, they found that the porters had brought tents for only four of the seven people, and no stoves or fuel.

"We were able to melt enough snow to make one pot of cold noodle soup that allowed each of us one cup," Feith wrote.

One investigator developed signs of pulmonary edema—a life-threatening accumulation of fluid in the lungs—and had to descend the next morning; another developed altitude sickness at the crash site. Feith's team spent a day digging through deep snow around the plane and located the portion of the tail where the flight recorders should have been, but weren't.

It would be decades before anyone went looking for them again.

~~~~~~

After finding so much—wreckage, body parts, Judith Kelly's memorial—Isaac starts to think that the flight recorders have to be here somewhere.

"A couple days ago, I would have told you—I think I did tell you—that I don't really care about finding the black box," he says. "But I find myself becoming more and more obsessed."

The next day, Dan is low-energy, but Isaac's on fire, scrambling around the debris field, trying to cover it all. We crawl through glacier ice melted into curious spires. We hop over crevasses and peer into glacial caves, because we've exhausted all the safest places to search.

"Have you found it yet?" Dan and Isaac ask each other every few minutes.

"No, but I'm about to," the other invariably responds.

At one point, Dan finds a human neck with what looks like a dog tag embedded in the flesh. But when he digs the metal out, it turns out to be just another piece of aluminum. "I was hoping I could get an ID," Dan says. "But this unlucky guy just took some plane metal straight to the neck."

By midday we're beat. Isaac walks 150 yards to his gear and barely makes it back to the group; Dan sits down next to an engine. I can't stand without feeling like I've stepped onto a merry-go-round. We give up. Jose and Robert head back to camp to start dinner; Dan and Isaac say they just want to search a little longer.

But instead of searching, they start digging up a metal beam angled out of the ground. When I ask them why, Isaac says, "I don't know, I just started digging."

Just as we're beginning to accept that we've failed, that we still don't know whether the flight recorders were stolen or destroyed or maybe still covered in ice, that we've given up and will have nothing to tell Stacey Greer and George Jehn and all the other people who are still following the crash. . . . Just as we're coming to terms with all that, something amazing happens: Isaac finds the cockpit voice recorder.

It's on the ground, ten steps from where we ate lunch, a chunk of smashed metal sitting orange side down in the rocks. Isaac picks it up. Dan comes over to examine it.

There's a wiring harness on one end, with a group of cables leading inside, labeled CKPT VO RCDR. It's bright orange, crushed almost beyond recognition. Like many recorders manufactured before the mid-eighties, its outer shell is made of aluminum.

"This is it; this is the black box," Isaac says.

We've been finding pieces of it—of both flight recorders—the entire time.

~~~~~~

When we get back to La Paz, Dan and Isaac call Stacey Greer. "Why didn't anyone find it before?" she says. "It just feels like there are so many unanswered questions."

Indeed. Why didn't anyone find the flight recorders on the first, second, or third expeditions? Who threatened Bernardo Guarachi, and why? Who was smuggling reptile skins to Miami? What brought the plane down in the first place?

Flying home, we thought we still might have a shot at answering the last one. We had that roll of magnetic tape Dan found on the first day of searching. And based on nothing more than photos we could find online, it looked pretty similar to what would have been inside a flight recorder.

Before we found anything, the plan had been to turn all notable materials over to the US embassy in La Paz. But with orange metal in hand, giving them to a bureaucrat seemed like a good way to get them locked away forever.

When Dan and Isaac got home, they told a friend who had worked at the FAA about what they'd found, and he said, "I just hope you didn't bring it home."

By taking the flight recorders and tape back to the United States, they discovered, they had violated Annex 13 of the Convention on International Civil Aviation, a document that lays out the rules for international air travel. It says that wherever a plane crashes, that country is in charge of the investigation. Moving evidence to a different nation could be seen as undermining that authority.

The NTSB told Dan and Isaac that the Bolivian government would have to request the agency's assistance before it could get involved, and it's the only agency with equipment to analyze the tape.

Unfortunately, relations between Bolivia and the United States are pretty frosty. In 2008, Bolivian president Evo Morales accused both the US ambassador to Bolivia and the Drug Enforcement Administration of plotting a coup, and expelled them from the country. Then, in 2013, Morales's personal plane was forced to land in Austria because of a rumor that Edward Snowden was on board. Morales was so mad he threatened to close the US embassy.

I tried reaching out to retired crash investigators at Boeing and to various aviation museums, hoping that someone might help us figure out whether the tape was from the black box, but no one would touch it until the legal situation was resolved. Meanwhile, we couldn't get any answers out of La Paz or the Bolivian embassy in Washington. From June to September of 2016, we made phone calls that weren't returned, sent e-mails that weren't acknowledged, and mailed certified letters that went unanswered.

"This surprises me not one iota," George Jehn wrote in an e-mail when I sent him an update. "It's like that crash is toxic. Nobody wants to go near it."

~~~~~~

Conspiracies breed in the spaces between solid facts, and unless the NTSB decides to further strain diplomatic ties with Bolivia or gets permission to look at the tape and finds usable information—and both scenarios seem pretty unlikely—there will always be gaps in the story of Flight 980. But when you're solving mysteries, the simplest explanation tends to be the right one. After we got back from Bolivia, we knew that Guarachi didn't steal the flight recorders and that a bomb didn't suck all the bodies from the plane before it hit the mountain. As we reevaluated the facts about the flight, a plausible story began to emerge.

The descent into La Paz, for example, was even more difficult than we first realized. In addition to the lack of radar at the airport, language problems sometimes plagued communication between flight crews and controllers on the ground. When Eastern purchased the routes to South America, it issued a memo warning pilots to exercise a "dose of pilot-type skepticism" when in contact with the tower. There was little training on how to do this, however. Before going into La Paz, the captain was required only to watch a video about the landing. Then, on his first trip, a check pilot—someone who had flown the route before—would ride in the cockpit.

Flight 980 crashed on what would have been pilot Larry Campbell's second landing in La Paz. Check captain Joseph Loseth was aboard, but had been seated in first class.

What's more, the navigation technology at Campbell's disposal was rudimentary. Nine months after the crash, Don McClure, the chairman of ALPA's accident-investigation board, was part of a separate inquiry into the overall safety of flying in South America. His report details a number of shortcomings, particularly with an onboard navigation system called Omega. He noted that on flights between Paraguay and Bolivia, the system steered aircraft 4 miles off course in the direction of Mount Illimani—though this alone wouldn't have caused Flight 980's impact.

Meanwhile, the aircraft's other navigation system—called VOR, for "very high frequency omnidirectional range"—relied on localized radio transmitters that told pilots only where the beacons were, not where the plane was.

"All the navigation facilities on this route are so weak and unreliable that there is no good way to cross-check the Omega," McClure wrote. Even if the pilots suspected that they were off course, it would have been impossible to verify.

Maybe none of this would have mattered if there wasn't also a storm southeast of the airport. Maybe a more-experienced crew would have gone south around that storm instead of north, toward Illimani. (Or maybe not—other airlines had maps of the valley with terrain hazards labeled prominently, but Eastern didn't.) We can speculate that the storm, combined with lackluster navigation equipment, inexperience, and bad luck, led Flight 980 straight into the side of Illimani, but it's still conjecture. Instead of case closed, it's case slightly less open.

Or maybe that's missing the real point. In July, Stacey Greer was in Boston for a week of classes and met up with Dan to talk about the expedition and look at pictures of the debris field. He also brought a couple of small plane parts and gave them to her.

"This is my dad, right here," Stacey said as Dan clunked the pieces down on the table. "This is the closest thing I have to the last time I saw him."

When her young kids called at bedtime, she had them talk with "the man who found Grandpa's plane." Then she and Dan called her mom, Mark Bird's widow.

"Do you have any idea what happened?" she asked.

"We have lots of ideas," Dan said. "The problem is we're no better than anyone else at picking the right one."

But now that there's evidence of the bodies and flight recorders, and any notions of mysterious journeys to the summit have been dispelled, the questions we're left with seem much less nefarious.

Did a storm push the flight off course, or was it a problem with the navigation systems? Did the cockpit crew spot the mountain and try to make a frantic emergency turn? Or were they calmly pulling on the oxygen masks that they would have worn all the way to the gate? Were they sitting in nervous silence as lightning flashed around them and weather beat at the cockpit? Or was Mark Bird wishing everyone a happy new year and telling a joke? If his voice is on the magnetic tape sitting in Dan and Isaac's kitchen, will anyone ever hear it?

NUT JOB

PETER VIGNERON

~~~~~~

In California, millions of dollars' worth of almonds, walnuts, and pistachios have gone missing since 2010. Farmers are perplexed, the cops are confused, and the crooks are getting richer. We sent our writer to the Central Valley to investigate what's become an unusual new side hustle for sophisticated organized-crime syndicates.

~~~~~~

At 11:22 a.m. on Thursday, June 20, 2013, an orange Freightliner tractor trailer arrived at Crain Walnut Shelling in Los Molinos, California. The truck's driver, a man in his mid-thirties wearing a gray T-shirt, introduced himself as Alex Hernandez. He said he was from K and G Transport Services, a company contracted to take a load of Crain's walnuts to Bulk Barn Foods Limited, a Canadian food retailer located 2,600 miles away in Ontario. Hernandez had arrived before the pickup had been scheduled, which initially made Crain's logistics director suspicious. But after double-checking the paperwork that he provided, she directed employees to load 630 cartons of walnuts, worth $85,000, into Hernandez's trailer.

At 12:06 p.m., Hernandez left Los Molinos and headed south through California's Central Valley into Glenn County, where he picked up a second batch of walnuts intended for Bulk Barn from a processor called Carriere Family Farms. While leaving, Hernandez's Freightliner got stuck in a field. He called a tow truck to pull it out, then drove off.

By Monday, June 24, neither batch of walnuts had arrived in Canada. A representative from the shipping brokerage that arranged the exchange tried but failed to reach K and G, and alerted Crain to the possibility that the nuts had been stolen.

On June 27, Chad Parker, a then thirty-eight-year-old agricultural-crimes detective with the Tehama County Sheriff's Office, went to investigate.

Crain's chief financial officer showed Parker a photograph from June 20 and provided him with the Freightliner's plate number and a photocopy of Hernandez's commercial driver's license. What Parker found made little sense: The plate came back registered to a different model of truck, and the license number belonged to a thirty-year-old woman. Later, when Parker pulled records for the phone number Hernandez had listed on the paperwork, he found that it was a prepaid cell phone with a Miami area code. It had been activated for the first time only two days before the pickup and then disconnected on June 29. Tractor trailers do not disappear easily, and Parker considered issuing a be-on-the-lookout for the Freightliner. But more than a month after the theft, he decided it was likely long gone.

Petty thefts of walnuts are not uncommon in central California. Several counties even ban the sale of nuts before harvest is complete, to discourage black-market sales. But the Crain theft, along with similar heists in 2011 and 2012, seemed different to Parker. They were committed by people who appeared to understand the trucking business, identity theft, and computer security. Neither of the earlier crimes had given Parker much to investigate, and at first this one looked no more promising. "I'm left holding a report saying 'Someone showed up,' and I've got a license plate that doesn't exist," Parker told me last winter. "They disappear into the night."

~~~~~~

Around the time of the Crain theft, Rich Paloma, a police officer turned reporter at the *Oakdale Leader*, a weekly paper based several hours south of Tehama County, began tracking high-value loads of nuts that had vanished. Paloma counted half a dozen heists, valued at more than $1 million, in the previous year. In the fall of 2013, he published an article speculating that the thefts were coordinated.

"When you look at the logistics needed to complete this crime," he told me, all signs point toward an organized group. "You steal 370,000 pounds of almonds, you're not going to sell it on the side of the road."

In recent years, nut theft has exploded into a statewide problem. More than thirty-five loads, worth at least $10 million, have gone missing since 2013. The number and style of the thefts—quick and professional, as if the characters from *Ocean's Eleven* had descended on the Central Valley—have drawn the attention of federal organized-crime investigators, and prompted the creation of a regional task force.

Why steal nuts? They're worth an awful lot of money. In 2014, the American Pistachio Growers association reported industry-wide sales of more than $1.6 billion.

The organization recently signed endorsement deals with British cyclist Mark Cavendish, big-mountain snowboarder Jeremy Jones, and the US water-polo teams.

California grows the majority of the world's almonds and is the second-largest producer of pistachios and walnuts. Many environmentalists blame their cultivation for exacerbating California's drought—nut trees are thirsty plants.

Last spring I visited the Horizon Nut Company, three hours north of LA in Tulare County. In November 2015, Horizon lost a load of pistachios worth $450,000. Kirk Squire, Horizon's grower-relations manager, said that the theft was embarrassing for the company. "You have to imagine, you're handing someone half a million dollars."

The Horizon plant is well defended. Visitors must have escorts, and the facility is enclosed by a tall fence topped with barbed wire. When I arrived, a security guard examined my ID. Squire and I met in a waiting area near his office, where I found a bowl of roasted and salted pistachios and took a handful. Inside the processing facility, we walked by an embankment of 2,000-pound bins of pistachios. Squire showed me a series of automated laser- and X-ray-guided sorting machines and the company's refrigerated storage warehouse, where nuts are kept for processing after being husked. The nuts in the load that went missing in 2015 retail for as much as $17.

A few hours after that theft, a Horizon employee had noticed that the driver's paperwork was out of order and called the police. Officers eventually tracked down the man, who had already delivered the nuts and didn't seem to know that he'd been involved in a crime. The thieves likely tricked him into delivering the load, then quickly transferred it. The nuts were never recovered.

The man tasked with finding missing nuts in Tulare County is sheriff Mike Boudreaux, and in 2015 he faced a growing problem. That year, thieves had stolen six shipments, valued at $1.6 million, from area processors, including Horizon. Recognizing a threat to the county's economy, Boudreaux assigned half a dozen detectives to a new unit—the Nut Theft Task Force. I met most of them at a conference for nut processors in Modesto last year. The men were barrel-chested and serious, wearing jeans, cowboy boots, and blousey white dress shirts. They looked as if the department had just then switched their assignment from bailing hay to organized crime. Boudreaux said nut theft had outstripped drug crime as his top priority and promised an aggressive investigation. Shortly after the conference got under way, news arrived that another processor in Tulare had been hit, and the team excused itself to work leads by phone out in the hallway.

Scott Cornell, who heads a special unit of cargo-fraud investigators at Travelers Insurance, told the audience that food and beverages overtook electronics as the most commonly stolen cargo in 2010. "We think the bad guys learned that food is a great category," he told me. "There's no serial number. You can't locate these things over the Internet. The evidence is consumed."

In fact, food is the easiest target in an ocean of easy targets. A private investigator and transit-company owner from California named Sam Wadhwani said that he had tracked cargo thefts of tires, Xboxes, computer equipment earmarked for the military, baby formula, tampons, and iPhones. Inventing a fake trucking company is easy, he said, as is impersonating a legitimate one. The only people in the shipping industry responsible for verifying truckers are brokers, who connect customers with trucking companies. Wadhwani looked into vetting practices at a major brokerage several years ago and asked the company to describe its process. An employee said, "We ask the trucking company to send documents, we pick them up off the fax, and we file them away. We don't look at them, we don't read them."

Roger Isom, president of the Western Agricultural Processors Association, said that the situation is further complicated by the fact that many nut processors have avoided contacting the police, worried that reporting thefts could jeopardize future business. "And not just the nut industry—the trucking companies, the shippers," he said. "They don't want to talk because they're embarrassed." No one is eager to be the laughingstock of the nut industry. When I visited Horizon, Squire told me that one processor, concerned about publicity, tried hiding GPS trackers in its shipments instead of calling the police. The company still lost two loads to thieves.

~~~~~~

The closer Chad Parker looked at K and G Transport, the more he grew convinced that the Crain theft was linked to a broader conspiracy. E-mail records for K and G revealed that someone had been accessing the company's account from public computers at libraries and Internet cafes around Los Angeles. (K and G is based in Miami.) Cargo thieves often pose as legitimate companies and bid for shipping contracts on load boards, which are sort of like Craigslist for truckers looking for jobs. A thief hoping to steal almonds might try to find transport jobs in nut-growing regions across the country, especially ones that ask truckers to be well insured or that leave late in the week, to give them a few extra days to get away. The Crain pickup, which occurred on a Thursday and was headed to Canada, was a perfect target.

Parker's first real break came when he discovered that Hernandez had made an error: Crain employees asked him to submit a thumbprint on June 20, 2013, and he agreed. Parker was shocked when the thumbprint generated a hit in the California Department of Justice database. Hernandez, it emerged, was actually a parolee named Marco Alberto Garcia, and he had recently been detained in the Los Angeles County Jail. Parker subpoenaed cell-phone records for Garcia's contacts, many of whom seemed to live and work in LA.

When interviewed, however, Garcia refused to answer any questions, and Parker wasn't optimistic about the case. "It went cold pretty fast," he told me. To help navigate the Los Angeles connections, Parker had sought out Marc Zavala, an LAPD detective who is widely regarded as the state's top cargo-theft investigator.

I met Zavala at a Starbucks in Van Nuys last year to discuss the crisis. These people "know that the punishment for theft is nothing. There's minimal jail time," usually measured in weeks or months, he told me. The thieves not only understand this, but "they make it complicated by stealing IDs."

Zavala put me in touch with a truck driver I'll call Andrei, who he arrested several years ago. I met Andrei last summer in Commerce City, Colorado, east of Denver. He is fifty-three and short, and was wearing sandals, a baseball hat, shorts, and a blue button-down shirt open to his belly. Andrei is ethnically Armenian and lived in the Republic of Georgia before emigrating to the Los Angeles area in 1995, where he did occasional work with a small trucking company.

In 2011, an accident put Andrei's truck out of commission. He needed money and approached a friend in the trucking business for help. The man had easy access to federal motor-carrier and Department of Transportation ID numbers. "We're going to put these stickers on your truck, because they know this company," he told Andrei. The man gave him a fake driver's license and a new truck, then sent him to collect a load of Budweiser. After Andrei delivered the beer successfully, the man had him steal a trailer full of beauty products. Investigators call these schemes "fictitious pickups," and they are a variation on the style of theft used in the Crain and Horizon heists. The idea is to convince victims that they are working with legitimate truckers—sometimes by making up a trucking company, sometimes by faking the paperwork of a legitimate business. Zavala happened to catch Andrei as the beauty products were being unloaded, then linked him to a 2011 almond theft in Madera, California, from a processor called Going Nuts.

Andrei told me he collected the load of almonds from Going Nuts as a subcontract while passing through Northern California on a run back to Los Angeles. He took them to a warehouse in Van Nuys, where two men—one of whom had an Israeli-sounding accent—paid him $600 cash. According to a criminal complaint in the case, the almonds were intended for Once Again Nut Butter in Nunda, New York, but never arrived. Zavala believes that they ended up in Mexico.

Andrei's lawyer advised him to plead guilty to stealing the almonds. He spent just shy of a month in jail and is now back to work as a driver. Though he admitted to me that he knowingly stole the Budweiser and beauty products, Andrei swore that he did not realize the nut transaction was illicit.

It appears that some drivers *are* genuinely unaware that they are participating in a crime. Kirk Squire at Horizon believes that a gullible driver picked up the company's pistachios, not knowing he was delivering them to criminals. In his experience, he says, "it's always been a subcontracted driver who doesn't know what's going on." Keeping drivers in the dark makes it significantly harder for police to trace missing nuts—theft on a need-to-know basis.

Andrei and I spoke at dusk in the parking lot of a shipping facility in Commerce City. The area reminded me of the sinister, depopulated city depicted in season 2 of *True Detective*—a warren of warehouses, empty lots, and tractor trailers. Andrei was likable and friendly, though midway through our conversation he mentioned that he fought with Soviet forces in Afghanistan in the eighties. This revelation was not intended to be threatening, but it did nothing good for my nerves. After we spoke, Andrei said he was scheduled to haul a load of coins from the US Mint in downtown Denver back to LA, a detail I found astonishing, given his prior convictions.

Before I left, Andrei gestured toward the shipping dock where his truck was parked and explained how easy it would be to execute a theft. "No security, no cameras, nobody else," he said. "It's simple—you've got a truck, you can change your motor-carrier number, DOT number, name, license plate." I asked if he believed that the people who hired him were part of a larger group. "My opinion," he said, pausing, "yes."

In late 2013, Chad Parker got a call from a nut broker in Brooklyn, New York, named Arthur Coussa. Coussa explained that one of his clients, a distributor in Detroit, was getting undercut on walnut prices; he believed that someone was selling hot nuts. "How do you go cheaper than cost?" Coussa asked. Parker convinced the distributor to become an informant and had him go undercover at a bakery near Detroit called Babylon Foods. Because the nuts had crossed state lines, Parker enlisted the help of the FBI to obtain a search warrant for Babylon Foods. There, agents found walnuts in packaging that matched a load stolen from Carriere Family Farms. When questioned, Babylon's owner said he had purchased several shipments of nuts from a Los Angeles bakery and food distributor called Lavash Guy.

A number of experts told me that selling hijacked food is easy. Stolen nuts often move through unscrupulous food brokers and end up in independent grocery stores or bakeries. When I asked an executive at the shipping-security company CargoNet what sort of person buys stolen food, he laughed. "You do!" he said. "You just don't know it. If you go to the back of a market—a smaller market—those guys are looking for a bargain. They're not looking for information on where the food came from. They're not asking questions."

Later that fall, Parker and federal agents searched Lavash Guy and questioned the owner. According to a police report, he could not explain where he had purchased the nuts he sold to Babylon Foods, or why he had written a check for $30,000 to a nearby business called Lopez Canyon Development Group, where Parker found an orange Freightliner matching the one used to rob Crain. (Lavash Guy's owner told me that he did not buy or sell stolen nuts and denied that there was anything incriminating about the $30,000 check. The police, he said, "were going around to a lot of places. They searched us, but it wasn't us. They didn't find anything.") Parker and the FBI also uncovered a relationship between Lopez Canyon and three men with Armenian surnames.

More than a half-dozen law-enforcement officials I spoke with said they strongly suspect that many nut thefts have originated with Armenian Power, a criminal group that is active in the Los Angeles area and linked to a broader Russian organized-crime network. One of the three men listed in a police report as being involved with Lopez Canyon has a criminal history that includes convictions for burglary, assault and battery, criminal trespass, and domestic violence resulting in injury; a second pleaded no contest to a charge of grand theft in 2014. Though the men have not been charged with any crimes in the nut case, Parker told me that they remain under investigation by the FBI. "We were trying to go up the food chain," he said.

~~~~~~

It took the nut industry more than two years to realize that it was under attack. In late 2015, a month after the Horizon theft, the Western Agricultural Processors Association held a meeting for nut companies and law enforcement, which it called, perhaps melodramatically, the Emergency Nut Theft Summit. "We thought we'd hold it for just a couple of people, because we'd had two companies that had been hit," the association's Roger Isom told me. "We had 147 people register. We realized right then, about the first of December, that this was way bigger than we'd been led to believe." (By January 2016, Isom had received information about twenty thefts. Three months later, that number grew to thirty-four.)

As the pace of thefts accelerated in 2015, police in the Central Valley scrambled to piece together information about Armenian Power, which arose in Glendale and North Hollywood in the eighties and nineties. Martin Estrada, a former assistant US attorney who helped prosecute more than one hundred Armenian Power associates for extortion, kidnapping, and gun charges in 2010, told me that its closest analogues are Mexican drug cartels. "I worked on US organized crime, but I also worked on many cartel cases," he said. "It's hard to quantify, because the cartels operate in a different country. But I would say, as a criminal enterprise, they're highly sophisticated."

Well before it became interested in nuts, Armenian Power made tens of millions of dollars in credit-card and medical-billing conspiracies. In 2010, dozens of people linked to the group were convicted in a Medicare fraud case involving more than $160 million in fake claims. Bob Zahreddine, a detective with the Glendale Police Department who supervised a multiagency task force that investigated the organization, told me that local and federal investigators have identified Armenian Power collaborators working inside the Armenian consulate in Los Angeles, the California Department of Motor Vehicles, and the federal court in LA. (In the latter case, a clerk named Nune Gevorkyan and her husband, Oganes Koshkzryzn, were convicted and sentenced to prison for leaking sealed information to group members.)

"When a truck driver gets arrested for stealing a little container of walnuts, and then hires a $100,000 attorney, he's not the guy running the organization," Zahreddine said.

In another police report, Chad Parker noted that, while digging through business records during his investigation, he discovered that one person of interest in the case had cosigned a loan to a Los Angeles County official worth $5 million.

~~~~~~

When I first spoke with Tulare County sheriff Mike Boudreaux in February 2016, he told me to expect arrests within weeks. Several months later, no arrests had been announced and Boudreaux sounded less assured. He said that his team, which was now also working with the FBI, was examining connections in other parts of the country.

"We're taking it where the money is," Boudreaux said. "These are not easy prosecutions. But we believe we have enough evidence." Armenian Power, he said, is active across the country. (The FBI declined to comment for this story, but confirmed to the *Los Angeles Times* last year that it had opened an inquiry.)

Federal involvement has both widened the investigation and slowed prosecutions. The advantages of a federal probe—manpower, technology, and the authority to work across state lines—may be somewhat outweighed by the reality that theft is a low priority for federal prosecutors, who prefer to build cases around charges of conspiracy or racketeering. One might say that they prefer to crack the organization first, nuts second.

Another detective told me he'd traced a group of walnut thieves to Glendale and Van Nuys, and served search warrants there, yet there have been no prosecutions in that case. "We were onto the right people," he said. "But it's not what you know, it's what you can prove."

In the summer of 2016, Roger Isom and Kirk Squire lobbied the California legislature to increase penalties for people convicted of stealing nuts and to fund a task force to combat the problem, but Governor Jerry Brown vetoed the bill. When we met in California, I asked Marc Zavala whether he was optimistic that law enforcement might stop nut theft. He was complimentary of recent efforts but said that local departments would eventually move on, or else the thieves would find something else to steal. "Cargo theft has been around since forever," he said.

In 2014, Marco Alberto Garcia pleaded guilty in the Crain theft and was sentenced to four years in jail. (His lawyer did not respond to a request for comment.) Other members of the ring, if prosecuted, are likely to get off easier: In California, a 2014 state law prohibits people convicted of grand theft from serving sentences in state prison, and because county jails are so overcrowded, theft convicts often serve dramatically abbreviated terms.

Meanwhile, the heists have continued. "You go down to Tulare County, Fresno County, to San Joaquin County, where some of these thefts are also occurring, and most likely by the same people or by associates of theirs—it continues to happen," Parker said. "It's frustrating."

Ultimately, Parker's bigger contribution to stopping nut theft had little to do with police work. In the wake of the Crain theft, he began training Tehama County nut processors in basic security precautions, and there have been no fictitious pickups there since 2013, despite increased problems elsewhere in the state. "The whole point of investigations like this is to get to the bigger fish," he said recently. "We've gotten to the bigger fish. We have the bigger fish identified." The hard part is catching them.

WILD CRIMES

MR. BLAND'S EVIL PLOT TO CONTROL THE WORLD

MILES HARVEY

~~~~~~

In the dusty realm of big-league map collecting, one man cut a darker figure than his milquetoasty colleagues. Armed with an X-Acto knife and an arsenal of fake identities, he systematically ransacked the nation's libraries, hoping in his own peculiar way to dominate the globe.

~~~~~~

The grand stack room of Baltimore's George Peabody Library, an elegant chamber built in 1878 and now run by Johns Hopkins University, has been aptly described as a "cathedral of books." Rising 61 feet from its marble floor to its glass skylight, appointed in ornate cast iron and gold leaf, suffused with the smell of moldering volumes, the place indeed radiates a sense of the sacred.

On the afternoon of December 7, 1995, Jennifer Bryan, curator of manuscripts for the Maryland Historical Society, was doing a little research inside the grand stack room when she started to get a bad feeling about a fellow patron. The man in question was sitting across the way from her, looking through some books that were obviously very old.

There was nothing unusual about his appearance—quite the contrary. A studious man in his mid-forties, wearing a blue blazer and khaki pants, he could have been mistaken for half the scholars who walk through the library's doors. He was a withdrawn, slight-framed person with a biggish nose, smallish chin, reddish hair and mustache.

Yet the man kept looking over his shoulder and flashing her "surreptitious" looks. Her suspicions soon deepened. "I just happened to look up and over in that direction and thought I saw him tear a page out of a book," she remembers. "And I thought, Well, now what do I do? Do I say something, or did I just imagine that?"

As time went on, the man seemed to grow flustered by her stares. Finally, he stood up and pulled open a card catalog drawer, purposely obstructing Bryan's view. For Bryan, that was the last straw. She got up and reported him to Peabody Library officials.

A short time later, when three security officers confronted him, the man hastily gathered up his belongings and dashed out the Peabody's front door. In a scene that might have come from some odd amalgamation of *The Nutty Professor* and *The Fugitive*, the bookworm led his pursuers through downtown Baltimore, all four of them in a jog. Crossing historic Charles Street, the procession threaded past a famous statue of Washington and around another of Lafayette. Finally, after ditching a notebook in a row of bushes, the man found himself trapped on the back steps of the Walters Art Gallery.

Donald Pfouts, director of security at the Peabody Library, spoke to the man first. "I would really like to invite you back to the library," Pfouts remembers telling him "because I think there are some issues here that we have to deal with."

The officers pulled the red spiral notebook—about the size of a steno pad— from the bushes and quickly discovered that Jennifer Bryan's suspicions had been well founded. Tucked into its pages were three maps from a rare 1763 book, *The General History of the Late War*, by John Entick, a modest trove that the library later estimated to be worth around $2,000.

Earlier in the day, the man had presented library officials with a University of Florida ID card bearing the name James Perry, a fake. Now he told them his real identity: Gilbert Joseph Bland Jr.

An hour later, in what would turn out to be a controversial decision, the library released him after he promised to pay $700 to restore the book. Bland was in such a hurry that he forgot to take his notebook with him—and within minutes of the thief's departure, Pfouts made a startling discovery. As he looked more closely at the notebook, he realized that it was essentially a hit list containing the names and prices of rare maps, as well as the names of several other major libraries at which they could be found. Then, as Peabody librarians went back through their own records, they discovered that more maps were missing from other texts that Bland had apparently handled during an earlier visit. "This guy was low," says Pfouts. "He was violating the trust of practically every community in the country, committing crimes against our history."

When Hopkins officials began to warn other libraries around the country about the unwelcome visitor, Pfouts's worst fears were soon realized. James Perry had been to the University of Virginia. James Perry had been to Duke University. James Perry had been to the University of North Carolina, and to Brown. At every stop, books handled by him now appeared to be missing maps and prints.

As news of the crime spread through Ex Libris, an Internet site for librarians and rare book traders, Pfouts started hearing from legitimate map dealers around the country. "They'd say, 'Look, we know this guy, and we know that he's been doing this for a while,'" recalls Pfouts. "They didn't know how he was getting the maps, exactly, but they said he always had the rarest maps and he always had multiples of them. They could never understand why he always had everything."

Soon the FBI would enter the case, and Bland's name would be on the lips of nearly everyone in the world of vintage cartography, his cross-country string of heists casting a chill over this small, musty profession. Eventually, Bland would be arrested for his crimes, and after entering a series of guilty pleas, he would serve prison time while his case followed a convoluted course through federal and state jurisdictions. Late last month, Bland was set to be released from a New Jersey facility, completing an incarceration that lasted only a year and a half. Though he still faces the possibility of further legal action, America's greatest map thief will be, for the time being, a free man—a prospect that leaves curators and map collectors considerably ill at ease.

On October 31, 1995—Halloween—Gilbert Bland had an especially good day. That morning he allegedly walked into the University of Chicago's Regenstein Library, signed in as James Perry, and calmly sat down in the special collections room. Then he opened one of the Western world's more extraordinary texts: a 1584 edition of *Theatrum Orbis Terrarum*, compiled and edited by Abraham Ortelius, the father of modern geography. Ortelius, a Flemish cartographer born in 1527, took up his trade at a fortuitous time, in the afterglow of the great age of discovery. Columbus had landed in the Americas, Magellan's expedition had circumnavigated the globe, Copernicus had made his case for a sun-centered universe. Yet cartography was behind the times. Maps came in a slapdash variety of sizes and styles, many of them based on ancient Greek notions of geography—which, of course, did not take into account the possibility of a North or South America. Ortelius set out to change that, painstakingly collecting the finest maps of places throughout the known world and bringing them together in a uniform size and format. Originally published in 1570, *Theatrum Orbis Terrarum* was the first modern atlas. Ortelius put the whole world at the fingertips of the traveler—a revolution in the human imagination.

Yet now the great master's text had wound up in the hands of a kind of anti-Ortelius, a professional scatterer of maps and destroyer of books. Bland apparently paged through the volume until he came to a cartographic gem labeled "La Florida," the first widely available map of the broad region that is now the southeastern United States. (Ortelius added it to *Theatrum Orbis Terrarum* in the 1584 edition.)

Although the book measures 17 inches by 12 inches and its pages are so thick that they faintly rumble when turned, Bland is believed to have removed "La Florida" and two more maps from the atlas, as well as ten maps from another book. The Regenstein's special collections room is a kind of fish tank built expressly for security; its walls are made of glass, and no briefcases or pens are allowed inside. Yet Bland seems to have sneaked the thirteen maps into his clothes and walked out undetected. For good measure, he also altered a librarian's pencil-written inventory at the front of the Ortelius book, making it appear that the pages he took had been missing for years.

But that wasn't Bland's only alleged theft during his brief Chicago stay. Only the day before, he'd paid a visit to Northwestern University's Charles Deering McCormick Library of Special Collections. Curator R. Russell Maylone remembers him as "the proverbial man in a raincoat" with "a pile of books on the table spread out in a not very orderly fashion." That day, Bland is believed to have removed six separate maps from the pages of several antique atlases, including a 1681 map of New York and three maps of the Caribbean. As Perry got up to leave, Maylone said, "I hope you found what you were looking for."

Ultimately eighteen institutions, including libraries at the University of Delaware, the University of Florida, and Washington University, would report that they had been visited by a James Perry. It was an invisible crime spree, hidden amid the seldom-opened pages of centuries-old books. And now librarians, a legendarily docile people, wanted blood.

"If that man gets in front of my car," said Northwestern's Maylone, "I'll run over him—but in a nice way. Oh, and then I'll back over him again."

~~~~~~

Gilbert Joseph Bland Jr. was something of a chameleon, a clever inventor of aliases. Over the years, law enforcement officials say, he went by the names James Morgan, Jason Pike, Jack Arnett, Richard Olinger, John David Rosche, Steven Spradling, James Bland, James Perry, Gilbert Anthony Bland, Joseph Bland. He changed careers and families without seeming to look back; when a daughter from his first marriage once asked him for a favor, she says he refused, telling her, "You're a stranger."

People who'd met Bland would describe him only in the vaguest of terms: "clean-cut," "quiet," "mild-mannered," "a shadow figure." His face was neither young nor old. Medium height, medium weight, middle-aged, middle everything, he was a cipher—in cartographic terms, terra incognita. "The man was totally nondescript," says Linda McCurdy, an official at Duke University's Special Collections Library. "Part of the way he operated was to make as few ripples as possible." Margaret Bing, a special collections curator at Florida's Broward County Library, puts it this way: "I remember thinking the first time I met Bland, 'Now this is a guy who fits his name.'"

Then again, the world of vintage cartography in which Bland so craftily operated is itself a decidedly staid realm. There are an estimated ten thousand antique map collectors in the United States, a punctilious subculture loosely bound together by organizations like the International Map Collectors' Society and the International Society for the Curators of Early Maps. Cartomaniacs, as these obsessive map-hounds sometimes call themselves, subscribe to periodicals such as *Mercator's World*, or the more scholarly *Imago mundi*, and avidly discourse on the Internet's Map History Discussion List, exchanging esoterica or trading cartographic jokes. (What did the mapmaker send his sweetheart on Valentine's Day? A dozen compass roses.) The cartomaniacs' calendars are dotted with trade fairs where they haggle over the price of a Willem Blaeu or a William Faden the way baseball-card collectors would bargain over a Hank Aaron or a Mickey Mantle.

"Cartomania is a sickness," says Barry Lawrence Ruderman, a dealer and self-confessed map junkie from La Jolla, California. "It's obsessive. Once you're in up to your ankles, you want to be in up to your knees; once you're in up to your knees, you want to be in up to your waist. I like to think that it's sort of a beautiful sickness, because all human beings need things that stimulate them intellectually and drive them to passion. But the secondary aspect is that many of us spend insane amounts of time dedicating ourselves to map collecting. It's a twisted pursuit. But where's the problem in that?"

"People collect maps for a wide range of reasons," says Edward Ripley-Duggan of the Antiquarian Booksellers Association of America. "It's a little world over which people can have total aesthetic control. And as in any economy, whether it's Wall Street or whatever, there's always a rogue element. Unfortunately, certain people are sticky-fingered where desirable artifacts are concerned."

Gilbert Bland developed his "beautiful sickness" relatively late in life, sometime in his early forties, and unlike most of the afflicted, his interest in maps seems to have had more to do with money than with an authentic passion for the discipline of cartography. In February 1994, a little less than two years before he was caught in Baltimore, Bland and his wife, Karen, opened Antique Maps & Collectibles in

The Gardens, a sleepy little office and retail complex in Tamarac, Florida. Tamarac is a Fort Lauderdale exurb, a placeless sprawl of strip malls and subdivisions. It's about the last spot you'd expect to find an antique map shop—but then again, this was one antique map shop that didn't want to be found.

Though his wife was the owner of record, Gilbert Bland was apparently the guiding force behind the store, which was located just a few miles from the home the couple shared with their two children in Coral Springs. The Blands kept a decidedly low profile at the mall. "The place was basically always empty," says one employee of a business whose windows faced Bland's shop. "We were sitting here one day thinking, 'I wonder how he makes money?' And then we were wondering, 'Who would be interested in those old maps?'"

When the store opened, Bland was a complete unknown in the world of antique maps. Nonetheless, he quickly built up a moderately impressive inventory and began to cultivate a long-distance clientele. Barry Ruderman was one early client. "Bland sent out a computerized list of maps for sale," recalls Ruderman. "It was semiprofessional-looking, nothing real fancy."

From the beginning, it was obvious that Bland was not an expert. As one inside observer later put it, "Some of the dealers were awfully wary of him— the man didn't seem to know dick about maps." Ruderman remembers that original offering as a "bizarre mix" of materials that included a lot of worthless junk. "The other thing that was a bit odd is he really didn't know his prices all that well," Ruderman says. "He really just wanted you to make offers. And he accepted most of the offers."

Ruderman, a bankruptcy lawyer, says he once "sort of cross-examined Bland" about the provenance of his materials. According to Ruderman, Bland replied that he and his wife had been involved in scripophily—the collecting of old stock certificates and bonds—and had incidentally been accumulating old maps. "That was an acceptable answer," says Ruderman, "because frankly there are two or three respected dealers who fit that general MO." In the end, Ruderman concluded, "Gil passed the smell test."

Bland's client base was growing. As Antique Maps & Collectibles sent out catalogs and advertised in international trade magazines, word began to spread that a little store in south Florida had an incredible supply of low- to mid-end maps. Some dealers grew a little suspicious of Bland's ability to find multiple copies of relatively scarce pieces. Others were beginning to raise eyebrows over what one dealer called Bland's "ridiculously low prices."

But no one apparently ever directly accused him of stealing, much less demanded an investigation into his practices. "It's a very close community," explains F. J. Manasek, a well-known Vermont dealer. "We're all friends, even though we compete in business. There's a lot of honor, which is probably why Bland could gain such easy entrée."

"The degree of trust in this business is staggering," agrees another prominent dealer. "We literally sell tens of thousands of dollars' of stuff around the world based on a phone call."

The Blands made high-profile appearances at the two big industry conventions in 1995—the Miami International Map Fair in February and the International Map Collectors' Society Fair, in San Francisco, in October. "Bland had a major presence at both fairs," recalls James Hess, who owns the Heritage Map Museum and Auction House in Lititz, Pennsylvania. "He was putting himself out there with the major dealers."

Ruderman, who had dinner with Bland at the San Francisco convention, adds, "Most of all, he was interested in being a wheeler-dealer. He was looking for big buys. He was definitely crunching numbers a lot more than he was learning maps."

"It got to the point," recalls one respected map antiquarian, "that dealers would be saying, 'My goodness, maps of City X have been selling rather well. Do you have any maps of City X?' And Bland would say, 'Let me check, and I'll get back to you.' And the very next week he'd call and say, 'Why, yes, I just happen to have a map of City X.'"

~~~~~~

If Gilbert Bland had dollar signs in his eyes, it's not hard to understand why. He had entered the trade during a boom time, when the fascination with ancient maps was steadily spreading from the esoteric fringes into the mainstream. Over the previous decade or so, cartomania had become something of a bull market in the United States. (The trend continues today. *Money* magazine, for example, devoted its March 1997 Hot Stuff column to map collecting. The headline: "These Old Maps Offer You a New Way to Double Your Money.")

Much of the growth in antique map collecting has been fueled by one person: W. Graham Arader III, an intense and sometimes intimidating man from Middleburg, Virginia. Arader's main residence, an 86-acre estate in rolling horse country just up the road from Paul Mellon's place, is one of four that he and his wife own. Arader has made his multimillion-dollar fortune almost entirely from trading old maps and prints. "I'm the biggest map dealer of the twentieth century," the forty-six-year-old Arader asserts. "There's no question about it. I sell $10 million in maps every year. I can pick up the phone and make $10,000 in a single hour. Yes, collecting has made me a very rich man."

Before Arader entered the business in the early 1970s, old maps were mostly the province of librarians, historians, and a few tweedy collectors. Young, impudent, and by all accounts extremely savvy, Arader was determined to expand the base of investors beyond this small, druidic group. Reaching out to people with cash to burn and corporations with offices to decorate, he transformed antique maps from historical artifacts into trendy commodities.

Critics, especially rare collections librarians, have sometimes disputed Arader's cutthroat business practices, but no one would argue with his success. Luring wave after wave of new and inexperienced buyers into the market, he jacked his prices to the sky. His competitors—many of whom were appalled by his brash style—followed suit.

"It's been straight up since I started collecting in 1971, increasing 5 percent to 20 percent a year," says Arader. Just to take one example, an edition of the ancient Greek geographer Ptolemy's famous map book, *Geographia*, printed in Ulm in 1482, could be had for $85 in 1884, $5,000 in 1950, and $28,000 in 1965. Today, if you could actually find a copy for sale, it might cost you as much as $400,000.

That's good news for Arader and his fellow map dealers but bad news for the nation's librarians, who suddenly find themselves sitting on gold mines—often without the resources to protect their riches. Predictably, a new generation of map thieves has swarmed in. In 1978, for example, Andrew P. Antippas, a professor of English at Tulane University, pleaded guilty to stealing five rare maps from Yale University. Also at Yale in the 1970s, two men disguised as priests confessed they were part of a conspiracy to steal ancient atlases and maps by sneaking them under their robes. In Britain in the mid-1980s, a man named Ian Hart sneaked a huge haul of maps and atlases out of Oxford's Bodleian Library, much of it hidden in his trousers. In 1988, Robert M. "Skeet" Willingham Jr. was convicted of stealing an enormous cache of rare books, documents, and maps from the University of Georgia, where he worked as the head of special collections.

In his usual pugnacious style, Arader lays the blame for this wave of thefts squarely on the shoulders of librarians, whom he claims are simply not vigilant enough. "Most librarians are incompetent, boring, and dull," says Arader. "And they have this easy life. Many of them view their collections as their personal fiefdoms. But really, they don't look after their material. You know, it's not hard to tell the difference between a thief and somebody who's legitimate. If you're not intelligent enough to see these guys coming, then you shouldn't be a curator."

Earlier in his career Arader had purchased maps that had been stolen by none other than Andrew Antippas, but nowadays the Middleburg dealer likes to portray himself as the Argus of the industry, arguing that many of his fellow dealers are less than meticulous in ascertaining the backgrounds of their inventory. "It's simple," he says. "All you say is, 'Where did you get this map?' Then you listen to the story and you say, 'Do you mind if I check your sources?' And then if he starts waffling, you say, 'Sir, get the hell out of my gallery!' And if you really think he stinks, then you turn him in. In their hearts, the dealers who bought from Bland knew what was going on. If something is too good to be true, then it's too good to be true."

~~~~~~

At the time of his brief detention at the Peabody Library, Bland provided officials only with a temporary address in Columbia, Maryland, the town where he had lived before moving to Florida in 1994. But as news of his crimes spread, Bland fled that address and disappeared. It took the authorities more than a week to catch up with him again—time that allowed him to dispose of much of his inventory.

By the early morning of December 15, Bland had emptied his store, reportedly leaving a note for his landlord that said, "See you later."

"I came in and a lot of the maps were gone," says Laurie Bregman, a tenant whose shop was located just across the way from Antique Maps & Collectibles. "He'd emptied the place in a middle-of-the-night kind of deal."

Within a week and a half of Bland's vanishing, FBI agents, working with a University of Virginia cop named Thomas Durrer, tracked him down at his residence in Florida and knocked on the door, a search warrant in hand. On January 2, 1996, Bland finally turned himself in to local police.

News of his arrest came as no great surprise to many people in the industry. But others, particularly those who'd had close business dealings with Bland, maintain that they were stunned when they heard of his arrest. "My jaw dropped," remembers Jonathan Ramsay, the owner of a map and print business in the Bahamas. "I mean, the guy was straight as an arrow. When something like this happens, you say to yourself, 'Wow, I just don't understand human nature.'"

Ramsay heard about Bland's legal troubles when a friend from Florida faxed him a newspaper story. "I called my friend up and I said, 'You've got to be kidding me!' Just then, I heard a noise in the shop and I turned around and there were these three guys standing there. And I said, 'Yes? Can I help you?' And one of them said, 'I'm an FBI agent.' He'd been standing right behind me as I talked on the phone. He said, 'Obviously, I can hear from your phone conversation that you've heard the news.'"

Another dealer who bought maps from Bland and met him face-to-face shared Ramsay's surprise. "Bland was the most soft-spoken and considerate guy," he says. "It was like a contradiction. On the phone and in person, he was so quiet, and then on the other hand, the crimes he committed were incredibly nervy. I guess he was a hell of a con man."

Like any good con man, Bland did not surrender without retaining a certain amount of leverage: The feds still didn't know where his inventory was stashed. Somewhere Bland had old maps of New Jersey, Virginia, and Maryland, as well as Italy, Sweden, and Norway. He had the fortifications of Montreal. He had the Missouri Territory. He had the Empire of China, the Empire of Japan, and India beyond the Ganges. He had the Eastern Hemisphere, the Western Hemisphere, and the North Pole. He even had the trade winds locked up somewhere—and he wasn't telling anyone the location. Figuratively speaking, he was holding the world hostage.

As part of his plea negotiations, Bland would agree to tell the FBI the whereabouts of the cache—a rather cunning offer that FBI agent Hank Hanburger would later describe as "a very effective bargaining chip."

So in February 1996, Bland finally directed authorities to a storage space in Palm Beach Gardens, Florida, that he had rented under an assumed name. When FBI agents looked behind its bright orange doors, they discovered an extraordinary booty, some 150 maps in all, dating from the sixteenth century to the twentieth. Taken together with the 100 or so other maps that authorities would gather from Bland's assorted clients across the country, the thief's total collection of some 250 maps would have had a market value estimated at as much as a half-million dollars. The inventory included the work of such seminal figures as Jodocus Hondius, whose seventeenth-century atlases popularized the now-standard latitude-longitude projection system of the great cartographer Gerard Mercator, and Thomas Jefferys, the eighteenth-century geographer who published one of the first important atlases devoted to North America.

FBI agents from Virginia flew down to impound the collection. Bland's "bargaining chip" had now been cashed in.

⌇⌇

Werner Muensterberger, a New York psychoanalyst who is a nationally prominent expert on collecting and the author of *Collecting: An Unruly Passion*, says that the map lovers he has met tend to come from broken homes or from families that have moved around a good deal. They throw themselves into their hobby, at least in part, as a way to connect with a parent or to ground themselves in a more permanent sense of place. "Looking for maps, especially antique maps," he says, "is really looking for the past—Where do I come from? Who were my ancestors?—and symbolically, finding security."

Whether this profile more accurately describes Bland or the more-avid collectors he preyed on, one does find certain resonances in Bland's background. Certainly his life has been a rocky one. His parents divorced when he was only three years old, and according to defense attorneys, he later suffered physical abuse at the hands of his stepfather. In June 1968 he graduated from high school in Ridgefield Park, New Jersey, a New York suburb. That same month, he had his first run-in with the law. Arrested for possession of a stolen car, he was found guilty of a lesser charge and fined $100.

A few days later, he enlisted in the army and served in Vietnam. His combat experiences would later haunt him, causing him to suffer post-traumatic stress disorder—or so his lawyers have recently claimed. While in the service, he continued to run afoul of the law. Among other things, he was charged and briefly detained for desertion and being absent without leave.

He was discharged in 1971 and later that year married Carol Ann Talt. The couple eventually had two daughters, but fatherhood didn't seem to soften Bland's wild streak. During the early 1970s, he had a string of arrests and convictions on various charges, including marijuana possession. Then, in 1976, after separating from his wife (they eventually divorced), he found himself in serious trouble with the law. Arrested for using fake identities to defraud the government in an unemployment compensation scam, he made a plea bargain and was sent to federal prison in El Reno, Oklahoma, to serve a three-year term.

After his release from prison, Bland evidently had very little contact with his children. "He's got two children that he totally abandoned and couldn't care less about," says Heather Bland, his twenty-four-year-old daughter by that first marriage. Nonetheless, Bland appeared to have turned his life around, at least for a few years. He married again, and he and Karen had two more children. After receiving an associate's degree from Broward Community College in Fort Lauderdale, he moved to suburban Maryland, where he worked for Allied Signal Corporation. In 1992 he and Karen opened their own computer leasing business.

It was sometime in the early 1990s that Bland became interested in maps. According to statements he made to the FBI, it happened almost by accident. "His story is that he bought a bunch of items that someone had left unclaimed at one of these U-Store-It places," says Gray Hill, a Virginia-based FBI special agent who's worked on the case nearly from the beginning. "Included were a bunch of maps. And someone told him, 'Hey, there might be some value here.'"

The Blands moved back to Florida in 1994, opening Antique Maps & Collectibles that February. In April, they purchased (in Karen's name) a four-bedroom house in an upscale subdivision of Coral Springs for $151,400. But their financial picture was nowhere near as rosy as it appeared from the outside. Their debts were mounting fast, eventually prompting Karen Bland to declare Chapter 7 bankruptcy in late October of 1995. Court documents show that at the time of the filing—a little more than a month before Bland's brief capture in Baltimore—Karen Bland owed more than $40,000 in credit card debt alone.

Bland's lawyers would later argue that it was the failure of his computer leasing firm in Maryland that led to these financial troubles and eventually to his crime spree. But that might not have been the only factor. "I'll put another scenario in front of you," says dealer Jonathan Ramsay. "He came over here [to the Bahamas] about four or five times—and he liked to gamble. He'd say to me, 'I'm over here on a gambling junket.' He would come in to see me and then he would go off to the casino."

Whether it was to pay off gambling debts or some other reason entirely, Bland clearly needed cash fast, and he seemed to know how to get it. "He found an easy avenue to make some quick money—and he really overdid it," says Lieutenant Detective Clay Williams of the University of North Carolina Department of Public Safety. "He got in way over his head. It became addictive. I don't think he had any conception of the federal charges that could come down on him."

And come down they did: In a federal court in Charlottesville, Virginia, Bland was initially charged with theft of major artwork and transporting stolen goods across state lines. He agreed to plea bargains in North Carolina and Delaware state courts, as well as in the federal courts. In exchange for a reduced sentence and limited immunity from further prosecution, Bland promised, among other things, to cooperate with federal authorities and to advise libraries on ways to beef up their security to prevent future thefts. In the end, Bland would be forced to pay $70,000 in restitution in the federal case (an amount he would contest to a judge, noting that the damages he'd caused were easily remediable, as the maps could simply be glued back into their original atlases), plus an as-yet-undetermined amount in the Delaware case. All told, he would serve only seventeen months in various prisons ranging from Virginia to North Carolina to Delaware.

Today, most people in the antique cartographic world are appalled by what they view as Bland's distressingly light sentence. "It's very easy for a prosecutor to say, 'He ripped a few pages out of a few books? I've got better things to do,'" says map dealer and lawyer Barry Ruderman. "To the 99 percent of people who don't understand the magnitude of what he's done, Bland just doesn't seem to represent a threat to society."

However, there is still a possibility that Bland may face further legal action. Brown University's John Carter Brown Library, which is still missing two of three maps allegedly stolen by Bland, is now considering bringing a suit against him. "But the truth is," notes library director Norman Fiering, "I would drop all the charges if he promised to come up with the missing pieces. There's an analogy to kidnappers: You're willing to let them go if they give you back your child."

The history of cartography is full of peculiar islands. One of the manuscripts the FBI eventually recovered from Bland, for example, is eighteenth-century British cartographer Herman Moll's map of North America. It shows a continent that looks a lot like the one we now inhabit, except for one striking detail. Running the length of the west coast is a sprawling independent land mass—a famous and widely repeated cartographic fiction known as the Island of California. Many antique maps contain even weirder isles. A twelfth-century map by the Arab geographer al-Idrisi shows El Wakwak, an island said to be filled with trees whose fruit, shaped like the heads of women, continually cry out the apparently meaningless chant "Wak-Wak."

A good portion of the antiques stolen by Bland have themselves been consigned to a kind of island within the FBI, one that might be called the Island of Lost Maps. The lord of this peculiar domain is Gray Hill, a lanky, voluble, middle-aged special agent. Normally, Hill's job is to track down lawbreakers, but now his role has been reversed: He hunts victims. Despite an exhaustive search, the Bureau has so far been able to positively identify the owners of only about 100 of the 250 maps in Bland's collection. The rest face an uncertain exile here.

On this day, Hill is sitting beneath a photo of grim-faced J. Edgar Hoover in a conference room at the FBI office in Richmond, Virginia. On the table in front of him is a mountain of plastic bags and file folders, a zip-up art portfolio, and a U-Haul moving box. Hill is taking an inventory of his kingdom, carefully unfolding one fragile document after another, some of them printed more than four centuries ago. "I live in fear of getting these things wet," he says, casting a suspicious glance at a can of soda sitting on the table's edge.

The maps are mesmerizingly beautiful. With the onset of copperplate printing in the sixteenth century, mapmakers had the ability to embellish their work with extraordinary detail. And in an age when art and science overlapped, the results were spectacular: Sea monsters float in the Atlantic, angels hover over the Pacific, fire-breathing horses gallop atop the Arctic Circle. Hill pulls out a map from the 1607 edition of the famous Hondius-Mercator atlas. "This is another one that I don't have any idea where it came from," he says.

As part of his federal plea bargain arrangement, Bland has been helping the FBI in its efforts to return the maps to their rightful owners. But even with his cooperation, the process has proven extremely difficult for Hill. For one thing, libraries don't always keep inventories of maps that are bound in books—so even if they discover one missing, they can rarely be sure when it disappeared. Moreover, most maps are unmarked. Some institutions put stamps or other identification marks on their maps, but to many librarians this practice is repugnant, the equivalent of stenciling PROPERTY OF THE LOUVRE across the *Mona Lisa*.

As a result, FBI experts have been forced to match each stolen map, jigsaw-puzzle style, with each damaged book, using ultraviolet light to make sure the edges line up perfectly and the paper stocks on both sides of the cut precisely match up.

Curiously, Hill sometimes finds that librarians remain in denial about thefts that have taken place under their noses, even when the evidence is incontrovertible. "I talked to one librarian who said, 'There's no way he could have stolen anything out of here.' Well, I said, 'I just know one thing. I know that Mr. Bland told me that he came to your library and stole maps.' But they won't accept it. They will not believe that they have had anything stolen."

Or maybe they believe it all too well. As Robert Karrow, curator of maps at the Newberry Library in Chicago, points out, "A lot of library thefts have gone unreported in the past. You're embarrassed, and maybe you say to yourself, 'What will the donors think?' And you're reluctant to talk about the whole issue because you don't want to give the crazies ideas."

On a bright, brisk day last December, in a federal courtroom just a few miles from Gray Hill's office, Gilbert Bland was scheduled to appear for a sentencing hearing, one of the many court dates that have dotted his life over the past two years. On his attorney's advice, Bland had steadfastly declined to speak with me about his case, so I'd come to Charlottesville in hopes of finally laying eyes on the man. At the appointed hour, Bland shuffled into the courtroom wearing blue prison scrubs. There were no well-wishers or family members seated in the gallery—just a few reporters quietly scribbling notes. Bland was a sunken man with a wan, jowly face. His eyes were dark and piercing. A couple of times, he leaned back and sneaked nervous glances at me, and I imagined just how Jennifer Bryan must have felt when he darted his "surreptitious" eyes at her in the Peabody Library that day: It was the look of a man who intensely dislikes to be observed.

Prison had not been good to Bland. Earlier in his incarceration, while staying at the Albemarle-Charlottesville Regional Jail, he'd written the US District judge to complain about having to live in crowded conditions with a number of violent criminals. He attempted to pass the days and months by reading, he said, but found it "impossible to concentrate" in a place where the television constantly blared, "with rap music videos, cartoons and wrestling [as] the mainstay."

"I have tried, with the help of antidepressant medication . . . to cope," he wrote, "[but] the stress is unbearable." Noting that two other inmates had hanged themselves since his arrival several months earlier, he said he was worried about "retain[ing] my sanity."

In court that day, Bland's attorney argued that his troubled emotions were indeed at the heart of this case. In urging a light sentence for his client, Roanoke-based lawyer Paul R. Thomson Jr. said that Bland's map thefts were connected to his experience in Vietnam twenty-five years earlier. "He has a pattern of problems largely triggered by depression, a very common problem of post-traumatic stress [disorder]," said Thomson, who assured the court that his client would remain in an outpatient treatment program once he returned home to Florida.

"He recognizes that this was singularly poor judgment," Thomson concluded.

For his own part, Bland offered no insights into the crimes, giving instead what amounted to a stock repentant-felon speech. He spoke in a meek voice that occasionally snagged with emotion. "The first thing I'd like to say, Your Honor, is that I'm truly sorry for what I've done—I'm ashamed of myself. In the year that has gone by, I've had a lot of time to think about why this happened. . . . It will never happen again."

Then Bland quietly slouched back to the defense table and seemed to melt into his chair, the soul of inconspicuousness.

FIRESTARTER

AS TOLD TO MCKENZIE FUNK

~~~~~~

*Before her 2005 arrest, ecosaboteur Chelsea Gerlach took part in nine Earth Liber-
ation Front actions, including the 1998 arson that destroyed Vail Mountain's Two
Elk Lodge. In an exclusive interview from behind bars, Gerlach opened up about
life on the run, destruction on behalf of the environment, and why she cooperated
with the federal investigators who smashed the ELF. Her honesty and candor offer
a unique perspective on how an aspiring young environmentalist gets radicalized.*

~~~~~~

On our way from Oregon to Vail, we stopped at every major store in every major
city in three states. We stopped at every RadioShack.

There are only so many, and we could get only so many components at each
one without raising suspicions. We bought everything in cash and in small quan-
tities. An alarm clock and maybe a bottle of water from a Fred Meyer. A box of
matches from an Albertsons. A spool of wire from a hardware store. We always
wore baseball caps to shield our faces from overhead cameras, just in case.

We stopped at a motel in Utah to assemble the timers for the incendiary devices.
It was a nightmare. Avalon had instructions, but he'd never built this kind before.
These timers were digital, with longer delays than the ones he'd used—delays long
enough for us to get down off the mountain and out of the area before the fires
started. Half the clocks we bought didn't end up working with the design. We
abandoned them altogether after we realized they wouldn't work in the cold.

Once we got to Vail, we tried to drive the fuel—some gas, some diesel—up
the mountain one night, but there was too much snow, and my truck got stuck.

We spent hours trying to dig it out. There were maybe 75 gallons of fuel in the back, it was starting to get light out, and there were hunters around. We stashed the fuel cans in the woods and got out of there. The fuel was still miles below our target, a string of buildings and ski lifts on a ridge at 11,000 feet; it would have to be hiked up the mountain. We drove a few hours away to meet some others who'd come out from Oregon to help. Now there were a half-dozen of us, but nothing was set. Most of the group just didn't believe it was possible, so they went back to Oregon. I wasn't really thinking that Avalon and I would end up doing it alone, but that's what happened.

I dropped Avalon where we'd hidden the fuel, and we set a meet time for a few days later—long enough for him to hike fuel can after fuel can several miles and hundreds of feet up the hill and hide them near each of the buildings. When I picked him up, he was exhausted. He rested for a few hours in the campsite I'd found, way up a logging road, but there wasn't much time: The bulldozers were supposed to start rolling the next day. We finalized our plans, and I dropped him back at a trailhead in Vail. I returned to my camp and waited. The night of October 18 was cold, but I couldn't make a campfire—it might attract attention. I just stood in a forest of pines and firs and took everything in. I barely slept at all.

~~~~~~

We weren't arsonists. Many of our actions didn't involve fires at all, and none of us fit the profile of a pyromaniac. I guess "ecosaboteur" works. To call us terrorists, as the federal government did, is stretching the bounds of credibility. I got involved at a time when a right-winger had just bombed the Oklahoma City federal building—killing 168 people—and anti-abortionists were murdering doctors. But the government characterized the ELF as a top domestic terrorism threat because we burned down unoccupied buildings in the middle of the night. It shows their priorities.

Now that it's all over, I don't mind talking about my own role in the actions, and I don't mind talking about what my codefendants have already said. But otherwise I don't want to say who did what or name names. Maybe that seems funny to people who have condemned me as a snitch. I understand the general principle that turning your friends in to the cops should be discouraged. I understand it in a more personal way than my critics, actually, since I'm doing nine years because my friends turned me in.

It was just that nearly everyone had already admitted guilt, committed suicide, or fled the country, and the idea of spending the rest of your life in prison isn't something you can fathom until you've faced it. I knew that if I refused to cooperate and became a martyr for these actions, I wouldn't have been able to be honest in my critique of what we did. I felt like it was important, for the movement, to speak the truth, and not just be a cheerleader. Other radicals need to learn from us. Simply dismissing us as snitches doesn't explain why we'd all abandoned these tactics years before we were arrested.

~~~~~~

I don't like the term *hippie*. It's too associated with dirty, drugged dropouts—which my parents definitely were not. They were back-to-the-landers from Philadelphia who came out west in 1975, bought 8 acres of forest outside Sweet Home, Oregon, and built a house. I was born at home, fed nutritional yeast and sprouts, and not allowed much TV. No Happy Meals. My mom was a preschool teacher, then a biology undergrad, and my dad worked at an electronics company. After they divorced in 1980, I lived some of the time in the Eugene area. At Mom's house we got mailings from Greenpeace and Sea Shepherd—urgent, graphic accounts of whales being slaughtered. My dad got the *Earth First! Journal*, and when I kept borrowing it, he got me my own subscription.

When I was fifteen, I worked for the Northwest Youth Corps, maintaining Oregon's hiking trails. I saw miles and miles of clear-cuts. By the next summer, my dad had given me his old Subaru, which he had a shop paint forest green for me. I drove it to Cove/Mallard, in central Idaho—a huge timber sale inside one of the largest roadless areas in the Lower 48. That's where I met Avalon, an influential part of the Earth First! campaign. He was twenty-eight, and I was sixteen— the youngest person there.

Through Earth First! I was exposed to deep ecology, the philosophy that all species have inherent rights, that humans don't have dominion over the Earth. From there it isn't a big leap to see that the only ethical society is a sustainable one in harmony with its environment. A sustainable society cannot use fossil fuels to make disposable plastics or produce most of the things that constitute our economy. When I saw that political and economic systems themselves were the problem, working within these systems began to feel not only ineffectual but almost unethical.

It may seem unrealistic to say the problem is civilization itself. To me it's equally unrealistic to say that something like carbon credits are a solution. Running ethanol in SUVs won't change anything. At all. We don't live in a plastic bubble; everything is connected. Things will have to change whether we're ready or not. We're smart enough to learn that if you shit in your water supply, you eventually get sick. As a species, we need to evolve past our self-destructive patterns.

I hesitate to say this, because I don't want to sound like a terrorist. But in 1995, when I was at the Evergreen State College, up in Olympia, Washington, I read the

Unabomber Manifesto, which had been published in the *Washington Post*. I didn't agree with what he did, but what he wrote made sense to me: that the Industrial Revolution had been a disaster, causing psychological suffering in the First World, physical suffering in the Third World, and great damage to the natural world. It was like someone put all this stuff I'd been thinking into words.

At Evergreen, I got involved with the local Earth First! group. We did a blockade of an old-growth-timber sale going ahead under the "salvage rider"—a 1995 congressional provision that exempted some sales from significant environmental regulation. After just a few hours, the blockade was broken up and the timber trucks were rolling. For me it was a turning point: If the people destroying the environment didn't have to follow the law, why should the people defending it?

I saw Avalon not long after that, and I told him I was becoming disillusioned with aboveground activism. He didn't say much to encourage me. I dropped out and soon joined an underground cell.

~~~~~~

The Earth Liberation Front wasn't a group as such, and Avalon wasn't our leader. In general, we didn't know each other's names, phone numbers, or addresses. We used the ELF label as a way of telling people, "That wasn't just a random fire." Avalon recruited some of us, but we were anarchists—you couldn't tell us what to do. When people had particular skills, like deploying incendiary devices, their experience was respected. I was often the communiqué sender. I was good with words and computers—all the message-relaying and encryption we did weren't intuitive.

Targets were chosen by individuals. For example, someone would find a logging company, do some research, and then talk with whomever else they wanted involved. The first recon was usually a drive-by in a car, and the last involved walking the site at night, wearing all black and watching for neighbors, dogs, security guards, late workers, etc. We looked for spots to place the devices—overhangs, alcoves, anything that would reflect back the heat.

A big factor in selecting targets was safety—our own and that of other people and nontargeted buildings. We never wanted to put anyone at risk. In Eugene in the late nineties, more than a couple of timber-company offices were saved by the proximity of neighboring homes. In contrast, the Childers Meat Company—a meat-distribution plant that we destroyed in 1999, on Mother's Day—stood away from any homes at the corner of an intersection. The incendiary device we developed involved an electrical current, matches, a road flare, and a bucket of fuel. The term *firebomb* is misleading. The fires started out with a very small flame that, over the course of ten minutes, got bigger and bigger. It went straight up. It never exploded. It was never a sudden, giant fireball.

We tried to be smart about imagining the ways we could be caught. We mapped out traffic cameras, ATMs, and gas-station cameras so we could drive around them. We cleaned the fingerprints off everything, even wristwatches, which I thought was overkill until I lost a watch climbing over a chain-link fence. We were very good at it. That's why the government didn't know who did these things until someone who was involved told them.

It was October 1998 when Avalon showed up at the cabin I shared with my partner, Stan, outside Eugene and asked if we wanted to take part in a really big action. It would be my first arson, and it would be Stan's first action of any kind. We said yes. We went on a walk in the meadow, because we never discussed anything indoors. A few days later, we followed Avalon east in my truck. We didn't know where we were going until we got to Colorado. He told us the target was the Vail ski area.

I had read about Vail's plans to expand into an 885-acre wilderness where, fifteen years prior, Colorado's last wild lynx had been spotted. Vail Resorts seemed like the worst of the worst: not only destroying critical habitat, but also destroying local businesses and communities. All for corporate profit earned by building second homes. There had been a large public-outreach campaign, administrative appeals, and lawsuits, but it was still going to happen. If any company deserved to be targeted, Vail did.

In the predawn hours of October 19, with everyone else but me gone back to Oregon, and with no timers, Avalon set all the fires himself, by hand. He had to travel on foot, running from building to building on the mile-and-a-half-long ridge. As he lit the last ones, the flames from the first ones were lighting up the sky. There were some scary moments. A hunter was sleeping in a heated restroom in one of the buildings. Avalon opened the door, saw him there, and left it alone.

Down below, I had no way to be sure he'd be back on time. When I was returning from my campsite to pick him up, I heard over the scanner that the police and fire departments were looking for a blue pickup, which was exactly what I was driving. There was nothing to do but keep going. I had to meet Avalon down in town, at a popular trailhead.

I got there right on time. It was morning, it was light out, and day hikers were showing up. I stayed in my truck and shuffled through my things, pretending to be getting ready for a hike. Up on the trail, Avalon had exchanged his black clothing for the hiker's garb that he'd carried in a backpack, and whenever he heard voices coming, he stepped into the woods and hid.

I waited ten minutes, then twenty. After a half-hour, as I was wondering if I should leave, Avalon appeared. He just walked up to the truck and got inside. He said two things: He was injured. And the action was successful. It wasn't the time to get details. I just drove.

The first thing we did was go to a library in Denver, and I looked up his injury: a strained Achilles tendon—he'd done too much running. It required ice, not surgery. We went to a second library. He could barely walk, so I entered alone and e-mailed the communiqué.

In the days that followed, I read the news, and it was funny to see speculation that was so completely off base: that at least a dozen people had been responsible, that it must have been an inside job, etc. People tend to think this stuff is much harder than it actually is. We did $12 million in damage—a big part of the $15,894,755.42 I'm supposed to pay in restitution. The expansion went forward—we didn't stop them—and insurance money paid to replace the buildings. But it didn't pay back the $13 million they lost in revenues. Call that the ELF tax.

And we were looking at a much larger canvas anyway, even if, as we later found out, we each had our own concept of what we were achieving. To some degree Avalon still believed in the political process. He thought we could shift the middle of the debate: By being so far at one extreme, we'd make the rest of the environmental movement appear more reasonable. That didn't really ring true to me from the beginning, and after the fallout from Vail—which turned out to be detrimental to local activism—it was even clearer. But even for Avalon, Vail wasn't really about Vail. It was about what we as a society are doing. It was about inspiring people, and that certainly did happen to some extent.

During the four years that I was most active with the ELF, there were parts of my life that were enjoyable. And there were parts that were not. Like being in a hotel room for days on end, everyone clad in painter's suits and face masks and hairnets and multiple layers of latex gloves, craned over tiny electronic devices and soldering irons. Nothing working out, and all of us sweating, frustrated, yelling at each other.

But then there was running around in the wilderness at night, and this incredible sense of being alive. You got to that point of just being totally in the moment. I felt connected to the natural world and really empowered in defending it. The emotion is hard to articulate—like we'd broken through the veil of what was possible. Like things didn't have to be the way they were. Some would call that idealism.

By 2001, everything was falling apart. People were getting more reckless just when I thought we needed to be more careful. There was reason to believe Jake was on the radar of investigators, but instead of keeping a distance, some of the others invited him along on another action. That spring's trial of Jeff "Free" Luers, an activist who had set fire to three SUVs at Eugene's Romania Chevrolet Truck Center the previous summer, was coming up, and pressure was building. One night in March, Avalon, Stan, and three others (but not Jake) went to Romania and burned another thirty-five SUVs—an attempt at solidarity.

Many of us who weren't involved in Romania thought it would result in a longer sentence for Free and increase the heat on the activist community. We were right on both counts. Free got twenty-three years, and, by a twist of fate, Jake ended up becoming a prime suspect in Romania, an action he hadn't done and knew nothing about. Coincidentally, the day after it happened, he was accused of having stolen his former housemate's truck. The cops found the timing of that suspicious—though it was actually unrelated—and he was served with a subpoena. He didn't talk then, but it was the beginning of his relationship with the feds.

Since 2000, we'd been holding meetings of what we called the Praxis Book Club—a forum to discuss techniques and share skills. There'd been one in Eugene, another in Tucson, another in Santa Cruz, another in Olympia. At the fifth and final Praxis meeting, in Sisters, Oregon, things came to a head. Romania had exposed fissures. We talked about them, about strategy in general, and suddenly it was clear that we all had very different ideas about what we were doing, and why. In the radical movement there is a lot of reading and philosophizing about direct action, and we'd wanted to focus on actually doing it. We should have had that discussion much earlier. There didn't seem to be any reason to meet again. I decided it wasn't safe for me to stick around, and I left Eugene.

A few months later came September 11.

I was in another hotel room, getting ready to do another recon. The TV in the next room was blaring: A plane had hit a building or something. So I turned on my own TV and watched all day. The newscasters kept talking about all the crazy security; everything was on high alert. Military jets kept flying back and forth overhead—the hotel was near an air force base. It was the wrong time to be creeping around in black in the middle of the night, and we called the recon off.

My aunt lives in Connecticut, and my grandmother was in Philadelphia, and that November my family and I went out for Thanksgiving. Before my flight back out of JFK, I took a few hours to visit Ground Zero. The World Trade Center and Pentagon had been the heart of an American empire responsible for a lot of violence around the world, so I wasn't shocked by the attack. But I wasn't hardened to it, either. It was a tragedy, and Ground Zero was a powerful place. I walked around sobbing.

After leaving Eugene in 2001, I spent six months hiding out in Canada. This time was like an extended retreat for me. In my years as an activist, I'd never taken any time for myself. The problems of the world were so urgent, I felt like it was self-indulgent to just relax and have fun. But it was a mistake not to have a balanced life. We'd sacrificed so much that our egos were enmeshed in our actions. We were so steeped in bitterness about the world that it spilled over into the group and broke us apart. Away from all that, I could see it more clearly, and I decided I wanted to do things differently.

My move away from my ELF cell was a gradual process, and it was hard. I was still underground. I'd started living with Darren, a Canadian activist who'd done time for animal releases, and he wasn't legally allowed in the country. We went to San Francisco, then Portland, both using fake identities. We couldn't talk to any of our new friends about our past. I had a prepaid cell phone to call my family, and I was very careful about when and where I turned it on.

In Portland I started DJ'ing. The beat that defines house music is the same beat as a human heart; the connection to life and the Earth is intuitive. I often played music with a subversive, overtly political message. It was January of 2005 when I played a party in Eugene and Jake showed up, already wearing his FBI wire. I didn't want to be rude, but I didn't spend much time talking to him.

The following October, he showed up in line at a Portland coffee shop. I made small talk and bought him some food, since he'd always been broke, but I didn't tell him anything. In late November of 2005, a week before my arrest, I played one of my best sets ever, at a martial-arts studio in Eugene. The studio had been decorated in a jungle motif—big plants and overhead netting—and I played African-influenced rhythms until the whole place was jumping up and down.

Jake just happened to stop by. The government had arranged to have a Childers Meat Company truck parked right out front, hoping it would prompt me to reminisce about the action. It didn't work. I was focused on performing, and the agents got to listen to *boom boom boom* all night.

The day I was arrested, I'd driven to a coffee shop in northwest Portland and was stopped outside. Two cop cars blocked the intersection in front of me, and one came up from behind. There were at least two others. The agents approached my door, guns drawn, and yelled, "Put your hands on the steering wheel." They pulled me out, handcuffed me, and stuffed me in the back of an unmarked sedan.

At the FBI headquarters, they showed me a picture of the Bonneville Power Administration tower we'd downed. They said other people had been arrested and were talking, and that I should, too. I asked if I could have a cigarette. They let me go outside. I don't smoke very often, but I knew I was going to jail for a while, and I wanted to take advantage of my last bit of freedom. I watched some birds and tried to take in the trees, wind, grass, and sky. When I came back in, I went to the restroom and threw up.

I resisted cooperating for almost two months. I argued and argued with my court-appointed lawyer. I didn't think it was ethical to put someone else in jail so I could get out of jail. Just before Christmas, Avalon killed himself in his cell. I learned that other people were beginning to talk, one after another. Soon I knew of at least eight, six of whom would testify against me. I was facing a mandatory minimum of thirty-five years, and it reached a point where I felt my cooperation wouldn't put anyone in jail. So I talked.

Later, some of my codefendants got a deal in which they were allowed to cooperate without naming names. This wasn't possible for me. They had minor roles in one or two arsons in Oregon. I could have been indicted for nine major actions in five separate federal districts spanning the entire period of the conspiracy, so I had much greater culpability. Colorado investigators were determined to get me to say who else was involved in the Vail arson. They were convinced Avalon and I couldn't have done it alone, and they seemed disappointed when I told them the truth.

Jail is overwhelmingly beige. I rarely get to see anything natural or beautiful here, except, occasionally, small bits of sky. I have a daily routine. Sleep through 5:30 a.m. breakfast. Lunch at 10:30. Read the newspaper. Exercise for two or three hours. Yoga. Shower. Write letters. Eat dinner. Work on whatever requires concentration after lights-out. Meditate for an hour or two. Sleep.

I'd never been a particularly spiritual person, but meditation came to me as a way to be at peace with a seemingly untenable situation. I've started to feel more grounded—more intertwined with the spirit of life while alone in my concrete box than I did during much of my time in the free world. Activists need to incorporate this internal work into the movement. It's the basis of true compassion. Once you realize that there's really no "them"—no other—moral action is not sacrifice. It's just aligning yourself with what is good.

Were we wrong? I don't know if I can answer that yet.

I don't regret doing what I felt was right. I don't regret trying to protect the environment. I had good intentions, and I don't regret that I dedicated so much of my life to this. I can't change the past, and I'm not sure I would. The actions were important for my personal evolution—and also for the evolution of the radical movement. I wouldn't be where I am without those experiences. I don't mean sitting in jail. I mean my mind-set.

Even now I can't say that destroying property is always wrong. Our main motive at Vail and in other actions was to inspire people, and we did that. But we were wrong to think more people would adopt our tactics. I can finally understand why they didn't. Activism is motivated fundamentally by compassion and a desire for peace. It's a big step to use force, and it should be.

It's an act of violence to close your heart to anyone, even for a moment. We were certainly guilty of that. We didn't really consider how our actions would impact individuals. We felt the pain of the Earth, and that was what we focused on. A few lost jobs didn't even measure on the scale of the extinction of species. But it doesn't matter what the scale is. You're hurting someone, and you have to grapple with the consequences of that.

True compassion has to apply to everyone: lynx and skiers. I apologized to my victims in court, and I meant it. I couldn't have done that two years ago. The primary responsibility we have as activists and as human beings is to ensure that whatever action we take is based on love. In my involvement with the ELF, we didn't do that, and in that sense we failed.

In martial arts there's a concept that you're not fighting against another person but taking a stand against violence itself. You use only the minimum amount of force necessary to stop an attack. I'm in jail. I'm not going to be doing any more direct action, and I'm not saying anyone else should. But what would a truly moral direct action look like? Maybe it would mean taking in the pain of your victims—opening your heart to them, being wholly present with them—and at the same time, truly taking in the pain they're causing to the natural world. Meditating on it. Fully contemplating it. And then, at the end of that process, perhaps deciding that the most compassionate thing in the world is to light their buildings on fire.

LAST RESORT

MIKE KESSLER

~~~~~~

For almost seventy years, former ski patroller and local legend Jim Blanning rode Aspen's evolution from broken mining outpost to chic mountain playground. But when his hometown spit him out, he came back with a vengeance. And bombs. Our writer investigates the explosive case that literally shook America's glitziest ski destination.

~~~~~~

DECEMBER 31, 2008, 2:32 P.M.

Chance Dannen, a banker at the Wells Fargo branch in Aspen, Colorado, looked down from his desk chair and stared at the bomb by his feet. It didn't appear to be the work of an actual terrorist. It was just a large plastic storage bin, really, its sides and lid sloppily covered with holiday paper, as if wrapped by a clumsy child. But there it was, staring back.

Twenty seconds earlier, an elderly man had strolled in wearing jeans and a parka, a black knit hat, and huge black glasses. He put the package on the floor and handed Dannen a small, empty pizza box with a typewritten note on top. The man was out the door by the time Dannen got through the first sentence, which read, YOU HAD BETTER BE ONE VERY COOL INDIVIDUAL AND NOT START A PANIC, OR MANY IN ASPEN WILL PAY A HORRIBLE PRICE IN BLOOD.

Dannen tiptoed around the package and took the letter to his manager. PUT $60,000 IN USED $100S IN THE WHITE BOX, it continued. DO NOT MOVE OR COVER THE

VERY BIG FIRECRACKER IN THE CONTAINER. UNIQUE CHEMICALS AND ELECTRONICS. ANY DYES, TRACKERS, OR OTHER BULLSHIT WILL CAUSE DISASTER TO ALL.

The note made cryptic references to "rag-head martyrs," along with Karl Rove, Dick Cheney, and their "monkey," George W. Bush. Wait twenty minutes, it said, and then take the cash-stuffed box outside for pickup. If all went according to plan and the "firecracker" went undisturbed, the device would deactivate in two hours. But there better not be any tricks. The letter stated that Aspen's three other banks were getting held up, too, with help from accomplices, and that another package was hidden in a "high-end watering hole" for "added insurance."

Nobody on the street noticed the suspect when he left Wells Fargo. Authorities theorize that he retreated to an alley half a block away, behind the Elks Lodge, where he picked up one of three more gift-wrapped bombs that he'd stashed next to a dumpster. He carried it a few yards to Vectra Bank, at the corner of East Hyman Avenue and South Hunter Street, delivered it with a note, and left, passing the bank's security camera at 2:36 p.m. He probably got to the corner of Hunter and Hopkins, looked down the block toward Wells Fargo, and, seeing the cops and the evacuees gathering outside, aborted his mission. Then he blended in with the crowd, whose New Year's Eve was about to be ruined.

Before long, Aspen police were swarming in and CBs were crackling all over northern Colorado. Every Crown Vic in the region was hurtling toward the Roaring Fork Valley: cops from Vail, FBI agents from Glenwood Springs, the Grand Junction bomb squad—190 responders in all. At 5:34 p.m., the Aspen Police Department (APD) issued a reverse 911 call to all the landline phones within two blocks of the crime scene; less than an hour later, they issued a second call, this time covering sixteen square blocks. Buses got rerouted. Traffic backed up. Residents and tourists, waiters and cooks, managers and merchants—everyone had to clear the area immediately. As for all those New Year's Eve parties and dinner reservations and free-spending downtown shoppers? No sale. Aspen finance director Don Taylor puts the loss to local merchants at nearly $2 million.

It was a dark moment, and it was far from over: The suspect was unknown and on the loose, and nobody could guess who he was. A few weeks after the events of that night, Chris Womack, forty-six, lead investigator for the Aspen police, told me that the bank's video wasn't any help. "We reviewed the image from Vectra's surveillance camera and released it to the public," he said, "but no one could ID the suspect. We didn't even know if it was someone local or an out-of-towner."

By the time the 911 calls went out, cops and sheriff's deputies were gathering three blocks from Wells Fargo and Vectra, in the basement of the Pitkin County Courthouse, where city and county law enforcement share office space. They interviewed bank employees and racked their brains. If it was someone local, who?

Among the many criminals, cranks, and jokers who'd passed through the Roaring Fork Valley over the years, who would choose Aspen's biggest night to threaten the town's 25,000 residents and visitors?

Nobody came up with a candidate, but a few hours later the answer would become head-smackingly obvious.

~~~~~~

His first name might as well have been "Fuckin'." As in: Who's that guy with the woman on his arm, a wad of cash in his hand, and a grin twice as wide as the Hotel Jerome bar? It's Fuckin' Jim Blanning! Did you hear about the guy who dropped his drawers at La Cantina and waved a dildo at the county commissioner? Ha! Fuckin' Blanning.

"People said that a lot over the years," Blanning's old friend Jackie Parker told me when I arrived in Aspen two weeks after the town's bizarre, headline-making New Year's Eve. "He'd be up to something, and every time we'd all just be, like, 'Fuckin' Blanning.' He had a way of surprising you, but at the same time, you expected it."

Even if he'd tried to lie low, Blanning—who was seventy-two on the night of the crime—had always been hard to miss. He was six feet tall and broad-shouldered, with a slow, confident stride. In his heyday, he was all bright blue eyes, thick brown hair, and a mellow-scratchy baritone.

Everybody knew Blanning. Hell, he'd been an Aspenite since the 1940s, when he was just five years old. If you'd ever caught the first gondola of the day, you probably saw the grown-up Jim grinning and gripping, saying things like "Glory morning!" If you'd ever had a nightcap at Little Annie's, then surely you heard him telling stories or marveling at life's little surprises. "Jim was always open to what the universe had to offer," says thirty-seven-year Aspen resident Joni Bruce, sixty-two, his fourth wife. "His favorite saying was, 'Fate is the hunter.'"

This was Jim Blanning from the days of Old Aspen, mind you, the wash-down-a-Quaalude-with-a-pull-tab-Coors-and-turn-up-the-Eagles Aspen of the seventies and eighties. Back then, Blanning didn't just show up for the party; he was the party. "I remember walking into the town's first disco back in '75," recalls Pitkin County sheriff Bob Braudis, a towering sixty-four-year-old who was Blanning's friend for more than thirty years, and whose native Boston accent has survived four decades in the Rockies, "and there's Blanning, dancing away in his cowboy boots and Wranglers. He could have fun with a bar full of miners or the prince of Thailand's nephew."

"Jim was the last of the wild men," says Bruce. "He was a tremendous character with a huge presence. He was a partyer, a prankster, totally gregarious and good to his friends." Blanning was the kind of dude who would hold court at the Pub or the Jerome, buy rounds, excuse himself to go tow a friend's truck out on Highway 82, and still make it back for last call. "He was one of my most generous friends," says Jim Wingers, sixty-four, who met Blanning in the early sixties. "One winter, when I was laid up with a broken leg and couldn't work, he came by and gave me four grand, no questions asked."

When Blanning had money, it usually was the result of a complicated real-estate transaction involving one or more mining claims. Pitkin County's back-country was loaded with old claims—10- to 20-acre parcels established during the silver boom of the early 1870s—most of which were abandoned during a market crash two decades later. But where prospectors had found failure, Blanning saw dollar signs—he was one of the first to grasp how easily old mining claims could be flipped into lucrative real-estate opportunities. By the mid-1960s, he'd already bought several, which could go for as little as $300 back then.

Blanning wasn't the only person to buy and sell claims, but his devotion to the trade was legendary. The potential was limitless, he'd insist, beaming with optimism at buyers or investors. There were untapped veins of silver! You could build cabins and subdivisions on those old parcels and have your own little slice of paradise! The cash came in sporadic chunks—$3,000 here, $25,000 there—but, Wingers says, "Blanning always had a place to hang his hat." Usually it was a trailer on one of his properties, recalled fondly by an old bedmate as "the stabbin' cabin."

The only thing that rivaled Blanning's passion for mining was his appetite for women. "Right when I moved to town, I told a girlfriend that I'd met this guy, Jim Blanning," Bruce recalls. "And she just laughs and says, 'Oh, Jim's the first guy you date when you move to Aspen.' When it came to women, he was the town greeter."

By the mid-seventies, when Bruce married Blanning, he was forty, three times divorced, and an estranged father of two. Wife number one had taken the kids—a boy and a girl—and hit the road early. Wives two and three had come and gone so fast that no one remembers their names. Bruce, who wore a gold "4" medallion while married to Blanning, filed for divorce after eight months, partly over concerns that her husband's hound-dogging might be pathological.

"After his final marriage, Jim went through women like they were nothing," says his younger brother Bill Blanning, now seventy-one and living in Denver. "Aspen was bad for Jim in that regard. These women would show up on vacation, and Jim's handsome and strong, a real mountain man. He'd tour them around town, take them up in the backcountry. Women just loved it."

For all his party-boy charm, Blanning was also prone to erratic behavior. He'd buy dinner for the gang one night and borrow for it the next, pleading poverty. According to consistent and oft-told legend, he initiated countless police chases around town, usually involving alcohol and a snowmobile. In 1986, on the night of his fiftieth birthday, Blanning got busted for a DUI while tearing through Aspen in an old Jeep—on the sidewalk.

Many old-time Aspenites recount these stunts with a sort of quaint fondness. But Bill Blanning is less sanguine. "Jim did what he pleased, when he pleased, no matter what it meant to other people," he says, offering as an example a party in the sixties that took an unpleasant turn when Blanning spiked the punch and locked everybody in the house. "Maybe he was what you call bipolar. You never knew what you were gonna get with Jim. When things were looking up, he was your best friend. He was gonna make millions and take you around the world. But he'd get some wild thing in his head. He could turn on you just like that and become a monster. And the next week the monster would be gone, and he'd be sorry and respectful."

Not everyone got Blanning's respect, especially the police. From the sixties through the mid-eighties, Blanning's name landed on seventy-three incident reports with the APD—traffic violations, failure to appear, petty theft, assault with a deadly weapon. That Blanning never spent more than a night or two in jail back then is a miracle, though Braudis chalks it up to his charm and intelligence.

"He usually knew how far he could push things," Braudis says. "He knew what to say and when to say it for maximum benefit." But Blanning's get-out-of-jail-free card didn't last forever; he did serious time starting in the late nineties. As Braudis would ultimately figure out, his crime back then—a racketeering conviction that put him in a federal prison from 1996 to 2002—was the key to what he did on New Year's Eve 2008.

5:30 P.M.

About an hour after sundown, when Grand Junction's bomb squad arrived in Aspen, authorities found two more packages in the alley behind the Elks Lodge, sitting on a black plastic sled. The contents were unknown, so the three-man crew sent in a robot to assess their weight and determine whether they contained liquids. Even now, bomb-squad member Matt Carson won't say exactly how the devices worked—he's worried about copycat bombers—but he emphasizes that the threat was real. "We gathered enough information to know that it wasn't a hoax," he says.

That night, Carson and his partners opted to use a "remote opening tool," essentially a high-pressure water cannon that obliterates and extinguishes any bomb parts or flames in its path. By 7:30 they were almost ready to make short work of the devices in the alley.

Meanwhile, everyone in Aspen had accepted that the night was officially a bust. The big fireworks show was postponed. People with dinner reservations retreated to overcrowded establishments outside the danger zone. Down-valley residents with up-valley plans stayed in Woody Creek and Carbondale and Basalt. Mexican and Salvadoran dishwashers hopped on the bus back to Glenwood Springs. A man at a bus stop panicked and passed out, causing a minor scene.

Out at Aspen High School, volunteers set up a refugee camp for about two thousand hotel and condo dwellers with nowhere to go. Aspen mayor Mick Ireland prepared to ride his bike to the school to perform ambassadorial duties with the tourists, to assure them that everything would be back to normal soon. But just before he left, police hurried him off to an undisclosed location, citing a new threat.

This fact emerged at around 7:45, when the managing editor at the *Aspen Times*, Rick Carroll, found a handwritten note by the paper's front door, on Main Street. "For the first two years in prison I woke up every [day] wishing I was dead," it read. "Now it comes to pass. I was and am a good man." The note named two people: Sheriff Braudis and Mayor Ireland. "May Bob help to understand it all," it read. "May Mike Ireland rot in hell."

Carroll rushed the note, which had a Denver address written on it, over to the courthouse. When Braudis saw it, his eyes went straight to the signature at the bottom. He immediately recognized Jim Blanning's scrawl. He'd seen it many times, on incident reports and on letters that Blanning sent him from prison. And as far as he knew, Blanning had been living in Denver since he got out on parole in 2002.

"Anyone who knew Blanning came to expect some pretty bizarre behavior," he explained. "I knew him to be manic, and also to be depressed, but never violently so." Nevertheless, when Braudis read the letter, he had a premonition: "I knew we'd find his body by morning."

APD radioed the bomb squad to announce that they'd identified a suspect and that he had a history of arrests and disputes with Aspen officials. When the bomb squad neutralized the packages in the alley, the contents dispersed like shrapnel. The detritus consisted of cell-phone parts, mousetraps, and bladders of gasoline— items that, in Braudis's opinion, were pieces of a viable device.

"A cell phone receives a call and vibrates, setting off a mousetrap," he explains, theorizing about Blanning's bombs. "The mousetrap snaps down on a well-placed strike—a match or a road flare—igniting a spark or a flame. Flame meet vapors from five-gallon plastic bladder of gasoline. Boom."

"If your father was alive," Bill Blanning recalls his mother saying to little Jim, "he'd have straightened you right out." But James Blanning Sr., an officer in the army's 26th Cavalry, had died as a sick and starved POW in Japanese custody when Jim Jr.

was five, Bill was four, and Dick, the last child, was two. (Dick declined to be interviewed for this article.) The Blannings were from Des Moines, Iowa, but they'd bounced from base to base and were living in the Philippines when James Sr. died. Sistie Blanning took the kids to Colorado Springs, where her parents were living. She and the boys traveled to Aspen regularly to learn how to ski. They settled there permanently in 1945.

Few Aspenites are left from those days, but former *Aspen Times* editor and long-time columnist Mary Eshbaugh Hayes, eighty, remembers Sistie as "a bohemian, an artist." With help from a generous local baroness, Sistie bought and ran the Garrett House, a rooming establishment on West Hopkins Avenue, where Jim and his brothers grew up.

As the oldest of three boys, Jim was the ringleader. "He was strong and powerful," Bill recalls. "He pretty well got his way. He pounded my brother and me when we were little. We were constantly terrorized by him."

According to Bill, if Jim wanted a toy, he'd take it. If he needed money, he'd pawn something, never mind that it usually wasn't his to sell. "He took anything he wanted, anytime he wanted," Bill says. "He didn't have a whole lot of conscience about using other people's things. He'd say, 'Oh, I traded you for it—I can't remember what I traded, but now it's mine.'"

In the mountains, Jim became fascinated with mines. He'd seen the old mining maps and photos in the Hotel Jerome, where the family lived for their first few months. But the real thing blew his mind. There were tunnels and shafts under thousands of county acres—a giant honeycomb playground where he could explore and, according to Bill, experiment with old tools and explosives left behind by prospectors after the Panic of 1893.

After graduating from Aspen High in 1954 and then bashing gates with the Aspen Ski Club and doing a stint as a ski instructor, Blanning headed to the University of Colorado at Boulder. College being college, and Blanning being Blanning, he once floated a stick of dynamite down a small runoff channel that passed underneath a sorority house. "I don't think he got caught for that one," Bill says. Not long after, during a school parade, Blanning and some friends flipped the master switch controlling the power. "One of the other guys snitched," Bill says, "and Jim got expelled."

In '56, Blanning joined the air force, where, according to Bill, the regimented military life kept his wilder instincts in check. After serving three years, he returned to Aspen in 1959 and began odd-jobbing—shuttling tourists into town, working at ranches, driving a delivery truck. In '61, he left town to help cut trails at a new Colorado resort called Breckenridge. There, he got to know Dieter Bibbig, a young German who'd recently moved to Aspen.

"We were on the same crew, and I was telling someone how I wanted a gun for elk season," Bibbig says. "Blanning walks up to me and says, 'Hey, Dieter, I've got a rifle I can sell you.' It was a .30-30 Winchester. I gave him $40 for it." It was the only good deal he would ever get from Blanning.

8:00 P.M.

In the basement of the courthouse, authorities started calling Blanning's friends, asking about his whereabouts and whether they thought he really intended to hurt anyone. Soon, Blanning's pal Jay Parker and two Aspen police officers took a trip up to Smuggler Mine, northeast of town. Parker, a co-owner of the defunct mine, had spent plenty of time palling around with Blanning in its tunnels and shafts. Back in 1994, their good friend Stefan Albouy, a mining buff and claim developer, had committed suicide at Smuggler, and Parker was worried that Blanning might follow his friend's example. But Blanning wasn't there.

Meanwhile, a police background check had turned up a green 1997 Jeep Cherokee registered to one of Blanning's LLCs. The landlord at his Denver property said the Cherokee had a spare tire on the roof. Word went out over the radio.

Leads came in and fizzled. At 10:18, someone reported having seen Blanning at the Steak Pit earlier in the day. Another saw an elderly man shaking a police barricade near Wells Fargo. A man who'd been at Ace Hardware that afternoon said he'd seen a man buying black plastic sleds, just like the one Blanning had used to tow his packages. But it wasn't Blanning; it was a guy who runs the horse-drawn-carriage business on Ute Avenue. He'd shown up at the stables that morning to find that his horse-manure sled had been stolen. Police assume that Blanning swiped it to haul his bombs.

Around 11:00, cops headed out to Midnight Mine, a road that passes several of Blanning's former claims. Every law-enforcement officer available cruised Aspen, looking for a Cherokee with a tire on the roof. Blanning could easily have fled town, but some speculate that he stuck around to watch the hubbub. Jay Parker thinks Blanning "probably drove to a spot with a good view of town so he could look out over the whole scene and see the mess he made."

There is, however, another possible scenario—that Blanning was driving around looking for Mayor Ireland. The police took this possibility seriously. Ireland was brought to an "undisclosed location," where he would wait out the night's events with police protection. He was as surprised as anybody to hear that he was a target of Blanning's rage. "I'd been negatively referenced by constituents before," he said later, "but this was unusual. I don't know why he had all this animosity toward me."

The answer to that starts with Blanning's up-and-down track record as a businessman. His first notable venture was a bar called the Molly Gibson, which he opened in the winter of '63 in a Hyman Street space now occupied by a Quiksilver store. Business was brisk, but Blanning was a lousy bookkeeper, and the place folded in less than a year. He got over it. By that time, he'd also embarked on his life's work as a buyer and seller of mining claims.

For the next three decades, Blanning sank all his time and money into this work. Sometimes he'd look at a claim map, decide which parcel (or parcels) he wanted, track down the heirs of the original name on the deed, and buy them out for a few hundred dollars. The land was remote and lacked infrastructure, so most owners were happy to dump it. This method was labor-intensive, but it was cheap, and legal.

Blanning had other methods, however, that were less straightforward. One involved close scrutiny of the 1872 Mining Act, which requires counties to advertise mining-claim sales and auction the parcels off at a specified time every year. If Blanning could find proof that no such advertising or auctioning had taken place for a specific deed, well, too bad for Pitkin County—Blanning would lay claim to it.

Usually, though, Blanning searched for claims that were the property of old corporations—prospecting businesses that had packed up and left decades before. There were hundreds of them. Blanning would discover one, establish a new corporation with the same name as the defunct one, and become the rightful owner. "Jim referred to this as 'resuscitating' a corporation," says Chip McCrory, fifty-four, a former Pitkin County assistant district attorney. "But Blanning wasn't resuscitating anything. He'd adopt an old corporation's name just to take ownership. Then he'd turn around and sell it as a piece of real estate, regardless of its intended use."

Conservationists view the 1872 Mining Act much like gun-control advocates look at the Second Amendment—as an antiquated piece of legislation created in a context that no longer exists. "The Mining Act is outdated and obsolete in many ways," says Ireland. "Land pirates" like Blanning, he says, "were trying to parlay that obsolete law to their advantage and buy up mining claims for subdivision. No one could have foreseen this in 1872."

Even so, Blanning did his share of legitimate business, selling cheap land in the seventies and eighties to ski bums and service workers. Several houses on Ute Avenue—at the base of Aspen Mountain ski area—sit on former Blanning claims, as do a few homes in the Castle Creek area and an 8,000-square-footer on top of Red Mountain. "I think the price on that claim was $5,000," says Jim Wingers. "It's worth a lot more now."

According to everyone who knew him, Blanning was relentless about taking possession of every square inch of a parcel. "He had some claims that were being encroached upon by Ruthie's Restaurant," Wingers says, referring to the popular eatery at Aspen Mountain. "Jim put up a rope and made the skiers go through a six-foot-wide area so he could count the number of people passing through his property. This drove D. R. C. Brown, the resort's owner, up a wall. Jim settled for two lifetime ski passes and some cash."

~~~~~~

Mick Ireland moved to Aspen in 1979 to be a ski bum but switched tracks in '85 and enrolled at the University of Colorado Law School, in Boulder. He first heard about Blanning in the summer of '86, while on break. Blanning, by way of his land research, was convinced that the town was in danger. "We'd had a big winter followed by a wet spring," Ireland explains, sitting at a conference table inside city hall. "Blanning claimed that a seismograph showed the mountain was cracking and was wet enough to slide and bury the town near Wagner Park." Blanning was wrong, but he meant well. He was convincing enough that officials briefly evacuated the area.

Out of law school and back in Aspen, Ireland took a job as a reporter for the *Aspen Times* in the summer of '88. He'd heard about a group that was buying up mining claims with the intention of selling the land for development, and he began reporting the story. To Ireland, people like Blanning were using claims "for reasons other than their intended purpose." A few years later, Ireland was appointed county commissioner. One of the first projects he was involved with was a land swap involving 125 acres near Mount Sopris, which sat atop more than fifty mining claims northwest of town. The rub: Blanning's name was on some of the deeds. Blanning signed on to a lawsuit against the US Forest Service and won. But the case went federal, and the judge ruled against Blanning, saying that his ownership of the claims was based on duplicitously acquired deeds.

That battle, in part, inspired a legislative move by the county to rein in residential development on old mining claims. After several months of debate, the measure passed, placing strict limitations on rural building. By this time, of course, Aspen was a world-famous destination resort. Workers were being priced out of town and forced down-valley to Basalt and Carbondale and even Glenwood Springs, 40 miles away. Blanning, whose entire livelihood was tied up in mining claims, and who wasn't known for squirreling away cash, found himself left out of the game.

He had to make a statement. One evening in 1994, he threw a hardbound copy of the US Constitution through a courthouse window. While preparing for the stunt, he'd called up Sheriff Braudis's girlfriend, Dede Brinkman, a filmmaker, and asked her to document the crime. "It's a two-camera shoot," he told her.

Later that summer, he climbed the stairs to the roof of the Pitkin County Courthouse, tied a rope to the cupola, wrapped the other end around his neck, and stood at the edge of the building, threatening to jump. Braudis, along with several other law-enforcement officers and friends of Blanning, took turns trying to talk him off the ledge. "He's screaming all kinds of stuff," Braudis recalls. "'Bob, they ruined my life, these fuckin' elected officials. They're all wrong and I'm right. I can't live like this, man.'" When Blanning finally came down, he melted into the arms of the police chief and wept.

While psychiatric treatment, or at least a break, was probably in order, Blanning opted to stay in the land business. It would be his biggest mistake. In 1995, he learned that Dieter Bibbig, the German to whom he'd sold the rifle back in '61, kept his Aspen home not in his name but rather under the protection of a limited-liability company. Owning property under an LLC is a common way to protect assets in the event of a lawsuit. But just as a driver has to re-register a car, an LLC owner must renew the corporation every few years. Bibbig had let his LLC lapse. As far as Blanning was concerned, the property was up for grabs, just like the abandoned mining claims he'd scored over the years. He "resuscitated" Bibbig's LLC under his own name and then took out a $350,000 loan, using Bibbig's house—a Victorian on Park Avenue—as collateral. He defaulted on the loan, then sold Bibbig's house out from under him.

"It was not a real-estate transaction," says Chip McCrory, the former assistant DA. "It was a criminal act. He didn't resuscitate Bibbig's LLC. He stole it." Bibbig had to spend nearly a quarter-million on lawyer fees to get his house back. The incident prompted McCrory to investigate Blanning further. "The paper trail seemed endless," he says. "We found three or four mining-claim sales where Blanning was adopting these old corporations' names, passing property through a series of shell corporations . . . and trying to sell them. The county believed that he'd done business in violation of racketeering laws, so we charged him accordingly." That meant using the Racketeer Influenced and Corrupt Organizations Act (RICO), a federal law created to maximize punishment for organized-crime figures. Forced to choose between prison and a plea deal with financial demands he couldn't fulfill, Blanning opted to go to trial. The jury found him guilty, and the judge gave him sixteen years in prison.

Blanning had a few weeks of freedom after the sentencing, which he used to make a final statement. One Friday evening he walked into La Cantina, where county officials regularly met for after-meeting drinks. He approached their table, took off his clothes, and folded them neatly on a nearby chair. "All he had on was a Speedo, with this giant purple thing sticking out of it," recalls Ireland. "It was a huge purple dildo. He just stood there with his hands on his hips, staring at us."

The incident earned Blanning an indecent-exposure charge and got him branded a sex offender before he was shipped off to the federal pen in Cañon City, Colorado. "It was a totally draconian sentencing," Braudis says. "The Bibbig case should have been a civil case, not a federal RICO case. And the pervert thing, that was just excessive. Blanning got way more than he deserved. At that point, I knew his life was over."

In 2002, at age sixty-six, Blanning was released and given an "intensive supervised parole." He'd done six years. After a year in a halfway house in Denver, he rented an apartment in the city's Sloan Lake neighborhood. Every few months, his brother Bill would stop by to check in and occasionally leave money. Their meetings were brief, and Blanning did most of the talking—about mining claims or the nightclub he frequented on weekends, where he'd dance with the ladies and nurse a Coke to save money. Whenever Bill left, he'd say, "I'm glad to see you're doing all right and getting by, Jim." And each time, Blanning would respond, "Well, if worse comes to worst, there's always Plan B."

11:45 P.M.

Dieter Bibbig got the call just before midnight: Jim Blanning was behind the bomb scare and on the loose. He hung up, went into another room to get his rifle—the rifle Blanning had sold him forty-seven years earlier—and waited. But Blanning never showed; he was busy preparing his final message, a suicide note, handwritten and four pages long, addressed to Sheriff Braudis. He wrote, in part:

> I came loaded for bear, as you will see. I was going to do just as the bomb note [stated]. Could have done some serious damage. Oh well. Too tired—to the bone. . . . My body is shot and the ongoing black depression has [made] mush of my mind lately. . . . Many people know I had a wonderful life until Mick Ireland and JE [Jodi Edwards, another county attorney] got me. God knows I would love to have cut Ireland's and Chip McCrory's balls off before skinning them. I wandered around for hours this afternoon. God knows I have a long history—Aspen School, Air Force Nuclear Weapons—Ski Patrol and Instructor . . . more deeds/property, etc., than most anyone. Not sure where you will find me. Should be interesting to hear everyone tell stories about me.

Sometime in the early-morning hours, Blanning pulled into a small parking area next to the North Star Nature Preserve, about 2 miles south of town, toward Independence Pass. He turned off the engine, stepped out of the vehicle, put a .38 revolver under his chin, and fired. The bullet pinballed inside his skull, never emerging. Police found him at 4:27 a.m., faceup in the snow, legs outstretched, eyes open.

Moments later, Grand Junction's bomb squad deployed the "remote opening tool" on the Wells Fargo package, which they'd safely moved to the sidewalk. When the blast of water hit it, a four-story fireball shot into the sky. "We'll never know whether the devices would have actually worked," APD's Chris Womack later told me. "But I personally believe that Blanning intended to do damage."

He certainly had the firepower. In addition to the .38, he wore a fishing vest that held eight semiautomatic-rifle magazines and three .38 caliber speed loaders. In his Cherokee, authorities found maps of Aspen with several addresses marked, among them the homes of Ireland and McCrory. There was also an AR-15 rifle and enough camping gear for a person to survive in the woods for weeks.

Whether Blanning intended to do any real harm will be the subject of debate on Aspen's barstools and chairlifts for years to come. Some will demonize him, or categorize him as a slightly more personable version of the Unabomber. Others will mythologize him as a man driven mad by the forces of government. Braudis comes down in the middle.

"Jim Blanning was not Don Quixote fighting windmills," he says. "He's not a romantic figure. Some people ascribe his troubles to the closing of the door by government, but that's romanticizing Jim Blanning, and I'm not gonna do that. He was a friend. And he was one of many colorful characters I've met in Aspen. He had demons. He'd become critical, and critical people have to take things to the next level. Unfortunately he did that by fucking up New Year's Eve and then electing to kill himself."

Shortly into the new year, Vail police announced that Blanning was a suspect in two robberies from 2005 and 2006, both at Weststar Bank, in Vail Village. Blanning had made purchases and deposits equal in value to five-figure amounts taken from the bank, and the suspect in surveillance footage wore a hat, glasses, and jacket identical to the outfit Blanning sported in Aspen on New Year's Eve. The Vail suspect wore white gloves and bronze face paint. Authorities found matching gloves and tubes of bronze makeup in Blanning's Denver apartment—along with mining-claim maps, field guides, books, camping gear, and receipts dating back to the 1950s. Blanning had even saved the famous purple phallus from his visit to La Cantina.

At the time of the Vail robberies, Blanning didn't own a car. Police found no evidence of any car-rental transactions after his release from prison, and they have no leads as to a possible getaway driver. A friend of his in Denver told me that he thinks Blanning may have taken a bus—an audacious and crafty move, but not beyond the scope of his behavior. Detective sergeant Craig Bettis of the VPD believes that after the second robbery, Blanning may have simply walked out of Weststar, trekked up Vail Mountain, and camped out for a few days until the heat died down.

"He certainly was bold enough," Bettis says. "But at this point, all we can do is guess."

THE BALLAD OF
COLTON HARRIS-MOORE

BOB FRIEL

In 2008, a teen fugitive was making a mockery of local authorities the Northwest's San Juan Islands—and headlines around the world. He not only stole cars and broke into vacation homes, he pilfered planes and took them for joyrides. His ability to elude the police and survive in the woods earned him folk-hero status. But when our reporter began looking into the case, some wondered if the eighteen-year-old would make it out of the hunt alive.

Around ten a.m., everything went to shit. Sixty-mile-an-hour wind gusts grabbed the little Cessna 182, shook it, twisted it, threw it down toward the jagged peaks of the Cascade Range, then slammed it back up again.

Pilots of small planes obsess about the weather. Ill winds, icing, poor visibility—all can bring a flight to a terminal, smoldering conclusion. However, when you're a seventeen-year-old kid with exactly zero hours of flight training other than what you've gleaned online and from DVDs, and you're sitting in the pilot seat of a stolen airplane trying to make a quick getaway from a whole lotta law that's on your tail for busting out of a prison home and going on your second cop-teasing crime spree, well, you've got other things on your mind besides the weather.

It's believed the kid had cased the small airport on Orcas Island, in the San Juans off the coast of Washington, for at least a week, hiding in the trees behind a flimsy deer fence to watch takeoffs and landings, waiting patiently until a late-model Cessna

182 Skylane—fuel-injected dependability, easy to fly, rugged as hell—touched down and rolled into the hangar farm. Sometime after sundown, he'd pried his way inside the hangar, where he had all night to check out the plane, read the GPS and autopilot manuals, and dig around to find the ignition key the owner had tucked away in a fishing-tackle box. At sunrise, he'd raised the hangar's wide metal door, attached the tow bar, leaned his 6-foot-5, 200-pound frame against the 1-ton plane, and slowly rolled it out.

Between YouTube and flight sims, anyone who is computer-literate can find more than enough info to pilot a plane—in theory. Microsoft Flight Simulator reproduces the dash of the 182 exactly, and once the thief climbed into the pilot's seat, his fingers found all the gauges and controls quickly, adjusting fuel mixture and rudder trim. The newer fuel-injected engines turn over easily, and with so many private planes on Orcas, none of the neighbors took special notice of the early-morning growls of the Skylane's 235-horsepower Lycoming. He revved up and taxied south toward the still-sleeping town of Eastsound, then spun the plane until its nose aimed straight down runway 34—which ends abruptly in the cold, slate-gray waters of Puget Sound. He went full-throttle and popped the toe brakes. Instantly the plane lurched forward. The virgin pilot kept his cool, applying enough pressure on the right rudder pedal to counteract the propeller torque and keep the Cessna on the skinny, half-mile strip long enough to hit 60 miles per hour, lift off, and mainline an epic hit of euphoria.

From what the pilot's mom, Pam Kohler, tells me, this was not only her son's first solo takeoff, but also the very first time he'd ever been in a plane. Here's a kid who'd been told over and over, by teachers, by the police, by so-called friends, and by nearly every adult he'd ever had contact with, that he would never do anything. Suddenly he's flying high, soloing in a bright white plane with whooshing red stripes.

He banked toward the sun, which was rising above snowcapped Mount Baker, and turned south, flying alongside Orcas's Mount Constitution, at 2,402 feet, the highest point in the San Juan Islands. Within ten minutes, Camano Island, his home, came into view. There's a landing strip on Camano, but that wasn't an option—his face already adorned Wanted posters all over that island. So he continued south-southeast, leaving Puget Sound for the mainland and managing to avoid the heavy commercial air traffic around Sea-Tac. South of Seattle, he banked east, putting the frosty white bulk of Mount Rainier in his right-side window, and headed across the Cascades.

The mountains create a lot of weather, and on a good day, this means lively turbulence. On November 12, 2008, it meant wind gusts exploding against the little Cessna like aerial depth charges, causing one massive buzzkill.

"The ride would've been extremely uncomfortable," says Eric Gourley, chief pilot for San Juan Airlines and a flight instructor with somewhere north of 13,000 hours in the air. Gourley spent time as an Alaskan bush pilot, so "uncomfortable" to him means the equivalent of spinning inside a commercial clothes dryer. He's a fellow resident of mine on Orcas Island and taught the owner of the stolen plane—popular Seattle radio personality Bob Rivers—how to fly. Now he just shakes his head, considering a kid with no training over the Cascades that morning, saying it's "almost unbelievable" he made it.

The police believe it, though. Once past the violent updrafts, the kid flew on until eleven a.m., when he attempted to land in a scrub field on the Yakama Indian Reservation—about 300 miles from where he took off. The Cessna came in hot and hit hard, bouncing back into the air before impacting again and nosediving into a gulley, the propeller blades tearing up the earth. The pilot trashed the plane, but he walked—or ran—away, the minimum test of a successful landing. When police got to the scene, they found the cockpit splattered in puke. Other than bits of his breakfast, though, the pilot left no trace and disappeared into the woods.

Before he was suspected of stealing the plane, the kid had been just Colton Harris-Moore, high-school dropout, juvenile delinquent, and petty thief who sometimes left bare footprints at crime scenes. After he climbed out of the Cessna and disappeared in the wilds of Washington State—home of Sasquatch, D. B. Cooper, *Twin Peaks*, and *Twilight*—he became Colt, latest in a long line of gutsy outlaws to capture the world's imagination.

When you look at the facts, it's easy to understand why he's garnered so much attention: His name is Colt, carrying the gun-slinging resonance of the Wild West. He's escaped a jail (albeit a baby jail) and evaded several sheriffs, the Royal Canadian Mounted Police, and even the FBI for twenty months. He's underdogging it alone in the Northwest wilderness, yet he's followed by bloggers and Facebookers worldwide, the modern equivalent of yesteryear's sensationalized dime-novel hero. During his many close calls, the cops claim Colt has "vaporized," "vanished," and "[run] like lightning." When the posse does close in, he allegedly rustles luxury cars, boats, and even planes. And something no one's mentioned is that one of his hide-outs on Orcas Island, Madrona Point, is an honest-to-God, can't-make-this-stuff-up ancient Indian burial ground. Hell yeah, this looks like the birth of an outlaw legend.

"Colton was first suspected of theft in 2001, when he was ten years old," says Detective Ed Wallace, of the Island County sheriff's department, which has been chasing Colt almost constantly ever since. Born March 22, 1991, the young outlaw tended toward the childish in his criminal tooth-cutting—petty thefts and malicious mischief. Classmates remember him and a couple of cronies getting busted for breaking into their school, Stanwood Middle, located in mainland Snohomish County just across the bridge from Camano Island, where Colt lived with his mom in a single-wide. By December 2003 Colt had accumulated eight incident reports at school for theft and vandalism, among other infractions, resulting in multiple suspensions. According to Snohomish County court records, when confronted by the principal, Colt said he "could not stop stealing and didn't know why." In sixth grade, the kids at school began calling him Klepto Colt.

Christa Postma, one of his former classmates, says that while Colt was always getting into trouble, he was "a nice kid" and "seemed really smart, though he didn't know how to put that into his schoolwork." The two of them would hang outside the Stanwood Library after school, and that's where, she says, Colt met up with a future accomplice, a guy two years older, with the rebel-ready handle Harley Davidson Ironwing. "When Colt wasn't around Harley, he'd be totally chill," she says. "When Harley showed up, Colt would suddenly be all, I'm so big and bad." Ironwing, who's serving time in Washington Corrections Center, recently talked to an *Everett Herald* reporter for a story subtitled "Harley Davidson Ironwing says he trained Colton Harris-Moore how to survive by stealing."

By the age of fifteen, Colt had been to juvie more times than most kids his age had been to McDonald's. When not in detention, he often lived under a sentence of community service. In 2006, as soon as he finished one stretch at the Denny Youth Center, in Everett, police were already poised to arrest him for crimes they'd investigated while he was away. That July, one day before he was due in court, Colt disappeared into the hinterlands of Camano Island.

Roughly 70 percent of Camano remains wooded—primarily thick stands of cedar and maple with a soft sea of waist-high ferns filling the understory. From the road, you can't see past the first line of trees, and even when you hike in, the exuberant growth means you'd literally have to stumble onto anyone who kept a low-profile camp. No matter how lush, though, living off the land is harder than it sounds—and always dirtier, smellier, and hungrier. Going into the wild killed Christopher McCandless in Alaska. Eric Rudolph—the anti-abortion Olympic Park bomber—was finally nabbed when he slithered out of the Appalachian boonies to go dumpster diving for food. Tramping through Camano's many parks and preserves that butt against residents' backyards, Colt came up with an idea that remains his identifying MO: When your ecosystem is a vacation destination, the vacationers lie at the bottom of the food chain. Instead of camping full-time, he began breaking into Camano's 1,000-plus holiday homes—many of them empty much of the time—to shower, forage for food, and sleep.

Ever the opportunist, Colt found that, along with cans of tuna, people leave all kinds of property in their weekend homes. He helped himself to laptops, cash, jewelry, camcorders, cell phones, a telescope, a GPS unit, iPods, radio-controlled toys like boats and a helicopter, and a Trek mountain bike. There's not much evidence that he pawned the loot, just collected it. Sometimes the homeowners left behind credit cards. Another Colt innovation: Simply punch in those numbers online and you get custom burglary, with overnight delivery of such on-the-lam necessities as bear mace, aviation magazines, a police scanner, and "evidence eraser" software. This was a risky escalation, though, because Colt now had to return to the scene of the crime to collect his packages once they'd been delivered.

On February 9, 2007, seven months after he'd gone on the run, Island County cops finally corralled Colt when he screwed up and turned on a light in a supposedly vacant home. He surrendered after a short standoff and pled guilty to three of twenty-three counts of burglary and possession of stolen property. After a year in the max-security Green Hill School, Colt was transferred to the minimum-security Griffin Home, near Seattle, to serve out the rest of his three-year sentence. But around nine p.m. on April 29, 2008, he decided he'd had enough of confinement and reportedly climbed out a window.

Today, Colt remains at large, and getting larger, a suspect in more than one hundred crimes, mostly felonies. It's been twenty months since he busted out and began playing *Grand Theft Auto: The Reality Version*, and he's wanted in five Washington counties—Island, Snohomish, San Juan, Whatcom, and Kitsap—as well as in Idaho. The Royal Canadian Mounted Police joined the chase when he bolted north of the border this past September, allegedly stealing cars and breaking into homes to scrounge for food. And because they believe he flew across state lines in October in another stolen Cessna, Colt's got the FBI on his tail.

This time, the authorities were chasing a suspect alleged to be the lanky teen near the crash-landing site of a $500,000 Cessna 182 turbo that had been heisted in Idaho, flown back across the Cascades, and somehow set down in one cracked, racked, and jacked-up piece on a hillside clearing in Granite Falls, Washington. Police marshaled two counties' worth of SWAT in armored personnel carriers, canine units, a sheriff's helicopter, and a Department of Homeland Security Black Hawk. Their search of every outhouse, henhouse, doghouse, and meth house— Granite Falls has a rep—turned up nothing. Once again, the suspect melted into the Washington woods.

After this latest escape, the media set up all three rings, bringing in the *Today* show, CNN, CBS, Fox, CBC, and all the Seattle network affiliates and radio talkers to fetishize the fact that Colt had committed some crimes while barefoot, and to sling lazy shorthand references like Catch Me If You Can. The story had already gone viral online, and when it was picked up by print and TV worldwide, the Colton Harris-Moore Fan Club on Facebook was friended from as far away as Ireland, Italy, and Australia. A ballad about Colt showed up on YouTube, and T-shirt sales—FLY, COLTON, FLY! and MOMMA TRIED—soared.

The law—in particular, the sheriff's office of Colt's own Island County—was not, to put it mildly, amused. When he was asked on CBC TV about Colt's Robin Hood hero status, Sheriff Mark Brown's round-and-ruddy face turned a new hue.

"He's certainly not my hero," he said, adding ominously, "I hope that you and I and everybody else, when he does make that fatal mistake, are not responsible for something other than an arrest being made without an incident."

~~~~~~

Lying just 30 miles north of Camano and offering some three thousand ready-to-pluck vacation homes, the San Juan Islands—and, in particular, Orcas, the largest and most heavily wooded of the archipelago—became Colt's second-happiest hunting ground. Floating out here in Puget Sound, on America's far western frontier, Orcas collects more than its share of the anti-authority-minded. When about one hundred of us gathered around a huge bonfire just before Halloween to drink beer and chow on barbecued venison (called "hillside salmon" when it's out of season), talk naturally turned to Colt. Everyone knew his victims, or at least frequented their restaurants and shops. One guy had been hit twice, his store burgled and then his boat allegedly stolen and run aground during another getaway. Between slurred extremes of "I'm glad he's sticking it to the cops" and "Hope he sticks his head in my house, 'cause he'll die of lead poisoning," there was a universal appreciation of Colt's balls and brains.

With only some four thousand full-timers on Orcas, we're all at most one degree away from each other. Residents include ex-CEOs of chemical companies and defense contractors, millionaire Microsofties who optioned out in their thirties, Hollywood glitterati, an Apollo astronaut, and even *The Far Side*'s Gary Larson. And then there's the rest of us: retirees, a working middle class of small-business people, organic farmers, contractors, and cabinetmakers, and an eclectic mix of woodcarvers, potters, painters, musicians, and writers. Many struggle to cling to an island where the cost of living reflects its isolation. The cool Salish Sea, filled with killer whales, giant octopus, and Steller sea lions, acts as a moat, keeping the world at bay, but every single thing must be imported except fresh air, the spectacular outdoor lifestyle, and whatever you can find at the farmers' market. It's worth it, though: It's that wonderful. This is the kind of place where, B.C.—before Colt—ignition keys lived in the car's cupholder, and very few of us locked our homes.

This past summer's crime wave appeared limited to Eastsound, Orcas's zero-traffic-light and one-cow town. (The cow's name is April and she lives at the top of Enchanted Forest Road.) Madrona Point, the Lummi Indian burial ground where Colt secretly camped, is a thickly wooded peninsula dangling below town, conveniently located just steps away from all the shopping. Eastsound was easy pickings for Colt, and since it lies half an island away from the rural cabin where my wife, Sandi, and I live, Colt was the furthest thing from my mind on this August 22, when I woke to a noise at three a.m.

All manner of deer, raccoons, mink, otters, owls, and other critters rustle around here at night, but none had ever moved lumber. The sound of wood clacking also roused our dog, a Leonberger named Murphy, and he padded heavily into the bedroom, snuffed at the window screen, and raised his hackles. The first rain we'd had in more than a month plinked off the metal roof, and the thought of pulling on shoes and a rain shell, finding a flashlight, and stumbling around under the cabin—which perches at the edge of a rocky cliff—seemed way too exhausting, especially since this was probably just a deer bombed on fermented huckleberries. The following night, again, around three a.m., I woke to the eerie sensation of someone staring at me in the pitch blackness of the bedroom. Murphy was on alert at the window again, hackles raised.

I sat up and listened but couldn't hear anything except the rain.

The next day, I learned that during those two nights someone had broken into a B&B, a restaurant, a marina, and a dock store, all within a mile or so of our place. When I realized that the dense woods surrounding our cabin connected directly to all of those spots, my hackles went up, too. That's also when Sandi started talking about putting up curtains while we turned the cabin upside down looking for our one house key.

Usually, life on our little island remains so blissfully devoid of what a city dweller would call "action" that our hormone-charged teens call it "Orcatraz." Before Colt, we read the sheriff's log for its Lake Wobegon–like entertainment. My favorite entry from this past summer: On August 3, "an eighty-three-year-old Eastsound woman reported . . . one pair of fur-lined moccasins . . . and three almost-new pair of beige women's underwear were stolen from an unlocked old fruit-packing barn."

The last time an Orcas crime was even considered newsworthy for the mainland papers was twenty-two months ago, when a numbnuts who'd drifted ashore for a while decided to punish the "rich, white people" of the island for the death of Luna the killer whale (who'd swum into a tugboat's propeller 185 miles north of Orcas, up in Canada). He jumped a fence at a power station and, fully protected by Playtex kitchen gloves, tried to cut a high-voltage line with a polesaw. When a lineman got to the scene, the vigilante's pants were still smoking. No matter how delusional, though, at least that guy had a message, something Colt has yet to feel the need to offer.

"Jesse James and other outlaws weren't celebrated just because they were criminals," says professor Graham Seal, author of *The Outlaw Legend: A Cultural Tradition in Britain, America and Australia*. "They were seen to embody a spirit of defiance and protest, allowing the dispossessed to strike a vicarious blow against their oppressors." Seal says that Colt "sure sounds like an outlaw legend in the making," especially considering his elusiveness, style, and growing number of supporters. So who's living vicariously through Colt? So far, he's a blank screen, ready for projection. Rebelling against the government, the cops, your parents? Colt's got you covered.

The only hint of a motive I can dig up is a note Colt wrote to his mom after the Camano Island deputies found one of his campsites, filled with stolen merchandise. His dog, Melanie, was at the camp, and the police took her. "'The cops wanna play, huh?" Colt wrote. "It's war! Tell them that."

Davis Slough runs wet at high tide, making Colt's home turf, Camano, officially an island, even though it's a drive-to. Over the past twenty years, most of the island's rustic fishing and crabbing camps have fallen to luxe waterfront homes, but the talk still tends toward what's biting and how Dungeness crab season is shaping up.

Heading toward the lower end of the island, where Colt grew up, I pass the dinky prefab that serves as a base for Camano's small group of sheriff's deputies and their black-and-gold patrol cars. Soon the homes spread out and it's mostly wooded acreage, private property as well as parks, with plenty of room to hide. I leave the pavement at Haven Place, marked by a long line of mailboxes and several FOR SALE signs.

After reading a couple hundred pages of Island County court documents concerning Colt's childhood, I got the impression that, at times, this place had been anything but a haven for him. Reports name a dozen Child Protective Services referrals dating from the time he was one. They also reference "numerous" reports that "Colton's mother has been heavily affected by alcohol abuse throughout his formative years," and state that his father was gone by the time Colt was four, though back for at least one family barbecue, which ended with Colt calling 911 and the father being chased through the woods and arrested on outstanding warrants. The court documents state that Colt's stepfather was a heroin addict. A third potential male role model was described by Colt's mom as "not playing with a full deck." A court psychologist's evaluation says that young Colt was diagnosed with ADHD, depression, and intermittent explosive disorder, and placed on four medications. Quotes from Colt at age twelve include "I am tired of this stuff" and "I need help."

I turn down a dark driveway, slowly roll past several no-nonsense NO TRESPASSING signs, and park beside three other pickups in varying states of decay. Across a small clearing slumps a dingy white single-wide trailer with extra bits and pieces cobbled on, including a small wooden deck. I climb the loose cinder blocks, piled three high, that stand in for steps. Looking out from atop the rain-slicked deck, it's a beautiful, peaceful piece of property, completely screened by lush green drapes of cedar. The junk cars, the busted lawn furniture, the aluminum shed frozen in mid-collapse—nothing is really so far out of the ordinary for the rural areas around here. It's just a little more so. At the far side of the clearing, amid the soaring cathedral of cedars 100 feet tall, stands some kind of statue. It's about 4 feet high, without much shape, but could be a Virgin Mary.

"That's an armadillo that used to stand outside a liquor store," says Pam Kohler, Colt's mom. "The chickens got to it, though, and pecked off some of the Styrofoam." The statue, she says, like the trailer, was on the property when she bought it twenty-four years ago. She leads me inside, where I'm greeted by 20 pounds of wagging tail named Melanie.

"Colt wanted a beagle, so we went to the shelter and they brought this one out," says Pam. "I think she's some kind of hunting dog. This summer she got one of the biggest snakes I've ever seen, and just last month she's barking at something in the yard, so I walk over, and it's a SWAT guy hiding in the trees in his full G.I. Joe outfit."

The first time I talked to Pam on the phone, we were interrupted when six police officers showed up at her door. All the jurisdictions have been there and, lately, officers from an auto-theft task force who, she says, have told her they think Colt has stolen between forty and sixty cars. "Those guys brought me a plate of chocolate-chip cookies," she says. "It's all weird."

I get the sense, though, that the weirdness started before Colt's current troubles. Pam, at fifty-eight, appears literally hunched over from the weight of a life that hasn't been what she expected. We sit down at a small table in the kitchen. She's not smoking, but the air is so saturated—Pall Malls, by the butts in the ashtray—that it claws my eyes. She talks of a marriage to an air force man (she was Pam Harris then), a life in Southern California, another in St. Louis, and then moving back to her home state, Washington, cashing in her retirement fund to buy these five acres on Camano, where, after five years of trying, and, twenty years after the birth of her first son, along came Colt. Pam says she had a federal job back then, in the accounting department of the National Park Service down in Seattle. "Commuting three hours a day when I had a newborn baby, that was awful." The air force husband was gone, and Colt's biological father was in and out of the trailer, and their lives. Pam remarried when Colt was four, giving him a stepfather named Bill, a Vietnam vet whom, she says, he was very close to. "They did every-thing together," she says. Then one day, when Colt was ten and Bill had gone off to help move some relatives to Florida, the phone rang.

"Someone from Island County sheriff called and asked if I was Bill's wife. I said yes, and they just said, 'Well, he's dead.'" No funeral, no closure other than the jug of ashes in the closet—and Bill, she says, never wanted to be cremated. Pam doesn't know how he died. "They wanted me to pay for a coroner's report, and that just don't jive with me—not cool.

"After Bill died, I freaked," says Pam. "I cried all the time, and I drank a lot and went into a deep depression. I'm sure it affected Colt, too." Her job ended, and the only money coming in was from Social Security widow's benefits. She took some criminal-justice and psychology classes at Skagit Valley College. "I wanted to be a lawyer," she laughs, then sighs. "But then crap just started happening, trucks breaking down, nobody to help me." She stopped going, and money got tighter. "We starved," she says. Court documents from around that time report, "Colton wants mom to stop drinking and smoking, get a job, and have food in the house."

Melanie climbs onto the couch in the living room, where a nice TV stands next to the woodstove. A hallway so narrow that my arms brush both walls leads back to a bathroom and the bedrooms beyond, including Colt's, the one that a deputy's affidavit says sported a padlock hasp one time when they showed up looking for him, so Pam took a hatchet to it. In the kitchen, I sit below a piece of plywood screwed into the wall where there used to be a window. Three years ago, Pam says, a neighbor who accused Colt of stealing his car stereo terrorized them every night for a month by throwing potatoes, a can of corn, and circular-saw blades at them, breaking windows in both the trailer and her truck.

Neighborly relations do seem complicated along this stretch of road. One of the times the local police came closest to catching Colt was when they spotted a black Mercedes owned by Carol Star—who lives next door to Pam—driving erratically. When they gave chase, the Mercedes turned into the parking lot of the nearby Elger Bay Cafe and out jumped Colt while the car was still moving. He disappeared into the woods as the car rolled between a propane tank and a wall with inches to spare, coming to rest against a dumpster just a couple of yards from a 20-foot cliff. Star says Colt had already robbed her house several times, and it was from a stolen camera found in her car that Island County detective Ed Wallace recovered the now-infamous picture that Colt had shot of himself and then deleted. It shows Colt relaxing amid the ferns, wearing a Mercedes polo and a Mona Lisa smile. It's the same picture that now graces Wanted posters throughout the state.

"That's a terrible photo of him," says Pam, though she likes another Wanted pic taken by a security camera at the Island Market, on Orcas. "We didn't take many photos when he was growing up," she says, handing me a dusty frame holding a 1997 group shot of a Stanwood/Camano Junior Athletic Association soccer team, along with a portrait of Colt in his uniform. In the pictures, he's a cute towhead with a big, bright smile. When I spoke with the parents of another kid on that team, though, they said that Colt had come to only the first couple of practices and the photo session, and that he never actually got to play. It's a shame, because from the accounts of a half-dozen deputies who've chased—but never caught—fleet-footed Colt in the woods of Camano and Orcas, he's a natural athlete.

"He was a fat, happy baby," Pam remembers. "I used to call him Tubby." She pauses for a moment, then recalls other nice memories from Colt's childhood: camping in the Cascades ("Maybe I shouldn't have taught him all that survival stuff"), summer days on the water, she and Colt dancing to Sinatra's "Summer Wind" out on the deck. Pam remembers once taking Colt to a local beach but having to leave him there alone because she had a headache. "When I went back to pick him up, he'd set up a whole Robinson Crusoe camp, propping his towels up on sticks for a shelter." Colt had also dived up forty Dungeness crab in deep water without a mask or any other equipment. "He had them all lined up on the beach," she says. "I told him to pick the five biggest to take home for dinner, and he let the rest go."

Colt's problems with the police, Pam says, started on his eighth birthday, when she bought him an expensive bike. "He goes out to ride it, and next thing an Island County cop car pulls into the driveway with Colt inside. The deputy gets out and opens the trunk. He says, 'Is this Colt's bike?' I got pissed! Just because we live in this kinda dumpy old trailer, they figure, 'How could Colt get a nice bike like that? Well, he musta stole it.' I know Colt was scared, and it had a big effect on him." Since then, Pam says, everything that happens on the island is blamed on Colt. "He hasn't been alive long enough to do all the crimes they say he's done." Of the burglaries he is responsible for, Pam doesn't think he's stealing because he wants things. "Anything he needed, I always found a way to get for him," she says. "He had a computer, a PlayStation, then the new PlayStation, a whole bunch of James Bond movies I got on eBay—he loves those. He also had two flight-simulator games."

Pam brings out an art project Colt did while in detention. It's a psychologist's wet dream of a collage, packed with luxury brand names and images of Rolexes, cruise ships, smartphones, gold bars, credit cards, and, most prominently, a private jet. One snipped quote reads: Make Money Not Mistakes.

Pam says she was never able to control Colt. "He always did just what he wanted," she says. "Like now, with him running from the cops; he's doing it because he likes to see if he can. He thinks it's easy . . . and he's sure making them look like fools." Pam says Colt calls her from the road and they get along fine now, talking for hours about everything and laughing a lot. "When he was younger, though, we fought about everything . . . you name it." And after Bill died, she says, everything got worse. I ask her about the medications they put Colt on to manage his behavior. "A psychiatrist had him on something," she says, "then wanted to keep raising the dose and trying different things. One day, Colt came over to me in the yard and sat down—and he would hardly ever sit down—and he just hung his head. God, he was so depressed. So I said he's not going to be used as a guinea pig, and I took him off the drugs and stopped taking him to that doctor."

Colt grew up with the roar of low-flying jets as a daily event—Camano Island lies curled just east of its big sister, Whidbey Island, home to a large naval air station—and Pam says he always loved planes. She bought him sheets of balsa wood to make models, and he thumbed through his plane-identification book so much that it fell apart. "From the time he was a little kid," she says, "he could look up at any plane in the sky and tell you what make it was, what engine it had, when it was built, and whether it was a good, safe one."

Colt listed "pilot" as his occupation on his MySpace page, and Pam says she and his aunt promised him flying lessons if he graduated high school. She shrugs. "Evidently he didn't need flight school."

I page through a new book—*Jane's Aircraft Recognition Guide*—that Colt sent Pam last Christmas. ("He's smart enough not to send things direct; he first sends them east and has them forwarded to me.") She's very interested in which ones he flew. "I'm not saying it's right," she says, "but if he flew those planes, I'm very, very proud of him." She does hope, though, that Colt will take her advice and get himself a parachute before he steals another one.

The risk to Colt grows greater each passing day, with each alleged new crime and each additional jurisdiction pulled into the hunt. He can't walk into a Quickie Mart anywhere within 500 miles without being recognized. But still they haven't caught him.

The FBI fields an entire cyber-crime task force using advanced CIPAV spyware to find all kinds of ether-based bad guys—and obviously the Bureau has plenty of experience tapping phones and tracking cells. But the FBI remains close-lipped about the ongoing investigation.

At the county level, there's a lot of frustration mixed with embarrassment. The cops try to minimize it, but you can tell they're getting more pissed the longer this drags on. According to his spokesman, Island County sheriff Mark Brown is "way over" talking about this case. These small departments are in a tough position, hammered by residents on one side for not pulling out all the stops to catch Colt, and on the other for wasting too much of their dwindling budgets chasing what is, at the end of the day, simply a property thief, not a rapist or murderer. The FBI is busy hunting terrorist sleeper cells, and the police in Washington State have had five of their own murdered in the past year. In the overall law-enforcement scheme, Colt is—as several cops have told me—just "a giant pain in the ass."

When the Island County sheriff's deputies failed to quickly recapture Colt, some locals considered taking matters into their own hands. Joshua Flickner, whose family owns the Elger Bay Grocery, remembers Colt from the time he was a kid, and describes the "evil" in his eyes. Flickner says the crime that sent Colt into the woods for the first time happened at his store. "We had him on the security camera emptying our ATM using a stolen credit card four or five days in a row. That woman was his first identity-theft victim, and she was just in here. I've talked to dozens of his victims. You don't see the victims. All he's doing is hurting people—financially, psychologically, he's hurting people, yet here we are putting him on a pedestal, glorifying him, idolizing him. He's got a Facebook site. . . . I want to vomit, okay?"

Flickner went to Sheriff Brown about forming a posse to comb the Camano woods, but the offer was declined.

Up here in San Juan County, Sheriff Bill Cumming is also surprised Colt hasn't been caught. "Burglary, burglary, commercial burglary, burglary, commercial burglary, commercial burglary . . ." Cumming runs down a long, long list of felonies—almost all of them on Orcas—that he believes Colt may have committed. "We've processed all of these crime scenes, and some we're sure was him; others may go nowhere because the suspect wore gloves . . . others, maybe he'll tell us about them someday."

With a criminology degree from UC Berkeley, an easy laugh, and a visage that's part Gene Hackman and part Jimmy Buffett, the sixty-one-year-old Cumming hits the right tone as sheriff of the laid-back San Juans; he's held the job for twenty-four years. He doesn't believe Colt committed every unsolved crime on his books, but he also doesn't think his department knows yet the extent of his activities.

For most of Colt's time on the lam, Cumming reminds me, the feds and others haven't been involved; it's just been too few underfunded deputies tasked with shaking a few million bushes. He offers a "no comment" when I ask him about a rumor I heard around the bonfire that one of his deputies had been sitting in an Orcas home when Colt came to pick up a package he'd ordered online. The story goes that by the time the cop got out of his chair, Colt had leapt off the porch without touching the stairs and vanished into the trees. Like the Island County sheriff's department, Cumming's guys have had Colt in their grasp—there just weren't enough hands there at the time to hold on. On September 13, 2009, Orcas deputies got close enough during a foot pursuit to positively identify Colt, but he danced away. "We could hear him laughing," one deputy involved in the chase told me. Colt ran through a churchyard and into the woods, circling around to Brandt's Landing, where he stole a boat and rode off into the sunrise, escaping to Point Roberts, on the mainland.

What happens once they do catch him? "There are no easy answers," says Cumming. "We arrest people—we're not social workers—and from an enforcement point of view, the longer we can lock him away, at least we know he's not committing more crimes during that time. However, any thoughtful person who looks at long-term protection issues knows that this person will come back to the community—and who do you want to come back?"

A local woman who spent years as a crisis worker counseling at-risk youth, and who asked to remain anonymous, says she believes "Colt didn't intend for all this to happen. It's gotten away from him now."

She met Colt when he was about fourteen and had been sentenced to serve a week of community service at the park where she works. She says Colt showed up without food or anything to drink but had to work full days outdoors. "I fed him, gave him water, and he was just so very grateful." Colt worked hard sawing and hauling wood, pulling weeds, and cutting brush, she says, and was very smart, showing a "ridiculous amount" of knowledge about the local plants.

Colt, she says, wasn't anything like the extreme cases she's seen. "He really struck me as a good-hearted kid who'd always been looked at with negative expectations and didn't have a lot of motivation to feel good about his life. Yet when given an opportunity, I mean, he just worked his butt off. How is it possible," she wonders, "that all these groups of people and systems in place miss children like this, over and over again?"

Two weeks after Colt finished his community service, he rode his bike the 10 miles back to the park. "He was kinda shy, handed me three small bags, and just said, 'Here.' I'd told him we had a very small budget for new plants, and he'd gone out and hand-harvested seeds from local flowers that he thought would grow well in the park. I said, 'Oh my God, thank you so much!' And he's like 'Yeah, all right.

Well, I guess I'll go, bye.' He started to walk away but then turned around and said, 'Thank you for being so nice to me.' I was literally teary-eyed."

Colt, unfortunately, has escalated beyond youth programs—he turned eighteen last March. "One of the problems of our justice system is that he'll be tried as an adult for any new crimes, so he'll end up in jail," says Eric Trupin, a child psychologist and director of the University of Washington's Division of Public Behavioral Health and Justice Policy. "That's unfortunate for this kid, but, again, he is a risk to the community. He's gonna hurt somebody if he keeps this up."

~~~~~~

November is the shittiest month on Puget Sound. Halloween leaves behind malevolent winds and drooling skies. The shockingly short days have to compete with the four months of sunny, 72-degree days and nine p.m. summer sunsets that went before. Down on Camano, another wave of burglaries sweeps across the island like a cold front. One woman's home is hit twice within a week. She knows Colt's back because, she claims, over the years he's robbed her eight times, always for cash and food. She says this time he took some pizzas.

On my last trip down to Camano, a black-windowed SUV pulls up as I sit in front of the Elger Bay Cafe. The four deputies inside are loaded for bear, and I'm told they're a search team. When I stop by Pam's trailer, a friend of hers shows me his plans for booby-trapping the property with modified shotgun-shell "toe-poppers" in order to keep the cops and the media and the weirdness away. Pam's very interested in the price of bulletproof vests. "I'm going to get Colt one," she tells me. "I don't care if he wants it or not. I'm getting him one and he's going to wear it. Sometimes a mother has to put her foot down."

With multiple warrants for his arrest plus cash rewards offered by the Orcas and Camano chambers of commerce, Colt can't trust anyone, can't risk turning on a light in a house that's supposed to be empty, and hopefully won't risk breaking into an occupied home. The islanders are edgy. While this remains the safest and friendliest place I've ever lived, nearly everyone I know, from the most liberal tree hugger to the most conservative clear-cutter, is armed—some disturbingly so—and has been since long before Colt showed up.

When homes started getting hit again on Camano, Pam's neighbors say, police helicopters were up searching at night. The colder it gets outside, the easier it is for the thermal-imaging gear to pinpoint a small campfire or a warm face poking out of a sleeping bag. The fact that the infrared hasn't spotted him means that Colt's back to house-hopping, he's slipped loose of the dragnet yet again, or—just to help along the legend—he's a vampire.

In another strange twist, Ed Wallace says that Island County is now seeing copycats. "Burglars are hitting homes, stealing cash, and then grabbing a potpie before they leave. That way, everything gets blamed on Colt."

Speculation on how this will all end remains a popular local pastime, second only to coming up with ways to catch Colt using various combinations of tranquilizer darts and tiger traps. If he doesn't surrender peacefully or wind up forming the red bull's-eye in a burnt circle of ground where a stolen Cessna augers in, a lot of people think Colt will end up gunned down by the police. A shot fired during the Granite Falls chase and an assault rifle stolen from a deputy's car—with Colt a suspect in both events—could lead to quick draws. That's not what the cops are saying, though. In fact, they're not saying much about the case anymore. "I'm very cognizant of the fact I don't want to be part of the problem with this young man by giving him notoriety, creating myths behind him that endanger the community and do not bode well for him in the long run," says Bill Cumming, who along with Trupin believes that Colt narcissistically digs the infamy and that it may cause him to escalate to tragic levels.

Colt's Facebook fan club now has more than nine thousand members. A big Swedish contingent came aboard recently, along with a number of marriage and wanna-do-you proposals and plenty of helpful suggestions for the "Barefoot Burglar," such as "You should steal the space shuttle."

Pam calls me one Sunday morning to say that Colt phoned her the previous night. "He's safe and in good spirits," she says. "And he's nowhere near Camano Island. He's on the mainland, staying with friends at a house protected by all kinds of high-tech security and cameras." Colt, she says, does computer work for them and gets paid $600 a week. "I told him to send me some money," she laughs.

Pam says Colt told her before that he may lie low for a while, maybe a year, to let things die down before coming in from the cold and turning himself in. She doesn't think, however, that he'll get a fair trial. Pam believes the best place for him would be out of the country, someplace without an extradition treaty. She said Colt's goal was always to fly wealthy people around in jets until he got rich enough himself to buy a yacht and live on a tropical island. "That's still what his plans are," she says. "He wants to come get me, and we'll go live the good life."

Back home on Orcas, walking down the path toward my little cabin, I hear a noise in the woods. It's dusk and raining. Maybe it's just a bird rapping its bill against a tree, but something's a little off. Since all the break-ins, every simple sound seems to echo a little louder. I move into the trees and pick my way carefully down the steep slope to a spot under a big fir where bald eagles like to perch and eat. The skulls, spines, and fine bones of fish and seabirds litter the forest floor.

There's no one around and no sign anyone has been. All I hear now is tree frogs, the only living things besides the resurgent moss that are happy about the ceaseless rain. I look up at the cabin. My wife has switched on the lights, and through the big window I can see her moving around the bedroom. As I stand here in the woods, in the dirty blue light and cold drizzle, the sight of the cabin's honeyed glow epitomizes the idea of warm and cozy, of safety, of home.

I climb back up the hill, duck under a wet cedar branch, and walk inside, where I'm greeted by my big dog and a toasty fire. I feel sorry for Colt. And then I lock my door.

STEAMED

ERIC HANSEN

~~~~~~

In the late 2000s, a surprising war was being waged in coastal Maine, where rene-
gade crustacean gangs were forcing locals to grope for their guns. Our writer headed
for the boiling waters of Matinicus Island—the site of a 2009 dockside shoot-out
between feuding lobstermen—to find out why families that had shared these grounds
for generations were suddenly going after each other tong and claw.

~~~~~~

Around ten a.m. on July 20, 2009, a slight breeze started to pick up on Matinicus
Island, Maine, the most remote inhabited island on the Eastern Seaboard. Alan
Miller eased his sleek lobster boat, *Hustler*, past the rock breakwater and into the
sheltered harbor. Although Miller had a permit to lobster the crustacean-rich seafloor surrounding Matinicus, islanders had made it known that the mainlander
wasn't welcome.

About a month earlier, Miller, a wealthy sixty-year-old lobsterman with a
second home on the island, had chosen to ignore the islanders' unofficial decree
and boldly set four hundred traps, valued at $20,000, in Matinicus waters. Two
weeks after, he discovered that about half of his wire-mesh pots had been cut free
from their buoys and heard rumor that Weston Ames and Chris Young, two for-
ty-something stepbrothers and Matinicus residents, hidden by fog, had snipped his
lines. Reportedly, Ames and Young soon found some four hundred of their traps
knifed—and suspected Miller, of course.

Earlier on the morning of July 20, Young had tried to force a confession out of
Miller's sixty-nine-year-old father-in-law, a longtime Matinicus lobsterman named

Vance Bunker. According to court documents, Young had illegally boarded Bunker's boat and accused him and Miller of molesting his gear. The argument escalated. They ended up wrestling, then Bunker pepper-sprayed Young in the face.

A couple of hours after the fracas, the stepbrothers sought out Miller while he was hauling traps off Matinicus. According to Miller, they intercepted his boat and, supposedly just inches from bumping rails at 30 miles per hour, tried to run it aground on the shallow rock ledges. Miller managed to escape, but he suspected that the stepbrothers might be waiting for him back on Matinicus. As a precaution, he decided to radio the Marine Patrol and inform them of the situation. Ultimately, one of their officers decided to board Miller's boat and accompany him to the island, where, hiding belowdecks, the officer might overhear Ames or Young make threatening remarks or confess to vandalizing Miller's traps.

All seemed to be going according to plan when Miller approached Matinicus's cement wharf around ten. The stepbrothers, as predicted, were waiting for him at the edge of the dock. As soon as Miller tied off, Ames and Young began spouting accusations, calling him names, and pounding on the canopy of his pilothouse.

Unbeknownst to Miller, however, his wife, Janan, and father-in-law were about to screw things up. From the window of the home that the Millers own on Matinicus, Janan had seen the men waiting for her husband and decided to take matters into her own hands. She had grabbed a shotgun from the bedroom and run down to the wharf. Bunker was also enraged. Still smarting from his earlier altercation with the stepbrothers, he and his deckhand (or sternman, as they're called on lobster boats) were bouncing toward the showdown in a blue pickup with a heavy arsenal: a .22 caliber revolver, a .45 caliber handgun, and an AK-47 assault rifle with nine loaded clips.

As the shouting between Miller and the men grew louder, Janan arrived with her 12-gauge and leveled the barrel at the stepbrothers.

"Hey," she barked.

"Shoot me, you stupid bitch," Ames purportedly replied.

Miller yelled for the Marine Patrol officer, who was still hiding. Bunker, who had skittered onto the scene moments earlier, stepped onto the pier. When Ames made a move toward Janan's shotgun, Bunker cocked his .22 and fired at him. The bullet whizzed past his head.

"Dumb fuck, you missed me," Ames taunted, according to Bunker. Ames instead says he pleaded, "Wait a minute!"

Ames then allegedly lunged at Bunker, who fired again, this time at Young, who collapsed at Ames's feet. The bullet had struck him in the left side of his neck and would leave him partially paralyzed on his left side.

The entire altercation had lasted only a few minutes, but rumors of a possible showdown had already made their way around the tiny, 2-square-mile island. Many of its forty-seven residents, some of them allegedly armed, had descended on the wharf en masse. The Marine Patrol officer finally made it into the open, pointed his service revolver at Bunker, and told him to stand down.

~~~~~~

A typical working lobsterman is thickset, clean-shaven, and red around the jowls and lives in a modest inland home; he doesn't need to live beside the coast like some part-timer from "Mass-a-two-shits." He never harvests egg-bearing females or undersize juveniles, honoring regulations that are nearly impossible to enforce, and is proud that the lobster population in the 36,000-square-mile Gulf of Maine might be the healthiest, most sustainable fishery in the world. Whether he's a successful "highliner," who can afford to party away the late-winter off-season in the Caribbean, or a "dub," who doesn't know how to move his gear to follow the critters' migrations, he values hard work.

In a single year, the very best captains can harvest 100,000 pounds of soft- and hard-shell lobsters. This puts a couple hundred grand in each of their pockets and spurs on the state's $250 million lobster industry. When they motor out to hunt sea bugs in the July-to-November high season, quite a few are packin' heat.

Altercations in the 350-year-old fishery are nothing new, of course. As social anthropology professor James M. Acheson revealed in his groundbreaking 1988 book, *The Lobster Gangs of Maine*, fishing for the crustaceans is a low-grade turf war, with the delicious invertebrates as the drugs. (The disputes also inspire good fiction, as Elizabeth Gilbert's first novel, *Stern Men*, demonstrates.)

While lobstermen don't necessarily think of themselves as gangs, and few people commonly refer to them as such, that's essentially what they are: informally organized groups of men from rivaling harbors. (Few women lobster.) The guys based out of nearby Monhegan Harbor, for example, are simply known as "the Monhegan boys" or "the Monhegan fishermen." Most members come from long-established Maine families, live in the same town, keep their radios on the same channel, and help each other out if, say, a prop shaft breaks. When disputes arise, members generally follow the lead of the best and most magnanimous lobsterman in the harbor, though some harbors make collective decisions in regular, private meetings. For the most part, they interact only with the nearby competition; the only thing the Georges Islands gang might know about the roughly two hundred other gangs along the Mid Coast is where their own turf abuts the Bremen boys' and overlaps with the Pleasant Point punks'.

While gangs occasionally host cookouts or raise money for charity, one of their main functions is to "defend their bottom"—i.e., guard the seabeds where they drop their pots. Informal and long-standing lobstering boundaries, often referred to as "imaginary lines," crisscross the Gulf of Maine like a spiderweb. Landmarks and dividing lines used to be handed down by word of mouth—e.g., "from the Western Pollock shoal at the 30-fathom mark, head toward the Hogshead lighthouse . . ." Now, lat-long coordinates are simply programmed into onboard GPS units. The state doesn't recognize these imaginary lines or give them any legal weight, but defending and respecting them has become an honored tradition. Competitors will set their buoys within 10 feet of each other without problems, but if a lobsterman from Boothbay crosses into the area claimed by South Bristol, then, well, things happen.

"That's the exciting part of the business," enthused Ryan Post, a fourth-generation lobsterman I met one sunny afternoon at the Port Clyde lobster feed. "We have to fight for what we got."

Traditionally, fighting rarely if ever results in bloodletting. And it usually stays at sea. ("What happens on the water stays on the water," the old red-clawed maxim goes.) First, the interloper is often verbally warned, then telltale knots might be tied in his buoy lines, lobsters stolen, threatening notes left inside bottles, lines cut, or traps even flattened with a sledgehammer or carved up with a chain saw.

Over the past two years, however, the retaliations have grown progressively more severe. Shotguns have been brandished, boats surrounded. Traps have been cut almost daily; a stack was torched in a man's yard. One boat was doused in gasoline and set ablaze on its mooring ball. Two others—their engine intake hoses cut— were sunk to the muddy bottom. Atop this steepening curve of violence stands the Meltdown on Matinicus, the first time in memory that a trigger was squeezed.

Initial newspaper reports suggested the economy spurred the gun show. A few years ago, lobstermen were discussing their investment portfolios on the VHF. Now wholesale lobster sells for $3 a pound, roughly half the peak price in 2005. Lobstermen are scraping by and on edge. They were looking for fights, the papers suggested.

Others blamed Matinicus, an isolated fist of rock 20 miles east of Rockland, where legend has it the last resident cop was run off twenty years ago by a cheering mob. And off the south shore of which, for a week after the July 20 incident, a couple of Coast Guard boats were anchored, to protect the peace. Without the civilizing influences of police, summer folk, and regular ferry service, the island's residents—many descended from just three families—have been practicing a form of renegade justice so long that Matinicus has earned the nickname Pirate Island.

"They have their own systems and norms out there," said a government employee who wished to remain anonymous. "You'll see brothers clubbing each other in the mud at low tide with oars. Over what? Who knows?"

While many details of the incident remain murky, Vance Bunker was ultimately charged with two counts of elevated aggravated assault; Janan Miller, with reckless conduct; and Chris Young and Weston Ames, with criminal trespassing, among other infractions. The trial wouldn't hit Knox County Superior Court until the spring, but I couldn't wait that long to go to the island and ask a simple question: What the hell is going on?

~~~~~~

Not long after reaching Rockland, in the Mid Coast area, in November, I rang Alan Miller up. He wasn't home, Janan cheerily informed me, before telling me that neither of them would talk about the shooting without first consulting their lawyers. But, she politely offered, had I tried her father?

While awaiting trial, Bunker was living in his home on the mainland, near Rockland. Not two hours later, I pulled into the driveway of a tidy red shake house with a short-cropped lawn. Bunker is a huge man, 6-foot-1 and 265 pounds, and wore heavy-duty suspenders and begrimed work pants. Even at sixty-nine, stiff with arthritis, hard of hearing, and facing up to thirty years in prison, he still hauled traps every other day. He was raised on Matinicus by a rum-running dad, has been "buggin'" all his life, and made headlines one frostbitten winter for the daring rescue of the crew of a sinking tug. Everyone I'd talked to respected him. Except, I soon learned, the parrot.

Perched on a hoop in the living room was a battery-powered bird that squawked when its motion sensor was triggered. "Who's a fucker now?" it asked mercilessly. We sat at the laminated breakfast table. Bunker spoke quietly and sometimes rubbed his fingers in his palms. The reason Miller wanted in, he explained, was simple: The lobstering around Matinicus was exceptionally good. While Miller wasn't expecting balloons and a welcoming party, he figured they'd at least tolerate him.

"It was only a couple or three that was upset or pissed off about Alan," Bunker claimed.

As Bunker continued, his wife, Sari, appeared with a roast chicken. "It's a Dodge City mentality," she opined.

The lobstermen of Matinicus, Bunker continued, had been debating what to do about Miller since he started dating Janan, a Matinicus native, in 2000. He was usually just one of many items they discussed in the island's one-room schoolhouse or in the damp basement of the Congregational church. Bunker, who attended only some of the meetings, declined to share any specifics, but a rare 2007 court document, given to me by a source who wished to remain anonymous, allows us to imagine it.

The three-page photocopy, entitled "Matinicus Island School Lobster Meeting / Clown Show / Clusterfuck," is from a meeting in June 2003. It may be the only tangible evidence of such gatherings to surface in 350 years of lobstering, and it includes telling items like "#5: Are we going to allow someone to fish two boats and sets of tags?" This, despite the well-known state law that every lobsterman use only one boat and one set of licenses.

A subsequent agenda item raises the issue of a neighboring gang lobstering beyond its bounds: "What's going to be done about the Criehaven punks pushing the line, and who is really going to do what?" Another page lists the names of three people who wanted to lobster around Matinicus. (Miller wasn't seeking permission at the time.) Everyone was asked to circle "Yes" or "No" and bring their opinions to the meeting.

Decisions made at such meetings are legally meaningless, as was the islanders' eventual choice to deny Miller access to their lobstering territory. But it's the way things are done. Bunker doesn't have any problem with that. What irked him about the rejection of his son-in-law was the apparent change in the rules for joining the gang. In the past, he said, an island home and family legacy was all that was required to earn the right to harvest lobsters around Matinicus.

"I figured he's got as much right to fish out there as about fifteen other families," said Bunker.

"The whole island is full of incest," Sari offered.

As dusk fell, Bunker became even more forthcoming about the island's insular politics, which other sources would later corroborate and expand upon. Bunker and the stepbrothers, including the one he shot, had been friends for decades, it turned out. And while I would later learn that Weston Ames had been convicted of sexually assaulting a minor in 1993, the general consensus was that he's basically a decent guy. Few lobstermen had kind words for Miller, though. They alleged that he had amassed a fortune by taking advantage of the loophole in the law that allowed you to fish two boats, and was unliked even in his home port of Spruce Head. As one Matinicus lobsterman would later put it, "We have enough assholes of our own. We don't need to import more."

I finally decided to ask the question I'd worn on my chest like a sandwich board since arriving: "Why did you shoot?"

"I can't tell you," he replied, looking hangdog. "I was scared. Afraid."

~~~~~~

He wasn't the only one. Although I heard a few idyllic anecdotes about life on Matinicus, most were ominous.

Like the one about a bitter ex-resident, nicknamed Uncle Knifeblade, who tossed ashore a passel of hungry, nonnative raccoons. Or the sternmen who arrived each summer, heroin addictions in tow. Or the one about the island's fire chief, "Rambo," normally an upstanding member of any community, threatening a fellow islander with nunchucks. Or the axes swung through car windshields. Or the lobsterman stabbed in the chest with a kitchen knife, for allegedly burning down his assailant's house.

While it was clear that the incidents had taken place over the course of many years, the savage rumors still cast a long shadow. Plus several people had warned me, "You go out there, no one's gonna talk to you."

Indeed, Ames and Young had retreated behind a shroud of loyal friends and changed-number notices. Even the island's self-appointed spokesperson to the press, Clayton Philbrook, and his friend Nat Hussey, a supposedly affable former lawyer who recently moved to the island to practice guitar and work as a sternman, didn't call me back right away. (Although I did stumble upon Hussey's surprisingly excellent lobster-rock video, "Haul 'Em Up," which you can watch on YouTube.)

The only person whose number I had but didn't dial was Ames's sixty-nine-year-old father, R. K. Ames. The supposed "kingpin of the cartel," according to one local, was the only islander I had been specifically warned not to cross. So I started off by doing as much snooping as I could on the mainland. I wandered around the Journey's End Marina, in Rockland, where Young's $250,000 lobster boat was on blocks, up for sale. A workman with a burn-swirled half-face claimed he didn't know anything at all about the incident.

Lobster wholesalers, neighbors of those involved, the officers at Marine Patrol headquarters—people either didn't want to talk or had nothing informative to add. In a darkened office one drizzly afternoon, I had an off-the-record conversation with a trap builder who began by summoning his mute secretary to bring us black coffee in Styrofoam cups and finished with vague, unhelpful allusions. A visit to the Knox County Courthouse, in Rockland, one rainy morning was equally unfruitful. Convictions and complaints about the assailants and victims were minor and random—hunting without orange clothing, drunken boating, threats to destroy septic fields. I was learning very little but growing unduly, conspiratorially suspicious nonetheless.

One evening I attended a dispiriting gathering of the Lobster Advisory Council. The main topic was the severity of an upcoming shortage of herring, the primary bait used by lobstermen. Massive amounts of information were displayed in dizzying PowerPoint grids. Eyes glazed over behind wire-rim accountant glasses. New sustainable sources of inexpensive bait weren't obvious, and attendees worried about lobstermen losing their livelihoods.

In the past four years, as demand dwindled and costs creeped higher, highliners and dubs alike had seen their incomes drop by almost half. If the price of bait doubled, or if bait wasn't available, due to new laws restricting the amount of herring you can catch, one of Maine's few great economic engines—a billion-dollar industry, once you factor in all the multipliers—was likely going to implode. The phrases "Hail Mary" and "Take it on the chin" were repeated.

"It's gonna weed guys out," predicted a somber attendee, "especially those who live on islands."

The only bright spot was that, through a connection at the meeting, I was finally able to track down Chris Young, who'd been in and out of the hospital. He was irate to learn that I'd been given the unlisted phone number he'd switched to after the shooting. When I tried to explain myself, he cut me off. "You've talked to Vance?! This conversation is over," he declared, and hung up. Twenty minutes later, his wife called, chewed me out for a few minutes, and hung up.

The next morning, after spending the night at the tony Camden Harbour Inn, I discovered that the front-desk attendant in the pressed polo shirt had sterned offshore for a couple of summers. "No one messes with Matinicus," he declared, a note of awe and menace in his voice. I chuckled, a bit uncomfortably, and then slumped into an Adirondack chair on the wraparound porch overlooking the ocean.

Only a few moments later, as if on cue, a maintenance man strode by in a black hoodie featuring a graphic of an assault rifle, crosshairs, and the obscure but unmistakable words MATINICUS TACTICAL TEAM.

~~~~~~

In October, a ferry runs just three times a month to Matinicus. You can also pay to hitch a ride on the single-prop Cessna that delivers the mail most mornings, or, for a few bucks more, simply hire a charter. After fifteen minutes aloft, my air taxi touched down on the gravel airstrip. There were no other guests at the Tuckanuck Lodge bed-and-breakfast, just the eccentric old proprietor, a spartan room, and the included breakfast and dinner—but not lunch, which is odd when you consider that there isn't a restaurant, grocery store, or even a coffee shop on the island.

I dropped my bag and walked past boggy pine forests over a knoll to the wharf. In the peaceful solitude, it was difficult to reimagine the crime. Just as I was about to leave, Philbrook and Hussey happened to step ashore in the dusky late-afternoon light. Philbrook handed me a plastic bag full of fresh lobster and invited me to his house for a beer.

"Every lobsterman who doesn't fish Matinicus has to believe Matinicus lobstermen will cut his lines," Philbrook explained, sitting at a living-room table strewn with electrical wires and other detritus. With only 39 lobstermen to defend a perimeter of imaginary lines that elsewhere might have 390, the more overblown the island's pirate reputation, the better. The real secret, according to Philbrook and Hussey, was how amazing it was to live there. "I left twice last year, and it was two times too many," said Hussey.

What they described did sound great. The one-room schoolhouse. Two-word addresses and four-digit phone numbers. A pervasive esprit de corps whenever the town pulled together during power outages or to rescue someone lost at sea. Everyone gathering at the church for the Christmas potluck, regardless of any differences, and singing carols and exchanging Secret Santa gifts. Stars so thick you'd think it was snowing.

A century ago, there were some three hundred such inhabited islands in Maine, populated mostly by immigrant granite workers and Grand Banks fishermen. Now there are maybe a dozen, peopled by descendants of those Swedes and Italians and Canadians, but with a frontier culture diluted by tourists and a real-estate market thrown out of whack by vacation homes.

If Matinicus was going to survive, Philbrook reasoned, every lobsterman who hauled traps around Matinicus needed to live, year-round, on the island. And according to him, that logic was at the center of the debate: Miller wasn't allowed because islanders simply doubted he genuinely wanted to join the community. "His little place isn't winterized," Philbrook said.

It all made perfect sense. I put down my pad and pen, had another beer, and, half joking, ran through some of the crazy rumors I'd heard. When I told the one about the man being stabbed in the chest by a kitchen knife, Philbrook interjected.

"Well, that one's true," he said, shrugging casually and lifting his T-shirt to show his short pink scar.

~~~~~~

Philbrook had invited me to go buggin' with him the next morning, but bad weather turned us back at the dock, so I tried again to get in touch with a few other islanders. Most were either fishing or off-island or not where their fellow islanders told me they'd be, like in a white truck by the diesel-run powerhouse.

Running out of leads, I decided to try the infamous R. K. Ames. Even after I promised not to inquire about hidden beefs or the shooting of his stepson, he didn't want to talk. Ten minutes later, however, he mysteriously changed his mind and called back. "I'll give you a tour," he said when he picked me up in a red, big-block Chevy dump truck.

Even by the outsize standards of a typically enormous lobsterman, Ames was a hulk. He wore a gold hoop earring in his left ear, a la Captain Kidd, a frayed, sun-faded ball cap, and a heavy chinstrap beard that gave him the scowling mien of a Southern hanging judge.

We stopped first at the graveyard, where he'd already planted his own head-stone in the grass. The marble slab, featuring a carving of his lobster boat, wasn't far from that of Stephen Ames, a son who died of a heroin overdose, and Marina Ames, a relative who'd also OD'd. "We dig our own graves," he explained. "This is how we live out here."

Everywhere we drove, he narrated the stories of whichever relative had lived in whatever New England–style home we bounced past. "Is inbreeding a problem?" I ventured.

"We have two types of family trees: the flagpole and the wreath," he said. "We don't call it inbred; we say thoroughbred."

He told me he owns some fifteen pieces of property on Matinicus and the mainland. His gear collection, part of which I ogled in the hangar he calls his "toy box," is just as impressive: thirty-two boats of varying size, a Piper Cub airplane, a 1977 Corvette, a full purse-seine fishing-net rig in a sawed-off school bus, a cus-tom-built, Captain America–style panhead Harley chopper.

Ames was easy to like. He seemed to epitomize all the moxie, grit, and vigor of a Matinicus lobsterman. But he wasn't so charming when it came to relations with living people. Ames women were either plump and faithful, like his lovely third wife, Emily, or skinny and promiscuous, like his daughter on the mainland, whom he wouldn't talk to or support and repeatedly called a "slut."

We admired his lobster boat, with its souped-up 400-horsepower engine and trim paint "the color of a teenager's nipples." Noting the skull-and-crossbones insignia on its prominent red riding sail, I asked about the Pirate Island reputa-tion. "That's a crock of shit," he spat. Sure, islanders end up in a fair number of fights, but that's just because, like fishermen across the world, they work too hard and drink too much. Anyway, the island polices itself just fine, he said. I wanted to point out that shooting a man's son in the neck might not qualify as fine law enforcement, but I stuck to my word and bit my lip.

Visiting the sprawling house he was building for Emily—"new bird needs a new cage," he explained—I went too far. I raised the allegation, unearthed while sifting through courthouse records, that he'd stolen this gently declining spread by the sea to make a backyard runway. One moment we were celebrating how he'd sealed his shingles by dousing them in a "secret sauce." The next, he was standing stock-still, turning me into ice.

"My family has lived here for two hundred years," he growled lowly and evenly. "I don't ask permission for much."

We eventually made up over strong rum-and-Cokes back at the house, but I was still looking over my shoulder later that afternoon when I boarded the next plane out.

"It's the Wild West," a Rockland-based detective named Dwight Burtis would later tell me. "I think it's probably more common that we don't find out about incidents."

~~~~~~

In March, after a four-day trial and ten hours of deliberations, Vance Bunker and Janan Miller were acquitted of all charges. (Chris Young—who has since regained some mobility and begun lobstering again—and Weston Ames pleaded guilty to trespassing and paid a small fine.) The eight women and four men of the jury, all from the mainland, found that the father and daughter had acted in self-defense— or, perhaps more accurately, it wasn't proven beyond a doubt that they hadn't acted in self-defense.

Bunker and his daughter both wept openly upon hearing the verdict. The step-brothers chose not to be in the courtroom. They awaited the decision in the district attorney's office, one floor below. After hearing the decision, they declined to talk to the press.

The next day, someone slashed all four tires of the truck Bunker kept parked at the Matinicus airstrip. Soon after, it was further vandalized with spray paint. Bunker has since returned a few times to his log cabin on Matinicus, but he and his wife now spend most nights at their home on the mainland.

Two months later, in an unrelated and little-publicized incident, two sternmen attacked another at his house in Matinicus, stole his pistol, threatened to break his hands off at the wrist, and left him with a smashed nose and a pummeled face.

THE DEVIL ON
PARADISE ROAD

BRUCE BARCOTT

~~~~~~

What happens when a domestic terrorist targets one of America's iconic National Parks? On New Year's Day 2012, a rare bluebird winter morning in the Pacific Northwest, a lone gunman murdered a Mount Rainier ranger and then fled into the park's frozen backcountry, putting the place on lockdown. Every climber, skier, and camper suddenly became a suspect—and a potential victim.

~~~~~~

Thirteen miles of two-lane blacktop connect the fir-and-cedar forests of Longmire, Mount Rainier National Park's ranger headquarters, to Paradise, the mountain's 5,400-foot subalpine playground. Technically, it's a section of Washington's State Route 706, but locals know it as the Paradise road. Beautiful and treacherous, the road winds its way up the mountain's lower flanks, offering visitors views of misty waterfalls and glacial river valleys—and, when the clouds part, a spooky glimpse of Rainier's 14,410-foot ice-clad summit.

January 1, 2012, looked like it would be a busy day at the mountain. The holiday always draws a crowd to the park, and the Paradise snow-play area, with its long, rolling sled runs, would finally open for the season.

Margaret Anderson, a thirty-four-year-old park ranger, crossed into Rainier a few minutes after seven a.m. The forest around her was still night dim and frozen. It hadn't been easy to rise in the winter darkness and leave her husband, Eric, and their sleeping girls—one nearly four and the other eighteen months—at home in Eatonville, a charming burg 22 miles west of the park. But Eric, also a ranger at Rainier, would be working the second shift. He'd be coming on at eleven. Maybe she'd see him.

In the meantime, she had a lot to manage; she'd hired four new seasonals, and this was their first day working the sledding hill. Anderson was a law-enforcement (LE) ranger. By custom, National Park Service rangers are jacks-of-all-trades, but today they follow several distinct career tracks: law-enforcement ranger, interpretation ranger, or, in mountain parks like Rainier and Yosemite, climbing ranger. Interpretive rangers are often wildlife specialists or cultural-resource experts, while climbing rangers rescue stranded mountaineers. LE rangers undergo extensive training at the Federal Law Enforcement Training Center in Glynco, Georgia, but with budgets tight, they are tasked with a growing list of handyman chores. Anderson drove patrol, organized the park's EMT training, and dug road signs out of the snow when necessary.

Anderson passed by Longmire, where the two other LE rangers on the early shift, Dan Camiccia and Kraig Snure, were stationed. The road to Paradise had iced overnight, so Camiccia was setting up a tire-chain checkpoint. Anderson continued on up to Paradise.

She had spent New Year's Eve with her family. After they put the girls to bed, she and Eric talked about the coming year. The couple had met in 2002 at Bryce Canyon National Park—two young seasonals working the rim roads of southern Utah—but it wasn't until they left for other postings that they realized they'd fallen in love. Since then, Eric had punched his ticket at four parks, Margaret at two. Finding openings for a married couple at any national park is rare, so when two positions came up at Mount Rainier in late 2008, the Andersons jumped at them.

Now, three years later, they were talking about getting out. The burdens of a two-child, two-ranger family were heavy. The couple played tag-team with their shifts, and they often saw each other only on weekends. Margaret was working toward her nursing degree. Eric, who had been a firefighter before joining the Park Service full-time, loved being a cop, but an LE ranger's day can often feel like only 51 percent law enforcement—or less. He wanted more LE in his LE ranger's job. Margaret, who had a master's in biology, enjoyed the resource-management aspects of her work, but she shared some of Eric's frustrations.

The Andersons were looking at 2012 as their last year at Mount Rainier National Park. The girls' grandparents lived back east. It was time for a change.

~~~~~~

At Paradise, Anderson exchanged greetings with the interpretive rangers opening the Jackson Visitor Center (JVC). Although the snow had arrived late this year, it was piling up. Paradise usually got around 650 inches, enough to bury the historic Paradise Inn—which closes for the winter—up to its gabled dormers. It looked like a tough day ahead. The parking lot was sheet slick. One interp was fighting the flu, and Anderson wasn't feeling so hot herself. She told a friend she might knock off at eleven, when Eric and the other second-shifters came on.

At 9:30 a.m., Camiccia began waving chain-equipped vehicles up the mountain. The first visitors arrived in Paradise a little before 10:00. Anderson worked the parking lot, giving directions, moving signs.

At 10:20, a car drove past the chain checkpoint without stopping. A blue Impala.

Camiccia discussed the blow-by with Snure. It wasn't a big deal. Foreigners visited the park every day. The driver might have been confused. Was it worth going after the guy? Probably so, they decided. Better to stop him now than tow him out of the snow later.

Camiccia jumped into his NPS pickup. He called in the plate as he accelerated: Washington 791XZL. Dispatch called back. The plate was clean, which meant the car hadn't been reported stolen. Owner: Barnes, Benjamin Colton. White male, 5-foot-9, 160 pounds, twenty-four years old.

The ranger caught up to the Impala about two minutes later. He rolled his lights. No response. He hit the siren. Nothing.

Trouble.

Camiccia let the Impala gap him on the hairpin. Then he gunned it and caught up, lights still flashing. But the Impala kept on.

He called for backup as the two cars wound their way up the icy hill, locked in a low-speed switchback chase.

At Paradise, Camiccia's voice squawked out of the radio on Anderson's hip. She took a quick situational inventory. There were a few dozen cars in the parking lot. That meant upwards of a hundred visitors.

Camiccia and the Impala would reach her in about fifteen minutes. During summer the road continues into the Gifford Pinchot National Forest. But in winter it dead-ends at Paradise, blocked by a wall of snow. Anderson wanted to stop the driver before he got that far. She was, in a way, the perfect ranger for the job. She had a cop's knack for reading people and solving problems. She could cool a hot situation with a few words and a disarming smile, but the use of handcuffs and force were not foreign to her experience.

Anderson jumped into her white Chevy Tahoe and roared down to Barn Flats, where the road unkinks into a 250-yard straightaway. It took her a little over a minute to get there.

At the Flats she parked sideways, blocking both lanes.

Then she waited.

Coming up the hill in the Impala was Benjamin Barnes, an Iraq War veteran. Troubled since high school, the newspapers would later report, he was the son of a marine, a California kid who'd found a home in the military—and then managed to get himself booted out for drinking and driving. Barnes embraced warrior culture. He kept his hair in a jarhead shave, inked his body with words that evoked the epic. A neck tattoo listed four of the seven deadly sins: PRIDE ENVY GLUTTONY LUST. The skin over his heart read ODIN, the Norse god of battle, victory, and death.

Of course, none of this was known to Margaret Anderson. Barnes was just a suspect leading her colleague in a two-car parade.

At 10:42 a.m., fourteen minutes after she arrived at the Flats, the blue sedan came into view.

Immediately in front of him, Barnes saw Anderson's SUV blocking the road. Behind him, a ranger on his tail. Beside him sat a loaded AR-15 assault rifle, the civilian version of the M16 he carried in Iraq.

Barnes braked, swung open his door, aimed, and fired at Anderson. The gun went off in bursts. Anderson slumped at the wheel.

When Camiccia rounded the corner, Barnes wheeled on him and squeezed off four quick rounds. The bullets pierced the ranger's windshield in a four-corners pattern that outlined a box around Camiccia's head. One tore through his seat belt just above the shoulder. But he wasn't hit. He jammed his truck into reverse and retreated.

Anderson, bleeding badly, backed her Tahoe into the snowbank so hard the tailgate crumpled. Executing a two-point turn, she moved her vehicle about 100 yards up-mountain—still in the Flats straightaway but blocking the downhill lane. Camiccia spit into the radio: "Shots fired, one officer struck."

Camiccia's attempts to rescue Anderson were met with gunfire. Barnes had a semiautomatic assault rifle, battlefield firepower.

The park dispatcher called Anderson's number over the radio. "Seven-four-one, come in."

There was no response.

At Paradise, the interpretive rangers working at the Jackson Visitor Center had been following the Impala's progress closely. Within seconds of the shooting, they and members of the park's road crew began herding visitors inside.

Interpretive rangers carry no weapons. They're trained to remove themselves and visitors from dangerous situations, not to confront the threat. So the Paradise interps decided their best strategy was to turn the JVC into a fortress. "We've got to do a lockdown," said one.

Out in the parking lot, Lisa Hill, a fifty-one-year-old dental hygienist from nearby Graham, was eager to hit the trail and try out her new Jetboil stove. She'd talked her boyfriend, Brian Hess, a forty-year-old electrician, into a New Year's Day snowshoe trip.

Then Hill heard a voice. "This is an emergency! Everybody into the building!"

Instinctively, she looked up-mountain. If an avalanche was coming, she wanted to know which way to run.

Once Hill and Hess entered the visitor center, a ranger radioed the Rainier dispatcher: "JVC is in lockdown." Hess glanced at a clock. It was 10:48 a.m. Most visitors at the JVC didn't know what was going on. But Hess stayed close to the door so he could overhear the rangers' radio traffic. "It didn't take me long to figure out a couple of things," he said later. "Somebody had been shot. The guy was still on the loose. And the staff at the visitor center were unarmed."

The JVC rangers hatched a plan. Rebecca Roland, a forty-four-year-old interpretive ranger, huddled with a few colleagues. They asked ranger Gavin Wilson to take charge. Wilson had been trained in ICS, the Incident Command System, which prevents federal, state, and local cops, firefighters, and EMTs from working at cross-purposes. A handful of visitors were still out on the mountain, oblivious to the emergency. Longmire park volunteer Jim Miltimore—who, with his wife, Carol, has logged more than 12,000 hours of service at the park—strapped on his snowshoes and charged up the cross-country trail to warn any skiers.

When stragglers approached the visitor center, a ranger searched them for weapons. Paradise was a short fifteen-minute hike from Barn Flats. Anybody could have been the shooter. Could he be in the JVC already? Could this be some sort of holiday terrorist strike? The most maddening, hateful acts of our era are known by their geographic location. Columbine. Virginia Tech. Norway's Utøya Island. That Mount Rainier would be added to the list remained a frightening possibility.

~~~~~~

Eric Anderson kissed his daughters good-bye and dropped them at a babysitter's around ten a.m. on New Year's Day. Mama will pick you up soon, he told them. Margaret's shift ended at three, but she'd told her husband she might knock off early. As Eric made his way up the Mountain Highway, the main artery to Rainier, a Pierce County sheriff's cruiser roared past him. Anderson called the Rainier dispatcher to see what was going on. The dispatcher asked him to report directly to park headquarters at Tahoma Woods, 17 miles west of Longmire. There'd been a shooting, he was told.

Park superintendent Randy King arrived at headquarters a few minutes before Anderson. Soft-spoken and solidly built, King had assumed the park's top job only eight weeks earlier, but he'd been Rainier's deputy superintendent for eight years. He knew the park and its people. "There's been a shooting near Paradise," he told Anderson, confirming what Eric had already heard. "Margaret was involved." Nobody knew much more than that, King said. He asked Anderson to sit tight.

The next few minutes and hours: what they were for Anderson, only he knows. It's not a memory he cares to relive.

~~~~~~

Half an hour after the first shots, Margaret Anderson remained in her Tahoe. Her radio was silent, and the suspect—Barnes or whoever was driving his car—continued to fire on anyone approaching.

From the Canadian border to northern Oregon, word flashed over law-enforcement wires: officer down, shooter loose. The Pierce County Sheriff's Department—which is headquartered in Tacoma but maintains a mountain detachment in Eatonville—was the first to respond. A ranger flagged down Deputy Frank Brown near Longmire, handed him a park radio, and pointed him up the road. A few minutes later, Brown raced past two empty Park Service vehicles and had nearly reached the Flats when he heard the radio call him back. Rangers Camiccia and Snure had briefly abandoned their trucks, but when they saw Brown drive by, they scrambled back to stop him from stumbling into the shooting alley.

Up at Paradise, a group of rangers and maintenance workers debated mounting a rescue effort. They had an ambulance and a sanding truck they thought they could use to reach Anderson.

She was so close. One minute away. And yet the risks were enormous. The shooter was still squeezing off rounds. The folks at Paradise had no weapons and no protection, not even a service vest. It's still not clear who made the call, but in the end the mission was deemed too dangerous.

"It was the right decision," superintendent King would later tell me. "A tough one, but the right one. Not responding, that's the hardest thing in the world. Because all you want to do is help."

That didn't make it any easier for Anderson's colleagues. She sat just a few hundred yards from Paradise, wounded and possibly dying. Another twenty minutes went by.

At 11:42 a.m., rangers Camiccia and Snure met with a group of Pierce County deputies at a turnoff called the Stevens Canyon Y, about 500 yards south of the shooting site. In addition to Deputy Brown, Sergeant Nick Hausner and deputies Brian Coburn, Kevin Reding, and Ara Steben had answered the call-out. An hour had passed since Anderson's last radio contact. Shooter or no shooter, they decided they had to go in.

The team gathered what gear they had. Brown had an armor-plated vest. Hausner found a ballistic shield in his SUV.

The deputies strapped on helmets and piled into the back of Camiccia's bullet-pocked pickup. Each held a rifle. "If the suspect engages," Hausner told the team, "immediate return fire is authorized."

The men jammed the armored vest into the truck's bullet-shot windshield and stuffed the shield along the driver's door. Kraig Snure volunteered to drive. As the truck rolled toward the Flats, shots rang out. The shooter was alive and active.

The deputies crouched in the flatbed, eyes sweeping the hillside. The high snowbank gave the shooter a massive tactical advantage. With an assault rifle, he could let off five rounds before the cops had time to react. "It was one of those moments," Coburn later told Tacoma's *News Tribune*, "where you prayed that you survived this call."

At the Flats, they passed the Impala. The driver-side door hung open. The shooter was nowhere in sight.

Anderson's SUV was nosed into the snowbank about 100 yards up the road. Engine still running, transmission in drive. She was upright at the wheel, buckled in, her body still. A radio microphone sat in her lap. Coburn and Brown quickly moved her to the back of the pickup.

"We have her," Coburn told dispatchers.

As the truck tore off down the hill, Hausner put two fingers to the fallen ranger's neck. He found no pulse.

"She's gone," one of the deputies said.

The team relayed the information to park headquarters. At Tahoma Woods, despair washed over the eyes of Superintendent King. He straightened his shoulders and delivered the news to Eric Anderson.

Up at Paradise, Ranger Rebecca Roland entertained visitors' kids with Junior Ranger workbooks. When one finished, she'd stage a small ceremony, pronouncing the youngster an official Mount Rainier Junior Ranger. The locked-down visitors applauded each one.

Lisa Hill and Brian Hess sat at a picnic table by the door. Hess wanted to be there in case something happened. He had a card that had not been played: In his back pocket was a permit to carry a concealed handgun. In his front pocket was a .380 Ruger LCP.

At 12:20, one of the rangers guarding the door crossed the main foyer to the information desk. "He looked like he might throw up," recalled Hess. Anderson had not survived the shooting, the ranger told his colleagues. They absorbed the shock and held back tears.

A few minutes later, another child achieved Junior Ranger status. Roland gave him his due. Applause all around.

~~~~~~

All afternoon cops and armored vehicles streamed into the park. The FBI, the Pierce County Sheriff's Department, Tacoma police, and the US Forest Service scrambled their SWAT teams to Longmire, where rangers had set up an incident command center. Game wardens and state troopers responded. One veteran ranger, Uwe Nehring, had retired from a twenty-nine-year Park Service career on December 31. When news of Anderson's shooting flashed on the radio, he suited up and reported in. By midafternoon, so many officers had responded—there would be close to two hundred at Longmire in the end—that Rick Adamson, incident commander for the Pierce County Sheriff's Department, had to broadcast a hold-your-horses message to agencies across the Puget Sound region. "Do not self-deploy," he said.

A series of incident commanders—Adamson of Pierce County, chief ranger Chuck Young of the Park Service, Steven Dean of the FBI, and others—oversaw the mission as the day wore on. Each of them sought answers. Was Barnes the shooter? What were his intentions? Hour by hour, detectives worked up a profile. A routine check of court records revealed an ugly custody battle and a restraining order from Barnes's girlfriend. Her affidavit mentioned his military service. Calls to Joint Base Lewis-McChord, just south of Tacoma, confirmed that. Did he have specialized survival training? JBLM officials didn't know.

That remained one of the critical unknowns. Mountaineering district ranger Stefan Lofgren, Rainier's lead climbing ranger, has spent twenty years moving in the park in the toughest winter conditions. "If I'd bailed out of my car at the Flats," he told me, "I could make it to Longmire in an hour or two. I'd be out of the park by nightfall." But Lofgren knew the terrain, and he could survive a freezing night in a snow cave. Could Barnes?

Nobody knew how fast or how far he could travel, but he had options. He could kill a snowshoer and walk out in the victim's gear, so the cops took no chances with anyone emerging from the backcountry. At Narada Falls, a trailhead half a mile below Barn Flats, a group of snowshoers returning from an overnighter were greeted at the parking lot by a SWAT team, guns drawn. "Keep coming out one at a time," the officers told the shocked visitors. "Slowly. Hands in the air." They asked the snowshoers to stand like birds on a wire while the SWAT team retrieved everyone's ID from their van. A Pierce County deputy then told the group to stand by the van. "If something happens," he told Robert Conrad, the group's guide, "get down and stay down."

~~~~~~

The more the cops dug, the more dangerous their shooter appeared to be. Barnes wasn't some two-strikes car thief. Uncle Sam had taken him on as a raw recruit in 2007, molded him into a soldier—a communications specialist—and posted him to one of Joint Base Lewis-McChord's Stryker brigades, the ground units that lived on the point of the spear in Iraq and Afghanistan.

His unit served a yearlong deployment in Iraq in 2007–2008. Upon his return, Barnes did not adjust well. A DUI arrest and a weapons charge led to his discharge in 2009. He drank too much, made few friends, and spent his money on tattoos and guns.

In late 2010, Barnes's girlfriend, twenty-two-year-old Nicole Santos, gave birth to a girl named Aubrey. Fatherhood did not suit Barnes, who, according to Santos, found the baby an annoyance. She left him and took Aubrey on January 1, 2011. Barnes responded with a text: "If you come home don't be surprised to find my brains splattered all over the walls."

The next twelve months played out in a flurry of court papers. Santos filed for legal custody of Aubrey and for a restraining order against Barnes. In affidavits taken last summer, she described him as a violent, unstable man with "possible PTSD issues." A close reading of the documents revealed a character who, PTSD or not, had plain old asshole issues: Santos's statement alleges that Barnes played cruel mind games with her and screamed at and abused the baby.

Despite Barnes's domestic problems, motive remained a puzzle. Why would he head to the mountain with an assault rifle? Suicide was a possibility: suicide by self, by cop, or after taking a whole lot of people with him. Throughout the early afternoon, it remained unclear whether the shooter was seeking more victims or trying to flee. "We had to prepare for both," said Pierce County sheriff's detective Ed Troyer. "The thought was to keep him trapped up there on the mountain. Keep him on foot. Keep the area contained."

At 2:19 p.m., a deputy standing watch on the Nisqually River Bridge, about a half-mile west of the Flats, reported seeing a head pop up over a snowy ridge and duck back down.

At the incident command center, Ranger Lofgren told his colleagues what he knew of the terrain. To be spotted from the bridge, the shooter would have had to move west from the Flats along the road's shoulder.

That wasn't good news for the 125 visitors locked down at the Jackson Visitor Center. Commanders in Longmire couldn't send in reinforcements as long as the suspect remained on the road's high snow berms. Fortunately, the Pierce County Sheriff's Department had its armored BearCat rolling toward the mountain. The vehicle, which looks like a cross between a Hummer and a Brinks truck, has heavy plating capable of stopping any high-caliber-rifle or assault-weapon round.

When the BearCat reached the rangers and deputies at the Stevens Canyon Y, the group hustled up a plan. Ian Canaan, a Forest Service law-enforcement officer, would lead a small team of rangers, including the just-retired Uwe Nehring, into the visitor center. Pierce County sergeant Mark Berry wanted Rainier rangers on the inside because they knew the building and the interps working it.

Eleven officers pressed into the back of the BearCat. It was a tight fit and a hushed ride. A few minutes later, they arrived at the Paradise parking lot.

The doors of the visitor center flew open just after three p.m. "Everybody down on the floor! Put your hands on your head!"

Brian Hess counted five or six SWAT team members. They moved quickly through the JVC, assault rifles drawn.

Do not move, Ian Canaan told the visitors. He asked Rainier LE ranger Ken Worstell to verify the identities of each interpretive ranger, one by one.

A chill from the concrete floor worked into Lisa Hill's body. She realized for the first time that the gunman might be among them. She shivered. A woman nearby reached out and asked if Hill was okay. It was a simple gesture, but she took great comfort in it.

Brian Hess had other concerns. Son of a bitch, he thought. These guys are looking for an armed man, and I've got a gun in my pocket. This will not go well.

Canaan spoke up.

"Is anyone here armed?"

Hess and another man slowly raised their hands. The other man spoke first. "I'm an off-duty police officer," he said.

Hess didn't have time to get any words out. An assault rifle was trained on his face. "You touch your gun," the SWAT team member told him, "and we're going to shoot you."

"Understood," Hess replied.

"Where is it?"

The officer removed Hess's Ruger and told him that the gun would be returned to him before he left the park.

With the JVC secured, Canaan briefed the visitors. An evacuation would happen, but probably not anytime soon.

"We're all going to be spending some time together here," he said.

A few hundred yards down-mountain, an active manhunt was under way. Ted Holden, a veteran game warden with the Washington Department of Fish and Wildlife, had spotted some tracks off the road, below the Stevens Canyon Y. Holden has years of experience tracking poachers across snow. "You get a lot of divots made by snow plopping from trees, but those divots are random," he told me. "What I do is cue in on patterns."

The SWAT guys found climbing notches in the roadside berm and postholes leading into the trees. No innocent park visitor would continue to posthole up to his crotch. This had to be their guy.

Heads swiveled. The Y had been a forward tactical post for the past three hours. All that time, it was now clear, the shooter had been moving above them, below them, all around. The team strapped on snowshoes and followed the holes.

Around the next bend, a second SWAT team searched Barnes's Impala. One officer cut the car's distributor-cap wires to disable it. From the trunk, deputy John Delgado removed a lever-action rifle, several packs of AR-15 ammunition, and heavy body armor. Another officer pulled an AK-47 and several .223 magazines from the passenger seat.

Meanwhile, calls were coming in from cops throughout Washington and Oregon wondering whether the Rainier shooter might be involved in unsolved crimes in their jurisdictions. This wasn't uncommon. One cop was especially insistent. Detective Mike Mellis, from King County, which encompasses Seattle, kept calling back. A Pierce County dispatcher finally conveyed the urgency to Longmire. The King County guys were saying that Barnes had shot four people just the night before.

Pierce County sergeant Trent Stephens radioed Mark Berry, who was up-mountain overseeing the SWAT trackers. "Barnes is a confirmed shooter in a quad shooting incident early this morning in King County," he said. The picture became clearer. And more tragic.

New Year's Eve had found Barnes drinking at a house party in a low-rent suburb in South Seattle. Some of the drunken young men began bragging about their guns. The clock moved to two a.m. The gun talk turned to show-and-tell. Argument ensued.

Booze, honor, young men, pride.

Sometime around three a.m., King County sheriff's deputies rolled up to find four people shot. They would all survive, and they fingered Barnes. He'd stolen a car, they said, and fled.

In the wee hours, Barnes returned to his North Seattle apartment and loaded his own car with weapons. He told friends he was heading to California.

Nobody knows why he drove to the mountain instead of the state line. But it wasn't a simple errant turn. You don't just end up at Mount Rainier. It's a two-and-a-half-hour drive from Seattle, down lonely country roads. A man who drives to the mountain has the intention of driving to the mountain.

When trouble finds people, sometimes that's where they go. An old friend of mine, a former ranger at Mount Rainier, once told me that one of the toughest parts of his job was finding suicides. "People come up here for a lot of different reasons," he said. "Sometimes they want it to be the last place they see."

~~~~~~

Darkness comes early to the Cascades in winter. Dusk at 4:30, lights out by 5:00.

East of the Paradise road, two Pierce County SWAT units used the failing light to track Barnes. One set of tracks led up from the shooting site, toward Paradise, and circled around a sewage-treatment building—just a few hundred yards below the JVC. They followed the fall line west, to the ridge where the deputy had spotted a head at 2:19 p.m. With cops covering the Nisqually River drainage, he took off east, crossing and recrossing the road, and headed toward Paradise Valley.

The teams moved slowly, not knowing whether Barnes might be waiting to ambush them. They watched his divots disappear down a bank into the Paradise River.

A Black Hawk helicopter, courtesy of the US Customs and Border Protection Air and Marine unit, 150 miles away in Bellingham, Washington, circled overhead. A chopper does triple duty in any manhunt. In addition to scanning for the suspect and providing intelligence for ground-based trackers, it has a little-known third purpose. "You put a helicopter overhead, anybody who's running tends to stop running," customs pilot Chris Rosen told me. "They don't want to be seen by the helicopter. That gives the ground team time to catch up."

But at around five p.m., the ground teams were forced to halt. Darkness gave Barnes the drop on his trackers. Now it became a question of survival. The temperature had fallen into the 20s. If Barnes was dressed for the weather and knew what he was doing, he could dig a snow cave and shelter overnight. If he didn't, his chances were slim. It's not uncommon for lost climbers and campers to die of exposure in the Rainier backcountry. Tracks leading into the Paradise River were a telling sign. Surviving overnight was tough enough; wading into the river put a man's chances near zero.

As officers equipped with night vision took up posts along the river and armored vehicles patrolled the roads, a veteran wilderness tracker—who has not been identified by law enforcement—leaned over a map in the incident command center, letting his eye fall into the natural V's of the topo lines. By this time, detectives had determined that Barnes probably didn't possess advanced survival skills. They figured he must be exhausted. But the moment he went into the creek, the tracker knew Barnes had cut his survival time from hours to minutes. The tracker put his finger on a spot northeast of Narada Falls. "This," he said, "is where we'll find him."

~~~~~~

Up at the Jackson Visitor Center, staffers raided the closed Paradise Inn for blankets and pillows. Parents dashed out to their cars under armed escort to find diapers and medicine. A couple of SWAT members retrieved some Disney DVDs from a car for the kids.

Finally, at around midnight, a ranger whispered to Lisa Hill and Brian Hess. "Are you guys ready to go?"

An armed ranger escorted Hess to his Jeep. He brought it around to the door of the visitor center, behind a Washington State Patrol cruiser. In front of the cruiser was a sanding truck. An armed SWAT member rode shotgun in both vehicles. Four other visitors eased their cars into the queue. Another trooper pulled in at the end of the convoy.

Quickly, the passengers moved from the JVC into the cars. A police officer returned Hess's pistol. "Please don't load it until you get in the vehicle," he said.

"The drive down was nerve-racking," Lisa Hill recalled. "We thought about Brian's kids, about my eighty-four-year-old mother, who lives with me. About what if something happened to us." They passed Margaret Anderson's SUV and the suspect's Impala. Hill realized how close the scene was to Paradise. How she would have been standing there in the open when the shooter arrived. She thought about how Anderson had risked her life to keep that from happening.

"Keep your eyes peeled on the ridges," Hess told her. So she did. And she prayed.

~~~~~~

The final convoy of Paradise visitors exited the park at around 3:30 a.m.

Half an hour later, customs pilot Chris Rosen reported to work in Bellingham. He was eager to get a helicopter down to Rainier at first light. His copilot, Dave Simeur, had navigated the Black Hawk in the previous day's manhunt and thought they'd do better in an AStar helicopter. The AStar is a smaller, nimbler craft, and customs' unit had an infrared camera system.

As the Cascade foothills rushed beneath them, Rosen and Simeur had a discussion about contingencies. "If I get shot," Rosen told his partner, "your only way of knowing might be that the AStar starts acting screwy. Be sure and take the controls."

The pilots checked the shooting site, then moved to nearby campsites. "Our concern was that this guy would find some campers, kill them, and take their gear," Rosen said.

They found two tents on the edge of Reflection Lakes. Infrared sensors turned up two warm bodies in each. Good sign. Rosen hovered above the tents until one of the campers, a web designer named Brian Vogt, emerged. The pilot tried to communicate via a loudspeaker, but the noise from the blades was too loud. The camper held his hands up in the universal "can't understand" gesture.

Rosen looked around. The only place to land was on the frozen lake, which might not be frozen enough. He couldn't chance it.

"Hand me your coffee cup," Simeur told Rosen.

On both pilots' paper cups, Simeur wrote a message. He poured water into the cups to make sure they didn't fly up into the whirling blades. Then he dropped them.

Vogt raced over to the cups.

"A ranger has been shot," the note said. "Shooter at large. Take road to falls and sheriff. We will keep an eye on you. Do not drive from Paradise w/o armed escort."

Vogt gave a thumbs-up. He began breaking camp.

~~~~~~

At 9:30 a.m. on January 2, three SWAT teams moved east on foot from the Paradise road. Two Pierce County units had followed Barnes's posthole tracks for about

200 yards before coming within sight of the berms sloping into the Paradise River. They held their position while the AStar overflew the river. No sign of the shooter.

The SWAT teams proceeded ahead. As the river itself came into view, someone spotted a piece of blue clothing in the water. He called out. "Suspect." Everyone froze. They radioed their location to the chopper.

Rosen hovered over the site. His copilot ran the infrared camera up and down the river. Any warm-blooded life would show up as a white blotch. "Man, there is nothing hot in that riverbed," said Simeur.

"We're not getting any clear signature," Rosen radioed the ground team. "Whatever is in that river is cold."

The SWAT team approached cautiously. One by one, they peered over the snowbank into the river. A body, facedown in the shallow riffles. Like a rock in the stream. White male, gray pants, blue T-shirt, one sneaker missing. No bullet wound. If this was the shooter, the mountain alone had killed him.

About 50 yards upstream, an AR-15 assault rifle rested under a few inches of water. In the front pocket of the man's pants was a Glock .45 magazine. In his back pocket, a cell phone minus its battery pack. Barnes knew enough to disable the tracking abilities of his phone.

Barnes's body was about 250 yards from where the tracker had predicted he would be found—and less than 100 yards from the Narada Falls trailhead, where Brian Vogt's group was headed and where Robert Conrad's campers had exited the previous afternoon.

As they documented the scene, one of the deputies pulled the collar of the suspect's shirt down to expose his neck. He saw a word tattooed on his skin: PRIDE.

Margaret Anderson received a hero's funeral. Thousands of family members, friends, and law-enforcement officers packed the Olson Auditorium on the campus of Pacific Lutheran University in Tacoma. Interior secretary Ken Salazar, Washington State governor Christine Gregoire, National Park Service director Jon Jarvis, and Randy King delivered tributes.

"Find yourself on Mount Rainier injured, lost, or threatened, Margaret Anderson would help," King said. "Find the park threatened, she would intervene."

Rob Danno, Anderson's first boss at Bryce Canyon National Park, recalled her extraordinary integrity and character, "her internal compass." Rangers wearing crisp uniforms ceremonially folded an American flag. Interior Secretary Salazar presented it to Eric Anderson, sitting in the front row.

Mount Rainier National Park remained closed for five days. When it reopened, visitors poured in to offer flowers, cards, and sympathy. Some employees couldn't bring themselves to return to work for days and weeks, and rangers from Olympic, North Cascades, Glacier, and other national parks volunteered to fill in. For weeks, Rainier officials held a daily call-in session for staff to talk over their recovery.

Still, the park has not been the same for many of those who punch in every morning. Something will come up during a conversation, the talk will turn to Anderson, and everyone will go silent. Some rangers have a hard time sleeping. One keeps a book, *Emotional Survival for Law Enforcement*, next to his desk. Others have considered transfers, wondering if the best way to put New Year's Day behind them is to put the mountain in their rearview mirror.

Time heals. It can also bring fresh trauma. On June 21, climbing ranger Nick Hall died during a rescue mission on the mountain's Emmons Glacier. The memorials continue.

~~~~~~

Eric Anderson and his daughters will be dealing with January 1 for the rest of their lives. I reached him in early May, four months after his wife was killed. He was, understandably, still torn up. And angry. He believes the New Year's Day shooting was an incident that had been long coming—and that the park's law-enforcement unit was unprepared for.

"There's a lot of disturbed people out there who see this mountain shining at them," he told me. "How long before some nut says, 'I can go to that mountain and slay a shitload of people and be on the news in a matter of minutes'? We're close enough to the metro area. There are plenty of opportunities to run into any type of crime.

"In terms of law enforcement, we were stretched way too thin and have been for years," Anderson said.

Compassion demands that his complaint be heard. And the Park Service is listening. In May, a board of review heard his testimony, along with others', as part of an effort to determine how to prevent similar incidents.

It's a dicey thing, discussing the murder of a ranger in the context of staffing and training. It is true that Randy King, like other park superintendents, is expecting more cuts to his budget this year. Do more with less: It's become a standard marching order in a service perennially starved by Congress. In 1980, the Park Service employed 1,841 full-time rangers to protect 220 million annual visitors. By 2010, the number of rangers had declined to 1,417—a loss of nearly a quarter of the force—while visits surged to 281 million.

Hiring more law-enforcement rangers and giving them sufficient tools would make our parks safer. But a malevolent individual like Benjamin Barnes is a bolt from the sky. Anyone with a gun, ill will, and the element of surprise can murder a law-enforcement officer. Better training and backup do not give a ranger the power to read minds or predict the future.

"We still don't know what Barnes was going to do up there," Pierce County detective Ed Troyer told me. "Kill himself? Take people out? Go survivalist and hide? The only person who knows what he was going to do was him. If Margaret Anderson hadn't stopped him, who knows what would have happened. What we do know is, he had the means and ammunition to kill a lot of people."

Anderson and his daughters will be leaving the mountain soon. The Park Service has found him a posting at the National Interagency Fire Center in Idaho. The former firefighter will work as a training specialist in structural fires. "The Park Service has been trying to do well by me," he said. He sounded genuinely appreciative.

I wish I had your job. Rangers hear it so often, it's like white noise. While most of us understand the drawbacks—low pay, working holidays, bureaucratic hassles—we still have a pang of envy when we see a ranger out on the trail on a bluebird day. What a life!

It *is* all that, some days. And most rangers join the National Park Service for the same reasons the rest of us visit them. They love the scenic beauty, the chance to work outdoors, the sense of positive mission. But they also absorb the bad acts that go on in the parks. They seek the negative so the rest of us can pitch our tents and hike in our snowshoes without having to worry about who's driving past the tire-chain checkpoint. Rangers see those glaciers and old-growth forests stained with violence, with ugliness and tragedy and loss. They absorb it, they deflect it, they capture it. Rangers like Margaret Anderson run to it and stand in its path.

TAKE THE MONEY AND RUN

GORDY MEGROZ

~~~~~~

Search the web for Dean Reinke and you'll soon be scrolling though a rap sheet of consumer complaints about how he and his for-profit road-race company, USRA Half Marathon, do business. Is he a fraud who has stayed one step ahead of the law, or an upstanding man who's been slimed by his enemies? Our writer cracked the code on one of the most bizarre sports-business stories you'll ever hear.

~~~~~~

On August 12, 2012, Maureen Lampa, a sixty-one-year-old retired teacher, her daughter, and her daughter's friend all piled into Lampa's Chrysler convertible for the three-hour drive from their home in Westminster, Massachusetts, to Freeport, Maine.

In May, the women had signed up for a race called the Freeport Half Marathon, and they'd spent four months running 5 to 10 miles a day, five days a week, to prepare. This would be Lampa's fifth half marathon. For her daughter, Katherine, and her daughter's friend Lauren Laserte, both twenty-one, it was their first.

On August 13, after spending the night in a nearby hotel, the group pulled into downtown Freeport an hour before the race's scheduled seven a.m. start time. But when they arrived, there was no sign of a race. No start banner, no water stations, no police directing traffic, no markers indicating the course route. Lampa walked into L.L.Bean's flagship store on Main Street to ask about the event. Nobody knew anything about a Freeport Half Marathon. Did Lampa have the wrong day? The wrong location?

The women drove back to their hotel room. As soon as they arrived, Lampa sat down and sent an e-mail to the race's organizer, Dean Reinke, the sixty-year-old

CEO and president of a five-year-old nationwide series he calls USRA Half Marathon, a company he founded in 2009.

"I am sitting in my hotel room with no race to run," Lampa wrote. "I spent over $100 to register my daughter and me for this race and spent $150 for a hotel room, because we live three hours from the supposed race site. . . . I want my money back!"

Three hours later, Reinke responded to Lampa—and other runners who'd sent bewildered e-mails—claiming that Howard Spear, the director of a popular annual event in Portland called the Maine Marathon, was to blame for the race getting canceled, apparently acting out of spite. Anybody with a complaint should take it up with him.

"With registration open and plans fully under way, just a few months ago Maine Track Club's Howard Spear submitted some false accusations and lies about the USRA to local politicians," Reinke wrote. "Spear had done the same thing a year ago but was rebuffed by the Freeport USA Tourism Group, who were very happy with us and the event. . . . Due to his actions, our agreement to use the approved course was reneged on despite the support of Freeport USA, Portland Convention & Visitors Bureau, and the State of Maine Tourism." To Lampa, Reinke wrote that Spear "has proven he is a pathological liar."

Lampa and several other runners contacted Spear, who was shocked by the accusation. "I've never even met him," Spear told me when we spoke on the phone. "And I certainly didn't try to block his race." That's true. Spear had nothing to do with the cancelation of Reinke's event. The strange reality is this: The 2012 Freeport Half Marathon was never even scheduled to happen.

A year earlier, Reinke had hosted a half marathon in Freeport and it had gone off without any problems. But after the race, Reinke didn't pay the $1,325 he contractually owed the Freeport police department for traffic-control services. In the meantime, Reinke had already started collecting entry fees for a 2012 race in Freeport, even though he didn't have any permits in hand, and hadn't applied for any.

In spring 2012, James Hendricks, a Freeport town-council member, called Reinke and asked him to come to Maine and answer a few questions. Reinke flew in and insisted that there had been a mix-up about the delinquent payment. He wrote a check on the spot and submitted a special-events application for the 2012 event. At meeting's end Reinke was informed that, before his 2012 application could be approved, the town council would have to meet and decide whether to grant him a new permit. "We shared our concerns that we were not happy that the event was advertised as a set event when in fact the Town of Freeport had not approved it," Gerald Schofield, chief of the Freeport police department, told me in an e-mail.

Reinke was invited to attend but told the council he couldn't make it. On May 1, the seven council members voted unanimously to deny his permit. Reinke was informed of the decision, but the USRA website, which he owns and operates, continued to promote and collect entry fees for the race, as did Active.com, a separate online-registration forum for people seeking race opportunities. In all, roughly one hundred people reportedly paid the $60 entry fee for the race, and thirty complained to Hendricks that they did not receive refunds.

Hendricks encouraged Lampa and other runners to contact the office of Maine's attorney general to file a complaint. The Maine AG referred them all to the Florida AG—Reinke's company is based in Winter Park, near Orlando—who told the runners that the office didn't handle small claims, and suggested that they file a complaint with the Better Business Bureau. If the runners wanted their money back, they'd need to lawyer up and take Reinke to court.

"That's not worth it," Lampa says. "You'd end up spending more on legal fees to recover the money than on the entry fee itself."

And that's where the matter died. The 2012 Freeport Half Marathon, the race that never happened, made Dean Reinke a slightly wealthier man.

To people in the running community, the Freeport incident wasn't surprising. Google Reinke's name and you'll see why: Most results will lead you to angry blog posts and message-board complaints by runners or people linked to running organizations. Going back to 2010, there are stories about charities that worked with Reinke and then never received any of the proceeds they were promised. About races that never happened and refunds that weren't paid. About police departments, race officials, and T-shirt companies that say they were never compensated for the work they did on USRA events.

One blogger describes Reinke as a "con man." A commenter labels him a "snake oil salesman." A poster to a message board called LetsRun.com sympathizes with a fellow runner who "fell prey to yet another shady race situation in the long, sordid history of this individual as a race director." In a Runners-World.com thread about Reinke, one runner stated that "Reinke managed a half marathon in Lexington, Kentucky, this past March. It was the most poorly facilitated race I've ever seen. Reinke only cares about making profit and has no concern for the runner's experience."

The Better Business Bureau gives a solid F to Reinke Sports Group—the LLC behind the USRA Half Marathon Series—and lists twenty-three user complaints on its website, including allegations of poor race management. There's also a Tumblr site called Reinke Sports Group Race Reviews, which is dedicated to "chronicling the negative reviews and race failures of the USRA Half Marathon Series."

The site contains a glut of negative information, including a letter from the Convention and Visitors Bureau in Bentonville, Arkansas, stating that Reinke never paid two charities—the Bentonville Public School Foundation and the Northwest Arkansas Food Bank—proceeds he'd promised them from a 2010 race, and that Reinke still owed money to the Clarion Hotel and Convention Center for space used during a prerace expo and packet pickup. The visitor bureau eventually covered the amount owed to the charities and the hotel.

Also available on the Tumblr site is a link to a letter from John Sensenig, the owner of John's Run/Walk Shop in Lexington, Kentucky. In it he states: "We had a very bad experience with Mr. Reinke and his USRA race that was held here in Lexington in spring of 2010. John's Run/Walk Shop, the city of Lexington, and even the sponsored charity dropped our support of his race and refused to support him in future races in Lexington."

Sensenig didn't respond to my request for an interview about what went wrong, but I was able to reach Anna Seitz, the client-relations and marketing assistant at Fasig-Tipton, a Thoroughbred-auction firm in Lexington that lined up a facility used during the start and finish of the race.

"What didn't go wrong?" Seitz says with a sigh. "He wouldn't pay the charity, Blue Grass Farms, or the vendors, and we ended up doing most of the work." When Reinke walked into a meeting with city officials requesting permits for a 2011 race in Lexington, he denied everything. "Voices were raised," says Seitz. "Then we said, 'We're not going to sit here and argue with you. We're recommending that you not be granted a permit.' It was the first time he shut up."

Not surprisingly, Reinke has had his share of legal disputes. In 2010, in a partnership with the city of Joplin, Missouri, he staged the Mother Road Marathon, an event that drew 1,929 runners. After that race, the city council decided that city employees had done a disproportionate amount of the work and told Reinke they were severing ties. Nonetheless, he moved forward, promoting his own Mother Road Marathon in Joplin. The city of Joplin sued Reinke for rights to the race's title, but he prevailed. According to reports at the time, Joplin settled out of court, paying him $20,000 to give up the name.

Also that year, Reinke petitioned the city of West Lafayette, Indiana, and Purdue University to hold a half marathon that would weave through the city and the Purdue campus. He was denied permission, but he began promoting a race 30 miles away, calling it the Home of Purdue Half Marathon. Purdue sued Reinke for using its name without permission. As part of a settlement, he was barred from appropriating the school's intellectual property and banned for three years from holding races anywhere in Purdue's home county, Tippecanoe.

In 2013, the city of Worcester, Massachusetts, also sued Reinke over unpaid bills, and the city of Barnstable is considering similar action. "I don't understand how he keeps getting away with stuff like this," says Sergeant Andrew McKenna of the Barnstable police department, which worked one of Reinke's races. "Why do places keep hiring him?"

~~~~~~

McKenna asked the obvious question. Based on his track record, how is Dean Reinke still in business?

To start with, it's important to note that not all USRA races are flops. Reinke holds twenty-three events nationwide, and a few are consistently successful, following a simple model that works for race organizers around the nation: charge an ample entry fee, keep costs under control, realize profit. Runners have proven to be remarkably tolerant of fees closing in on $100 for non-marathons and $100 to $150 (and sometimes more) for marathons. Still, profit margins are pretty narrow. If you attract 1,500 people to a half marathon at $60 each, and keep municipal expenses modest, you'll earn a ballpark $15,000.

In 2014, Reinke will oversee three races that have been put on three times before and four that will hit their five-year mark. Since Reinke started his race series, 25,000 people have participated, and the USRA website is plastered with photos of happy runners proudly displaying their finisher medals.

"The USRA races are fun, simple, and low-key, but with an upbeat environment," says Todd Lytle, a race director for several charity events in Clermont, Florida, who has run five of Reinke's races. "The courses are through nice state parks and scenic downtown areas, and they're usually in smaller places where you wouldn't normally find a half marathon. A lot of times, there's bands and pizza after the race, and that's pretty unique."

Reinke also has good working relationships with several people in the towns where his races are held, some of whom defend him. After I called the Las Cruces, New Mexico, police department, looking for information about a late payment Reinke owed the city for a race held there in September 2013, I got a separate call from Ed Carnathan, sports director at the Las Cruces Convention and Visitors Bureau. Carnathan said that in the four years he'd held races in Las Cruces, there'd never been a problem.

What about the late bill?

"You've never had a late bill before?" he said. "I've asked him to pay it. I can only ask him so many times."

An essential source for answering questions about Reinke, of course, is Reinke, but for the first few months that I researched this story, he failed to respond. I was able to piece together a basic portrait from various places, so I knew that he was sixty, was on the shorter side, and was a former college athlete who'd run varsity track for Indiana University in the 1970s. I also knew that he had close-cropped brown hair and a toothy grin, and was considered a sales genius by some people who'd met him.

"The best I've ever seen," says Mark Crepeau, a consultant in Ormond Beach, Florida, who worked for Reinke from 1989 to 1991, and credits his ex-boss with teaching him how to sell and market events. "He's high-energy, a dynamic presenter, and unbelievably disciplined. He has a schedule and routine, is organized as hell, and has a steel trap for a memory." Others described Reinke as gregarious, extremely smart, and willing to promise just about anything to close a deal.

"That's the problem," said Crepeau, who has mixed feelings about Reinke. "He'll promise the universe but only deliver twenty or so galaxies."

To pitch events, Reinke attends biannual conventions that bring together visitor bureaus, sports commissions, hoteliers, and the like. Typically, he goes after the local tourism center, and to seal the deal, he'll guarantee to get people in hotel beds and at restaurant tables. That's usually enough to prompt the visitor bureaus to sign on. At that point, Reinke often connects with a local liaison, usually somebody from a running club, who'll help map out the course, secure permits, and lock down portable toilets, volunteers, and other race essentials.

But almost always, city officials and others involved in the race go back to their desks and start to research the man behind the USRA Half Marathon Series. They usually run into the flak about him that appears online, and that's when the master salesman really demonstrates his charm and skill.

One person I spoke with—I'll call him Tom, because he asked that I not use his real name—was Reinke's liaison for the Tri-Cities Half Marathon in Richland, Washington. Not long after signing on with Reinke in 2011, Tom confronted him over the phone about reports of unpaid bills in various cities. He says Reinke offered a multitude of excuses.

"Dean told me that those cities had experienced great success with his races," he recalls. "Then they decided they could do it without him and they kicked him out. The way he saw it, based on that, he didn't owe them any money."

Okay, but why had Reinke opened registration for the Tri-Cities race prior to securing permits? Tom remembers Reinke saying: "I've been doing this a long time, and this is how we do it."

"Everything had an answer, and it seemed to make sense," Tom says. "I decided that there were two sides to every story and that he was telling me the truth."

In February 2012, the Tri-Cities Half Marathon was executed perfectly. The race drew 659 participants, and Reinke spared no expense to make it a first-class experience. There was plenty of food and refreshment at the finish—pizza, cookies, Gatorade—a band played, and each runner received a T-shirt and a high-quality finisher medal. "The die-cast ones," said Tom. "Not the kind with stickers on them."

The next year, Reinke was determined to grow the event, with the goal of drawing at least one thousand runners. He also wanted to hold a health and fitness expo in one of the hotel convention centers on the afternoon before the race, something runners would cruise through while they picked up their numbers. To sell vendor spots at the convention, Reinke hired Wendy Harris, a local stay-at-home mom. For each vendor Harris brought in, she'd earn a 15 percent commission.

Tom continued in his role as liaison, but things seemed different to him this time. The year before, when Tom had submitted receipts to Reinke for purchases, Reinke had sent him a check almost immediately. Now it was taking months. "He blamed it on his billing system," Tom says.

Meanwhile, Tom had discovered that Reinke owed the nearby Yakima Valley Sports Commission $1,500 for a race that had taken place there earlier in the year. "Dean told me he'd applied for a grant and that it had fallen through," Tom explains. "He'd planned on paying that bill using the grant money. It should have raised a red flag, but I was just so excited about what we were doing that I was blinded."

Eight hundred and forty runners turned out for the 2013 Tri-Cities Half Marathon. Reinke was so pleased that he decided to move his Yakima race (the one he still owed $1,500 to the city for) to the Tri-Cities area and hold it in July, calling it the Columbia River Half Marathon.

But soon after the 2013 Columbia River event, Tom started getting complaints. Mighty Johns, the company that supplied the portable toilets for the Tri-Cities race, was still owed $550; Russ Zornick, who'd timed a race for Reinke in Edmonds, Washington, was owed $750; Wendy Harris hadn't received all of the commission she'd earned; and the local charity, the Union Gospel Mission, which had provided the volunteers and was promised $225, hadn't been paid, either.

After a local TV station ran a report about the unpaid charity, Reinke immediately sent them a check. As of December 2013, however, Mighty Johns, Zornick, and Harris still hadn't been paid, even though each of them had contacted Reinke several times requesting what they were owed.

By the time Harris found out that other people were still waiting for checks, she was already selling vendor spaces at another health and fitness expo for Reinke's Columbia River Half Marathon. At that point, shortly before the July race, Harris quit, sending Reinke an e-mail that said, "I am not paid to be at the expo or the race. Nor have you paid me for the booth spaces filled. . . . My time is valuable. I do not and will not work for free."

Reinke replied, calling Harris "unprofessional."

"I am very disappointed," he wrote. "I expected a lot more from you. I guess you don't care what you leave behind since you are leaving the market."

Harris and Tom, who had also told Reinke that he was stepping down from his post, took their case to the Tri-Cities Visitor and Convention Bureau, telling officials about the unpaid bills. When Reinke caught wind of it he was furious, and Harris says he left a threatening voice mail. "He said I better hope he doesn't run into me the next time he's in town," Harris told me.

But what happened after that is the most puzzling. The Visitor and Convention Bureau ignored the warnings and allowed Reinke to move forward with a 2014 race anyway. Why? "They said they didn't want to get wrapped up in the politics," says Tom.

~~~~~~

Dean Reinke is on the phone, and he sounds pissed off. A few weeks ago, I sent him an e-mail requesting an interview. He declined, saying he was too busy. I followed up a week later, telling him I realized he was probably hesitant to speak with me because of allegations made against him in the past, but that I'd love to fly to Florida and give him the opportunity to discuss it. That e-mail went unanswered.

Now, however, he seems fully aware that I've been tracking his business practices. "I'm getting calls from people saying you're trying to bring me down!" Reinke shouts. "I don't need somebody who's trying to do a hatchet job on me. Do you even know anything about me? Have you ever done any of my races?" The conversation is brief, with Reinke repeatedly saying, "I've been doing this for thirty-plus years!"

As Reinke says, he's been involved in the running industry since the early 1980s. Prior to that, he was a track and cross-country star at Andrew Jackson High School in South Bend, Indiana. After graduating, in 1971, Reinke went on to compete for Indiana University, where he ran a 4:02 mile and represented the school at several NCAA championship meets. "He was a light-footed runner," recalls Sam Bell, eighty-five, Reinke's coach at Indiana. "We had a pretty good team, and he was our number-two man. He was outgoing, congenial; people liked him."

Reinke graduated from Indiana in 1976 and by the early eighties had landed a job as promotions director at Brooks Sports, the running-shoe company that, at the time, was located in Hanover, Pennsylvania. His job was to sponsor athletes and work out sponsorship deals with running events.

But Reinke's departure from Brooks was acrimonious. George Dietel, Reinke's boss, fired him after learning about what he viewed as shady business deals. For one thing, he discovered that Reinke would sometimes provide better sponsorships to race directors if they brought him in as a speaker—somebody to provide an inspirational message. For that, Reinke would be paid separately.

When I called Dietel and told him what I was researching, he chuckled and said, "I'd just as soon have nothing to do with it." But in a 1989 story published in a newsletter put out by Road Race Management, a membership organization, Dietel said that the firing stemmed from "very flagrant double dipping" and involved "a considerable amount of money."

After leaving Brooks, Reinke went back to South Bend, where he was hired by the St. Joseph's Medical Center to create, promote, and direct a 10K that he called the Sportsmed. According to news reports at the time, after three years at the helm of the race, he stopped working with St. Joseph's in 1984, for reasons that I couldn't pin down.

Rather than walk away quietly, Reinke began promoting his own race, one that would take place the same day as the hospital's event. St. Joseph's sued, and Reinke was slapped with a temporary injunction that barred him from "promoting, organizing, sponsoring, advertising, directing, or conducting" any race that overlapped with the St. Joseph's 10K.

According to reports, Reinke ignored the injunction and moved forward, promoting what he called the Sportsfest 10K. At that point, the judge in the case issued a permanent injunction and decreed that Reinke was responsible for paying St. Joseph's $20,000 for damages to the hospital's reputation, plus attorney fees. Reinke agreed to back off, but he couldn't afford to pay the hospital. The court recognized his inability to pay the judgment.

A few months later, Reinke announced that the Chicago Vultures, a team in the American Indoor Soccer Association (AISA), would play an exhibition against the Chicago Sting, from the Major Indoor Soccer League, at the University of Notre Dame. But the Vultures hadn't signed off on the game. "He did not get our permission, nor do any of our teams want to play in anything that is connected with Dean Reinke," Martha Makay, executive assistant to the AISA commissioner, told the *South Bend Tribune* at the time. "Reinke wants to get paid for promoting our soccer teams, and we have told him before that we can take care of our own promotions. He has caused our league nothing but trouble."

In 1985, it was reported that Reinke filed for Chapter 7 bankruptcy. He owed large sums to various media outlets that had promoted other running events he'd staged in the area, as well as to utility companies and lawyers, to name a few. Roughly $200,000 worth of Reinke's belongings were liquidated and used to pay off the debt, and Reinke moved to Winter Park.

But just two years later, Reinke started an even bigger business, Dean Reinke and Associates, which promoted nearly one hundred running races nationwide, including a masters racing circuit for elite runners forty and older. The masters races attracted big names like Boston and New York City Marathon winner Bill Rodgers, Olympians Marty Liquori and Frank Shorter, and Kenyan sensation Wilson Waigwa. Reinke wanted to do for running what other senior circuits had done for golf and tennis, and by many accounts the races were well produced. But the circuit wasn't without controversy.

According to Rodgers, Reinke skimmed money from appearance fees owed to the celebrity runners. Rodgers recalls a race in Macon, Georgia, that was sponsored by Arby's. "The fee that Dean had given me seemed low," he says. "So I asked the guy from Arby's what I was supposed to get, and it was double what Dean had paid me. I confronted him, and he hemmed and hawed and said, 'You know, Billy, I treat you so well, and I take you to a lot of races.' He was like that. He was always looking to hustle people."

Reinke also continued to have trouble paying his bills. The Road Runners Club of America's *Footnotes*, *National Masters News*, and *Running Times*—all of which were owed advertising fees—approached Imperial Chemical Industries, Reinke's main sponsor for his masters circuit, to ask it to step in and force Reinke to pay up.

By 1991, the masters series was over. For the next decade, Reinke continued to promote races on a small scale while also taking on a variety of other clients. In the mid-nineties, he served as executive director of the United States Croquet Association. "He just sandbagged his way through that job," says Bob Alman, publisher of *Croquet World* magazine. "He would take credit for things he had nothing to do with. Everyone wanted him fired." By 2004, he was working for a publisher of sports books.

In 2010, Reinke started the USRA Half Marathon Series, seizing on the surging popularity of the 13.1-mile races. Since 2003, half marathons have grown faster than road races of any other distance. From 2006 to 2012, the number of finishers increased by 10 percent or more each year. During the past five years, Reinke has expanded from ten to twenty-three races, with plans for more events. In a November 2013 newsletter e-mailed to past USRA participants, Reinke wrote that he had just attended a conference in Salt Lake City, and that he was interested in organizing races in twenty-five cities. "We love to increase the number of areas where we are placing our events, and would love your feedback if you'd like us to come to your area," he wrote.

~~~~~~

A little over a week after our first phone call, Reinke agreed to a real interview, with the condition that it wouldn't be recorded. This time there's a different guy on the phone. Reinke speaks very fast but he's jovial. He asks me where I'm from.

I grew up in Vermont, I tell him.

"You see your Catamounts basketball team last night?" he excitedly asks, referring to the University of Vermont's near upset of Duke.

I tell him I missed it.

"Too bad! It was a great game!"

I can't help but like this Reinke a little, and I can see why people might find him easy to trust. He tells me about growing up in South Bend, how he'd wanted to be the quarterback at Notre Dame but realized he was built to be a distance runner. He tells me about his family: three children, one of whom has special needs. And he talks about his father, the head of a construction company who "busted his ass" and taught young Dean that if you "work hard, you get rewarded."

But when I start asking about unpaid bills and canceled races, he gets defensive.

"I don't owe anybody any money," he says firmly.

What about Marathon Sportswear and Gordon Lovie, the T-shirt makers who say they're owed roughly $12,000 and $2,300, respectively? Or Val Lofton, a race timer who claims she's still owed $1,000? Or Mighty Johns? Or Russ Zornick? Or Wendy Harris? Or the Barnstable and Las Cruces police departments?

Reinke pauses. "The thing that you need to understand," he says, "is that I'm not always responsible for the bill. Sometimes it's the convention and visitor bureau, sometimes they were supposed to be paid through a grant, sometimes it's a sponsor that owes them money."

I ask Reinke why, then, he doesn't tell these people that they need to contact somebody else to get paid? Why does he ignore their calls and e-mails?

"I don't ignore them; I've told them this."

I move on to canceled races without refunds. Earlier, I'd spoken to Phil Stewart, editor and publisher at Road Race Management, a company that publishes newsletters and how-to guides about organizing running events. Stewart told me it's common practice for road races to have a no-refund policy for canceled races, but that it usually applies only when a race is shut down because of bad weather or some other circumstance out of management's control—not because the race director failed to secure permits. And when directors do cancel, they typically roll over the entry fee to the next year's race.

When Reinke cancels races, he allows runners to transfer into one of his other twenty-two events, but those are often several months later, and several hundred miles away from the original location. When I ask Reinke about this, he stresses: "But I do offer refunds."

This contradicts several people I spoke with, who told me they'd requested refunds after canceled USRA races in Tracy, California; Greenwood, South Carolina; and Freeport, Maine. All have failed to get a refund.

In addition, responding to an online article published after the canceled Greenwood race, Reinke had this to say in the comments section: "Like most major races throughout the country, we too have a no-refund policy as stated in our waiver, standard in the industry."

Reinke and I speak for nearly two hours, and he continues to deny allegations. When I ask him why he was fired from Brooks, he tells me he wasn't. "The company wasn't doing well," he says. "I decided to move on." But usually Reinke is focused on trying to shift the conversation toward the great things he's done for people and the sport of running.

"We're creating a tourism destination event to get people active and support a charity," he says, sounding sincere. "I look at people who've had a heart attack or cancer or people whose husband just left them. We take a serious look at these people and how our races change their lives."

When it comes to road races and possible games of deception, Reinke isn't alone. According to Jean Knaack, the executive director of the Road Runners Club of America (RRCA), small-scale con artists across the country set up races, collect entry fees, then flee town—never to be heard from again. In 2012, an Indiana company called Rapid Running Event Management pulled the plug on three races it never received permits for, pocketing the entry fees and not refunding any of the participants. It subsequently went out of business. "But nobody does this on Reinke's scale," says Knaack.

For its part, the RRCA booted Reinke from its membership (something that Knaack says rarely happens), established a race-management code of ethics, and published an online story called "Buyer Beware," which advised runners to do several things before signing up for any race, including "Google the company or promoter."

But none of that has real teeth. RRCA membership is essentially just a label, and Reinke can always figure out another way to sell his races. In fact, he's already begun going around tourism offices, pitching city mayors and city managers directly. So the real question is this: Is Reinke acting criminally?

"Only if there's intent to deceive," says professor Robert Weisberg, an expert in white-collar crime at Stanford Law School. "But if he's doing these things over and over, you could make the case that he's doing it on purpose. And that's larceny."

Reinke has probably pocketed at least $25,000 through unpaid bills and by refusing refunds, which would certainly be enough for the attention of a prosecutor.

Weisberg says that if Reinke is using the Internet to collect entry fees, thereby reaching across state lines, he could be charged with a federal crime. "But federal prosecutors probably have bigger things to deal with, so they aren't concerned with something like this."

If any law-enforcement agency is looking into criminal charges, it certainly isn't deterring Reinke from pressing forward.

Last December, he e-mailed me a few references—people who he says can vouch for his character and professionalism. One is Chris Hamilton, the executive director at the Aurora, Illinois, Convention and Visitors Bureau. I call Hamilton, only to find out that he has been let go. Instead, I'm directed to Charlie Zine, Reinke's liaison for the inaugural Fox River Trail Half Marathon, held in Aurora in May 2013. Zine tells me that the race went pretty well, but Reinke never paid the charity, the Rosary High School track team, which did all the volunteer work and was owed at least $200.

"We use that money to put on meets, buy equipment, and buy food for the races," says Vic Mead, the school's coach. "We do this for a lot of races, and we're usually paid within a month, but I'm still waiting."

Later I speak with Dale Berman, the mayor of North Aurora, a city where part of the race took place. He's aware that the charity hasn't been paid, and tells me that "there won't be a race here if I have anything to do with it. The Convention and Visitors Bureau wouldn't support his permit, and as mayor of North Aurora, I wouldn't allow him to race here."

Given that information, it appears unlikely that Reinke's 2014 half marathon in Aurora will happen. But when I log on to the USRA website, I'm able to sign up for the race anyway, paying a $50 entry fee with my credit card. I don't expect to ever run it. And I don't expect to get my money back.

HORNSWOGGLED

PAUL KVINTA

~~~~~~

Back in 2010, South African Johnny Olivier was just looking for an easy job to pay the bills. But after agreeing to help a golf buddy collect lion bones for his boss, an international wildlife-trafficking kingpin, he found himself in the middle of an unprecedented poaching scheme that involved imported prostitutes, heavy gambling, bags of cash, and the slaughter of more than thirty rhinos. Welcome to the bizarre, bleeding edge of wildlife crime.

~~~~~~

He saved fifty rhinos. But he's still a con man.

—Investigator, South African Revenue Service

He turned a corner in the Emperors Palace Casino and froze. Peter, Chai, and the others lingered near some slot machines. He stared at them for a moment, looked left and right, then headed for the exit.

Had they seen him?

It was June 2010. He had cut off communication two years earlier, after the deal had gone bad. They'd lied to him. He'd ended up in a reeking 13-by-20-foot jail cell with twenty-three other guys for three days in the boondocks east of Johannesburg. Sure, Chai had paid his $20,000 fine. But where was Chai when his identity—John Olivier, fifty-one—appeared beneath the headline "Two Guilty of Possession of Rhino Horns"? Where was Chai when he'd lost his job and was unemployed for fourteen months? Johnny was friendly with the owner of a seafood restaurant at the casino. He popped in to visit occasionally. But the last person he wanted to bump into was Chai.

"Johnny!" said Peter, rounding a bank of slot machines.

"Peter."

"How are you, Johnny?"

"I'm fine, Peter. Chai."

"Johnny."

In the beginning they'd seemed harmless enough. They were lion-bone traders. According to his friend K.K., they bought the bones from South African game farmers and sold them to a guy in Laos. Asians used them for medicine or something. It's all legal, K.K. had said. It certainly helped the farmers. They sold lion hunts to rich Americans, and after exporting the trophy heads, they had a pile of bones. Why not sell them to the Asians?

Maybe it was a stretch to call K.K. his friend. He didn't have many friends. It's not that he wasn't friendly. He was. But ever since his company—he worked for an auto-parts business—had relocated him from Durban to Joburg in 2007, he'd never found his niche. His wife was back in Durban, and the big city could be lonely for a graying, middle-aged man living by himself. Johnny had close-cropped hair, leathery skin, and a trim white mustache. It didn't help that he'd lost most of the hearing in his left ear during his military service in the 1970s and '80s, when an antitank mine exploded in Angola. He didn't drink, so bars were out. He liked watching rugby on TV, or he'd go to the golf course. That's where he'd met K.K. All you had to do was sit in the clubhouse and you could pair up with someone to play a round. That was nice.

K.K. was Thai and worked at the airport, for Thai Airways. Johnny spoke some Thai, which K.K. was thrilled to learn. Would Johnny consider helping his friends in the lion-bone business? There were four or five of them, all from Thailand, and their English was limited. The Afrikaner farmers struggled just pronouncing their names. That's why they'd adopted nicknames. Punpitak Chunchom was Peter. Chumlong Lemtongthai, the ringleader, was Chai. Johnny recalled the blissful months he'd spent in Thailand as a young man. What a paradise! The beaches, the scuba diving. The young girls. Whatever you wanted! Sure, he'd help K.K.'s friends. They paid him $100 for each complete skeleton, and he needed the money, what with rent in Joburg and his mortgage in Durban.

"Come work for us again, Johnny," said Chai, the slot machines jingling and clattering around them.

"No way," said Johnny.

"We have lots of business."

"Forget it, Chai."

"We're only doing lion bones. Everything's legal. No rhino horns."

Rhino horns had been the problem, hadn't they? After initially doing lion bones, they'd instructed him to find rhino horns. What did he know about rhino horns? He certainly didn't know the bloody laws about rhino horns. Look, when he was a kid growing up on a farm, if he wanted to shoot a buck, a guinea fowl, whatever, he could go shoot it. You didn't need permits or crap like that. Chai said rhino horn sold for more than the price of gold in Vietnam, more than cocaine. So Johnny found a guy, a safari operator. It was October 2008. They all agreed to meet at a restaurant (in a little town outside Joburg called Delmas). The Thais whipped out a scale right there in the parking lot. After weighing the three horns, they began pulling $100 notes from their socks, $60,000 worth. They loaded the horns into Johnny's white Mazda and took off. That's when a bunch of cars raced up, gravel flying, cops screaming. Next thing Johnny knew, he had a plastic zip tie around his wrists.

"I'm not interested, Chai."

"Think about it, Johnny."

"I was just leaving, in fact."

"We'll call you, Johnny."

~~~~~~

> She knew she was coming here to work as a prostitute. That's in her statement.
>
> —Investigator, South African Revenue Service

She realized something was wrong even before entering the house. A Thai woman named Mau met her in the driveway and grabbed her passport. The signature page listed her as Boonta Kongklin, but everyone called her Joy.

"You won't need this," Mau said.

She wasn't used to people snatching her things. She was thirty-four years old and tiny, not 5 feet tall, maybe 90 pounds. But she was feisty. Years earlier, when her boyfriend had smashed her in the face, she'd fought back. She'd sustained a cracked cheekbone, a gash over her eye, and three days in the hospital. But she'd fought back. And she left him, despite being four months pregnant. She didn't take shit from anyone.

But this was different. She didn't know where she was. There was a farmhouse and an empty swimming pool near several cages with colorful birds. She was exhausted from the flight from Bangkok. A white woman had collected her that morning at the Johannesburg airport, and they'd driven thirty minutes. It was October 2010. "We're going to Mau's house," the woman had said. Who was Mau?

Inside the house were five other Thai ladies chatting. Mau approached them and slapped one so hard her head snapped back. Silence. "I told you no talking." Joy was to share a room with them. There were no beds, only blankets.

Her pulse quickened.

Back in Thailand, her friend had been vague about the details. All that registered was "good job in South Africa, good money, great boss." What choice did she have? In Pattaya, the beach town where she was living on her own, she was close to starving. Fewer *farang* (foreigners) were coming for the white sand and turquoise water. At the laundry where she worked, her pay had been cut to $80 a month. Most of that she sent to her grandmother and her seven-year-old son, four hours away in the small city of Nakhon Sawan where she grew up. Her parents were dead.

Life had not always been about survival. When Joy was sixteen, she discovered that she could sing. Her rock band played gigs across Bangkok, mostly clubs for officials and rich people. She wore 4-inch heels and red-carpet outfits. But then her vocal cords failed, and the doctors said no more singing. That was ages ago. When her son arrived, sometimes she could feed him only rice and water.

In Bangkok, a woman she didn't know had handed her a plane ticket and a visa. On the flight she told herself over and over, "If something isn't right, I will go to the police."

Now Mau stood over her. "I get your first 60,000 rand [about $8,700]. After that you can have your passport back."

Rademeyer is used to hanging out with unsavory characters.

—Yolandi Groenewald, reporter, Johannesburg *City Press*

By the spring of 2010, well before he knew about Johnny and Joy, Julian Rademeyer couldn't imagine South Africa's rhino-poaching crisis becoming more outrageous. How could it? Rademeyer was an investigative reporter for South Africa's Media24 newspaper group, and he'd covered wars, corruption, and his share of crazy African stories. But the crisis threatening South Africa's 21,000-some rhinos was surreal from the start. From 1980 to 2007, a total of 260 rhinos were killed for their horns, an average of 9 per year. But in 2008, poachers killed 83 rhinos, and in 2009, the number jumped to 122. A year later 333 were slaughtered, and the figures would continue to skyrocket: 448 in 2011, and 668 in 2012. Rademeyer couldn't read a newspaper without wincing at yet another gruesome photo of a dead rhino with its face hacked off.

He found the situation stranger in light of South Africa's conservation history. A few decades before, the country had been lauded for saving the white rhino from global extinction, an intervention considered possibly the greatest conservation story ever. Africa's two species of rhino, the white and the black, had once roamed much of the sub-Sahara. But by 1900, colonial big-game hunting had left maybe 50 white rhinos standing, all of them huddled in a corner of KwaZulu-Natal province. In the 1960s, wildlife officials created new parks and allowed rhino sales to private game farms. Aggressively managed for population growth, rhinos were relocated across the country and into former habitat states like Zimbabwe and Namibia. By the twenty-first century, there were 20,405 white rhinos in eight countries. South Africa had also become the primary redoubt for black rhinos, with about 40 percent of that species' 5,055 animals.

The poaching crisis threatened all this. As best Rademeyer or anyone knew, the horn trade (banned in 1972 by CITES, the Convention on International Trade in Endangered Species) was fueled by Vietnam, where a high-level official was rumored to have cured his cancer by downing a tonic of ground-up horn and water. On the streets of Hanoi, an expanding middle class was buying rhino horn for $65,000 a kilo, despite zero evidence that it cures anything. Asia's three species of rhino had almost disappeared. Meanwhile, poachers had decimated rhino herds in the countries north of South Africa, and they were now invading Kruger National Park from Mozambique. The government had dispatched the army and effectively turned its flagship park into a war zone. South Africa's four hundred private rhino owners, who managed a quarter of the nation's herd, didn't have armies, and soaring security costs were forcing them to auction off their animals. Rhino prices were collapsing. By 2010, a dead rhino was worth more than a live one.

Rademeyer had never covered the environment, nor did he consider himself a tree hugger. He'd made his bones investigating the mob bosses and hit men of Johannesburg's underworld, where personalities tended toward the flamboyant and brazen. But in the spring of 2010, Rademeyer began looking into the poaching syndicates, and one thing became clear: Joburg's mobsters had nothing on these guys. For starters, poaching gangs were chock-full of people charged with protecting rhinos—game farmers, veterinarians, park scouts, government officials. One outfit consisted of Afrikaner game farmers and vets who acquired and killed rhinos, dehorned them, then buried their bodies in a giant pit. Another syndicate, the Musina Mafia, featured a convicted South African poacher exploiting the economic collapse over the border in Zimbabwe, dispatching other poachers to target rhinos in the country's last remaining conservancies. Still another network involved Vietnamese diplomats trafficking horns through their embassy in Pretoria and avoiding prosecution through diplomatic immunity.

But the story of Johnny and Joy achieved a degree of creative immorality that surprised even Rademeyer. It was a tale of greed, guns, sex, and corruption that involved not one but two types of trafficking, all used to manipulate and exploit South Africa's vaunted wildlife-conservation system. Had prosecutors not so mishandled it, Rademeyer could have stuck to chronicling the misdeeds. But in the end, to make things right, he had to become part of the story himself.

~~~~~~

Johnny is mostly interested in money.

—Julian Rademeyer, investigative reporter

After their chance meeting at the casino in the summer of 2010, Johnny agreed to moonlight for Chai again. After the arrest, he'd been unable to find work in Durban, so he'd returned to Joburg and found another job in the auto-parts business. Still, money was tight, especially now that he was living on his own again. He agreed to source lion bones for Chai, nothing more.

Johnny visited game farms with Peter, marveling at his colleague's dexterity with lion bones. Peter could empty a bag on the floor and arrange the entire skeleton in ten minutes. For a good 6-to-8-pound set, Peter would pay the farmer $1,000, maybe $1,500 with the skull and paws. Teeth and claws were especially valuable—although Johnny wasn't sure why—and there was an urgency to get them to Laos faster than the five days their regular bone shipments took to arrive. So Peter gave the teeth and claws to K.K. at Thai Airways, who slipped them to the flight crew, who delivered them to Chai's guy in the Bangkok airport. It took less than twenty-four hours. Transporting them this way wasn't exactly legal, but the rest of it was. The bones had CITES permits and everything.

When they weren't working, Chai insisted on going to the casino. For someone who loved money, Chai hated handling it. Peter followed him everywhere with a black shoulder bag emblazoned with the words BAD BOY. That thing was stuffed with cash. Peter was a sonofabitch about it. Nobody got near that bag. Chai would pick a slot machine, ask Peter for up to $5,000, then get completely absorbed. Peter would get bored and start casing the floor for hookers. He had a thing for the black ladies. He'd book a room with a couple of them, and sometimes the other guys joined in. It was all done with Chai's money, but he didn't mind.

Johnny liked Chai. He wasn't rowdy like Peter. He rarely lost his temper. And he was generous. He always bought clothes for the guys, whatever they wanted. On Chai's birthday, he insisted Johnny drive him to a poor neighborhood to give money to beggars. Chai said that's what you do in Thailand on your birthday. Of course, it also gave him a chance to show off. That was Chai. He made sure everyone knew about his seven Rolexes, about his extensive handgun collection. He photographed or videotaped every transaction he made, downloading the images on his Sony laptop. Then he could show friends back in Bangkok how large he was living.

When the guys needed a new place to stay, Johnny found them a house in Edenvale not far from the casino, a four-bedroom with a garden out back and a big kitchen for Peter to cook all the crazy shit Peter cooked. Chai spared no expense on furnishings—giant Samsung flat screen, surround sound, karaoke machine, leather lounge suite. He insisted Johnny live with them. Johnny figured what the hell.

Life was good. They were making steady money. But in the late summer of 2010, they started looking into a loophole in South Africa's conservation system that was too good to be true. Apparently, with the right permits and documentation, rhino hunting was legal in South Africa. They had Johnny research it. There were rules, of course. A person could shoot only one rhino a year, for example. But you could export the trophy—the mounted horn—to your home country. Chai was ecstatic. South Africa's hunting laws allowed him to ship rhino horns out of the country? Legally? He'd need to find a lot of hunters, but that wouldn't be a problem. He threw a party to celebrate.

~~~~~~

The more I dug, the more horrified I became.

—Julian Rademeyer

The scheme Chai envisioned was nothing new. As Rademeyer investigated South Africa's rhino-poaching crisis, he found that several Vietnamese criminal syndicates had previously exploited the country's hunting laws to traffic horns to Asia. To understand how they did it, one had to understand the controversial role that hunting played in South African wildlife conservation.

South Africa and Swaziland are the only countries in the world that allow hunting white rhinos (hunting of the more-endangered black rhinos is allowed only in

Namibia), and while environmentalists decry the practice as a colonial relic, advocates view it as critically important. National parks and private game farms auction off excess rhinos—older bulls, for example—to other game farmers, some of whom sell hunting safaris. Those farmers reinvest profits into more land and rhinos, which expands the animals' range. Ever since the country resumed legalized white rhino hunting in 1968, the population had increased tenfold, to 18,910. CITES allows the export and import of personal "sport-hunted" trophies, calling it noncommercial trade. A hunter is allowed to kill one rhino per year, and the industry typically markets the animal as one of the iconic Big Five—along with the elephant, lion, Cape buffalo, and leopard—that hunters can legally bag in South Africa.

But Rademeyer noted something curious in the historical record. From 2003 through 2009, most hunting permits didn't go to the usual deep-pocketed Hemingway types from America and Europe. Instead, the permits went to applicants from Vietnam, a country with no tradition of big-game hunting. And these "hunters" hardly seemed wealthy. They came from crowded Hanoi tenements and hardscrabble villages. During this seven-year period, they "hunted" at least 329 rhinos, resulting in 658 horns (two per rhino) being "legally" exported to Southeast Asia.

These weren't hunts at all but pseudo hunts, staged by Vietnamese wildlife traffickers who flew in Southeast Asian peasants to pose as hunters. Far from being showcased on living-room walls, those 658 rhino horns landed in Vietnam's medicinal black market, fetching $200 million to $300 million. This was an open secret in South Africa's hunting industry. Usually, the rhinos were killed not by the permitted hunters—who'd typically never fired a gun before—but by the South African "professional hunter" required by law to accompany safaris and allowed to dispatch only wounded animals.

By transforming a conservation tool into a smuggling pipeline, Rademeyer figured, these Vietnamese gangs had sinned twice. First, they'd bagged 329 rhinos, which may or may not have been killed in legal hunts. Second, those initial pseudo hunts fed early demand for horn and expanded the market in Vietnam. By 2008, rhino poaching had exploded to feed that market. As much as anything, pseudo hunting had sparked South Africa's raging poaching crisis.

And yet, those fraudulent hunts went unpunished. So Chai, it seemed, had nothing to fear when he decided to stage a few himself.

~~~~~~

This crisis has attracted every scumbag imaginable to South Africa.

—Pelham Jones, chairman, South African
Private Rhinos Association

Toward the summer of 2010, a safari operator Johnny knew offered to facilitate a hunt. For roughly $140,000, he could procure two rhinos and relocate them to North West province, where obtaining hunting permits was easy. Peter and the guys went to the casino to tap a couple of ATMs. With the security there, they wouldn't be robbed. They drew and drew, $275 a pop, using Chai's card with unlimited withdrawals. They had so much cash they had to stuff much of it down their pants. Finally, more than five hundred withdrawals later, a message appeared: "Out of commission." They'd sucked the machines dry. They walked out like stiff-legged cowboys.

In September, Peter and another of the Thais went hunting, and afterward a taxidermist mounted the horns on decorative shields. (CITES issued permits only for proper hunting trophies.) Then Chai shipped them to Bangkok. It was easy.

The guys soon lost interest in lion bones. Rhino horns meant exponentially bigger money. They were getting greedy, Johnny thought. His parents hadn't raised him that way. But these guys? Hell, one day Chai announced that he wanted a Hummer. It was late Saturday afternoon, and the dealerships were closed. But Chai wanted it now. Johnny called around and found a dealer who'd open for someone paying cash. They hit the casino ATMs again, and that evening they dumped a pile of money on the dealer's desk. It took him forty minutes to count it. Naturally, Chai videotaped the whole thing. Then he drove home in a silver H3 and called all his friends over.

A game farmer they'd bought lion bones from, Marnus Steyl, could arrange as many rhino hunts as they wanted. Since a hunter could shoot only one rhino a year, they would need hunters. Lots of hunters. Southeast Asian hunters.

Chai knew where to find them.

~~~~~~

> Even if she knew she was coming for sex work, it doesn't matter. If there was deception, or if she was held against her will, that's human trafficking.
>
> —Loren Landau, director, African Center for Migration and Society

For a week after her arrival in South Africa, in the fall of 2010, Joy did nothing. On the eighth day, Mau said, "You make *pam-pam* with the *farang*." Then she delivered Joy to the Flamingo Club in Pretoria.

It was two p.m. Her eyes needed a few seconds to adjust. The place was dark and cavernous, with thumping music. There was a stage. Naked women gyrated and spun around poles. She saw a man in an overstuffed chair leaning back, with a woman grinding against him.

She found the bar. She didn't speak English, but she pointed, and the bartender served her a hard cider, Savanna Dry. She drank without looking up. She ordered another. Then another. She wasn't going to make *pam-pam* with anyone. Leaving Thailand had been a terrible mistake. How could she approach the police about this?

Mau returned twelve hours later. She was furious. Joy had booked no men. "You are so fucking ugly. None of the *farang* wanted you."

Mau hauled her to the Flamingo twice more, with similar results. She drank Savanna Dry and tried to talk Mau's other girls into joining her at the bar rather than working. When Mau caught wind of this she went ballistic. Joy was bad for business, she said. Mau picked up the phone and dialed a man named Anthony. They negotiated a price, and soon Anthony was at the front door. He was young, tall, and good-looking. Compared with Mau he seemed nice. But how nice could he be? He'd just purchased Joy for $1,800.

Anthony drove her to a small two-bedroom townhouse, where at least half a dozen other Thai women were staying. After a couple of days, Joy was dropped off at a club in Krugersdorp, a mining area in the western suburbs. It was filthy, and the place terrified her. She spent the entire evening in the garden outside.

Her new pimp was not pleased.

Two days later, she was driven back to Mau's place, where she received some bewildering news. "Tomorrow," Mau said, "you will go rhino hunting."

~~~~~~

Johnny knew he was involved with illegal activity, that he was facilitating it.

—Paul O'Sullivan, private forensics investigator

Two Thai men arrived at Mau's at six a.m. Joy was still wondering about the rhino hunting—wouldn't the gun be bigger than her?—when Mau instructed her to do anything these men requested. Anything. Joy and three other Thai women climbed into a couple of vehicles, one driven by an older *farang*.

It was November 2010.

As he drove, Johnny contemplated how sweet the girls had it. They were basically being paid 5,000 rand ($440) each to go on holiday at Marnus Steyl's farm in North West province. Mau had already provided Chai with their passports to secure the hunting and CITES permits. Now, beyond posing with dead rhinos for the CITES-required photos, the girls were free to sun themselves by the pool and sip cocktails. And when he turned into the local police station so the girls could be fingerprinted—another hunting requirement—Johnny was further comforted with how legal all this was.

At the guesthouse, the poolside barbecuing and drinking began in earnest. Johnny noticed immediately that Joy stood off by herself. Joy noticed he was the only one not drinking. He wondered why she seemed sad. She wondered why he seemed less threatening than the Thai men. Hello. Hi. I'm John. Joy. Nice to meet you. You speak Thai? Yes. Hmm. Something wrong? She burst into tears. He looked to see if anyone noticed. She explained her situation. He listened attentively. Could he help her? He didn't know how to help. The tears continued. Okay, he said. Okay.

Peter noticed them talking and later pulled her aside. "Johnny can't help you," he said, laughing. "He has no money." But that evening, as the women were divvied up—they were still on the job, as far as Peter was concerned—Johnny spoke up forcefully. "Not Joy. She's with me."

The next morning they spent out in the bush, lounging in the back of a pickup, looking more like shoppers than big-game hunters. The girls wore T-shirts and shorts. Johnny had on Crocs. They fanned themselves in the blistering heat and nibbled sandwiches. Somewhere across the scrub landscape, Steyl, the game farmer, and Harry Claassens, a licensed professional hunter, were stalking rhinos. Legally, Claassens was allowed to shoot only if the permitted hunter wounded the animal. In this case, the permitted hunters were drinking sodas and were nowhere near any rhinos when shots rang out. Then Steyl's voice came over the radio with instructions on where to find them.

The sight of the dead rhino splayed in the red dirt shocked Joy. It was bigger than a car. But a couple of the girls laughed, and Chai was giddy. He handed Joy a rifle, told her to stand next to the animal. She could hardly lift the gun. She and the rhino stared blankly as they clicked the photo. Then Steyl's farmhands worked a long, thin knife around the base of the horn until it popped off, sounding like chicken bones snapping apart at the joint.

Over four days they bagged four rhinos. Chai paid Steyl by horn weight, 60,000 rand a kilo. With the rhinos producing about 4 kilos apiece, Steyl pocketed more than $140,000. The horns would sell for eight times that in Southeast Asia.

Afterward, Joy stayed with Johnny and the guys at the Edenvale house for two days. Mau called in a spitting fury, warning that if Joy didn't return, there'd be consequences. Johnny returned her. Mau took Joy's 5,000 rand for the hunt and sent her back to Anthony.

Two nights later, when she was taken to an underground brothel, a man tried to coax her into a room. They argued. The owner got involved. She ran outside and called Johnny. He had to come, now! This was dicey territory, Johnny thought. But he got in his car, found her, and brought her home.

The next day, he informed Mau that Joy wasn't returning. Mau said it was Anthony's problem, he owned her now. So Johnny called Anthony.

"Anthony, Joy is with me. I believe you bought her."

"Yeah, she's mine."

"She doesn't want to be with you."

"Is that a fact?"

"Yes."

"You gotta pay me then."

"What for?"

"What for?"

"I'm . . ."

"You're gonna pay me 18,000 rand."

Maybe they'd crossed paths for a reason, Johnny thought. Maybe he was meant to help her. He had the money from all the lion bones. He devised a contract saying the payment released Joy of all debts, that nobody owned her, that she could live as she pleased. The pimp signed it and returned her passport.

Joy was free.

~~~~~~

Johnny's a wheeler-dealer, always hatching schemes that never really work out.

—Julian Rademeyer

In November 2010, Joy moved in with Johnny at the Edenvale house. Where else could she go? She had no resources. And while she missed her son in Thailand, she had no opportunities there. As for Johnny, look, he was happily married. He had a wonderful wife in Durban. But helping Joy was the Christian thing to do.

She moved in as Chai was ramping up the rhino hunts. Everyone had a role. Peter began trolling Joburg's strip joints and brothels for Thai passports. He'd leave the house at seven p.m. and be back by nine with half a dozen. It was an easy sell, Johnny thought. Free food and drink for a weekend and the equivalent of three months' salary in Thailand? Johnny scanned the passports—he made $100 per rhino—and forwarded the information to Steyl, who applied for the hunting permits and acquired the rhinos. Steyl could practically steal the animals at auction, what with the poaching crisis escalating and farmers unloading rhinos left and right. After moving them to his farm, he'd signal that it was time to hunt. Peter typically accompanied the hunting parties, while Chai traveled between Bangkok and Joburg, monitoring the horn shipments.

Hovering over all this, virtually, was a mysterious man named Vixay Keosavang. Johnny knew nothing about him except that he lived in Laos and operated Xaysavang Trading Export-Import Company. He'd never been to South Africa. During long video chats, he and Chai spoke rapidly in Thai and Lao, and Johnny couldn't follow. One time, Chai called Johnny over to meet the big boss. The middle-aged man on the screen greeted him, but that was the extent of their interaction.

Unfortunately, Johnny dealt mostly with Steyl and Peter. In addition to breeding lions and conducting safaris, Steyl, thirty-nine, raised show horses and had business interests in Dubai. This apparently made him too good to call Johnny "Uncle," a common practice among Afrikaners when addressing an older man. He usually ignored Johnny altogether, arrogant bastard.

Peter, meanwhile, was becoming more erratic by the day. He'd developed insatiable cravings for one of Mau's girls, and one night he got wasted, jumped into the Hummer, and went looking for her. He shanghaied Joy to navigate. He swerved the wrong way down one-way streets and monster-trucked his way across town doing over 100 miles per hour. When a cop pulled him over, Peter shoved $600 at him from the BAD BOY bag. He later bragged that you could do anything in South Africa for a price.

Another time, Johnny found him with the guys in the backyard huddled around a gray blob the size of a barber pole. It was a rhino penis. They wanted to make jerky. One of them held back the foreskin while the others hacked away at the pink member with knives. They built a fire right there, charred the individual pieces, and laid them in the sun to dry. Clouds of flies soon descended, along with an overpowering stench. The landlady complained, and Peter ended up burying the whole mess in the garden.

The situation deteriorated from there.

By spring of 2011, Johnny and Joy had learned to flee whenever Peter hosted a party. One morning, returning from the quiet shelter of a hotel, they found the yard littered with bottles and condoms. The landlady was homicidal. She lived next door, and the all-night karaoke and shrieking prostitutes had shell-shocked her grandkids. Johnny confronted Peter, who was still clutching a glass of wine. Having spent time in Thailand, he knew these guys grew up with Thai boxing. He'd studied it a bit himself. So when Peter grabbed his shirt, he predicted the sonofabitch would come with a right knee to his crotch. But Johnny delivered a vicious head butt that laid Peter out and opened a deep gash across his nose. When two of the other Thais moved toward Johnny, Joy grabbed a kitchen knife and jabbed it at them. "You touch John, I'll kill you!" she screamed. Then, with Peter bloodied and groaning, she couldn't resist a little smack talk. "You think you're Superman? Why don't you take this knife and John takes a knife, and we'll see who wins?"

In three days the Thais moved out, leaving the house to Joy and Johnny.

~~~~~~

> He was motivated by several things. The fight with Peter. They owed
> him money. But I think that order for fifty rhinos affected him.
>
> —Julian Rademeyer

"Why do you hurt my people?" Chai asked Johnny over the phone from Bangkok. "We are family. We must work as a family." It was self-defense! Peter attacked him. But Chai sent Johnny what amounted to a contract stating that he would have to abide by Chai's rules.

That wasn't the only troubling document from Chai. He'd recently sent Johnny something to forward to Steyl, an order for fifty rhinos. It explained that Xaysavang Trading was prepared to shoot fifteen rhinos a month for the next several months. Steyl would be paid by horn weight, 65,000 rand ($9,700) a kilo. Steyl had complained that the girl hunters would attract attention and that male hunters should be flown in from Thailand. The order suggested that those hunters had already been lined up. Assuming 4 kilos of horn per rhino, Steyl stood to make nearly $2 million.

Jesus, that was a lot of rhinos. Was that really hunting? Had it ever been? If Johnny was fuzzy about the morality of their previous activities, he wasn't fuzzy about this. Fifty rhinos was harvesting, not hunting. It wasn't right.

But what could he do about it? Chai had unlimited funds to bribe the police. Johnny was mulling this over one day in early 2011 when he bumped into an acquaintance at McDonald's. They started talking. By total chance, Johnny's acquaintance was an informant for a private forensics investigator named Paul O'Sullivan. O'Sullivan had extensive contacts in Joburg's underworld and a reputation as a Lone Ranger–style crime fighter. Johnny knew about his exploits from the news, as did most South Africans. He'd been the driving force behind some significant takedowns, most notably the country's corrupt former national police commissioner.

Johnny told the informant everything.

A few months later, on May 11, he repeated it all to O'Sullivan, giving up names, dates, phone numbers, and addresses. The order for fifty rhinos was especially damning. If it stuck, Chai would become the highest-level operative nabbed for wildlife trafficking in recent African history. Johnny urged O'Sullivan to confiscate Chai's laptop. The entire case was right there. Chai recorded everything.

O'Sullivan delivered Johnny's statement and supporting documents to both the police and the South African Revenue Service. SARS took an immediate interest. On June 13, investigators arrested Peter at his new residence for unpermitted possession of lion parts. That same day, they confronted Chai at the airport, where he'd just arrived from Bangkok with five men permitted to hunt rhinos. They confiscated his laptop and released him. Two weeks later, Peter was convicted for violating South Africa's Biodiversity Act and deported. In July, SARS arrested Chai after the rhino hunt, charging him with fraud, customs violations, and illegally trading in rhino horns. Investigators had found hundreds of e-mails, hunting permits, receipts, and videos on his laptop. Johnny's story was true. He and Joy would get immunity, but they would have to testify against Chai. They'd also have to vacate their house immediately.

~~~~~~

When the heat's on, he rats out his mates to save his skin. People were not happy with him.

—Paul O'Sullivan

Soon after moving into their new place, a tiny, one-bedroom apartment in Edenvale, they heard the news: Chai put out a 100,000 rand ($15,000) bounty on them. Johnny remembered a party months earlier when Chai had photographed everyone in the room. He then announced that if anyone snitched, their photo would be circulated among people who deal with snitches.

The cops reassured them. Joy and Johnny needed to hunker down. Go to work, come home, that's it. But then the photographs began arriving on Facebook. One series was of a woman Johnny recognized as Chai's girlfriend. The first photo showed her holding a kitten. In the second photo, one of her stiletto heels was jammed through the kitten's eye socket. The final image showed the animal stomped flat as a tabletop. Another series depicted a man and a woman being hanged. Yet another showed a beheading. The last photos were of a girl in a bathtub with her throat slashed, blood splattered everywhere.

The cops told Johnny to stay offline.

It felt like the walls were closing in. The trial was repeatedly postponed, and weeks turned into months, months into a year. At least Johnny could still go to his auto-parts job. Joy felt like she was in jail. She hadn't seen her son in two years. When the authorities denied yet another request to leave the country, she called Johnny one day and screamed, "I will kill myself!" He raced home to find her holding a knife, her wrists bleeding. But the wounds were superficial.

He tried to alleviate the pressure. He bought her a karaoke machine with Thai lyrics. He got her Thai magazines and romance novels. They adopted a wiener dog. She tried to think outside herself. She cooked Johnny elaborate Thai meals. She placed water before her Buddha statue to quench his thirst, and she fed the spirits of their apartment, leaving them meals outside with burning incense. Still, it was hard not to be constantly terrified. Johnny was once followed most of the way home from work, the mystery car peeling off only after he called the police. Joy regularly reported suspicious cars on their street.

As another trial date approached, in the fall of 2012, Joy received a text message from someone claiming to be a cop. "We've got documents for you," it said. "Please provide us your address." The police told them to ignore it. But the messages continued, along with threatening phone calls. "We're closing in on you," a voice said. "You'll never see the inside of a courtroom."

<hr>

What Julian did was absolutely critical.

—Investigator, South African Revenue Service

On November 5, 2012, Rademeyer arrived at Kempton Park Regional Courthouse in Joburg to find what had become common at rhino-poaching trials: protesters raising hell. It had been more than a year since he'd broken the story of Chai's pseudo hunts, and now he had completed a book about the rhino-hunting crisis, *Killing for Profit*. Outside the courtroom, the public wanted justice. Amid the inflatable rhinos and photos of grisly de-hornings were signs showing Chai's image in crosshairs. Rhinos had become a middle-class cause célèbre in South Africa, what with poaching exploding and the authorities floundering. Experts predicted that by 2015, poaching deaths would outnumber births.

Inside, Rademeyer saw the whole motley bunch standing in the dock. Chai had initially pled guilty in hopes of being fined and deported, but he later withdrew the plea. Peter had returned to South Africa to pursue smuggling deals, but officials promptly rearrested him. Steyl turned himself in shortly after that, and then Harry Claassens, the professional hunter, was arrested at his farm. Rademeyer also saw Johnny sitting in the hallway. He looked terrified.

Rademeyer couldn't blame him. As he'd discovered while reporting on the gang's rhino scheme, Johnny had been working for the Pablo Escobar of wildlife trafficking, Vixay Keosavang. Rademeyer had traveled to Laos and learned that the kingpin was moving tons of live animals and animal parts around the world, including rhino horns, elephant ivory, lion bones, and scaly anteaters. He was emptying forests of wildlife. A single sales contract in 2009 showed that he'd supplied a Vietnamese company with 40,000 rat snakes, 30,000 cobras, 20,000 water monitors, and 20,000 endangered yellow-headed temple turtles. Keosavang had held political office in Laos, and in 2004 he'd accompanied the future prime minister on an official trip to Vietnam. He was untouchable. (In November 2013, US Secretary of State John Kerry announced a $1 million reward for information leading to the dismantling of Keosavang's global smuggling network, which the State Department called "one of the most prolific international wildlife trafficking syndicates in operation.")

Rademeyer didn't know what to expect from this trial. Few poachers had faced serious consequences since the crisis began in 2008. Initially, arrests were rare, and judges mostly issued fines or suspended sentences; only a few underlings, mostly black, had done prison time. But this case had received extensive media coverage, and the government couldn't ignore it. Chai and his crew had killed at least thirty rhinos, and had Johnny not blown the whistle, they would have killed at least fifty more. After their arrests, officials had changed big-game hunting regulations and sharply curtailed pseudo hunting, but rhino poaching in its more-traditional form continued unabated. South Africa needed a big win in court.

The verdict surprised everyone. The good news: Chai unexpectedly pled guilty. He claimed that Steyl and Claassens knew nothing of the fake hunts, and he begged for mercy. The judge gave none. He sentenced Chai to forty years in prison. The bad news: Prosecutors let everyone else walk free.

Whoa. Forty years for Chai was fantastic, Rademeyer thought. But Steyl walks? Seriously? The idea that Steyl knew nothing about the fake hunts was a joke. The most damning proof was a video clip of a hunt from January 2011. Rademeyer had acquired a copy. It showed Chai and Peter walking through the scrub with Steyl and Claassens. They spot a slumbering rhino. Steyl fires his rifle. The rhino screams. Steyl shoots again, but the animal struggles to its feet. Steyl's third shot is followed by one from Claassens. As they approach, the rhino is still whimpering. Steyl pumps a fifth bullet into it. Chai laughs. Trailing the party is another Thai man, the permitted hunter. He never touches a weapon, even though legally he's the only one allowed to shoot a rhino.

In the scrum after the trial, Rademeyer overheard someone ask the prosecutor about the literal smoking-gun video. "What video?" he said. What video?

Rademeyer thought. It was the most compelling piece of evidence. The prosecutor hadn't bothered watching it? Are you kidding?

South Africa's National Prosecuting Authority never explained why the video went unwatched or why it agreed to Steyl's release. Maybe prosecutors felt that the customs aspect of the case was more worthy than the hunting aspect. Maybe they felt that getting Chai was enough. Or maybe they were just incompetent. Whatever the case, Rademeyer was furious. If prosecutors weren't interested in the video, fine. The South African public would be.

In the days that followed, television news programs showed the footage of the illegal hunt, with Rademeyer providing commentary. The video was heavily tweeted, and public reaction was swift. "Cut Steyl's horn off!" one respondent wrote. Others suggested merely killing him. In Parliament, justice officials were thoroughly grilled.

Three weeks later, succumbing to public pressure, authorities rearrested Steyl.

On one of the news programs that showed the video, Rademeyer had talked Johnny into being interviewed. Johnny was still plenty scared, but he wanted to help. With his face and voice altered, he spoke at length. Near the end, the host pressed him on whether blowing the whistle had been worth it, given the death threats and his cloistered existence for sixteen months. Johnny paused. He then collapsed into heaving, remorseful sobs, unable to speak. Yes, he managed, finally. He said it was probably the greatest thing he'd ever done.

~~~~~~

He'd been involved in an ugly thing, and maybe he wasn't fully truthful. But basically Johnny's a good person.

—Julian Rademeyer

Since the trial ended in November 2012, life has been easier. Johnny can come and go without fear. Chai is in prison. (His sentence was reduced to thirty years.) Mau, under pressure, fled back to Thailand. Peter eluded arrest and somehow slipped out of the country, too, even though authorities still have his passport. As for Steyl, Johnny is prepared to testify against that bastard, if they ever try him. The trial has been postponed several times, but prosecutors insist that they're pressing ahead. Claassens has apparently agreed to testify against Steyl, too.

Joy, before visiting Thailand to see her son, scrawled a warning in permanent black marker across Johnny's living-room wall: "No have lady come in home. If come, bad for Johnny." What a jokester! Look, Johnny is happily married. Sure, Joy has since returned to Joburg a couple of times, and yes, she stays at his place. But someone has to help her, don't they? She wants to open a little Thai restaurant in Joburg. Or maybe a hair salon. He's simply helping her with her visa.

Johnny still works for the auto-parts business, and he follows news of the poaching crisis when he can, in the papers, on TV. It's getting worse. In 2013, 1,004 rhinos were poached, the highest annual toll ever. Apparently, the government is so desperate to stop poaching, it is now proposing legalizing the horn trade. A rhino horn is made of keratin, same as human fingernails. You cut it off, it grows right back. Some farmers are already dehorning their rhinos to deter poachers. It's strange, the thought of harvesting and selling rhino horns the way you might harvest and sell, say, corn. But South Africa is bringing the idea to the next CITES conference in 2016.

Johnny hopes there will still be rhinos around for his grandchildren to see. But the way things are going, it's hard to predict. People are just so greedy. So damn greedy.

THE THROUGH-HIKING CON MAN

BRENDAN BORRELL

~~~~~~

For more than two decades, Jeff Caldwell has lured in hikers, couch surfers, and other women (and they're almost always women), enthralling them with his tales of adventure. Then he manufactures personal crises and exploits their sympathy to rip them off. Our writer corresponded with Caldwell while he was still on the run, and came away with an intimate look at the life of a serial scammer who's found his easy marks in the outdoor community.

~~~~~~

On a Thursday in late April, Melissa Trent, a single mother in Colorado Springs, Colorado, logged into her account on the dating website Plenty of Fish and had a new message from a user called "lovetohike1972." "I can't believe a woman as pretty as you is on a site like this," he wrote. Trent clicked open the man's account. The photos showed a smiling, clean-shaven guy in a Marmot puffy with chunky glasses and shaggy hair curling up from under a baseball cap. Trent thought he looked cute. There were shots of him atop Pikes Peak, hanging out with through-hiking buddies at a hostel in Seattle, and climbing into a tractor in Montana. "I love adventure," he wrote in his profile. "Anything in the outdoors." His interests included hiking, biking, skiing, craft beer, and the occasional toke.

Trent, who is in her forties, hadn't had much luck with online dating, but this guy seemed promising. He was smart and good-looking and she especially liked that he was outdoorsy. After exchanging a few messages, she gave him her number.

When he called that evening, he introduced himself as Jeff Cantwell. He said he was born on Kodiak Island, Alaska, and had recently moved to Colorado Springs, where he was training to be an arborist. Most guys Trent had spoken to from dating sites were gross, bringing up sex during a first phone call. "Jeff didn't do that," she says. "He wanted to know about my favorite flower." They ended up talking for ten hours.

Two days later, Trent and Cantwell met for burgers. The connection they made on the phone seemed to deepen in person. They talked about Pikes Peak, which he claimed to have climbed over two hundred times, and he also told her how he had lost his parents in a car crash when he was eighteen. When the bill came, Cantwell paid. A few days later he came over and made spaghetti with meatballs for Trent and her two daughters.

Over the next week, they texted and talked every day. To Trent, it seemed like they grew closer with each conversation. She asked if he had ever been married, and Cantwell revealed more about his history of heartache and loss. During the car accident that killed his parents, his fiancée and his five-month-old baby were also killed, he said. He enlisted in the army and deployed to Afghanistan, where he was the victim of a severe knife attack. He apparently found some consolation in nature, however. He showed Trent tattoos on his calves that he said he earned for completing hiking's so-called Triple Crown—the Pacific Crest Trail, the Continental Divide Trail, and the Appalachian Trail.

That weekend, when Cantwell said his bank card had stopped working, Trent lent him a couple hundred dollars. She trusted him. On Monday morning, when she let him borrow her blue Audi A4 to go get a new bank card, she figured he wouldn't be gone long. About thirty minutes later, however, Cantwell texted that he'd need to go to the branch in Denver, more than an hour away. He asked if he could use the credit card she left in the car to get gas. Trent gave him the go-ahead, but now she was getting nervous. She didn't remember leaving her card there.

Cantwell's behavior grew stranger that afternoon. He claimed the bank in Denver had already closed by the time he got there. "I'll have to sleep in the parking lot," he told Trent. She knew something wasn't adding up, but she didn't want to believe the worst. "I thought we had a connection," she says.

When Cantwell's texts became increasingly erratic that night, Trent finally called the El Paso County Sheriff's Department. They used Cantwell's cell-phone number to identify him as forty-four-year-old Jeffrey Dean Caldwell, a Virginia native who'd been locked up in three states for seven felonies, including burglary, writing bad checks, and attempted escape. Most recently, he'd been paroled in September 2016, after serving time in Colorado for identity theft. But in April, shortly before he met Trent, he had stopped reporting to his parole officer.

Still, Trent couldn't quite convince herself that the man she'd met had such a dark side. "Can I hear your voice one more time?" she begged him in a text. Part of her wanted to trick him into returning the car. Part of her still believed the man she'd fallen so hard for had to exist somewhere. "I don't want you to go to prison. We have to figure out a way out of this. Can we leave the state?"

Caldwell did call her one last time, but when she started sobbing, he hung up. "I'm sick in the head," he texted her. "Write to me in prison."

~~~~~~

The cops put out a warrant for Caldwell's arrest, but he wasn't known to be violent, and no one expected he'd be locked up anytime soon. "These con men are transient and move around a lot, without any way to track where they are," says Lieutenant James Disner of the Larimer County Sheriff's Office, which had arrested Caldwell almost a decade ago. "I have been successful in a few of these types of cases, but only by reaching out to the communities they prey on."

Caldwell's victims typically fell into one of two communities: elderly people and women, whom he often found by participating in Facebook and Meetup groups for hikers, by using the website Couchsurfing.com, and by hanging around trailheads, hostels, and outdoor gear stores. By the time he met Trent, he had been traveling across the West, presenting himself as a free-spirited outdoor archetype, for over a decade. On his Couchsurfing account, he used the name John McCandless, the same middle and last name as Christopher McCandless, the charismatic wanderer profiled by Jon Krakauer in *Into the Wild*.

A pattern emerged with each of Caldwell's cons, too. He'd scope out a victim, share his tale of woe, then enthrall her with his adventures ("31 wolves talking to each other!") and quixotic pursuits ("I'm buying land. 155 acres. You can come stay with me . . . putting up a yurt"). Next, he'd give her a sentimental gift—say, an Alaska shot glass or an Appalachian Trail patch—and send her selfies from the mountains. Finally, he would orchestrate a personal crisis that ranged from the plausible to the bizarre, and finish it off by asking for a small loan, or else he'd just steal what was lying around. The con might be over within days. In a few cases, he was able to stretch out such a relationship for years.

At the end of each con, he would apparently be racked by regret, sending messages to victims that often began with him sounding apologetic and self-pitying, then switching to angry and entitled. "You were a means to an end. Adios," he wrote one woman. "No crime done, just sniveling broads." The moment the authorities caught Caldwell, he would confess everything.

As I learned about Caldwell's exploits, I wondered if there was something about the outdoor community and our sympathy for such wanderers that may make us especially easy marks. When we see a man with a trail-worn Gore-Tex jacket and a decade-old Dana Designs backpack, we instinctively trust him. We can't help but envy his authenticity, his freedom. He's not just a weekend warrior—he's living the life we want. Or at least, that's how it seems.

~~~~~~

For six weeks, I texted Caldwell at a number that Trent had given me, but he never responded. Then, on June 27, he finally sent me a text along with a photo of himself sporting a blue flannel shirt while lounging on a rolled-up fleece in a pine forest. When we spoke on the phone a couple days later, I could hear birds chirping. At first he told me he was in northern Arizona. Later, he claimed he was near the popular Barr Trail on Pikes Peak. "I know Pikes Peak," he said, "I can hide on this mountain for a long time."

He agreed to speak with me because he hoped that, by coming clean in public, he wouldn't be able to take advantage of anyone ever again. "There has got to be a reason why I'm here," he said. "There's got to be. It can't be to keep scamming people."

Over the next week, we talked for several hours and exchanged hundreds of text messages. "Living like this gets lonely," he said. He estimated that he's conned twenty to twenty-five people over the course of his life, but it doesn't seem like there are clear lines in his head between a friend, lover, or potential victim. "I don't go into meeting somebody thinking I'm going to use them," he said. "It just happens when I'm down and out." He wasn't always honest with me, minimizing some of his crimes and the extent to which he manipulated people. Still, he was more transparent than I expected, providing me with access to his e-mail and Facebook accounts. I checked everything he told me with public records and through interviews with dozens of people who had met him.

Caldwell was born in Roanoke, Virginia, on October 26, 1972, the son of a navy captain and an office worker. His parents split when he was ten months old, and he and his mother, Susan, moved to southern California. Money was tight, and Caldwell says his mother was too busy with boyfriends to give him much attention. (I couldn't confirm this, as Susan Caldwell died in 2015.) As a teenager, Caldwell says he became a troublemaker. Skipping school, breaking windows, and staying out all night became routine.

When Caldwell was around sixteen, Susan turned him over to the Baptist Children's Home, a family services organization in Virginia that bounced him between foster families and group homes. He never finished high school, and the day he turned eighteen, he set off on his own.

Caldwell spent his first few weeks of freedom camping out in a creek bed in the woods behind the Hanging Rock Golf Club in Salem, Virginia. But he felt unmoored. In August 1991, he enlisted in the Army Reserve. After thirteen weeks of basic training, the Reserves just required him to report to duty for one weekend each month over the next two years. (He'd be honorably discharged after two and a half years.) The rest of the time he was back in Roanoke, sleeping on couches and attaching himself to a group of outdoorsy potheads who were starting college or working day jobs. Caldwell didn't have his own car, but he had a knack for picking up young girls who could shuttle him around. "I liked him, and he was fun to hang out with," recalls one friend, Heather Riddle.

In June 1993, Caldwell finagled a job as a tennis instructor at Virginia's oldest girls' camp, Camp Carysbrook, by presenting himself as a student at Roanoke College. Toward the end of the summer, he snuck into a shed by the lake and stole some camping and rock-climbing gear and sent it back to Roanoke with a friend. Then, he says, he hiked a section of the Appalachian Trail from McAfee Knob north to the James River. It's a distance of only 60 miles, but Caldwell spent three weeks out there with friends. "We weren't pushing for miles," he says.

When Caldwell returned to Roanoke, he says he started betraying the people closest to him. He snagged a checkbook from one buddy. From another, he stole a camera. The Camp Carysbrook theft caught up to him that winter when a friend's mother ratted him out and he was handed his first prison sentence—two and half years in Tazewell, Virginia.

After Caldwell was released in 1996, he worked odd jobs in the Missouri Ozarks, yet failed to pay the restitution he owed. A year later, he got arrested again, this time for writing a bogus $10.16 check to a convenience store from a bank account that didn't exist. He could have wiped out the resulting three-year sentence with three months in prison under the state's "shock incarceration" program, which tries to rehabilitate nonviolent offenders. But he violated the terms of his parole three times and got locked up again each time.

In 2004, Caldwell fled from his parole obligations once again and took off to Topeka, Kansas, where he met a woman who was working at the homeless shelter he was staying in. According to Caldwell, they went on a camping trip to Colorado, fell in love with the Rockies, and made plans to move there. But when she became pregnant, he balked at the idea of marriage. Her family convinced them to move back to Kansas to have the child, but his heart wasn't in it. "Everything started to go downhill after that," he says. (Through her family, the woman declined to speak about the relationship.)

The couple never married, and Caldwell drifted in and out of his daughter's life over the next three years. He failed to pay child support, according to court records. One night, drunk on margaritas, he broke a window, got arrested, and was sent back to Missouri. In May 2004, he forfeited his parental rights.

Not surprisingly, Caldwell's actual backstory was quite different than the one he shared with Trent and other victims, even if some of the details, like the name Cantwell, had some vague connection to reality. He wasn't an injured war veteran, but he had been in the Reserves. He hadn't lost a child in a tragic accident, but he was a father. And his family wasn't dead. Well, of that he wasn't sure. But he imagined they were. It was easier that way. "I didn't want to tell people the real story," he says.

In the summer of 2006, Paul Twardock was at his office at Alaska Pacific University in Anchorage, where he's a professor of outdoor studies, when his phone rang. He glanced at the caller ID and was surprised to see that it was from Missouri's King County Correctional Center.

Jeff Caldwell introduced himself as an incoming student—his high GED scores had made him eligible for a full financial aid package—and he said that he was eager to get some academic advice. "While we were talking, I asked him what he was doing in jail," Twardock recalled recently. Caldwell admitted that he had passed some bad checks. "He seemed remorseful."

By the time he arrived in Alaska, Caldwell, then thirty-four, was styling himself as a real adventurer, sporting mountaineering boots when he strutted into Kaladi Brothers, the local coffee chain. Caldwell says he genuinely wanted a fresh start, but couldn't handle the class schedule. He didn't even last a semester.

Within weeks, he was stealing from friends and roommates, marking the start of his strategy of flattery and deception. He says he wasn't motivated so much by the money or adventure. He longed to get close to people—almost exclusively women—to be swaddled, pampered, and mothered by them. "They keep offering to help, so you say 'Okay,'" he says. "It's so comfortable. I am a nice person, but I have that evil person that's also there."

Con men like Caldwell have been known to spend years pretending to be someone else, building a relationship for a financial payoff that is, quite often, dwarfed by the investment in time. Maria Konnikova, psychologist and author of *The Confidence Game: Why We Fall for it . . . Every Time* says that the true motivation of the swindler is never money. "They want to have power over other people," she says. "What is more controlling than the most intimate thing of all?"

Caldwell eventually left Alaska, staying ahead of the law for a while as he hopped across the West. In August 2007, he met Erika, a mountain biker with long blonde hair who had just started graduate school in Montana and needed a friend. (Erika asked that her last name not be used in the story.) "He was kind of a charmer and had these amazing stories," she says. "I was enamored by the idea of living in the middle of nowhere in Alaska." They hiked to the "M" overlooking town, and Caldwell brought a bottle of red wine that they shared at the top.

Yet over the next month, Caldwell never invited Erika into his place. That seemed odd to her. He tried to brush off her questions about it, but he also got clingy, showing up at her place late at night or meeting her after class with flowers. When she confronted him about his behavior, he said he was working undercover for the DEA, and taking her to his house would put them in danger. Caldwell says he didn't want to tell her that he was really living at the Poverello Center, a homeless shelter downtown. He was in love with her. "I was nervous about telling her the truth," he says.

A month after they met, she loaned him her truck while she was in class. When she got home, he had stolen her backpack and an enormous jar of change. He left the truck in the parking lot of a nearby grocery store—the keys in the ignition and a thank-you note in the cab.

The grifts continued. The next year, Caldwell swiped a credit card and $1,900 in cash from a woman he met at a bar in Fort Collins, Colorado. He took a train to Lynchburg, Virginia, then used the stolen credit card to load up on $800 of camping gear, including a Jetboil stove and a SteriPen. The cops learned that he had checked into a motel that night, but by the time they arrived, he had made a dash for the Appalachian Trail.

Caldwell says he spent the next month hiking south more than 500 miles—a breakneck pace which, if you believe him, would require climbing and descending an average of 4,500 feet over 20 miles every day. "I can do ten by lunch," Caldwell insists. On October 30, he was coming out of a grocery store in Robbinsville, North Carolina, when a cop ran his ID and arrested him for the theft in Colorado.

Caldwell spent the next six years in and out of prison and halfway houses, but he never dropped his outdoor persona. While he was on parole in July 2015, he headed to Glory Badges Tattoo in Colorado Springs and had the three through-trail symbols inked on his calves. Then, thanks to the Western chapter of the American Long Distance Hikers Association, he flew to Portland, Oregon. The group had given him their through-hiker scholarship to attend their annual gathering because he claimed to have just completed the Triple Crown. He told people his trail name was "Mr. Breeze," but even that was stolen. He had evidently lifted it from another hiker. Caldwell convinced an older couple at the conference to loan him $500, which he never repaid. "Being in the trail community, I couldn't believe that somebody would do this to another hiker," says ALDHA-West president Whitney LaRuffa.

Caldwell used the money to buy a train ticket to Whitefish, Montana. He hiked around Glacier National Park and answered a Craigslist ad for a live-in caretaker at the All Mosta Ranch, a livestock rescue center run by Kate Borton, a woman in her sixties who goes by "Granny Kate."

Borton says she knew something was off about Caldwell the moment she let him stay with her. He talked about wanting to hike around Europe and about buying an off-the-grid property, but she doubted he had the wherewithal to accomplish any of it. After a few months, she and her husband asked Caldwell to move on. They later discovered he had used her credit card without permission, but she didn't resent him. She felt sad. It seemed like he was following someone else's dream, Borton says, going through the motions of a life that he could never truly live.

"What was missing?" she says. "The heart."

⁓⁓

We all create narratives about ourselves, about who we are, where we come from, and who we want to be. Caldwell told me he lied about the Triple Crown because it was "an accomplishment that people are amazed by," but it was "a useless lie, like most lies I tell." He said he didn't necessarily target people in the outdoors community; they just happened to be the people he liked to spend the most time with.

Whenever I asked Caldwell to explain what motivated him, he seemed unwilling or unable to reflect on his behavior. Maybe he manipulated people simply because he could. He told me he became better-looking in his thirties, discovering then how much he could get away with. When I said it seemed like he'd given up on a normal life, he scoffed. "Who's EVER going to give me a chance at a decent job, Brendan? No one. I'm a modern-day leper," he texted. I pressed him again a few days later. "U asked why i tell lies? Pretend to be someone else," he wrote. "Ever heard of self-aggrandizement? If not, look it up (:"

In late June, as we corresponded, Caldwell was still driving around in Trent's car, and told me his goal was to make a little honest money before he turned himself in. He asked if I would pay for a motel or help him out in any way, but I said I could only pay for us to talk on the phone. I knew he was starting to see me as another mark, but I still felt guilty about saying no. I saw how easy it was to be charmed by him. He was bright and had a self-deprecating sense of humor. When I broke the news to him that his mother was dead, he told me he was despondent. "I'm truly alone," he texted. He longed for something better for himself, and I wanted to believe that he was ready to turn his life around.

I didn't hear from Caldwell for a few days. He had assured me he wasn't leaving the state, but on July 1, he was arrested coming out of a coffee shop in Spearfish, South Dakota, where he'd gone to work a carnival. I reached him a couple days later at the Deadwood Jail. "I'm glad this is over, actually," he said. As a repeat offender, he was potentially facing twenty-five years in prison for stealing Melissa Trent's car and joyriding in it. He was almost looking forward to the prison time. "Maybe, deep down, I'm comfortable in there." He told me he'd texted Melissa Trent to apologize. "I do feel bad for everything."

A few weeks later, when he was transferred to Washington County Jail in Akron, Colorado, he wrote me several letters. He was on an antidepressant, Wellbutrin, and taking three classes: Time for a Change, Healthy Relationships, and Anger Management. "Being a writer for *Outside* magazine must be an exciting job," he wrote. "I had so much potential. I could've possibly been in the cubicle next to you, working on my next story." In the next letter, he sounded optimistic about his case, and planned to plead not guilty. "[Melissa] gave me the keys and she got her car back with no damage. We'll see!"

~~~~~~

That's one way to put it. After all, it was the cops in Spearfish who gave her back the car after he was arrested. Trent says it was a mess. He had blown out the speakers, and the engine had to be replaced because he had driven it for so long while it was low on oil. His dirty clothes were in the trunk and there was part of a condom wrapper under the front seat. Trent's ex-husband helped her clean it up and scrape off all the brewery and gear-company stickers that Caldwell had plastered on the back windshield. As she went through Caldwell's things, she found a little black notebook of Caldwell's in the backseat. It contained all of his contacts, and even some of his passwords.

On July 26, Trent used the information from the book to access his Facebook account, which had become, in recent years, a living record of the man that Caldwell longed to be. Trent decided to start editing it, to make it reflect, more clearly, the man who he truly was. She took down the profile picture of him as a bearded mountain man and replaced it with a shot of him in an orange prison jumpsuit. "I am a con man," she wrote under his introduction. "I befriend people posing as a nice, hiking fellow. I steal from them, then disappear."

Then, she added a post about Caldwell's next adventure. "Going to prison," it read. "Hopefully, they'll put me away for a very long time."

CONTRIBUTORS

Caroline Alexander has written for *Outside, National Geographic Magazine,* and the *New Yorker.* She is the author of nine books, including *The* Endurance*: Shackleton's Legendary Antarctic Expedition, The* Bounty*: The True Story of the Mutiny on the* Bounty*,* and a new translation of Homer's *Iliad.*

Bruce Barcott is a contributing editor at *Outside,* the deputy editor of *Leafly,* and a contributor to *National Geographic* and the *New York Times Magazine.* He lives near Seattle with his wife, the writer Claire Dederer, and their two children.

Brendan Borrell is a correspondent for *Outside* and has written about science, crime, and the outdoors for many publications, including the *Atlantic, Bloomberg Businessweek, National Geographic,* the *New York Times,* and *Smithsonian.* He lives in Los Angeles, with two bikes and a dog.

Bryan Di Salvatore is an English professor and a longtime contributor to the *New Yorker.* He lives in Missoula, Montana.

Tony D'Souza is a Florida-based writer, college football fan, author of three novels, and many articles for magazines, including the *New Yorker, Playboy,* and *Esquire.* A recent single-speed-bicycle ride took him through Estonia, Latvia, Lithuania, and Poland. Other single-speed trips have seen him ride through West Africa, the Middle East, Europe, and Japan.

Peter Frick-Wright is the host and producer of *The Outside Podcast.* A contributing editor for the magazine, he has reported from Bosnia, Burma, Burundi, and Bolivia, but most of the time lives in Portland, Oregon.

Bob Friel is a writer, photographer, and documentary filmmaker. His book, *The Barefoot Bandit: The True Tale of Colton Harris-Moore, New American Outlaw*, has been optioned for a feature film. Friel lives in a cabin on a cliff on a small Pacific Northwest island where he hikes with his dog, Quinn, and produces the eco-adventure video series *Salish Sea Wild*.

McKenzie Funk wrote the PEN Award–winning book *Windfall*, and contributes to *Harper's, Rolling Stone, National Geographic*, and the *New York Times Magazine*. He lives in the Pacific Northwest with his wife, Jennifer Woo, and their two sons.

Eric Hansen is a contributing editor at *Outside*, an award-winning magazine writer, and director of external relations at the international medical nonprofit Partners In Health. From 2006 to 2010, he wrote the magazine's "Out of Bounds" column.

Miles Harvey's books include the national and international bestseller *The Island of Lost Maps: A True Story of Cartographic Crime*. His latest, *The King of Confidence* (to be published in 2019), tells the story of a swindler with dreams of ruling the world. A former Knight-Wallace journalism fellow, Harvey teaches creative writing at DePaul University in Chicago, where he is cofounder of Big Shoulders Books.

Mike Kessler is a longtime journalist whose work has appeared in *Los Angeles, Esquire, GQ*, the *New York Times Magazine*, and many others. His articles have been nominated twice for National Magazine Awards (for Public Interest and Reporting) and anthologized in the *Best American Magazine Writing* book series. He lives in Los Angeles.

Dean King is the nationally best-selling author of *Skeletons on the Zahara, Unbound*, and *The Feud*, and is the biographer of Patrick O'Brian. He lives in Richmond, Virginia, with his wife, Jessica, and their schnoodle, Poppy.

Paul Kvinta is a contributing editor for *Outside*, and has written for many other publications. His article on human–elephant conflict in India, "Stomping Grounds," won the Daniel Pearl Award, was a finalist for the National Magazine Award, and appeared in *The Best American Magazine Writing*. His awards and fellowships include the Knight Journalism Fellowship at Stanford University and the Templeton Journalism Fellowship in Science and Religion at Cambridge University. He lives in Atlanta, where his surfing options are extremely limited.

Deirdre McNamer is a novelist whose books include *Red Rover* and *My Russian*. She teaches writing at the University of Montana.

Gordy Megroz is a contributing editor for *Outside* and lives in Jackson, Wyoming. His work has regularly appeared in *Men's Journal, Ski, and Bloomberg Businessweek.*

Megan Michelson got her start as an intern at *Outside* after college, and is now a correspondent and regular contributor. She is also a senior correspondent for *Powder* magazine and an editor-at-large for *Backcountry* magazine. She lives in Tahoe City, California.

Matthew Power was an award-winning journalist who wrote regularly for *Outside, GQ, Men's Journal,* and *Harper's*. He died on assignment in Africa in 2014. An annual grant established in his name, the Matthew Power Literary Reporting Award, has been supporting the work of journalists since 2015.

Grayson Schaffer is an editor-at-large at *Outside*, where he started as an intern in 2002. He lives in Santa Fe, New Mexico, with his Labrador dog, Cooper.

Brandon Sneed is a writer-at-large for *B/R Mag* at Bleacher Report, and has written stories for *Outside, ESPN The Magazine,* and *GQ*. He is the author of four books, including *Head in the Game: The Mental Engineering of the World's Greatest Athletes.* He is also the head writer for the narrative podcast *Why Sports Matter*. He lives in eastern North Carolina with his wife and two young sons.

Christopher Solomon is a contributing editor for *Outside* who has written about severed feet in the waters off Vancouver, British Columbia; hapless homemade boats in the Hudson River; Seattle's Bike Batman; Italy's tradition of making the world's best climbing boots; Utah's wilderness wars; and an Alaskan scientist who climbs inside whales, looking for what killed them. He lives in Washington State.

Mark Sundeen is the author of *The Unsettlers, The Man Who Quit Money, The Making of Toro,* and *Car Camping*. He lives in Albuquerque, where he teaches at the University of New Mexico.

Earl Swift is a frequent contributor to *Outside* and the author of six nonfiction books, including *The Big Roads* and *Auto Biography*. His latest, *Chesapeake Requiem,* chronicles the lives of crab fishermen on Tangier Island.

David Vann's nine books have been published in twenty-three languages and have won fourteen prizes, including best foreign novel in France and Spain. He wrote the true-crime account *Last Day on Earth: A Portrait of the NIU School Shooter*, and in his novels, usually somebody dies.

Peter Vigneron is an *Outside* correspondent. He lives in Santa Fe, New Mexico.

Ned Zeman is a contributing editor at *Vanity Fair*, where he covers Hollywood, crime, politics, and many other topics. He's written about the lives and deaths of wildlife adventurers Timothy Treadwell and Bruno Zehnder. He's also the author of a memoir, *The Rules of the Tunnel*, published in 2011 by Gotham/Penguin.

Tim Zimmermann is a contributing editor at *Outside*. When he isn't writing about our relationships with nature and other species, he spends as much time as he can on the water, on a bike, or trying to make vegan cooking delicious. He lives in Washington, DC, with his wife and two teenaged kids.